SUSTAINABLE DEVELOPMENT, INTERNATIONAL AVIATION, AND TREATY IMPLEMENTATION

In 1944 the Chicago Convention set out the foundations of public international law regulating international air transport, but until 2016 no international agreement existed to limit its environmental impact. *Sustainable Development, International Aviation, and Treaty Implementation* explains why the CORSIA scheme adopted by the International Civil Aviation Organization in 2016 should be implemented in 2020, even though the adequacy of this scheme is still open to doubt and criticism. This book seeks to examine the many dimensions of the effort to contain greenhouse gas emissions from aircraft in a manner consonant with the principles of sustainable development, and examines the development of international law and policy in an area that has remained largely outside the general framework of international environmental law. International civil aviation is a significant polluter of the atmosphere, and in this volume a group of air law and sustainable development law specialists considers how the international community can respond.

Armand de Mestral, CM is an emeritus professor of law and former acting director of the Institute of Air and Space Law at McGill University. He teaches and writes on international law, international trade law, air law, EU law, and constitutional law, and has served on dispute settlement and arbitral panels under CUFTA, NAFTA, and WTO.

Dr. Peter Paul Fitzgerald, MBA, DCL, FRAes, FCILT is a former member of the Canadian Transportation Agency and an adjunct professor at McGill's Institute of Air and Space Law. He is an internationally recognized expert in aviation law who has taught, lectured, presented, and published in Canada, the United States, Western Europe, the Middle East, South Asia, and Singapore.

Dr. Md Tanveer Ahmad, DCL, is an Associate Member and was the Executive Director of the Centre for Research in Air and Space Law at McGill University. He lectured in Canada, China and Bangladesh, and extensively published in the area of aviation law and environmental law.

TREATY IMPLEMENTATION FOR SUSTAINABLE DEVELOPMENT

Over the past three decades, a series of international treaties have entered into force to address pressing global concerns of social and economic development and environmental protection. On climate change, biodiversity and biosafety, desertification, agriculture and seeds, and trade and investment liberalisation, new regimes have been established to implement global commitments related to sustainable development, many with nearly universal membership. Successful domestic implementation of these international treaty regimes is one of the most significant challenges facing international law today. Although much has been written on the content and form of treaty law, there is relatively little that examines the transition from international legal theory and treaty texts to domestic regulation and practice.

This series of books addresses this need and provides a serious contribution to ongoing global debates by conducting a detailed analysis of how myriad new treaty regimes that cover the future's most pressing concerns can be made to work in practice.

Series Editors:

Marie-Claire Cordonier Segger

Markus Wilheim Gehring

Volumes in the Series:

Sustainable Development, International Aviation, and Treaty Implementation
edited by Armand de Mestral, Peter Paul Fitzgerald, and Md Tanveer Ahmad (2018)

NAFTA and Sustainable Development
edited by Hoi L. Kong and L. Kinvin Wroth (2015)

Legal Aspects of Implementing the Cartagena Protocol on Biosafety
edited by Marie-Claire Cordonier Segger, Frederic Perron-Welch, and Christine Frison (2013)

Sustainable Development, International Criminal Justice, and Treaty Implementation
edited by Sébastien Jodoin and Marie-Claire Cordonier Segger (2013)

Sustainable Development, International Aviation, and Treaty Implementation

Edited by

ARMAND DE MESTRAL
McGill University

PETER PAUL FITZGERALD
McGill University

MD TANVEER AHMAD
McGill University

CAMBRIDGE
UNIVERSITY PRESS

CAMBRIDGE
UNIVERSITY PRESS

University Printing House, Cambridge CB2 8BS, United Kingdom

One Liberty Plaza, 20th Floor, New York, NY 10006, USA

477 Williamstown Road, Port Melbourne, VIC 3207, Australia

314–321, 3rd Floor, Plot 3, Splendor Forum, Jasola District Centre, New Delhi – 110025, India

79 Anson Road, #06–04/06, Singapore 079906

Cambridge University Press is part of the University of Cambridge.

It furthers the University's mission by disseminating knowledge in the pursuit of education, learning, and research at the highest international levels of excellence.

www.cambridge.org
Information on this title: www.cambridge.org/9781107153110
DOI: 10.1017/9781316594216

First published 2018

Printed and bound in Great Britain by Clays Ltd, Elcograf S.p.A.

A catalogue record for this publication is available from the British Library.

Library of Congress Cataloging-in-Publication Data
NAMES: De Mestral, Armand L. C., editor. | Fitzgerald, P. Paul, editor. | Ahmad, Md Tanveer, editor.
TITLE: Sustainable development, international aviation, and treaty implementation / edited by Armand de Mestral, McGill University; Paul Fitzgerald, McGill University; Tanveer Ahmad, McGill University.
DESCRIPTION: Cambridge, United Kingdom ; New York, NY, USA : Cambridge University Press, 2018. | Series: Treaty implementation for sustainable development | Includes index.
IDENTIFIERS: LCCN 2018021309 | ISBN 9781107153110 (hardback : alk. paper)
SUBJECTS: LCSH: Aeronautics, Commercial–Law and legislation. | Aeronautics, Commercial–Environmental aspects. | Sustainable development–Law and legislation. | Environmental law, International.
CLASSIFICATION: LCC K4108.E58 S83 2018 | DDC 344.04/634–dc23
LC record available at https://lccn.loc.gov/2018021309

ISBN 978-1-107-15311-0 Hardback

Contents

Figures

Tables

Contributors

Md Tanveer Ahmad, LLM, DCL (McGill) is an Associate Member of the Centre for Research in Air and Space Law, McGill University. Previously, Dr. Ahmad served as Executive Director of the Centre for Research in Air and Space Law, McGill University, a Sessional Lecturer and an Erin J.C. Arsenault Postdoctoral Researcher at the Institute of Air and Space Law, McGill University, and Editor of *Annals of Air and Space Law* (vol XLI). He was an Assistant Professor at the Department of Law, North South University, Bangladesh, and a Lecturer at the School of Law, BRAC University, Bangladesh. He has lectured in Canada, China, and Bangladesh, and authored a book on *Climate Change Governance in International Civil Aviation*. He was a coeditor of a book on space commercialization and a codesk editor of a book on global space governance. He also authored, among others, several peer-reviewed journal articles, book chapters, book reviews, policy papers, and working papers, mostly dealing with aviation law and environmental law.

Kuan-Wei (David) Chen obtained his undergraduate degree in law and politics from the School of Oriental and African Studies (SOAS), University of London. Later, he obtained an LLM (*cum laude*) in public international law from Leiden University and an LLM in air and space law from the Institute of Air and Space Law, McGill University, where he was also a Boeing fellow in air and space law. In addition to being Executive Director of the McGill Centre for Research in Air and Space Law, Kuan-Wei is a Sessional Lecturer at the Faculty of Law of McGill University and Deputy Project Manager of the project to draft the McGill Manual on International Law Applicable to Military Uses of Outer Space (MILAMOS). He was formerly Editor of *Annals of Air and Space Law*.

Emilie Conway is a Canadian lawyer member of the Quebec Bar. She holds a B.A. in international relations and international law, and an LLM in public international law, both from Université du Québec à Montréal (UQÀM), as well as a BCL/LLB from McGill University Faculty of Law. Her master's thesis, entitled "La protection du consommateur à l'épreuve de l'Organisation mondiale du commerce," was published in 2012. While studying law, she was Editor-in-Chief of the *Quebec Journal of International Law* and a coordinator of UQÀM's Groupe de recherche en droit international et comparé de la consommation. After finishing her studies, she clerked for the Honourable Justice Mr. Marc Noël of the Federal Court of Appeal in Ottawa, Canada, and their Excellencies Mr. Peter Tomka and Mr. Mohamed Bennouna, at the International Court of Justice. She is now an Associate Legal Officer at the International Court of Justice.

René David-Cooper is a lawyer and holds a Commercial Pilot Licence with over a decade of flying experience. He obtained his LLM from the Institute of Air and Space Law at McGill University where he served as the Boeing Fellow in Air and Space Law. He also holds a Licentiate in Civil Law (LLL) and a Juris Doctor (JD) from the University of Ottawa. After clerking at the Federal Court of Appeal for the Honorable Mr. Justice André F. J. Scott. René now works at the Transportation Safety Board of Canada in the Air Investigations Branch.

Armand de Mestral, CM, AB (Harvard), BCL (McGill), LLM (Harvard) has *honoris causa* doctorates from the University of Lyon and Kwansei Gakuin University. He has taught constitutional law, law of the sea, public international law, international trade law, international arbitration, the law of the European Community, and public international air law. His current research interest is the law of international economic integration. He has prepared books, articles, and studies in English and French on international trade law and on Canadian comparative and constitutional law and international law. He has served on WTO and NAFTA dispute settlement and arbitration tribunals. He was made Member of the Order of Canada in December 2007 and received the John E. Read Medal from the Canadian Council on International Law in 2017.

Peter Paul Fitzgerald, MBA (Western Ontario), DCL (McGill), FRAeS, FCILT, is a former member (judge) of the Canadian Transportation Agency whose decisions have been favorably reviewed by Canada's Federal Court of Appeal and the Supreme Court of Canada. He is an Adjunct Professor at the Institute of Air and Space Law (IASL), McGill University. He has been the driving force behind Canada's Open Skies agreements with Iceland, New Zealand, Barbados, the Dominican Republic, South Korea, and the European Union, and has successfully fought against regulatory initiatives that would have harmed the airline industry. He has lectured in aviation law in Canada, the United States, and India. His work has been published multiple times in five different air law journals, in book chapters, as an author, and as part of airline industry conference proceedings.

Markus W. Gehring, JSD (Yale), MA (Cantab), LLM (Yale), Dr. of Law (Hamburg), is an expert in the Centre for European Legal Studies (CELS), fellow and director of studies in law at Hughes, and a fellow of the Lauterpacht Centre for International Law at the University of Cambridge. Dr. Gehring is also the Arthur Watts Senior Research Fellow at the British Institute for International and Comparative Law (BIICL), a senior fellow with the International Law Research Program (ILRP) at the Centre for International Governance Innovation (CIGI), and Lead Counsel for Trade with the Centre of International Sustainable Development Law (CISDL). He is a member of the Ontario and Frankfurt am Main Bars and an affiliate member of Landmark Chambers in London.

Nicole Gonzales is a Dutch Antilles lawyer. She holds an LLM in air and space law from McGill University's Institute of Air and Space Law in Montreal, Canada, and an LLM in General Civil Law from the University of the Netherlands Antilles in Curacao. She has been active in the international aviation industry since 2012, including managing IATA's Cabin Safety department and the IATA Cabin Operations Safety Task Force as well as assisting ICAO's Air Navigation Bureau (ANB) in the Safety and Air Navigation Oversight Audit Section.

Ömer L. Gülder is a Professor at the University of Toronto Institute for Aerospace Studies (UTIAS) since 2001 and was the Associate Director of UTIAS from 2007 to 2016. Before joining UTIAS as a faculty member, he worked as a researcher and then as the section head of the combustion laboratory at the National Research Council of Canada. Dr. Gülder completed his PhD at the University of Manchester, United Kingdom, and his undergraduate and MSc degrees at the Middle East Technical University, Turkey. His current research interests include high pressure combustion, soot formation, turbulent combustion, bio-fuels for aviation, and aviation fuel thermal stability. He has published over 250 papers on combustion-related subjects and served on the editorial boards of *Combustion and Flame*,

International Journal of Thermal Sciences, and *International Journal of Engine Research*. Dr. Gülder is a fellow of the Canadian Academy of Engineering.

Brian F. Havel is a Professor of Law and Director of the Institute of Air and Space Law at McGill University. He is also an Emeritus Distinguished Research Professor of Law at DePaul University College of Law, Chicago, and a Visiting Professor of Law at the University of Oxford, Leiden University, and University College Dublin. He was the Keeley Fellow at the University of Oxford, Wadham College, from 2011 to 2013, and previously served as the Fulbright Distinguished Chair in Comparative Law and Legal Pluralism at McGill. His most recent book is *The Principles and Practice of International Aviation Law* (Cambridge University Press, 2014, with G. Sanchez).

Jae Woon Lee is an Assistant Professor in the Faculty of Law of the Chinese University of Hong Kong (CUHK). At CUHK, he teaches aviation law and competition law. Having studied in Seoul (HUFS), Montreal (McGill), and Singapore (NUS), he has seven years of work experience in the airline industry. His work mainly consisted in advising on airline liability and government regulatory issues and handling competition law cases. He has also acted as consultant to the Ministry of Foreign Affairs of the Republic of Korea on aviation law issues, and attended the ICAO Legal Committee meetings and the Diplomatic Conference as a legal advisor to the Korean delegation. He has published many articles in international journals and a monograph: *Regional Liberalization in International Air Transport: Towards Northeast Asian Open Skies* (2016).

Benoît Mayer is an Assistant Professor in the Faculty of Law of the Chinese University of Hong Kong. He previously worked at the Research Institute in Environmental Law in the School of Law at Wuhan University, China. He studied at Sciences Po Lyon, the Sorbonne University, McGill University, and the National University of Singapore. His research focuses on the international law on climate change, in particular with regard to human mobility, loss and damage, and adaptation. He is the author of *The International Law on Climate Change* (Cambridge University Press, forthcoming).

Damilola S. Olawuyi, LLM (Calgary), LLM (Harvard), DPhil (Oxford) is an Associate Professor of Energy and Environmental Law at the HBKU Law School, Qatar, and Chancellor's Fellow and Director of the Institute for Oil, Gas, Energy, Environment and Sustainable Development (OGEES Institute), Afe Babalola University, Ado Ekiti, Nigeria. A prolific and highly regarded scholar, Dr. Olawuyi has published several peer-reviewed articles, books, and reports on climate finance, energy infrastructure, and extractive resource governance. His most recent publication is *The Human Rights-Based Approach to Carbon Finance* (Cambridge University Press, 2016). Dr. Olawuyi was formerly an international energy lawyer at Norton Rose Fulbright Canada LLP, Calgary, where he served on the firm's global committee on extractive resource investments in Africa. He has lectured on energy and environmental law in Europe, North America, Asia, Africa, and the Middle East. Dr. Olawuyi has been admitted as a Barrister and Solicitor in Alberta, Canada; Ontario, Canada; and Nigeria. He serves on the executive committees and boards of several organizations.

Alejandro Piera is a founding partner at the Asuncion-based law firm of Guanes, Heisecke & Piera Attorneys at Law (GHP). His areas of practice include corporate, competition, foreign investment, cross-border, environment, transportation, and sports law. The 67th FIFA Congress recently appointed Alejandro Vice-Chair of FIFA's Disciplinary Committee. At GHP, Alejandro is in charge of the firm's cross-border, aviation, and environment practices. Alejandro is an arbitrator of the Shanghai International Arbitration Center and he is a columnist for the business journal 5 *Dias*. Alejandro has written extensively. Among other titles, in 2015 he authored *Greenhouse Gases from International Aviation: Legal and Policy Issues*. Alejandro holds a doctorate (DCL) and LLM from McGill University. In 2016, the *Association des Professeures et Professeurs de Droit du Quebec* awarded him the prize of best doctoral thesis 2015. He also holds a BCL from the National University of Asuncion.

Cairo Robb, MA (Cantab), Lic. spéc. dr. eur. (ULB) was called to the Bar of England and Wales in 1993. She edited *International Environmental Law Reports* (Cambridge University Press), including volumes on trade and environment, human rights and environment, and international environmental law in national courts. On secondment from the University of Cambridge to the Department for Environment, Food and Rural Affairs (DEFRA) in London, Cairo spent two years working as a policy advisor at DEFRA's Sustainable Development Unit. She is currently a legal research fellow with the CISDL.

Maha Mousavi Sameh holds an LLM in air and space law from McGill University. She also holds a master's degree in international law, and has participated in several research projects dealing with different aspects of international law as well as air and space law. After completing an internship in the Legal and External Relations Bureau at ICAO, Sameh rejoined this organization in 2017 to work on the Next Generation of Aviation Professionals (NGAP) Programme in the Air Navigation Bureau.

Juliana Macedo Scavuzzi dos Santos is a Brazilian lawyer. She holds an LLM from the Institute of Air and Space Law, McGill University, where she completed her thesis on the liability of Global Navigation Satellite Systems (GNSS) used for air navigation in Brazil. She also earned her MSc in Juridical Science from UNIVALI, Brazil, in 2004, and is a member of the Brazilian Aeronautical and Space Law Society (SBDA) and Women in Aerospace (WIA). She is involved in the research on the protection of the space and Earth environment from harmful interference on satellite services.

Jeffrey J. Smith teaches law in the Norman Paterson School of International Affairs, Ottawa. He was previously law of the sea counsel to the United Nations during the transition of East Timor to independence in 2002. His current legal work includes advising marine classification societies on environmental governance policy and implementation of IMO MARPOL rules, and the regulation of ships to be converted to artificial reefs. His areas of scholarly research include measures for environmental protection in commercial shipping in the Polar Regions and evaluating the effectiveness of global chemical pollution treaties.

Joseph Wheeler is the Principal (Legal Practice Director and Founder) of International Aerospace Law & Policy Group (IALPG), and helps people and companies with domestic and international aviation legal issues. His practice focuses on pilotage, drone, space industry, and liability issues with advice and expertise provided to foreign aviation lawyers and claimants, plus international organizations and insurers. Wheeler is a member of both the Legal Committee and the Professional & Government Affairs Committee of the International Federation of Air Line Pilots' Associations (IFALPA). He serves as Aviation Legal Counsel to the Australian Federation of Air Pilots and consults as National Head of Aviation Law to Maurice Blackburn Lawyers, pursuing serious accident litigation for claimants worldwide.

David W. Zingg is in his thirtieth year as a Professor at the University of Toronto Institute for Aerospace Studies, where he was Director from 2006 to 2016 and is currently the University of Toronto Distinguished Professor of Computational Aerodynamics and Sustainable Aviation. His research areas include aerodynamics, computational fluid dynamics, and aerodynamic shape optimization. His current research is concentrated on applying aerodynamic shape optimization to the design of unconventional low-drag aircraft configurations motivated by the need to reduce greenhouse gas emissions from aircraft. He held a Tier I Canada Research Chair in Computational Aerodynamics and Environmentally Friendly Aircraft Design from 2001 to 2015, was awarded a prestigious Guggenheim Fellowship in 2004, received the McCurdy Award from the Canadian Aeronautics and Space Institute in 2012, and is a fellow of the Canadian Academy of Engineering. He serves on the Board of Directors of the Green Aviation Research and Development Network (GARDN), is the Director of the Centre for Research in Sustainable Aviation at the University of Toronto, and serves on an Independent Experts Panel currently conducting a review for the Committee on Aviation Environmental Protection (CAEP) of the International Civil Aviation Organization (ICAO).

Introduction

Sustainable Development, International Aviation, and Treaty Implementation

Armand de Mestral, Peter Paul Fitzgerald, and Md Tanveer Ahmad

I.1 BACKGROUND

This book addresses an important and urgent concern: the need to facilitate sustainable growth of the international air transport industry while dramatically reducing the emissions of greenhouse gases (GHGs) and other environmental and social impacts, which are currently the by-product of every commercial flight. This book argues that sustainable aviation law can integrate economic, social, and environmental concerns for the future of this important industry and the world alike. Many chapters of this volume focus on climate change, which presents perhaps the most immediate challenge to the social license of this global industry. As the world worked slowly past the Kyoto Protocol and toward the Paris Climate Agreement, the international civil aviation community adopted a wait and see attitude. All too often, rather than taking an active part in this global effort to reduce the emissions of GHGs, the international civil aviation community – commercial, industrial, and governmental – has maintained that it represents a small percentage of the phenomenon and should thus not be regarded as part of the problem. On the contrary, it has been asserted that international civil aviation is already doing all it can and that its options are limited by technological or economic imperatives. Successive sessions of the Assembly of the International Civil Aviation Organization (ICAO) paid lip service to the need to act and postponed meaningful action to the next session of the Assembly.

All this radically changed at the 39th Session of the ICAO Assembly in September to October 2016, which approved a mandate for the ICAO Council to implement a global market-based carbon offsets scheme, namely CORSIA, to reduce carbon dioxide (CO_2) after 2020. The decision taken by the 39th Session of the ICAO Assembly followed the decisions taken at the 21st Session of the Conference of the Parties (COP 21) to the United Nations

Framework Convention on Climate Change in Paris in December 2015. After that point, it was no longer possible for the ICAO to plead that civil aviation was not part of the problem or that it represented too small a source of GHGs to matter. International civil aviation is the only activity whose emissions principally occur in the upper atmosphere; it continues to grow at a significant rate and is expected to do so for the indefinite future. Nor will it be possible to plead that deliberate action to reduce GHGs will be too costly or that only one part of the international community should assume the cost. Landmark decisions were taken at Paris and Montreal to reduce GHG emissions, and it is now up to States and the international civil aviation industry to find the means of achieving this goal.

In late 2012, Students of the McGill University Institute of Air and Space Law (IASL) began to focus on the issues of sustainable development and climate change in the previous decade. The controversy surrounding the 2009 decision of the European Union (EU) to extend its Emissions Trading System (ETS) to international civil aviation proved to be an important catalyst focusing the interest of students upon these issues. However, the long-term concerns posed by emissions controls are only one facet of a much greater set of issues and this book attempts to respond to this fact. Most of the authors of the chapters of this book are graduates and academics associated with the IASL, most of whom have embarked upon careers in the field of international air law and are thus actively dealing with the issues addressed in this book.

Climate change and the need to reduce GHG emissions from international civil aviation constitute the most pressing series of issues addressed by this book. However, the challenges posed by a commitment to sustainable development policies are much broader, and this book attempts to highlight many facets of the challenges that are currently posed to international civil aviation.

1.2 CLIMATE CHANGE: THE CHALLENGE FOR INTERNATIONAL CIVIL AVIATION

One of the central challenges to international civil aviation and, hence, to the Member States of the ICAO, concerns climate change. International civil aviation significantly contributes to climate change through emissions of gases and particles from, *inter alia*, aircraft, ground support services, auxiliary power units providing electricity and air conditioning to aircraft parked at airport terminal gates, stationary airport power sources, and construction equipment operating at the airport. Aviation is a small but significant contaminator in a variety of ways. At present, civil aviation accounts for some 2 percent of total global CO_2 emissions, which is 3 percent of the total manmade contribution to climate change. This contribution is projected to grow around 3–4 percent per year. Aviation is responsible for 12 percent of total CO_2 emissions from the transportation sector and such emissions are projected to grow to 23 percent by 2050 unless effective measures to check such emissions are initiated. Aviation would have been the 17th largest emitter of CO_2 in 2010, if international aviation were a "country."

Concern over aviation's contribution to climate change has been rising, since the industry and related activities continue to outpace technological innovation in this field toward lowering emissions. Passenger traffic is expected to grow at an average rate of 4.8 percent per year through the year 2036. Aircraft engines emit gases and particles directly into the upper atmosphere that affect atmospheric composition by, *inter alia*, altering the concentration of atmospheric GHGs, prompting formation of condensation trails and increasing cirrus cloudiness. These effects of GHG emissions from aircraft accelerate climate change. It should also be borne in mind that natural catastrophic events caused by climate change are detrimental to the aviation industry, since those events cause disruption to air travel and air transport facilities. In 2017 alone, airports serving major cities, such as Boston, Chicago, Delhi, Houston, London, Miami, Montreal, Mumbai, New York, Philadelphia, Phoenix, Tokyo, Toronto, and Washington, were fully or partially closed at least on one occasion due to weather or weather related events. This demonstrates the need for immediate and firm action from the air transport sector to diminish the environmental footprint of aviation, if it is to attain sustainable civil aviation. Furthermore, global, simultaneous, and collective actions by all the sectors are required to combat climate change.

I.3 DEFINING THE REQUIREMENTS OF SUSTAINABLE DEVELOPMENT AS IT APPLIES TO INTERNATIONAL CIVIL AVIATION

I.3.1 *Sustainable Development Is the Objective*

Sustainable development requires that environmental, economic, and social dimensions be balanced with each other. For aviation, this means that climate concerns, the economic growth of the industry, and the social dimension of airline travel need to be balanced in a way that does not completely ignore any one of these dimensions.

The *Chicago Convention* adopted in 1944 must be interpreted in light of today's world, which since 2015 includes firm Sustainable Development Goals.[1] Sustainable development should thus be part of a living interpretation of the *Chicago Convention* itself. Nonetheless, it is also an objective for all ICAO Member States and as such becomes part of the interpretative canon for the *Chicago Convention* in accordance with the Vienna Convention on the Law of Treaties. Sustainable development has been identified as a concept around which all the international civil aviation community can rally. It can help to move away from the sterile debate between developed and developing States on the right to differential rates of environmental degradation to a more integrated world, in which all States participate and all industries focus on integrated sustainable economic, social, and environmental concerns.

This all reflects a shared duty to cooperate. For example, Annexes to the *Chicago Convention* contain standards and recommended practices (SARPs) that, though without the full force of an international treaty, entail legal obligations for the contracting States to the *Chicago Convention*. Such States have "accepted an explicit legal undertaking to collaborate in securing the highest practicable degree of uniformity in regulations, standards, procedures and organization in relation to [air navigation]."[2]

The ICAO SARPs are the current multilateral mechanism used to govern or guide, at the international level, the consequential national regulations concerning air transport. Compliance with these standards is of the highest concern for States. Without that compliance, cooperation and faith in international air transport are jeopardized. Article 33 of the *Chicago Convention* seeks to ensure compliance by ensuring that SARPs are recognized, on a reciprocal basis, by every contracting State.[3] This means that certificates of airworthiness, competency, and licenses "issued or rendered valid by the contracting State in which the aircraft is registered, shall be recognized as valid by the other contracting States, provided that the requirements under which such certificates or licenses were issued or rendered valid are equal to or above the minimum standards which may be established from time to time." Article 33, therefore, dictates that one State may not reject or

1 UNGA, "Transforming our world: The 2030 agenda for sustainable development," A/Res/70/1, www.un.org/ga/search/view_doc.asp?symbol=A/RES/70/1&Lang=E last accessed October 31, 2017, at 14.

2 M. Milde, "Problems of safety oversight: Enforcement of ICAO standards," in C. J. Cheng (ed.), *The Use of Air and Outer Space: Cooperation and Competition* (Boston: Kluwer Law International, 1998), 254.

3 *Convention on International Civil Aviation* (adopted December 7, 1944, entered force April 4, 1947) 15 UNTS 295, Can TS 1944 No 36, ICAO Doc 7300/9, Art 33 [*Chicago Convention*].

discriminate against the aircraft of another State, where that aircraft is complying with the minimum standards annexed to the *Chicago Convention*. States must, therefore, ensure that any initiatives put in place do not have the effect of invalidating another State's Annex-compliant air transport framework.

Adopting the goal of sustainable development for international civil aviation will have a profound impact on the airline industry as it is currently entirely dependent on carbon-based fuels. While other modes of transport have the possibility of electric or nuclear propulsion in the foreseeable future, the means of propulsion of the airline industry are primarily carbon-based, with the result that any reduction in GHG emissions is derived almost exclusively from decreased fuel consumption. Measures such as more efficient air traffic management practices, improved operation of airport slots, gates, and terminals, increasingly efficient engines, and the reduction of airframe weight through the use of composite materials like carbon fiber will all help to reducing fuel consumption and, consequently, GHG emissions. Given that fuel costs are one of the greatest components of an airline's expenses, any reduction in fuel consumption is greeted with great enthusiasm in airline boardrooms. Thus, initially, airlines are strong supporters of initiatives to make flying more fuel efficient.

However, there is an upward limit to the GHG emission reductions that can be achieved by increased efficiency. Moreover, while such progress might be impressive in terms of an intensity-based GHG reduction target, where progress is measured in terms of GHG emission reduction per unit of production, such emissions might actually grow if there is an expansion in units of production.[4] Thus, if GHG emissions are to be reduced 20 percent below 1990 levels by 2020,[5] this target will not be achieved simply by reducing GHG emissions per flight.

I.3.2 *Precaution, Inter-Generational Equity, and Common but Differentiated Responsibilities and Respective Capabilities*

Precaution is a key factor not only in climate change and environmental law in general, but also for the future approach to aviation and climate change.

[4] See D. Marshall, "Intensity-based targets: Not the solution to climate change" (David Suzuki Foundation, February 26, 2007) at 1.

[5] This is the EU's commitment under the United Nations Framework Convention on Climate Change 2011. See Center for Climate and Energy Solutions, "2020 country emissions targets," www.c2es.org/international/history-international-negotiations/2020-targets last accessed October 31, 2017.

A precautionary approach would suggest at least analyzing the risks involved in not acting or not acting decisively. At current rates, GHG emissions from aviation may increase by 176 percent over the next few decades as estimated by the ICAO, and might quadruple by 2050.[6] For this reason, inaction or *status quo* are no longer options.[7] The emergence of the precautionary principle in international environmental law[8] thus suggests taking measures as soon as possible. This would also correspond to demands regarding intergenerational equity.

However, especially in developing States, resistance to any robust new regulations is often based on arguments of common but differentiated responsibilities and respective capabilities (CBDRRC). As most of the GHGs currently in the atmosphere have been produced by developed, industrialized States, there is a feeling of injustice in developing States, which believe that they now have the right to exploit their natural resources accordingly. It has been pointed out by economists that a market-based measure, and an emissions trading scheme in particular, would be superbly placed to realize the necessary differentiation in a politically attractive way, through the allocation and administration of allowances.[9] From the starting point of a cap and allocation on a business as usual basis, the stringency of the regime can be tightened while also increasing differentiation of the burdens among State participants by means of differentiation in the allocation and administration of allowances, including, for example, the granting of preferential auction rights to some States rather than others. Ellerman calls this "inconspicuous

6 See "Aviation's contribution to climate change," in ICAO, Environmental report 2010, 44, ch.1, figure 3.

7 See also FOI, "Developing a sustainable framework for UK aviation: Scoping document – Consultation response from Friends of the Earth" (2011), https://friendsoftheearth.uk/sites/default/files/downloads/sustainable_aviation.pdf last accessed October 31, 2017.

8 So far, the precautionary principle can be only deemed to be an emerging customary norm; although included in various agreements, it lacks so far positive acknowledgment and confirmation through courts and tribunals, M. Pyhälä, A. C. Brusendorff, and H. Paulomäki, "The precautionary principle," in M. Fitzmaurice, D. M. Ong, and P. Markouris (eds.), *Research Handbook on International Environmental Law* (Cheltenham: Edward Elgar, 2010), 203–10. The ICJ mentioned the precautionary principle in the request for an examination of the situation in accordance with para. 63 of the Court's Judgment of December 20, 1974 in the Nuclear Tests Case (*New Zealand* v. *France*), [1995] ICJ Rep. 288, Order September 22, 1995, para. 35, but did not decide upon its legal nature in contrast to the dissenting opinions in the same case of, Judges Palmer, 412, and Weeramantry, 342.

9 See D. Ellerman, "The EU's emissions trading scheme: A prototype global system?" (MIT Report No 170, February 2009). See also his lecture "European CO_2 trading: Dead end or path to the future" (Bren School of Environmental Science and Management, University of California, Santa Barbara, March 29, 2011), www.youtube.com/watch?v=GeacfcaKNYo last accessed October 31, 2017.

differentiation." For this to work, formulae for allocation would have to be subject to multilateral decision-making, but the potential for inconspicuous differentiation in this way to address CBDRRC requirements is certainly a valid point that several States criticizing the market-based measure option do not seem to have fully considered.

More recently, the International Maritime Emissions Reduction Scheme (IMERS) has set out detailed proposals for dealing with CBDRRC concerns overtly in both the international maritime and aviation transport sectors. The IMERS proposals seek to use carbon pricing of international transport as a mechanism to increase mitigation and financing ambitions for climate change action, while at the same time delivering on equity.[10] IMERS calculations show the international aviation carbon footprint being concentrated in the North, and the potential burden of aviation carbon pricing – as a percentage of GDP – being largest in the South, impacting most on less developed countries, as they often disproportionately rely on international transport as a percentage of GDP. IMERS addresses the question as "not whether, but how" to relate differentiated climate principles and provisions to uniform carbon pricing for international aviation. The proposed scheme focuses on the inclusion of a Rebate Mechanism (RM). The RM could apply to any revenue-raising market-based measure, such as a levy/charge or emissions trading scheme. Under the scheme, all planes pay for their emissions. Developing States could[11] obtain rebates of the cost burden incurred by participating in the market-based measure to ensure they are at least not worse off.[12] The remaining revenue (net revenue) dedicated for climate action would, therefore, come from consumers in developing States only, complying with the UNFCCC principles. It would be disbursed by an agreed entity or entities (e.g. GCF, ICAO). The most vulnerable States would benefit through the relevant rules and provisions (SIDS, LDCs, African countries), and the aviation sector would also benefit, potentially through a new global Aviation Technology Fund. Rebates to developing States might amount to a third of revenue raised; the remaining two thirds would be a predictable and affordable source of climate change financing and research and development for clean international transport.

10 A. Stochniol, "Increasing mitigation and financing ambitions through action on international transport" (side event, Bonn Climate Change Conference, June 7, 2013).

11 The IMERS proposals also address the issue of "graduation," proposing that high income developing countries may agree voluntarily to forgo the rebate, or part of it, with such money potentially going toward South-South collaboration.

12 The IMERS proposals suggest the rebate key could be based, for example, on a country share of fuel uplifted for international flights, as proposed in the IMF/WB report for G20.

In line with the principles of precaution, intergenerational equity, and CBDRRC, the further development of technological improvements must be pursued as part of the solution.[13]

I.3.3 *Integration*

Integration suggests that, in the upcoming negotiations, social and environmental aspects have to be considered on an equal footing to economic considerations. Thus, any solution that ignores the different pillars of sustainable development should be rejected on principle.

I.3.4 *Sustainable Use of Natural Resources*

Especially in the aviation industry, it is of key importance to observe the principle that natural resources should be sustainably used. While ever lighter airplanes are constructed using less metal and more carbon-based materials, the use of fossil fuels in aviation will always be a key issue.

In this context, one might be tempted to question the way biofuels are treated under the EU-ETS scheme.[14] Aircraft flying with biofuel are technically exempted from the scheme. This is because emissions are calculated using the following formula: Fuel Consumption X Emission Factor. And, the emission factor for biomass is zero. This means that using biofuel would mean "zero emissions."[15] This complete exemption granted to aircraft flying with biofuel can be questioned from the perspective of sustainable development.

Whereas, on the one hand, it is commendable that industries, including the aviation sector, become more and more independent of nonrenewable resources, on the other hand, the *carte blanche* given to airlines regarding

[13] Measures likely to reduce emissions are not only new airplane designs and propulsion engines, but also changes to alternative energy sources in the form of low carbon intensive fuels and power sources, as well as improved aviation management, including more links with other means of transportation. D. L. McCallom, G. Gould, and D. L. Greene, "Greenhouse gas emissions from aviation and marine transportation: Mitigation potential and politics" (Pew Center on Global Climate Change, 2009), 1–2.

[14] L. Bartels, "The WTO legality of the application of the EU's emission trading system to aviation," *European Journal of International Law*, **23** (2012), 429, 431–32. Part B of Annex IV of Directive 2008/101/EC (November 19, 2008), amending Directive 2008/87/EC so as to include aviation activities in the scheme for greenhouse gas emission allowing trading within the Community.

[15] See European Commission, Directive 2008/101/EC of the European Parliament and of the Council of November 19, 2008 amending Directive 2003/87/EC so as to include aviation activities in the scheme for greenhouse gas emission allowance trading within the Community, OJ 2009 No L 8/3, Ann. [*Directive 2008/101*].

their allowance quota raises several problems. First of all, it compromises the pressure on airlines to develop more fuel-efficient systems and mechanisms that might be more expensive than the additional costs for biofuel. On a larger scale, it opens up an accumulation of other factors linked to biofuels. The farming of monocultures (which is the common method for the production of biofuel) not only has detrimental repercussions for the environment, but has also been linked to price increases for wheat and other grains on the stock markets, and resulting food shortages and even famine around the world. The blanket exemption of all biofuels, therefore, does not appear to be compatible with an overall objective of sustainable development. In order to implement the principle of sustainable use of natural resources, it would be appropriate to include fuel quality standards also for airplane biofuels. *This would require an amendment of the current EU-ETS*. An airplane flying with biofuel should be exempted depending on certain biofuel standards, i.e. second or third generation biofuels, and thus allow operators to actually reduce their emissions, and not be trapped in the ETS with no possible reduction of GHG emissions from their activities.[16]

1.4 IS THE *CHICAGO CONVENTION* ABLE TO ADAPT TO THE IMPERATIVES OF SUSTAINABLE DEVELOPMENT?

In a world preoccupied with climate change, addressing the GHG emissions from international civil aviation and the development of a legal framework based on principles of sustainable development are not simple matters. It must be discussed in an international forum and any GHG emissions strategy will include various elements. This book seeks to address primarily the legal considerations arising from promoting, designing, and implementing sustainable development in the aviation industry – a policy urged by the EU and now the policy of the ICAO. It thus serves to highlight the importance of the 1944 *Chicago Convention*, the primary source of public international air law, for broader sustainable development objectives.

Although the *Chicago Convention*, adopted in 1944, does not explicitly address protection of the environment or social development, various provisions of the Convention, including its Preamble, tacitly endorse sustainable development of international civil aviation. In its Preamble, the contracting parties to the Convention "agreed on certain principles and arrangements in order that international civil aviation may be developed in a safe and orderly

16 See M. Gehring and C. Robb, *Addressing the Aviation and Climate Change Challenge: A Review of Options* (Geneva: ICTSD, 2013), 20.

manner and that international air transport services may be established on the basis of equality of opportunity and operated soundly and economically." While the environmental dimension of the sustainable development concept is absent from the *Chicago Convention*, the agreement of States to develop international civil aviation in, *inter alia*, an orderly manner and to operate international air transport soundly and economically arguably encompasses sustainable development of aviation. The Convention tacitly confers responsibility on the ICAO to address aviation environmental and social issues. According to Article 44 of the Convention, one of the aims and objectives of the ICAO is "to develop the principles and techniques of international air navigation and to foster the planning and development of international air transport so as to ... promote generally the development of all aspects of international civil aeronautics." Certainly, reducing environmental and negative social impacts of aviation to ensure sustainable development are aspects of international civil aeronautics and, hence, the ICAO has a duty to regulate environmental impacts, such as emissions, from international civil aviation.

The ICAO Council adopted Annex 16 to the *Chicago Convention* to address aviation environmental issues. Annex 16, divided into three volumes, addresses aviation environmental issues. Volume I of Annex 16 deals exclusively with aircraft noise emissions, Volume II is devoted to addressing the issue of aircraft engine emissions, and Volume III provides for a new aircraft CO_2 emissions standard. Nevertheless, Annex 16 does not deal extensively with environmental issues mainly concerning engine emissions and further decisions will be forthcoming from the Council as it implements the decisions of the 39th ICAO Assembly.

In the absence of any global effective mechanism, contracting States can utilize their authority under Article 11 of the *Chicago Convention* to enact laws and regulations for the protection of environmental or social issues so long as those concern admission to or departure from its territory or concern operation and navigation while within its territory of aircraft engaged in international air navigation and so long as those are "applied to the aircraft of all contracting States without distinction as to nationality." Foreign aircraft are obliged to comply with such laws and regulations "upon entering or departing from or while within the territory of that State." Furthermore, under Article 12 of the Convention, every contracting State has an obligation to adopt measures to ensure that "every aircraft flying over or maneuvering within its territory and that every aircraft carrying its nationality mark, wherever such aircraft may be, shall comply with the rules and regulations relating to the flight and manoeuver of aircraft there in force." Although Article 12 further requires States to keep their regulations "uniform, to the greatest possible extent, with those established from time to time under this Convention," Annexes do not yet comprehensively address the issue of protection of the environment. States can thus utilize their authority under Articles 11 and 12 individually or jointly, under Article 77.

1.5 THE ROLE OF THE ICAO

As it currently stands, "sustainable" in international civil aviation means, according to former ICAO Council President Roberto Kobeh González, "safe, secure, and efficient air transport operations that provide airlines and airports with a reasonable expectation of profitability – while supporting competitive economies and promoting balanced regional development." This definition appears to stress safety and economic viability, but it does not exclude concern over the environmental footprint of aviation caused by GHG emissions. The Kyoto Protocol requires its Annex I Parties to pursue limitation or reduction of GHG emissions not controlled by the Montreal Protocol from aviation fuels working through the ICAO, thereby providing a clear mandate for the ICAO to be the authoritative body for aviation environmental issues. Hence, cooperation between the ICAO and Annex I developed State parties to the Kyoto Protocol with regard to international aviation has been mandated by the Protocol. For many years, the ICAO, working as a facilitator not regulator, experienced considerable difficulty in adopting a scheme to reduce emissions from international civil aviation. However, it would not be fair to solely attribute this failure to the ICAO as an organization. Due to differences of opinion among ICAO contracting States over various issues, such as the CBDRRC principle, the ICAO could not reach a firm decision to reduce aviation emissions in international civil aviation until 2016. Hence, it is the ICAO contracting States that are more responsible for this failure than the ICAO itself.

The EU responded to this failure by including civil aviation in its ETS in 2009.[17] However, unsurprisingly, this unilateral initiative of the EU did not fare well with non-EU States who responded by threatening to take retaliatory actions of various nature. Nonetheless, the pressure from the EU – which cannot be a full member of the ICAO – played a significant role in bringing Member States to a unanimous decision to act on GHG emissions in October 2016.

As mentioned, the ICAO Assembly, at its 39th Session in 2016, decided to implement CORSIA to address any annual increase in total CO_2

[17] *Directive 2008/101*, *supra* Note 15.

emissions from international civil aviation above the 2020 levels, taking into account special circumstances and respective capabilities of States. CORSIA will be implemented in phases: The pilot phase will apply from 2021 to 2023, the first phase from 2024 to 2026, and the second phase from 2027 to 2035. To establish the necessary mechanisms to implement CORSIA, the Assembly required ten initiatives, including the development and implementation of SARPs, the measurement and registration of emissions, and the production of guidance materials with respect to the sale of emissions units.[18]

The Assembly requested the Council to complete these tasks as soon as possible to enable the full implementation of CORSIA from 2020. Beginning in 2022, the ICAO Council will be required to conduct a review of the implementation of CORSIA every three years. This will serve as an important basis for the Council to determine the necessity of making adjustments to the next phase or compliance cycle and, as appropriate, recommend such adjustments to the ICAO Assembly for its decision. In the face of the many delays encountered in adopting a GHG policy in the past, this objective appears ambitious.

1.6 IS A MULTILATERAL SOLUTION PREFERABLE TO UNILATERALISM?

There can be little doubt that a multilateral solution to the adoption of GHG reduction measures and other sustainable development policies for international civil aviation is preferable to unilateral or regional approaches. As discussed in several chapters of this book, the ICAO has witnessed a first unilateral attempt by the EU to impose a GHG policy. This unsuccessful effort by the EU to expand the reach of its general GHG policies to international civil aviation was met with considerable hostility, including the threat of litigation, legislative and administrative bans of national airlines complying with the EU GHG scheme, and threats of commercial retaliation against the sale of aircraft produced in the EU. Furthermore, the attempt by the EU to give its GHG scheme extraterritorial effect only weakened the case it tried to make for the justification of its scheme.

[18] See ICAO, "Consolidated statement of continuing ICAO policies and practices related to environmental protection – Global market-based measure (MBM) scheme," Res A39–3, 39th Sess., ICAO Doc 10075 (2017), I-80 at I-85.

1.7 THE UTILITY OF PARTIAL OR REGIONAL SOLUTIONS?

The failure of the EU to impose its scheme demonstrated the extreme difficulty of any one jurisdiction, however powerful, imposing its own scheme unilaterally. Nevertheless, should ICAO-contracting States fail to reach an agreement regarding the full implementation of CORSIA at the 40th Session of the Assembly in 2019, is it possible to imagine concerted measures by several major aviation jurisdictions? The book attempts to assess the viability of regional solutions. Again, the best option is a multilateral solution worked out at the ICAO Assembly, but failing that it may become necessary to assess the viability of an approach adopted in concert by several major aviation jurisdictions, such as North America and Europe acting together with other like-minded States. Can a sufficient number of States adopt a parallel approach to cover a satisfactory volume of international air traffic, and would such an initiative convince or compel the rest of the world to live by the same rules? These are major and very difficult questions, and the answers are not obvious. What is clear is that the States of the world assembled in the ICAO have a duty to bring GHG emissions into a global scheme for their reduction along with GHGs from other terrestrial sources.

1.8 STRUCTURE AND SCOPE OF THIS BOOK

This book is a contribution to the current academic and political debate on sustainable development and aviation law analyzing the practical, legal, political, and economic problems encountered from a global perspective and especially implementation from a regional perspective. It considers, in particular, the interaction between sustainable development and aviation in the EU, North America, Africa, the Asia-Pacific region, and the Caribbean. The purpose of the book is to examine the questions that are currently posed to the international aviation community from different perspectives.

Part I outlines the current status of international civil aviation with respect to sustainable development. Attention is given to technology and existing regulatory systems designed to ensure the safety, security, and growth of international civil aviation. A central concern is the capacity of the *Chicago Convention* to authorize and adapt to the imperatives of new public policies, such as sustainable development. The *Chicago Convention* is considered as well as the working of the ICAO, which has been the central regulatory body since 1944.

Part II addresses regional aviation issues. The economic concerns of airlines of different regions of the world have to be considered and met if any system of regulating GHGs from international civil aviation is to work. Similarly, the concerns of developing States, which constitute the majority of ICAO Member States and who consider that they are not the principal source of the problems caused by the emissions of GHGs, must be met.

Part III deals with dispute settlement to determine whether or not required mechanisms to settle disputes concerning international civil aviation and sustainable development are available and to make necessary reform proposals. In this regard, the dispute settlement provisions under the *Chicago Convention*, namely Articles 84–88, and the application of WTO law are addressed.

Finally, in Part IV, the book explores how the industry may evolve in the future to grow in a more sustainable manner.

It is hoped that these chapters give a balanced picture of the many issues posed at the present time and show that the *Chicago Convention* can indeed adapt to the exigencies of sustainable development.

PART I

Current Status of Global Aviation and Sustainable Development

1

Technology Developments and Renewable Fuels for Sustainable Aviation

David W. Zingg and Ömer L. Gülder

This chapter describes the prospects for reducing the impact of aviation on the environment through operational changes, new airframe and engine technologies, and biofuels. The focus is on the in-flight impact on the environment with particular emphasis on climate change impact. Examples of operational changes include optimized profile descents, reduced vertical separation, multistage long-distance travel, formation flight, and large aircraft for short ranges. New airframe technologies described include active laminar flow control and novel aircraft configurations such as the double bubble and the blended wing-body. Various possible approaches to improve the efficiency of jet engines are described as well as means of reducing nitrogen oxide emissions, such as lean premixed combustion. Prospects for large-scale use of biofuels are discussed and the technical path that should be taken in developing and adopting alternative jet fuels is presented.

1.1 IMPACT OF AVIATION ON THE ENVIRONMENT

The sources of the environmental impact of aviation can be divided into three categories: (1) in-flight operations, (2) airport operations, and (3) manufacturing and disposal. In-flight operation impact includes noise, emissions affecting local air quality at ground level, and emissions at altitude contributing to climate change. Airport operations impact is related to power consumption associated with the operation of the airport itself, emissions during taxiing, byproducts of aircraft and engine maintenance, and contamination resulting from the use of deicing fluid. Finally, the impact of manufacturing and disposal is associated with materials of concern, contaminants, and energy use.

Concentrating on in-flight impact, noise concerns are predominantly associated with take-off and landing operations, which primarily affect those living or working near airports. There are many studies indicating that exposure to increased noise levels can cause adverse effects on human health.[1] Noise is generated both by the engines and the airframe, with the landing gear and high-lift devices being the primary contributors from the latter. Aircraft noise is tightly regulated such that aircraft and engine manufacturers must meet increasingly stringent requirements in order to certify an aircraft. These regulations typically represent a balance between what is technologically feasible and the health impacts on people living in the vicinity of an airport. As a result, current aircraft are much quieter than in the past. Initially, great strides were made in reducing engine noise to the point where during approach airframe noise is now comparable to engine noise. Consequently, increased attention is now paid to reducing airframe noise in addition to engine noise.

Local air quality at and near airports is similarly a health concern associated with pollutants emitted by aircraft at ground level during taxiing, take-off, and landing, including ozone, carbon monoxide, sulfate aerosols, and soot aerosols (particulate matter). A promising approach toward alleviating local air quality concerns is electric taxiing, either by powering the aircraft's wheels with an electric motor or through an electric tractor that tows the aircraft to and from the gate.

Turning to the impact of aviation on climate change, this is associated with aircraft emissions in the upper troposphere and lower stratosphere.[2] This includes the direct effect of carbon dioxide emissions, which have a lifetime of 50–200 years. In addition, emissions of nitrogen oxides have an indirect effect on climate change by causing changes in ozone and methane concentrations through chemical reactions. Ozone concentration is increased and methane decreased, with a net warming effect. This effect has complex dependencies on altitude, season, and latitude. Oxides of nitrogen have a lifetime of weeks in the atmosphere. A further impact of aviation emissions at altitude on climate change arises as a result of water vapor and particulate matter emissions, which under particular meteorological conditions can persist for hours and can spread into cirrus clouds. Contrails and aviation-induced

1 S. Morrell, R. Taylor, and D. Lyle, "A review of health effects of aircraft noise," *Aust NZ J Public Health*, **21**:2 (1997), 221.

2 D. S. Lee et al., "Aviation and global climate change in the 21st century," *Atmospheric Environment*, **43**:22–23 (2009), 3520.

cirrus clouds are believed to cause a net warming effect.[3] However, both their formation and their climate impact are presently not well understood in several respects and the level of scientific understanding of this phenomenon is still evolving.[4] Finally, smaller effects on climate change are associated with particulate and water vapor emissions.

The focus of this chapter is on the reduction of the in-flight impact of aviation with emphasis on climate change impact, which is the most important impact in the long term.[5] We will briefly review some opportunities offered by changes in flight operations followed by a discussion of airframe technologies, engine technologies, and biofuels.

1.2 FLIGHT OPERATIONS

Operational improvements offer limited scope for reducing aviation's impact on climate change, but have the advantage that many of them can be implemented with today's technology. Optimized profile descents can be utilized to reduce fuel burn and hence carbon dioxide and nitrogen oxide emissions during approach, with potential reductions in noise as well.[6] Reducing the vertical separation minimum can enable more optimal trajectories with associated reductions in fuel burn and thus emissions.[7] Another possibility to reduce fuel burn is provided by multistage long-distance travel, which enables the aircraft to begin the first stage with less fuel (and thus a reduced take-off weight) in comparison to flying the entire distance in one stage.[8] Moreover, contrail avoidance based on diverting around regions where the meteorological conditions are such that contrails are likely to form can reduce contrail and cirrus formation. This leads to a trade-off, since it will increase fuel burn, but given the possibly large warming impact of contrails and aviation-induced cirrus this may be worthwhile. An improved understanding of the impact of contrails and aviation-induced cirrus is needed before a quantitative assessment can be made.

3 Ibid.
4 U. Schumann, "A contrail cirrus prediction model," *Geosci Mode Dev*, 5 (2012), 543.
5 J. E. Green, "Civil aviation and the environmental challenge," *Aeronautical J*, 107:1072 (2003), 281.
6 J. P. Clarke et al., "Optimized profile descent arrivals at Los Angeles International Airport," *J Aircraft*, 50:2 (2013), 360.
7 A. Malwitz et al., "Impact of the reduced vertical separation minimum on the Domestic United States," *J Aircraft*, 46:1 (2009), 148.
8 J. E. Green, "Air travel – Greener by design – Mitigating the environmental impact of aviation: Opportunities and priorities," Royal Aeronautical Society (July 2005).

One of the more promising operational opportunities is afforded by formation flight, which has long been exploited by Canada geese. With formations of as little as two or three aircraft, substantial drag reductions are possible and would translate directly into reductions in fuel burn and emissions.[9] Further efforts are needed to identify and address the remaining challenges associated with this concept. There is also considerable discussion in the aircraft design literature of flying at lower altitudes, although this generally involves a redesign of the aircraft for reduced speeds. Contrail formation and the effects of nitrogen oxides are greatly reduced at altitudes between twenty and thirty thousand feet. This is typically accompanied by an increase in carbon dioxide emissions. Hence, it is unlikely that such an approach will be adopted unless the confidence in our scientific understanding of the effects of both contrails and oxides of nitrogen is significantly increased.[10] Finally, designing large aircraft for short ranges, known as the LASR approach, has the potential to reduce climate change impact for short routes with high passenger volume.[11]

1.3 AIRFRAME TECHNOLOGIES

During the cruise segment, the fuel efficiency of an aircraft is determined by several factors, including speed, altitude, the engines' thrust-specific fuel consumption, weight, and aerodynamic drag. Drag is the aerodynamic force acting in the direction opposite to the motion of the aircraft; lift is the aerodynamic force acting in the direction perpendicular to the motion of the aircraft. During straight and level flight at constant speed, the lift force is equal to the weight of the aircraft, and the thrust from the engines is equal to the drag force.

The drag force acting on an aircraft has three primary components. One is lift-induced (or simply induced) drag that is associated with the vortices shed most notably from the wing tips as a result of the production of lift. Another is viscous drag resulting from the viscosity of the air. The third is wave drag, which is caused by shockwaves that can arise if the local fluid velocity in the frame of reference of the aircraft exceeds the local speed of sound. At the cruise speeds of modern aircraft shockwaves are weak as a result of carefully

9 S. A. Ning, T. C. Flanzer, and I. Kroo, "Aerodynamic performance of extended formation flight," *J Aircraft*, 48:3 (2011), 855.

10 Green, "Civil," *supra* Note 5.

11 G. Kenway et al., "Reducing aviation's environmental impact through large aircraft for short ranges," AIAA Paper 2010–1015 (2010).

designed supercritical wing section shapes and swept wings. Thus, wave drag is small. Hence, the primary contributors to drag are induced drag and viscous drag.

In order to improve fuel efficiency, therefore, the aircraft designer seeks to reduce induced drag, viscous drag, and weight. The thrust-specific fuel consumption of the engines is discussed in the next section. It is important to recognize that drag and weight are often interconnected such that a measure that reduces one increases the other, and vice versa. For example, induced drag can potentially be reduced by increasing the wingspan, but this generally leads to an increase in wing weight. If the increase in weight (and the corresponding increase in lift) is too large, then the net effect may be an increase in induced drag. Similarly, an active flow control technology to reduce viscous drag will add weight and consume power. These trade-offs must be carefully considered such that an optimal configuration is designed. The current dominant aircraft configuration, often referred to as the *tube and wing*, is typified by the Boeing 707 and Douglas DC8, which came into service over fifty years ago. Over the past fifty years, this configuration has been continually refined and optimized to incorporate new technologies, such as supercritical airfoil sections and composite materials. Together with improvements in engine technologies, this has produced reductions in fuel burn per passenger-kilometer in the order of 70 percent.[12] Improvements in fuel efficiency have come from more efficient aircraft and more efficient engines in roughly equal measure. The tube and wing configuration is now well understood and highly optimized. Further large improvements in efficiency are unlikely to come through additional optimization of this configuration. Either new technologies or new configurations (or both) that lead to reduced weight and drag are required.[13]

Induced drag is strongly dependent on the wingspan, reducing as the span is increased. However, an increase in span typically results in an increased wing weight due to the additional structure needed to withstand the increased bending moments. Therefore, the optimal span balances this trade-off. Similarly, the induced drag is impacted by the spanwise load distribution, which also affects the wing weight. Therefore, the spanwise load distribution must be carefully chosen to provide the optimal balance between weight and drag such that fuel efficiency is maximized. Induced drag is associated with the vortices that arise when the higher-pressure air beneath the wing interacts at the wing tip with the lower pressure air above the wing. Therefore, a further means of

[12] Green, "Civil," *supra* Note 5.

[13] Ibid.

reducing induced drag is to reduce this interaction or displace the shed vortex through nonplanar wing geometry. The classic example is a winglet, variations of which can be seen on many modern aircraft. However, this concept can be taken further to C wings, split wing tips, box wings, and general closed-wing systems. These have the potential to reduce induced drag by as much as 30 percent.[14] However, their impact on weight and viscous drag must be taken into account in order to determine the net improvement in fuel efficiency.

Viscous drag is associated with boundary layers, which are thin layers of air near the aircraft surface in which the effect of viscosity is significant. Boundary layers can be classified as laminar or turbulent. Laminar boundary layers are characterized by smooth, orderly flow, while turbulent boundary layers are characterized by apparently chaotic, random motion of the air. On an aircraft wing in flight, the boundary layers typically begin with laminar flow near the leading edge of the wing and at some point on the wing transition to turbulent flow. Since a turbulent boundary layer produces more surface friction than a laminar one, it is advantageous to design the wing such that the transition from laminar to turbulent flow occurs as far aft as possible, and the extent of turbulent flow on the wing is minimized.

A wing can be carefully shaped to move the laminar-turbulent transition point quite far aft; this is known as *natural laminar flow* and can lead to significant reductions in drag. However, this approach is limited in its applicability, becoming increasingly difficult at high speeds and on highly swept wings. This has motivated the development of *active flow control* techniques. With active flow control some form of actuation is introduced that delays the onset of laminar-turbulent transition. A classical approach involves removing some of the air in the laminar boundary layer near the wing surface by drawing it into the wing through small orifices. This inhibits the amplification of small disturbances that is central to the transition process and hence moves the location of transition downstream, thereby reducing drag. It is important to recognize that, in contrast to natural laminar flow (or passive flow control), active flow control consumes power, which must then be counted against the reduction in drag achieved in order to determine the net benefit. This has motivated the development of modern flow control techniques that attempt to minimize the power requirements by selectively targeting unstable disturbances that are responsible for the transition to turbulence through actuators that require little power, possibly through closed-loop feedback based on

[14] I. Kroo, "Nonplanar wing concepts for increased aircraft efficiency," paper delivered at the VKI lecture series on Innovative Configurations and Advanced Concepts for Future Civil Aircraft (June 2005).

sensors placed on the wing.[15] Other drawbacks of active flow control include added weight and complexity. However, the primary issues to be addressed in order to bring active flow control into practice in civil aviation are reliability and safety. Therefore, it is most likely that active flow control will first be applied to vertical tails and engine nacelles.

Our ability to reduce the weight of aircraft is primarily dependent on the continued development of new materials with advantageous strength and stiffness to weight properties while retaining other characteristics essential for use on aircraft, such as fatigue life, thermal properties, and manufacturability. The latest generation of aircraft utilizes significantly more composite materials than previous aircraft. Further reductions in weight are possible by continuing to replace metallic materials with composites and plastics. Moreover, weight reductions can be achieved by improving our capacity to manufacture composite materials such that fully three-dimensional components can be designed, reducing our dependence on laminated plates. It is important to stress the interdependence of weight and drag. As a result, use of a new material with improved strength to weight properties can reduce the weight of an aircraft, but it can also reduce the drag by enabling a higher span or a thinner wing section. The ability to determine optimal designs is enhanced by recent advances in numerical multidisciplinary optimization.

It is also possible that a significant improvement in fuel efficiency will come through the use of an unconventional aircraft configuration other than the dominant tube and wing design. Among the most promising is the blended (or hybrid) wing-body configuration, which has no distinct fuselage and wing.[16] Instead the body of the aircraft holding the passenger compartment blends smoothly into the wing. Moreover, the body is shaped such that it produces lift, thereby reducing the lift that needs to be generated by the wings. The aerodynamic lift is thus better aligned with the loads, leading to reduced bending moments in the wing and hence lower structural weight. This configuration is believed to be most efficient for very large aircraft.[17] The blended wing-body configuration has numerous other advantages that can be exploited, such as opportunities for boundary-layer ingestion or distributed propulsion, leading to improved propulsive efficiency, and natural noise shielding obtained by locating the engines on the top of the aircraft. There

[15] P. Lavoie et al., "Towards model-based closed-loop control of transition and turbulence in boundary layers," paper delivered at the 3rd UTIAS International Workshop on Aviation and Climate Change (May 2012).

[16] R. Liebeck, "Design of the blended wing body subsonic transport," *J Aircraft*, 41:11 (2004), 10.

[17] C. L. Nickol, "Hybrid wing body configuration scaling study," AIAA Paper 2012–0337 (2012).

are challenges with this configuration as well, most notably dealing with the noncylindrical passenger compartment, which has the potential to add weight. This has spurred research into promising options to address this problem, such as pultruded rod stitched efficient unitized structure (PRSEUS), a new approach to composite design.[18]

The D8 or double-bubble twin-aisle configuration has also been proposed, based on having a fuselage that generates lift.[19] Although the fuselage is distinct from the wing as in the traditional tube and wing design, the fuselage is a wide lifting body, which enables the weight of the wings to be reduced. The aircraft is also designed to fly at a somewhat lower speed than current transport aircraft. Therefore, the wing has reduced sweep, further reducing the weight and facilitating natural laminar flow. A key aspect of this design is the use of a boundary-layer ingesting engine, potentially leading to reduced fuel burn in comparison to conventional engine placement.

Other promising novel aircraft configurations are based on nonplanar wing concepts with the potential to reduce weight and induced drag. These include the strut-braced wing and various closed wing systems.[20] For example, Lockheed-Martin has proposed a configuration that is a basic tube and wing design but an additional lifting surface joins the top of the winglet to the vertical tail, creating a closed wing system, and the engines are hung from that surface.[21] This configuration enables low induced drag with modest span, thereby reducing weight, and facilitates the use of ultra-high-bypass engines with reduced fuel burn, noise, and emissions. The strut-braced wing (also known as the truss-braced wing) is another promising approach, in which the wing is supported by one or more struts that also serve as lifting surfaces. This creates structural advantages, reducing weight and improved aerodynamic efficiency by reducing induced drag.

One of the challenges facing the designer of a new aircraft and the developer of a new aircraft configuration is the need for a suitable metric enabling consideration of environmental impact.[22] For example, how should

[18] A. Velicki, P. Thrash, and D. Jegley, "Airframe development for the hybrid wing body aircraft," AIAA Paper 2009–932 (2009).

[19] M. Drela, "Development of the D8 transport configuration," AIAA Paper 2011–3970 (2011).

[20] N. A. Meadows, "Multidisciplinary design optimization of medium-range transonic truss-braced wing transport aircraft," *J Aircraft*, 49:6 (2012), 1844.

[21] K. Martin, "Lockheed Martin Skunk Works green aviation: NASA ERA and N+2 supersonic projects," paper delivered at the 3rd UTIAS International Workshop on Aviation and Climate Change (May 2012).

[22] E. Schwartz Dallara, I. M. Kroo, and I. A. Waitz, "Metric for comparing lifetime average climate impact of aircraft," *AIAA J*, 49:8 (2011), 1600; Green, "Civil," *supra* Note 5.

environmental impact be weighed against conventional objectives, such as minimizing direct operating cost? This may well be driven by economic measures, such as emissions trading systems and carbon taxes. Even within environmental impact, there are measures that increase noise while reducing carbon dioxide emissions, while other measures have the opposite effect. These design decisions will be greatly influenced by the regulatory environment as well as economic measures. Hence, it is critical that these be carefully and objectively considered based on a global perspective and the latest scientific understanding in order to avoid unintended consequences. For example, excessive tightening of noise regulations will hamper efforts to reduce climate change impact. In order to design aircraft with reduced climate change impact, a significantly improved understanding is needed of the relative impact of carbon dioxide, nitrogen oxides, and aviation-induced cirrus. The next generation of aircraft will typically be operational for thirty years, so there is a great incentive to minimize their climate change impact, and it would be a serious mistake to design them based on an inadequate understanding of the relative impact of these three primary sources. Finally, aviation-induced cirrus and oxides of nitrogen have a more immediate shorter-term impact, while the impact of carbon dioxide is much longer lasting. It is not clear how these impacts should be weighted in the design of future aircraft.

To sum up this section, there are promising technological opportunities to develop aircraft with significantly reduced environmental impact. Active flow control and unconventional aircraft configurations are among the most promising technologies. Examples of unconventional aircraft configurations include (1) the double-bubble concept combined with a reduction in speed and low-sweep wings; (2) the blended wing-body; (3) strut-braced wings. These configurations can potentially be even more efficient when combined with active flow control.

In order to derive the maximum benefit from new technology, it is crucial that the regulatory environment be driven by the best possible scientific understanding of the various sources of the environmental impact of aviation. This will require continued investment in the necessary science. Furthermore, despite the high potential of the new technologies described here, a considerable amount of further research is needed to develop and de-risk new ideas and to mature existing ideas. This will require substantial financial investment.

1.4 ENGINE TECHNOLOGIES

The introduction of the gas turbine engine and the turbojet principle into aircraft propulsion more than seventy years ago led to a revolutionary change in transport technology. As a result of this transformation supersonic flight became possible, the cost of air travel and cargo transport was greatly reduced, and significant improvements in aircraft safety were achieved. The cost reductions were realized as a result of a combination of increasing flight speed and the ability to build much larger aircraft.[23] Prior to introducing gas turbine engines into aircraft propulsion, aircraft had piston engines to drive the propeller. As the performance and efficiency of turbine engines began to exceed those of piston engines, gas turbines became the dominant engines in aircraft. The adaptations of turbine engines in the form of turbojet, turbofan, and turboprop engines came with the different needs for thrust at various speeds. A simple way to compare the performance of the three main engine types is to look at their thrust-specific fuel consumption. This parameter gives the amount of fuel by weight required to provide a specific amount of jet thrust over a certain period of time. Thrust-specific fuel consumption characteristics of typical aircraft engines as a function of aircraft Mach numbers are given in Figure 1.1.

It is clear that turboprops have superior fuel efficiency over turbofans and turbojets, but they are disadvantaged by the limitation of the flight speed. This limitation is induced by the tip speed of the propeller, which should be below the sonic speed, hence limiting the engine shaft speed. The solution to this problem seems to be a geared propeller, that is, a geared transmission between the propeller and engine shafts. The gearbox is typically massive and requires extensive development effort to ensure reliability and durability; most of the time substantial speed reduction is necessary. The massiveness of the required gearbox becomes the limiting factor for relatively larger turboprop engines. However, for long-range subsonic aircraft high bypass ratio turbofan engines are still the only choice. The latest design of this type of engine incorporates a geared turbofan, which provides significant efficiency improvements. Another concept is the open rotor engine design that has the potential to provide appreciable fuel burn savings for single aisle aircraft as compared to that of an equivalent high bypass ratio turbofan engine. This concept is a follow up on known designs of unducted fans or fanprops, which have not been commercially produced. Open rotor engines are likely to be noisier than turbofan engines as there is no nacelle to absorb and attenuate the noise generated by the engine. Other approaches that could improve the efficiency of jet engines are to find solutions to increase the compression ratio and the turbine inlet temperature. Both parameters directly influence

[23] P. G. Hill and C. R. Peterson, *Mechanics and Thermodynamics of Propulsion*, 2nd edn. (Boston: Addison Wesley, 1992).

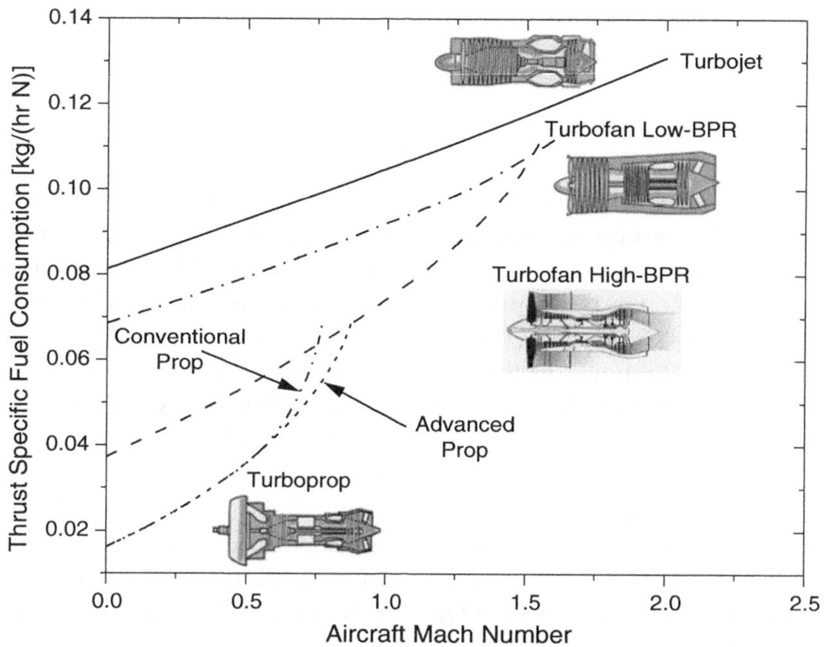

FIGURE 1.1 Thrust-specific fuel consumption characteristics of typical aircraft engines. BPR stands for bypass ratio, referring to the ratio of air mass flow around the engine pushed by the fan to the air mass flow that goes through the engine for combustion.
Source: Adapted from J. D. Mattingly, "Elements of propulsion gas turbines and rockets," AIAA Education Series (2006).

fuel efficiency. Today, the turbine inlet temperatures are limited by the blade materials available and the blade cooling technologies. Advances in these areas will further improve the fuel efficiency of aviation gas turbine engines.

The issue of high compression ratios and higher turbine inlet temperatures also has some negative implications since nitrogen oxide (NO_x) emissions increase with increasing pressure and temperature. NO_x control in current aviation gas turbine engines is achieved mostly by staged combustion schemes such as *rich burn/quick quench/lean burn*. The most promising technology now seems to be to operate aviation gas turbines in a premixed combustion mode instead of the current nonpremixed mode. Premixed combustion technology permits better control over NO_x emissions and completely eliminates particulate matter (soot aerosol) production and emissions. Known as *lean premixed* combustion, this technology has long been used in stationary gas turbines. It should be noted that applying this technology to aviation gas turbine engines is not straightforward, and there are concentrated research efforts at both universities and industrial laboratories to find innovative solutions.

1.5 BIOFUELS

It is estimated that the number of commercial aircraft in the world will double in the next two decades, reaching 40,000. Currently all commercial jet aircraft operate on a single fuel product obtained from fossil fuel sources.[24] Since the first turbine engine, aviation fuel has evolved into a tightly regulated commodity, and its specifications have narrowed as engine technology and refining methods have advanced. As a result, aviation gas turbine engine fuels today are the most highly regulated transportation fuels with the most extensive set of specifications.[25] Fuel specifications have material and manufacture requirements limiting the fuel feed stocks to petroleum crude oil, natural gas condensates, heavy crude oil, shale oil, and oil sands (i.e. hydrocarbons). The American Society for Testing and Materials (ASTM) is the governing body for establishing the requirements for aviation fuels, and the ASTM D1655 is the standard that lists the required specifications for turbine fuels.[26]

Two major biofuels are present in the global fuel market: bioethanol, which is largely produced by the fermentation of sugars or starches, and biodiesel, which is produced from the transesterification of vegetable oils such as rapeseed, soybean, or palm, as well as from animal fats. Ethanol and biodiesel are blended into gasoline and diesel fuels, respectively, in smaller percentages for ground transportation. However, unlike the use of biofuels in ground transportation, aviation gas turbine engines present more stringent restrictions on any candidate fuel due to several factors.[27] First, only a limited range of potential liquid fuels can satisfy the requirements for reliable and safe combustion taking place under the extreme conditions of a gas turbine combustion chamber. Second, any product proposed must be fully interchangeable with the current jet fuel product to avoid the logistic problems of airports handling multiple fuels of varying qualities and the commercial limitations this would impose. Finally, the long life of

[24] S. Blakey, L. Ray, and C. W. Wilson, "Aviation gas turbine alternative fuels: A review," *Proc Combust Inst*, **33**:2 (2011), 2863.

[25] G. R. Wilson et al., "Certification of alternative aviation fuels and blend components," *Energy & Fuels*, **27**:2 (2013), 962.

[26] ASTM International, *ASTM D1655–12: Standard Specification for Aviation Turbine Fuels* (West Conshohocken, PA: ASTM International, 2012).

[27] Wilson et al., "Certification," *supra* Note 25.

a commercial jet means any candidate fuel needs to be *backward* compatible and suitable for use in existing engine technology.[28] For these reasons, bioethanol and biodiesel are not fit for aviation gas turbines. The overarching criterion in developing biofuels for aviation has been the development of *drop-in* fuels that can be used in the existing fleet without any modifications.

Currently, synthetic paraffinic kerosene (SPK) produced by the Fischer-Tropsch (FT) process either from biomass sources or coal is allowed to be blended with conventional jet fuel up to 50 percent by volume.[29] It should be emphasized that SPKs from either source are mixtures of pure hydrocarbons of almost all paraffinic nature. Fatty acid methyl esters (FAME), which are the major components in biodiesel, are considered as contaminants in jet fuel because of their degrading effect on jet fuel thermal stability. In light of these concerns, it is clear that any biomass-based fuel should be first converted to pure hydrocarbon mixtures in order to be accepted as a jet fuel blending product. This limits, at least with the current technology, the potential biofuels for aviation to SPK obtained by the FT process from biomass and hydroprocessed esters and fatty acids (HEFA). HEFA is derived from animal and vegetable oils, but its composition is similar to SPK, that is, a mixture of pure paraffinic hydrocarbons. HEFA has also been approved to be blended with conventional jet fuel up to 50 percent by volume.[30]

The technical path that should be taken in developing and adopting any new alternative jet fuel that would satisfy the drop-in fuel requirements should go through the following three stages:

1. Testing to ensure that the following properties are within the current jet fuel specification range: physical and chemical properties, fundamental combustion properties, and emissions measured in benchmark lab tests.
2. Testing to ensure that the candidate fuel meets the following: thermal stability and handling requirements, specifications dictated by standards, and the *fit-for-purpose* requirements.
3. Finally, the following steps should be completed before certification: full engine tests, including simulated altitude and flight tests.

Of course, drop-in fuel requirements do not include any environmental credentials. The analysis of an alternative fuel's environmental credentials – which

[28] Ibid.

[29] ASTM International, *ASTM D7566–11a: Standard Specification for Aviation Turbine Fuel Containing Synthesized Hydrocarbons* (West Conshohocken, PA: ASTM International, 2012).

[30] ASTM International, *Evaluation of Bio-Derived Synthetic Paraffinic Kerosenes (Bio-SPKs)*, Research Report D-02–1739 (West Conshohocken, PA: ASTM International, 2011).

is expected to become a key requirement of an alternative fuel either due to political pressures or environmental legislations – can only be achieved by assessing emissions at all stages.[31] At the moment, development of biofuels for aviation is being driven by ensuring supply (energy security) and the sector's environmental footprint. The cost of reducing aviation carbon dioxide emissions about 30 percent by powering the world's fleet by 50 percent biomass-derived product seems unacceptably high at the moment. Despite current biomass feedstock being impractical, the search for and development of alternative high yield per ton feed stocks are the focus of current major research and development initiatives.

The influence of blending up to 50 percent of SPK with conventional jet fuel on engine-out emissions are not well-documented except a few studies that demonstrated NO_x, CO, and unburned hydrocarbon emissions similar to those of jet fuel and a measurable reduction in particulate matter emissions. This is one of the areas that require concentrated research and development efforts.

1.6 DISCUSSION AND CONCLUSIONS

There are numerous avenues available to reduce the environmental impact of aviation. As technology progresses, climate change impact is likely to emerge as the most important concern. It seems likely that nitrogen oxide emissions will be dramatically reduced in future generations of engines, leaving carbon dioxide and aviation-induced cirrus/contrails as the dominant problems. Much remains to be understood about the effect of aviation-induced cirrus and contrails, and it is relatively straightforward to reduce this impact if this turns out to be justified; hence the focus is on reducing carbon dioxide emissions. Some of the promising avenues include new aircraft configurations, new materials and advanced composite manufacturing techniques, new engine configurations, such as open rotors, active flow control for drag reduction, advanced materials and cooling technologies for engines, and biofuels. None of these provides the solution by itself, but many are complementary and can be combined. All will require considerable further research in order to have the desired impact while meeting the need for aviation safety, which of course cannot be compromised.

The ultimate goal is to meet the growing global demand for air travel while achieving the desired reduction in overall environmental impact, particularly

[31] Blakey, Ray, and Wilson, "Aviation Gas Turbine," *supra* Note 24.

climate change impact. Economic measures that succeed in reducing environmental impact simply by decreasing the amount of air travel cannot be said to achieve this goal, unless an alternative means of meeting the demand is provided. However, it is critical that the environmental impact of the alternative means of travel be properly measured. For example, in comparing the climate change impact of high-speed trains with that of aviation for routes where both are an option, it is important to consider the degree to which seats are filled on a regular basis, the nature of the energy source used, and the climate change impact of the construction of the necessary infrastructure in each case.

It is clear that the efficiency improvements historically achieved in aviation to date, which typically average between 1 and 2 percent per year, will not be adequate to enable both growth in air travel and a substantial reduction in total emissions. The preferred approach will involve measures that stimulate the research needed to achieve the above goal and, directly or indirectly, provide the funding required to support the required research and development.

2

Global Civil Aviation Emissions Standards

From Noise to Greener Fuels[Φ]

Md Tanveer Ahmad

The protection of the environment is one of the main components of sustainability and, hence, securing sustainable development of aviation requires initiatives from the aviation industry to lessen the environmental impacts of aviation while ensuring smooth growth of the industry. Emissions from civil aviation have become a great environmental concern, since such emissions pollute the environment, exacerbate climate change and are rapidly increasing with the fast growth of the aviation industry. Hence, emissions from aviation have to be reduced to protect the environment. This chapter addresses the question of whether or not the current global civil aviation emissions standards are sufficient to ensure sustainable development in the aviation industry and argues that these standards are not sufficient. The Chicago Convention has not set any such standards. The standards set by Volumes II and III of Annex 16 to the Convention are not binding and suffer from lack of modern effective provisions dealing with emissions from aviation. The ICAO's basket of measures in their current state cannot effectively reduce emissions from aviation. The difficulties that are hindering effective implementation of this basket have to be immediately addressed and solved.

2.1 INTRODUCTION

The protection of the environment is one of the main components of sustainability. Therefore, securing sustainable development of aviation requires

[Φ] A significant part of this chapter has been taken from the author's following two publications: *Climate Change Governance in International Civil Aviation: Toward Regulating Emissions Relevant to Climate Change and Global Warming* (The Hague: Eleven International Publishing, 2016) and "Environmental Law: Emissions," in P. S. Dempsey and R. S. Jakhu (eds.), *Routledge Handbook of Public Aviation Law* (Abingdon: Routledge, 2017) 195.

initiatives from the aviation industry to lessen the environmental impacts of aviation while ensuring smooth growth of the industry. Emissions from civil aviation have become a great environmental concern, since such emissions pollute the environment, exacerbate climate change and global warming, and are rapidly increasing with the rapid growth of the aviation industry. Hence, emissions from aviation have to be reduced to protect the environment. This chapter addresses the question of whether or not the current global civil aviation emissions standards are sufficient to ensure sustainable development in the aviation industry, and the author concludes that they are not.

2.2 CURRENT STATE OF GLOBAL CIVIL AVIATION EMISSIONS STANDARDS

In international law, the only legally binding instrument that specifically addresses emissions from civil aviation is the *Kyoto Protocol*.[1] Article 2(2) of the Protocol provides that the Annex I developed State Parties shall pursue limitation or reduction of emissions of greenhouse gases (GHGs) not controlled by the *Montreal Protocol*[2] from aviation bunker fuels, working through the International Civil Aviation Organization (ICAO),[3] which is the global forum for cooperation among its 191 Member States in all fields of civil aviation.[4] However, the Protocol has not further elaborated the provision and, hence, has not set any emissions standard for aviation. Moreover, the Protocol is not concerned with all types of gaseous emissions from aviation; it is only concerned with GHGs that are not controlled by the *Montreal Protocol*. It is unsurprising since it is not the *Kyoto Protocol* but the *Chicago Convention* that governs the area of law in the field of international civil aviation.[5]

1 *Kyoto Protocol to the United Nations Framework Convention on Climate Change* (adopted December 11, 1997, entered into force February 16, 2005) 2303 UNTS 162 [*Kyoto Protocol*].

2 *Montreal Protocol on Substances that Deplete the Ozone Layer* (adopted September 16, 1987, entered into force January 1, 1989) 1522 UNTS 3 [*Montreal Protocol*].

3 *Kyoto Protocol, supra* Note 1, Art 2(2).

4 ICAO, "Vision and mission," www.icao.int/about-icao/Council/Pages/vision-and-mission.aspx last accessed April 27, 2017.

5 *Convention on International Civil Aviation* (adopted December 7, 1944, entered into force April 4, 1947) 15 UNTS 295, ICAO Doc 7300/9 [*Chicago Convention*].

The *Chicago Convention* is the primary source of public international air law,[6] has established the ICAO,[7] and is often regarded as the "Constitution"[8] of international civil aviation. However, the Convention was signed in 1944 when international environmental law was at its first stage of development.[9] Thus, the need to protect the environment was not envisaged at the time of negotiation and drafting of the Convention in 1944 and, hence, no explicit provisions on environmental protection were incorporated therein.[10]

Nonetheless, the Convention tacitly confers responsibility on the ICAO to address aviation environmental issues. According to Article 44, one of the aims and objectives of the ICAO is "to develop the principles and techniques of international air navigation and to foster the planning and development of international air transport so as to … promote generally the development of all aspects of international civil aeronautics."[11] Since reducing environmental impacts of aviation for the protection of the environment is one of the aspects of international civil aeronautics,[12] it follows that the ICAO has a duty to regulate emissions from international civil aviation thus ensuring sustainable development of aviation.[13] To discharge this duty, the ICAO has adopted

6 M. Milde, *International Air Law and ICAO*, 3rd edn. (The Hague: Eleven International Publishing, 2016) 19. See also E. M. Giemulla, "Chapter 1: Chicago system: Genesis and main characteristics" in E. M. Giemulla and L. Weber (eds.), *International and EU Aviation Law: Selected Issues* (Alphen aan den Rijn: Kluwer Law International, 2011) 3, 5.

7 P. S. Dempsey, *Public International Air Law* (Montreal: McGill University, Institute and Centre for Research in Air & Space Law, 2008) 49.

8 Ibid. at 69; P. Mendes de Leon, "Enforcement of the EU ETS: The EU's convulsive efforts to export its environmental values," *Air & Space L*, 37 (2012), 287, 289.

9 C. Redgwell, "International environmental law," in M. D. Evans (ed.), *International Law*, 3rd edn. (Oxford: Oxford University Press, 2010), 687 at 687, 690.

10 See also ICAO, *The Convention on International Civil Aviation: Annexes 1 to 18*, www.icao.int/safety/airnavigation/NationalityMarks/annexes_booklet_en.pdf last accessed October 16, 2017; ICAO, "The postal history of ICAO: Annex 16 – Environmental Protection," www.icao.int/secretariat/PostalHistory/annex_16_environmental_protection.htm last accessed October 16, 2017.

11 *Chicago Convention*, *supra* Note 5, Art 44(i).

12 In fact, environmental protection is one of the five strategic objectives of the ICAO. See ICAO, "ICAO strategic objectives," www.icao.int/about-icao/Council/Pages/Strategic-Objectives.aspx last accessed April 27, 2017.

13 A. de Mestral and M. T. Ahmad, "A pre-analysis of Canada–EU aviation relations post-ICAO Assembly meeting concerning emissions trading system," policy brief, Carleton University Canada-Europe transatlantic dialogue (April 2013), 7, https://carleton.ca/canadaeurope/2013/a-pre-analysis-of-canada-eu-aviation-relations-post-icao-assembly-meeting-concerning-emissions-trading-system/ last accessed October 16, 2017.

Annex 16 to the *Chicago Convention* to address aviation environmental issues.[14] Importantly, the vision of the ICAO currently is to: "Achieve the sustainable growth of the global civil aviation system."[15]

The *Chicago Convention* facilitates the adoption of international standards and recommended practices (SARPs) as Annexes to the Convention by the ICAO Council, in accordance with Article 90,[16] to address new issues to meet the current global need.[17] The ICAO Council has an obligation to adopt SARPs in accordance with the provisions of Chapter VI of the Convention,[18] i.e. Articles 37–42. Among these provisions, Article 37 provides guidelines regarding such adoption:

> Each contracting State undertakes to collaborate in securing the highest practicable degree of uniformity in regulations, standards, procedures, and organization in relation to aircraft, personnel, airways and auxiliary services in all matters in which such uniformity will facilitate and improve air navigation.
>
> To this end the International Civil Aviation Organization shall adopt and amend from time to time, as may be necessary, international standards and recommended practices and procedures dealing with:
>
> … such … matters concerned with the safety, regularity, and efficiency of air navigation as may from time to time appear appropriate.[19]

Utilizing this authority, the ICAO Council adopted Annex 16. The SARPs are designated as Annexes to the *Chicago Convention* for convenience.[20] However, Annexes do not actually become part of the Convention.[21]

Since "[a]ircraft noise was the first major environmental issue raised with respect [to] aviation,"[22] noise emissions from aircraft engines were addressed

[14] For a brief discussion on Annex 16, see ICAO, *Annexes 1 to 18*, *supra* Note 10; ICAO, "Annex 16," *supra* Note 10.

[15] ICAO, "Vision," *supra* Note 4.

[16] *Chicago Convention*, *supra* Note 5, Art 90. According to Article 90, the adoption of annexes requires the vote of two-thirds of the ICAO Council at a meeting called for that purpose and shall then be submitted by the ICAO Council to each Contracting State, and that Annex or any amendment thereto shall become effective within 3 months after its submission to the Contracting States or at the end of such longer period of time as the ICAO Council may prescribe, unless in the meantime majority of the Contracting States register their disapproval with the ICAO Council. Ibid.

[17] Ibid., Art 37.

[18] Ibid., Art 54(l).

[19] Ibid., Art 37.

[20] Ibid., Art 54(l).

[21] See Dempsey, *supra* Note 7 at 75; M. Milde, "Aviation safety oversight: Audits and the law," *Ann Air & Sp L*, **XXVI** (2001), 165 at 168.

[22] Dempsey, *supra* Note 7 at 415.

by the ICAO before addressing gaseous emissions.[23] Hence, initially, Annex 16, adopted by the ICAO Council on 2 April 1971, only dealt with aircraft noise.[24] In international civil aviation, emissions from aircraft engines emerged as an environmental issue in the 1970s.[25] In May 1980, at the second meeting of the Committee on Aircraft Engine Emissions – which was established in 1977 to pursue a number of aspects of the subject of aircraft engine emissions – proposals were made for material to be included in an Annex. After amendment of the proposed material, the ICAO Council adopted the material to form the text of the Annex.[26] The ICAO Council agreed that it was desirable to include all environmental provisions in one Annex and, hence, Annex 16 was renamed "Environmental Protection" and divided into two volumes.[27] The then-existing text of the Annex became Volume I, exclusively dealing with aircraft noise, and the amended material became Volume II, devoted to addressing the issue of aircraft emissions other than noise emissions.[28] Recently, Volume III has been adopted to address only carbon dioxide (CO_2) emissions from aircraft.[29] Therefore, Volumes II and III of Annex 16 provide the current global civil aviation emissions standards.

Part II of Volume II contains the standards concerning vented fuel with respect to all turbine engine-powered aircraft manufactured after February 18, 1982 that are intended for operation in international civil aviation.[30] This Part stipulates that the design and construction of an aircraft shall be such "as to prevent the intentional discharge into the atmosphere of liquid fuel from the fuel nozzle manifolds resulting from the process of engine shutdown following normal flight or ground operations."[31] Certification related to the prevention of intentional fuel venting can only be granted on the basis of

[23] Ibid.

[24] ICAO, "International Standards and Recommended Practices: Annex 16 to the Convention on International Civil Aviation," Volume 1, Aircraft Noise (2008) at xi.

[25] Dempsey, *supra* Note 7 at 444.

[26] ICAO, "International Standards and Recommended Practices: Annex 16 to the Convention on International Civil Aviation," Volume 2, Aircraft Engine Emissions (2008) at ix.

[27] Ibid.

[28] Ibid.

[29] ICAO, "Annex 16," *supra* Note 10; ICAO, "ICAO Council adopts new CO2 emissions standard for aircraft" (March 6, 2017), www.icao.int/Newsroom/Pages/ICAO-Council-adopts-new-CO2-emissions-standard-for-aircraft.aspx last accessed October 16, 2017.

[30] *Annex 16: Volume 2, supra* Note 26 at ix, II-1–1.

[31] Ibid. at II-2–1.

satisfactory evidence that either the aircraft or the aircraft engines comply with this standard.[32]

Part III of Volume II provides for the standards related to emissions certification applicable to the types of aircraft engines specified in the individual chapters of the Part, "where such engines are fitted to aircraft engaged in international civil aviation."[33] Emissions certification shall be granted on the basis of satisfactory evidence that the engine complies with the minimum requirements set by the provisions of Volume II.[34]

Chapter 2 of Part III deals with turbojet and turbofan engines intended for propulsion only at subsonic speeds. Chapter 3 concerns turbojet and turbofan engines intended for propulsion at supersonic speeds. For the emissions certification for all types of engines, the following emissions shall be controlled: smoke and three gases, namely, unburned hydrocarbons (HC), carbon monoxide (CO) and oxides of nitrogen (NO_X).[35] Smoke emissions are measured and reported in terms of Smoke Number (SN).[36] The mass (D_P) of the gaseous pollutant – HC, CO or NO_X – emitted during the reference emissions landing and takeoff (LTO) cycle is measured and reported in grams.[37] Regulatory Smoke Number and regulatory gaseous emissions levels for different engines are specifically defined.[38] A certificate of compliance is issued if the mean of the values measured and corrected for all the engines tested does not exceed the regulatory level.[39]

In March 6, 2017, a new aircraft CO_2 emissions standard was adopted by the ICAO Council giving rise to Volume III of Annex 16.[40] The new standard "shall apply to new aircraft type designs from 2020, and to aircraft type designs already in-production as of 2023."[41] Those in-production aircraft which fail to meet the standard by 2028, "will no longer be able to be produced unless their designs are sufficiently modified."[42]

[32] Ibid. at II-1–1.
[33] Ibid. at ix.
[34] Ibid. at III-1–1.
[35] Ibid. at III-2–1, III-3–1.
[36] Ibid. at III-2–1, III-3–1.
[37] Ibid.
[38] Ibid. at III-2–3ff, III-3–3.
[39] Ibid. at App 6–1.
[40] ICAO, "Annex 16," *supra* Note 10; ICAO, "ICAO Council adopts," *supra* Note 29.
[41] ICAO, "Annex 16," *supra* Note 10.
[42] Ibid.

2.3 THE CAPABILITY OF THE CURRENT EMISSIONS STANDARDS TO ENSURE SUSTAINABILITY: AN ENVIRONMENTAL PERSPECTIVE

The current emissions standards for international civil aviation are provided in Volumes II and III of Annex 16 to the *Chicago Convention*. However, as noted already, unlike the provisions of the Convention, Annexes are not legally binding. Outside the *Chicago Convention* regime, the *Kyoto Protocol* provides a clear mandate for the ICAO to limit or reduce emissions of GHGs not controlled by the *Montreal Protocol* from international civil aviation.[43] However, the *Kyoto Protocol* includes emissions from domestic civil aviation requiring Annex I developed State Parties to regulate those but excludes emissions from international civil aviation, leaving such responsibility to the ICAO.[44] According to the Guidelines of the Intergovernmental Panel on Climate Change and of the *United Nations Framework Convention on Climate Change*,[45] emissions from both national and international civil aviation should be calculated as part of the national GHG inventories of Parties, but emissions from international civil aviation "should be excluded from national totals and reported separately."[46]

Certainly, a question arises of whether or not Annex 16, Volumes II and III can resolve the difficulty of the absence of a legally binding instrument dealing with emissions from international civil aviation. The answer will be in the negative for various reasons. First and foremost, Annexes to the *Chicago Convention* are not mandatory like the provisions of the Convention since, as

[43] *Kyoto Protocol, supra* Note 1, Art 2(2); Dempsey, *Public International Air Law, supra* Note 7 at 450.

[44] See Dempsey, *Public International Air Law, supra* Note 7 at 450; M. Milde, "The EU Emissions Trading Scheme: Confrontation or compromise?: A unilateral action outside the framework of ICAO," *ZLW*, 61:2 (2012), 173 at 175; J. Barton, "Including aviation in the EU Emissions Trading Scheme: Prepare for take-off," *J Eur Envtl Plan L*, 5:2 (2008), 5183 at 5184; M. D. Kasper, "The Air Transport Association's challenge to the European Union's extension of its Emissions Trading Scheme to international aviation: A legal analysis," *Issues in Aviation L & Policy*, 10:1 (2010), 145 at 153–54; D. B. Reagan, "Putting international aviation into the European Union Emissions Trading Scheme: Can Europe do it flying solo?" *BC Envtl Aff L Rev*, 35:2 (2008), 349 at 364.

[45] *United Nations Framework Convention on Climate Change* (adopted May 9, 1992, entered into force March 21, 1994) 1771 UNTS 107 [*UNFCCC*]; S. Eggleston et al. (eds.), *2006 IPCC Guidelines for National Greenhouse Gas Inventories* (Kanagawa: Institute for Global Environmental Strategies, 2006).

[46] UNFCCC, "Emissions from fuel used for international aviation and maritime transport (international bunker fuels)," unfccc.int/methods/emissions_from_intl_transport/items/1057.php last accessed October 16, 2017; A. Garg et al., "Volume 2: Energy," in S. Eggleston et al. (eds.), *2006 IPCC Guidelines for National Greenhouse Gas Inventories* (Kanagawa: Institute for Global Environmental Strategies, 2006) at 3.57.

noted earlier, Annexes do not become part of the Convention.[47] In reality, the adoption and legal force of Annexes are not "subject to the general international law of treaties."[48]

The Contracting States to the *Chicago Convention* are required to adopt measures to ensure that all aircraft flying over or maneuvering within their territory or carrying their nationality mark shall comply with the rules and regulations relating to the flight and man oeuvre of aircraft there in force.[49] In these respects, all Contracting States undertake to keep their own regulations "uniform, *to the greatest possible extent*, with those established from time to time under this Convention,"[50] i.e. with Annexes. Nevertheless, Articles 37 and 38 weaken the binding nature of the Annexes.[51] Both articles allow any Contracting State to the Convention to avoid implementing the Annexes.[52] Although Article 37 invites all Contracting States "to collaborate in securing the *highest practicable degree of uniformity* in regulations, standards, procedures, and organization,"[53] any State can refrain from doing everything possible by it since the phrase "highest practicable degree of uniformity"[54] has not been defined.[55] Article 38 allows deviation from any standard or procedure of any Annexes or any amendments thereto by any Contracting State.[56] If any State finds it "impracticable to comply in all respects" with any of those standards or procedures, it merely has to notify the ICAO of the discrepancy between its own practice and the respective standard or procedure.[57] What is meant by the term "impracticable"?[58] The Convention provides no guidance.[59] Again, although the deviating Contracting State must give "immediate notification"[60] to the ICAO of such

47 See Milde, *International*, *supra* Note 6 at 172; Milde, "Aviation," *supra* Note 21 at 168; M. T. Ahmad, *Climate Change Governance in International Civil Aviation: Toward Regulating Emissions Relevant to Climate Change and Global Warming* (The Hague: Eleven International Publishing, 2016), 61–63. See also *New Zealand Airline Pilots' Association* v. *Attorney General*, [1997] 3 NZLR 269 (CA).

48 Milde, *International*, *supra* Note 6 at 172; Milde, "Aviation," *supra* Note 21 at 168.

49 *Chicago Convention*, *supra* Note 5, Art. 12.

50 Ibid. [emphasis added].

51 Ibid., Arts. 37, 38.

52 See M. T. Ahmad, "Achieving global safety in civil aviation: A critical analysis of contemporary safety oversight mechanisms," *Ann Air & Sp L*, 37 (2012), 81 at 86.

53 *Chicago Convention*, *supra* Note 5, Art. 37 [emphasis added].

54 Ibid.

55 See Ahmad, "Achieving," *supra* Note 52 at 86; Milde, "Aviation," *supra* Note 21 at 168–69.

56 Ibid.; *Chicago Convention*, *supra* Note 5, Art. 38.

57 *Chicago Convention*, *supra* Note 5, Art. 38.

58 Ahmad, "Achieving," *supra* Note 52 at 86.

59 Ibid.

60 *Chicago Convention*, *supra* Note 5, Art. 38.

"differences between its own practice and that established by the international standard,"[61] the concerned State can avoid notifying since no defined time limit is set for that purpose.[62] The Convention is silent on the definition of the term "immediate."[63] Professor Dempsey has observed that, "[i]n practice, States have notified ICAO of impracticality of compliance with [Annexes] at any time, or indeed not at all, thereby violating the plain meaning of the phrase 'immediate notification'."[64] Interestingly, a sixty-day notification requirement is established for filing of differences with regard to any amendment to the Annexes.[65]

Twelve States, including the United States, have already notified the ICAO of differences that exist between their national regulations and practices and the SARPs of Annex 16, Volume II, while a large number of States remains silent.[66] It cannot be stated with sufficient certainty that only those twelve States are not complying with Volume II. At this writing, such information related to Volume III is unavailable, since the new aircraft CO_2 emissions standard has just been adopted. In fact, the overwhelming majority of States do not discharge their obligation to notify the ICAO of such differences.[67] The ICAO itself has admitted this unexpected fact.[68] Most importantly, "[t]here is no explicit sanction in the [Chicago] Convention for failing to notify."[69] Regarding the obligatory nature of the Annexes, Judge Buergenthal notes:[70]

> With some exceptions … the Contracting States have no legal obligation to implement or to comply with the provisions of the duly promulgated Annex or amendment thereto, unless they find it "practicable" to do so. This conclusion is supported both by the language of the Convention as well as by the practice of the [ICAO].[71]

61 Ibid.
62 Ibid.; Ahmad, "Achieving," *supra* Note 52 at 86.
63 *Chicago Convention, supra* Note 5, Art. 38.
64 Dempsey, *supra* Note 7 at 77 [footnote omitted].
65 *Chicago Convention, supra* Note 5, Art. 38.
66 ICAO, "Supplement to Annex 16, Volume II (Second Edition)," in *Annex 16: Volume 2, supra* Note 26.
67 Dempsey, *supra* Note 7 at 78.
68 Milde, *International, supra* Note 6 at 180; Milde, "Aviation," *supra* Note 21 at 170.
69 Dempsey, *supra* Note 7 at 79 [footnote omitted].
70 Thomas Buergenthal, *Law-Making in the International Civil Aviation Organization*, 1st edn. (New York: Syracuse University Press, 1969), 76.
71 Ibid.

Nevertheless, Professor Dempsey argues that "whatever *de jure* 'soft law' attributes SARPs may have, they appear to have corresponding *de facto* 'hard law' attributes as well."[72] This is due to the authority granted to the Contracting States by Article 33 to refuse to recognize certificates of airworthiness, and certificates of competency and licenses issued or rendered valid by another Contracting State if they do not meet the minimum standards established from time to time pursuant to the *Chicago Convention*.[73] If economically powerful States, such as the United States and the European Union Member States, elect to wield their authority under Article 33, States that fail to comply with annexes will lose their right to fly to those economically powerful States.[74] As a consequence, those non-compliant States will be isolated from the global economy, which can gravely affect their economic development.[75]

It is apparent that annexes are *de facto* "hard law" and, hence, Annex 16, Volumes II and III or any amendments thereto will force the Contracting States to comply with the emissions standards under these volumes. However, annexes should be made *de jure* "hard law" to ensure more effectiveness, given that, in the case of Annex 16, Volume II, the United States itself has notified the ICAO of differences.[76] This requires amending the *Chicago Convention*, a difficult and time-consuming process.[77] Therefore, amending Annex 16 so as to ensure its effectiveness in reducing emissions from aviation may be an easier, faster and more flexible process than amending the Convention.[78] It is worth noting that the International Law Commission considers Annex 16, Volume II, as one of the multilateral agreements relating to air pollution.[79]

[72] Dempsey, *supra* Note 7 at 79–80 [footnote omitted]. Similarly, Milde, "Aviation," *supra* Note 21 at 169, argues:

"However, in practice there is a powerful motivation for all States wishing to participate in international air transport to comply with such standards as closely as possible. The fact remains that these standards cannot be disregarded with impunity, and a phrase has been coined that their force can be compared with that of the 'law of gravity': compliance is simply unavoidable in practice."

[73] *Chicago Convention*, *supra* Note 5, Art. 33.

[74] Dempsey, *supra* Note 7 at 79.

[75] Ibid. See also Milde, "Aviation," *supra* Note 21 at 169; Milde, *International*, *supra* Note 6 at 179.

[76] Ahmad, *Climate*, *supra* Note 47 at 63.

[77] See also J. Liu, "The role of ICAO in regulating the greenhouse gas emissions of aircraft," *Carbon & Climate L Rev*, 5:4 (2011), 417 at 422; G. Guillaume, "ICAO at the beginning of the 21st Century: The 8th Beaumont Memorial Lecture, 5 February 2008," *Air & Space L*, 33:4/5 (2008), 313 at 317. To learn about the procedure, see *Chicago Convention*, *supra* Note 5, Arts. 49(j), 94(a).

[78] Liu, "The role of ICAO," *supra* Note 77 at 425.

[79] International Law Commission, *First Report on the Protection of the Atmosphere*, UNGAOR, 2014, UN Doc A/CN.4/667 at 19.

Besides not being legally binding, Annex 16 suffers from a lack of modern effective provisions dealing with emissions from aviation.[80] The ICAO has not yet included all the contaminants and GHGs emitted by aircraft in the list of controlled gases in Annex 16, Volumes II and III.[81] Most importantly, one of the major GHGs emitted by aircraft, namely, water vapor (H_2O), is not being regulated by Annex 16.[82]

Apart from Annex 16, the ICAO adopted several other legal measures dealing with emissions from civil aviation to fill in the gaps left by the *Chicago Convention* and Annex 16. These include: Assembly Resolutions A39–1, A39–2 and A39–3.[83] Nonetheless, resolutions do not have any legally binding effect since these are considered "soft law."[84] Resolutions are non-binding soft law, and are not law *per se*;[85] these instruments are a type of social rather than legal norms.[86] Hence, due to their non-binding nature, these soft

[80] See also Dempsey, *supra* Note 7 at 455–58.

[81] Contaminants from aircraft engine emissions include nitric oxide (NO), nitrogen dioxide (NO_2), carbon monoxide (CO), unburned hydrocarbons, sulfur oxides (SO_XO), particulate matter (PM), volatile organic compounds, ozone (O_3), semi-volatile organic compounds, metals, noise and odour. See ICAO, "Contaminants," www.icao.int/environmental-protection/Pages/Contaminants.aspx last accessed October 17, 2017. Aircraft emissions of relevance to climate change include: carbon dioxide (CO_2), water vapor (H_2O), NO, NO_2, SO_XO and soot. See World Bank, *Air transport and energy efficiency*, Transport Papers, TP–38 (February 2012) at 31, siteresources.worldbank.org/INTAIRTRANSPORT/Resources/TP38.pdf last accessed October 17, 2017; D. H. Lister et al., "Summary for policymakers: Aviation and the global atmosphere," in J. E. Penner et al. (eds.), *Aviation and the Global Atmosphere: A Special Report of IPCC Working Groups I and III in Collaboration with the Scientific Assessment Panel to the Montreal Protocol on Substances that Deplete the Ozone Layer* (Cambridge: Cambridge University Press, 1999), 1 at 3.

[82] See Ahmad, *Climate*, *supra* Note 47 at 63–64.

[83] See ICAO, "Consolidated statement of continuing ICAO policies and practices related to environmental protection – General Provisions, noise and local air quality," Res A39–1, ICAO Doc 10075 (2017), I-58; ICAO, "Consolidated statement of continuing ICAO policies and practices related to environmental protection – Climate change," Res A39–2, ICAO Doc 10075 (2017), I-72; ICAO, "Consolidated statement of continuing ICAO policies and practices related to environmental protection – Global Market-based Measure (MBM) scheme," Res A39–3, ICAO Doc 10075 (2017), I-80 [ICAO Res A39–3].

[84] See e.g. A. Boyle, "Soft law in international law making" in M. D. Evans, *International Law*, 2nd edn. (Oxford: Oxford University Press, 2006), 141 at 141–43; A. Kaczorowska, *Public International Law*, 4th edn. (Abingdon: Routledge, 2010), 64–65; D. Shelton, "Soft law," in D. Armstrong (ed.), *Routledge Handbook of International Law* (Abingdon: Routledge, 2009), 68 at 68–71.

[85] See e.g. Shelton, *supra* Note 84 at 68–71; Boyle, *supra* Note 84 at 141–43; M. Weston Janis, *International Law*, 6th edn. (New York: Wolters Kluwer Law & Business, 2012), 55.

[86] Shelton, *supra* Note 84 at 69.

law instruments will not succeed in effectively reducing emissions from aviation.[87]

2.4 OPTIONS UNDER CONSIDERATION: THE ICAO'S BASKET OF MEASURES

To address environmental concerns of aviation, the ICAO has developed and employed a basket of four mitigation measures, namely, technological improvements, operational improvements, sustainable alternative fuels, and market-based measures (MBMs). However, the basket in its present condition is fraught with difficulty and, hence, cannot sufficiently reduce emissions from civil aviation.[88]

With respect to technological improvements, no commercially viable aviation technology is in place that can ensure either zero emissions or even zero growth in emissions. Moreover, we cannot expect to see drastic technology advances in the near future to secure that solution since technological improvement, especially in the field of aviation, is a very expensive and time-consuming process.[89] Concerning operational improvements, such improvements cannot largely reduce emissions from international civil aviation, as shown in Figure 2.1, and new concepts for the purpose of improving operations suffer from several difficulties, including lack of implementation.[90] Although sustainable alternative fuels for civil aviation, where kerosene is the

[87] Ahmad, *Climate*, *supra* Note 47 at 94.

[88] For more on this, see ibid., c. 4.

[89] T. Barker et al., "Technical summary," in B. Metz et al. (eds.), *Climate Change 2007: Mitigation: Contribution of Working Group III to the Fourth Assessment Report of the Intergovernmental Panel on Climate Change* (Cambridge: Cambridge University Press, 2007), 25 at 36; S. Kahn Ribeiro et al., "Transport and its infrastructure," in B. Metz et al. (eds.), *Climate Change 2007: Mitigation: Contribution of Working Group III to the Fourth Assessment Report of the Intergovernmental Panel on Climate Change* (Cambridge: Cambridge University Press, 2007), 323 at 353–54; P. S. Dempsey and L. E. Gesell, *Airline Management: Strategies for the 21st Century*, 2nd edn. (Arizona: Coast Aire Publications, 2006), 314; Rob Corp, "Dreamliner trouble: A brief history of airliner problems," *BBC News* (January 17, 2013), www.bbc.co.uk/news/uk-21059525 last accessed October 17, 2017.

[90] See e.g. S. Sumner, "Regional forum: 'Creating more lift': ICAO Asia/Pacific Region," unpublished presentation delivered at the ICAO Performance-based Navigation (PBN) Symposium and Workshops, Montreal (October 16–19, 2012); A. Stealey, "Address," unpublished presentation delivered at the ICAO Performance-based Navigation (PBN) Symposium and Workshops, Montreal (October 16–19, 2012); C. Cirilo, "PBN: Global implementation situation," unpublished presentation delivered at the ICAO Performance-based Navigation (PBN) Symposium and Workshops, Montreal (October 16–19, 2012); A. Gittens, "Airports and PBN, will it make a difference?" unpublished presentation delivered at the ICAO Performance-based Navigation (PBN) Symposium and Workshops, Montreal

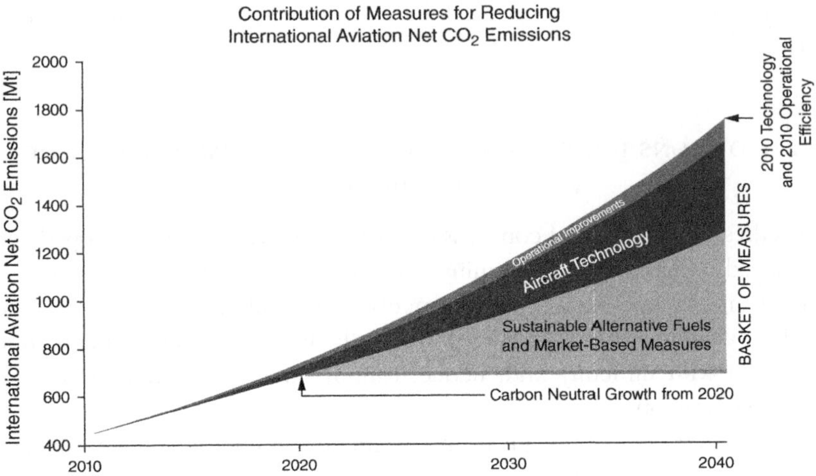

FIGURE 2.1 Contribution of measures for reducing international civil aviation net CO_2 emissions
Source: ICAO, "Environmental Trends," online: www.icao.int/environmental-protection/Pages/Environmental-Trends.aspx

primary energy source,[91] are essential as both a near-term and long-term solution,[92] as demonstrated by Figure 2.1, several challenges ranging from production to deployment still remain. Alternative fuels are still commercially unviable mainly because of the high and uncertain costs of such fuels and of an inability to meet the demand of the commercial aviation industry.[93] Even former ICAO Council President González asserted that "there is no alternative to current aviation fuel in the foreseeable future."[94]

(October 16–19, 2012). For an insight into the legal challenges in reducing GHG emissions through more efficient air traffic management practices, see c. 7.

91 See also Ribeiro et al., *supra* Note 89 at 334, 354; ICAO Sustainable Alternative Fuels (SUSTAF) Experts Group, "Sustainable alternative fuels: Challenges for the development and deployment of sustainable alternative fuels in aviation: Outcomes of ICAO's SUSTAF Experts Group," in ICAO, *ICAO Environmental Report 2013: Aviation and Climate Change* (ICAO, 2013), 126 at 126.

92 ICAO Secretariat, "Overview – Sustainable alternative fuels: Sustainable alternative fuels for aviation," in ICAO, *ICAO Environmental Report 2013: Aviation and Climate Change* (ICAO, 2013), 122 at 122.

93 See generally ICAO, "Alternative fuels: Questions and answers: 5. What are the challenges for the development and deployment of alternative fuels?" www.icao.int/environmental-protection/Pages/AltFuels-Challenges.aspx last accessed October 17, 2017. See also Barker et al., *supra* Note 89 at 51; Ribeiro et al., *supra* Note 89 at 355.

94 R. Kobeh González, "Towards a Transformed ATM environment – Working together," unpublished opening address by the President of the ICAO Council to the World ATM Congress 2013, Madrid (February 12–14, 2013), 2.

Regarding MBMs, no global MBM for international civil aviation is currently effective. At its 39th session in late 2016, the ICAO Assembly decided to implement a voluntary global MBM scheme "in the form of the Carbon Offsetting and Reduction Scheme for International Aviation (CORSIA) to address any annual increase in total CO_2 emissions from international civil aviation (i.e. civil aviation flights that depart in one country and arrive in a different country) above the 2020 levels."[95] As the title suggests and as emphasized in Resolution A39–3, CORSIA will regulate only CO_2 emissions from international civil aviation.[96] CORSIA will be implemented in different phases after 2020.[97] Thus, no global MBM for aviation will be implemented before 2020. MBMs are considered "to be an important gap filler"[98] to complement technological, operational and infrastructure measures.[99] The forecasts by the ICAO's CAEP show that, even after the implementation of technology and operational improvements and assuming 3 percent use of alternative fuels, "the emissions gap from carbon neutral growth in 2020 would be on the order of 500 Mt by 2040."[100] See Figure 2.1. Therefore, more participation of States in CORSIA is crucial.

2.5 CONCLUSION

It appears that the existing and envisaged global civil aviation emissions standards are incapable of significantly reducing emissions from aviation in

95 ICAO Res A39–3, *supra* Note 83 at I-81.

96 Ibid.

97 Ibid. at I-82.

98 ICAO Secretariat, "Overview – Market-based measures: Market-based measures," in ICAO, *ICAO Environmental Report 2013: Aviation and Climate Change* (ICAO, 2013), 138 at 138. See also International Coalition for Sustainable Aviation, "Effective market-based measures to address greenhouse gas emissions from international aviation," ICAO Assembly, 38th Sess., Agenda Item 17, Working Paper No 288, Doc A38-WP/288/Ex/100 (September 12, 2013), www.icao.int/Meetings/a38/Documents/WP/wp288_en.pdf last accessed October 17, 2017.

99 See ICAO Secretariat, "Market-based measures: ICAO's work on the development of a global MBM scheme for international aviation," in ICAO, *ICAO Environmental Report 2016: Aviation and Climate Change* (ICAO, 2016), 141; IATA, Press Release, "Historic Agreement on Carbon-Neutral Growth" (June 3, 2013), www.iata.org/pressroom/pr/Pages/2013-06-03-05.aspx last accessed October 17, 2017; P. Steele, "Aviation – Benefits beyond borders – ICAO destination green," unpublished presentation delivered at the ICAO Symposium on Aviation and Climate Change, "Destination Green," Montreal (May 14–16, 2013); A. Petsonk, "A Global MBM for aviation and climate Change: The time is now!" unpublished presentation delivered at the ICAO Symposium on Aviation and Climate Change, "Destination Green," Montreal (May 14–16, 2013).

100 ICAO, *Environment: Market-based measures and climate change* (August 2013), https://cfapp.icao.int/tools/38thAssyiKit/story_content/external_files/Flyer_US-Letter_ENV_MBMs_2013-08-30.pdf last accessed October 17, 2017.

their current condition. Hence, the current global aviation emissions standards are not sufficient to ensure sustainable development in the aviation industry. Annex 16, Volumes II and III, which provide for emissions standards, are not binding and suffer from lack of modern effective provisions dealing with emissions from aviation. The ICAO's basket of measures in their current state cannot effectively curb emissions from international civil aviation. The difficulties that are hindering effective implementation of this basket have to be immediately addressed and solved to contain emissions from international civil aviation. Unless the growth in emissions is restrained, sustainable development of aviation cannot be ensured.

3

Sustainable Flight Management and Aviation*

Peter Paul Fitzgerald and Md Tanveer Ahmad

Sustainable civil aviation is significantly dependent on successfully reducing greenhouse gases produced by commercial aviation. Lighter aircraft, more efficient engines and alternative fuels are the domain of scientists and engineers. It is now time for lawyers to act. The single largest remaining barrier to reducing the environmental impact from aviation is legal; literally those impediments that block "as the crow flies" routings or practices, such as "continuous decent." If environmental targets are to be met, and every milligram of gases emitted due to human activities is taken into account, it will be obvious that legal initiatives proposed herein must be adopted. This chapter argues that improvements in operations to ensure sustainable flight management should continue and new concepts for the purpose of improving flight management should continuously be developed. In this respect, this chapter addresses relevant provisions of the Chicago Convention, particularly articles 1 and 9, which concern airspace sovereignty and hinder the aviation industry's objective of achieving sustainable flight management, and provides recommendations to overcome those barriers.

3.1 INTRODUCTION

Reducing aviation emissions is central to achieving environmentally sustainable aviation, and the International Air Transport Association (IATA) believes that genuine progress in reducing greenhouse gas (GHG) emissions from

* This chapter has been adapted from the authors' article: "Efficient air traffic management: A precondition for reducing hazardous emissions from aviation: Is sovereignty getting in the way of progress?" ZLW: *German Journal of Air & Space Law*, 63:3 (2014), 386.

aviation cannot be achieved without necessary investments and reforms to optimize and modernize air traffic management.[1] Former International Civil Aviation Organization (ICAO) Council President Roberto Kobeh González agrees that current air traffic management (ATM) practices are an impediment to major efficiency gains.[2]

Operational improvements alone cannot ensure sustainable aviation since such improvements cannot reduce emissions to the level necessary to significantly diminish aviation's contribution to atmospheric pollution from human activities. Nevertheless, this environmental measure should not be ignored for at least two reasons: (a) every milligram of gases emitted due to human activities should be taken into account; and (b) no single environmental measure alone can effectively ensure sustainable aviation. Improvements in operations to ensure sustainable flight management should continue, and new concepts for the purpose of improving flight management should continue to be developed.

3.2 CURRENT STATE OF FLIGHT MANAGEMENT

Improving the ATM system is not a new strategy. The aviation industry has been gradually "working on ATM operational improvements … since the 1920s. The work accelerated with the onset of communications, navigation, surveillance and air traffic management [CNS/ATM] systems."[3] The ICAO has been facilitating operational improvements in various ways. For example, the ICAO, in close conjunction with IATA and the Civil Air Navigation Services Organisation (CANSO), introduced a new aviation system flight plan in November 2012 that would assist "aviation to more efficiently manage growing air traffic volumes and related capacity challenges while reducing" its carbon dioxide (CO_2) emissions.[4] "[I]n order to provide States and other stakeholders with information on a state-of-the-art variety of measures and best

1 See IATA, "Climate Change & CORSIA, fact sheets, facts & figures," Pressroom, online: www.iata.org/pressroom/facts_figures/fact_sheets/Documents/fact-sheet-climate-change.pdf last accessed October 17, 2017.

2 R. Kobeh González, "Towards a transformed ATM environment – Working together," unpublished opening address by the President of the ICAO Council to the World ATM Congress 2013, Madrid (February 12–14, 2013).

3 ICAO Secretariat, "ICAO's global air traffic management (ATM): Operational concept and global air navigation plan," in ICAO, *ICAO Environmental Report 2010: Aviation and Climate Change* (ICAO, 2010), 98 at 100.

4 ICAO, "Aviation groups unite to achieve instantaneous global system upgrade," Press Release, COM 19/12 (November 15, 2012), www.icao.int/Newsroom/Pages/aviation-groups-unite-to-achieve-instantaneous-global-system-upgrade.aspx last accessed October 17, 2017.

practices to reduce aviation emissions, ranging from weight reduction, to airport operations, as well as other operational improvements," the ICAO's Committee on Aviation Environmental Protection (CAEP) developed and updated the guidance material on operational opportunities to minimize fuel use and reduce emissions.[5] Additional guidance material on conducting CNS/ATM environmental assessment, referred to as *Environmental Assessment Guidance for Proposed Air Traffic Management Operational Changes*, was also developed by the CAEP and endorsed by the ICAO Council.[6] The ICAO publishes and updates the Global Air Navigation Plan (GANP), which is "an overarching framework that includes key civil aviation policy principles to assist ICAO Regions, sub-regions and States with the preparation of their Regional and State air navigation plans."[7] The fifth edition of the GANP is "designed to guide complementary and sector-wide air transport progress over 2016–2030 and is approved triennially by the ICAO Council."[8] Furthermore, "ICAO continues to develop and make available new tools to provide States with the ability to assess the environmental impacts of aviation operations."[9] The ICAO has also developed the Aviation System Block Upgrades (ASBU).[10]

5 ICAO Secretariat, "Overview: Global emissions," in ICAO, *ICAO Environmental Report 2013: Aviation and Climate Change* (ICAO, 2013), 96 at 96–97. To view the updated manual, see ICAO, *Operational opportunities to reduce fuel burn and emissions*, Circular 303-AN/176, ICAO Doc 10013 (2014). See also ICAO Secretariat, "Operations: Operational improvements to reduce global emissions," in ICAO, *ICAO Environmental Report 2013: Aviation and Climate Change* (ICAO, 2013), 112 at 112.

6 ICAO Secretariat, "Overview: Global emissions," *supra* Note 5 at 97; ICAO Secretariat, "Operations," *supra* Note 5 at 112. "ICAO has emphasized to States that early implementation of new communications, navigation, surveillance and air traffic management (CNS/ATM) systems would be an effective means of reducing fuel burn and avoiding unnecessary emissions." ICAO, "Environmental protection: Operational measures," www.icao.int/environmental-protection/Pages/operational-measures.aspx last accessed October 17, 2017.

7 ICAO, *Global air navigation plan*, 5th edn., ICAO Doc 9750-AN/963 (ICAO, 2016), 13, www.icao.int/publications/Documents/9750_5ed_en.pdf last accessed October 17, 2017. "'The objective of the GANP is to increase capacity and improve efficiency of the global civil aviation system whilst improving or at least maintaining safety. The GANP also includes strategies for addressing the other ICAO Strategic Objectives." Ibid. "The GANP outlines ICAO's 10 key civil aviation policy principles guiding global, regional and State air navigation planning." Ibid.

8 Ibid. at 2. "The GANP represents a rolling, 15-year strategic methodology which leverages existing technologies and anticipates future developments based on State/industry agreed operational objectives. The Block Upgrades are organized in non-overlapping six-year time increments starting in 2013 and continuing through 2031 and beyond." Ibid.

9 ICAO Secretariat, "Overview: Global emissions," *supra* Note 5 at 97. "For instance, ICAO … launched the ICAO Fuel Savings Estimation Tool (IFSET), which was developed to assist States to estimate the fuel savings and corresponding environmental benefits from the implementation of operational improvements." Ibid.

10 Ibid.

The ASBU concept has been developed to help the aviation community meet its dual challenges: "safety and operational improvements on a globally harmonized basis, while being environmentally responsible and cost-effective."[11] In fact, "[a] key challenge for the aviation community in recent years has been to prioritize and build consensus around the latest technologies, procedures and operational concepts … [since] a wide variety of national and regional ATM modernization programmes have been emerging worldwide."[12] ASBU aims to ensure at reasonable cost that:[13]

- aviation safety is maintained and enhanced;
- air traffic management improvement programs are effectively harmonized; and
- barriers to future aviation efficiency and environmental gains are removed.[14]

The ASBU "concept allows for a flexible global systems approach, enabling all States to advance their Air Navigation capabilities based on their specific operational requirements."[15] ICAO GANP includes ASBU "framework, its Modules and its associated Technology Roadmaps covering inter alia communications, surveillance, navigation, information management and avionics."[16] At its heart, ASBU "is a pragmatic system of Modules."[17] Each module is "comprised of technologies and procedures that are organized towards achieving a specific performance capability. Each of these modules is then linked to one of four specific and interrelated performance improvement areas."[18] These four areas are airport operations; globally interoperable systems and data; optimum capacity and flexible flights; and efficient flight paths.[19] These modules apply several other concepts that include continuous descent operations (CDO), continuous climb operations (CCO), collaborative decision making

[11] ICAO Secretariat, "Operations: ICAO block upgrades minimizing adverse environmental effects of civil aviation activities," in ICAO, *ICAO Environmental Report 2013: Aviation and Climate Change* (ICAO, 2013), 114 at 114.

[12] ICAO Secretariat, "Operations: Operational improvements," *supra* Note 5 at 113.

[13] ICAO Secretariat, "Operations: ICAO block upgrades," *supra* Note 11 at 114.

[14] Ibid.

[15] Ibid.

[16] ICAO, *Global air navigation, supra* Note 7 at 13.

[17] ICAO Secretariat, "Operations: ICAO block upgrades," *supra* Note 11 at 114.

[18] Ibid.

[19] Ibid.

to improve airport operations (A-CDM), and performance-based navigation (PBN).[20] At present, the ICAO's focus is on the development and implementation of PBN, CDO, CCO, and air traffic flow management (ATFM).[21]

In particular, PBN is crucial since it is essential for the implementation of ASBU, and is an enabler for CDO and CCO.[22] PBN "allows aircraft to fly even closer to their preferred 4D trajectory. Developed after the improvement of the air navigation system in the vertical plane, PBN improves the efficiency in the horizontal plane."[23] The ICAO defines PBN as "[a]rea navigation based on performance requirements for aircraft operating along an [air traffic service] route, on an instrument approach procedure or in a designated airspace,"[24] where "[p]erformance requirements are expressed in navigation specifications in terms of accuracy, integrity, continuity, availability and functionality needed for the proposed operation in the context of a particular airspace concept."[25] PBN provides the methods "for flexible routes and terminal procedures"[26] by applying Area Navigation (RNAV)[27] and Required Navigation Performance (RNP)[28] specifications.[29] The PBN concept represents a move "from sensor-based to performance-based navigation."[30] Under this concept, "generic navigation requirements are defined based on operational requirements."[31] Operators then assess options with respect to available

[20] Ibid.

[21] ICAO, *Global air navigation, supra* Note 7 at 21.

[22] ICAO, "PBN iKIT," www.icao.int/safety/pbn/PBNiKitV3/story.html last accessed October 17, 2017.

[23] ICAO Secretariat, "ICAO's global air traffic management," *supra* Note 3 at 100.

[24] ICAO, *Performance-Based Navigation (PBN) Manual*, 3rd edn., ICAO Doc 9613/AN/937 (ICAO, 2008), I-(xx); ICAO, "13 International Standards and Recommended Practices: Annex 11 to the Convention on International Civil Aviation: Air Traffic Services: Air Traffic Control Service: Flight Information Service: Alerting Service" (2001), 1–10.

[25] ICAO, *PBN Manual, supra* Note 24 at I-(xx); *Annex 11, supra* Note 24 at 1–10.

[26] ICAO, "ICAO performance based navigation programme: Overview," www.icao.int/safety/pbn/Pages/Overview.aspx last accessed October 17, 2017.

[27] RNAV is "[a] method of navigation which permits aircraft operation on any desired flight path within the coverage of station-referenced navigation aids or within the limits of the capability of self-contained aids, or a combination of these." ICAO, *PBN Manual, supra* Note 24 at I-(xix).

[28] RNP system is "[a]n area navigation system which supports on-board performance monitoring and alerting." Ibid. at I-(xx).

[29] ICAO, "PBN: Overview," *supra* Note 26. "RNAV and RNP systems are fundamentally similar. The key difference between them is the requirement for on-board performance monitoring and alerting. A navigation specification that includes a requirement for on-board navigation performance monitoring and alerting is referred to as an RNP specification. One not having such requirements is referred to as an RNAV specification." ICAO, *PBN manual, supra* Note 24 at I-(v).

[30] ICAO, *PBN Manual, supra* Note 24 at I-(iii).

[31] Ibid.

technology and navigation services that "could allow the requirements to be met."[32]

Nonetheless, PBN suffers from various difficulties, including a long and difficult implementation process;[33] a lack of global expertise;[34] difficulty understanding the PBN Manual[35] owing to technical incompetence and language barriers;[36] shortcomings in co-ordination between stakeholders;[37] lack of standardization;[38] a small number of older aircraft equipped for PBN;[39] lack of PBN procedures at some airports;[40] and difficulty of PBN-capable aircraft to fit in with non-PBN capable aircraft on same flight tracks.[41] Those difficulties need to be overcome to obtain full environmental benefit from the application of PBN, since ASBU cannot be implemented without PBN, thereby frustrating the ICAO's GANP.[42]

In line with the ICAO, States, groups of States, and regional organizations are also working to improve ATM systems. For example, in the United States (US), the Federal Aviation Administration (FAA) has been developing Next-Gen since 2003, which is an upgrade from World War II-era technology to

32 Ibid.

33 See e.g. S. Sumner, "Regional forum: 'Creating more lift': ICAO Asia/Pacific Region," unpublished presentation delivered at the ICAO Performance-based Navigation (PBN) Symposium and Workshops, Montreal (October 16–19, 2012); A. Stealey, "Address," unpublished presentation delivered at the ICAO Performance-based Navigation (PBN) Symposium and Workshops, Montreal (October 16–19, 2012); C. Cirilo, "PBN: Global implementation situation," unpublished presentation delivered at the ICAO Performance-based Navigation (PBN) Symposium and Workshops, Montreal (October 16–19, 2012).

34 See e.g. Cirilo, *supra* Note 33; Stealey, *supra* Note 33; M. S. Lewis, "PBN – A commercial data and service provider perspective – Are we ready to go?" unpublished presentation delivered at the ICAO Performance-based Navigation (PBN) Symposium and Workshops, Montreal (October 16–19, 2012).

35 ICAO, *PBN Manual*, *supra* Note 24.

36 See e.g. Sumner, *supra* Note 33.

37 See e.g. Stealey, *supra* Note 33; Cirilo, *supra* Note 33.

38 See e.g. B. Roturier, "RNP Approaches," unpublished presentation delivered at the ICAO Performance-based Navigation (PBN) Symposium and Workshops, Montreal (October 16–19, 2012).

39 See e.g. A. Gittens, "Airports and PBN, will it make a difference?" unpublished presentation delivered at the ICAO Performance-based Navigation (PBN) Symposium and Workshops, Montreal (October 16–19, 2012); P. Alibert Marchi, "PBN and regional aircraft: Legacy, turboprop and regional issues," unpublished presentation delivered at the ICAO Performance-based Navigation (PBN) Symposium and Workshops, Montreal (October 16–19, 2012).

40 See e.g. Gittens, *supra* Note 39.

41 See e.g. ibid.

42 M. T. Ahmad, *Climate Change Governance in International Civil Aviation: Toward Regulating Emissions Relevant to Climate Change and Global Warming* (The Hague: Eleven International Publishing, 2016), 134.

satellite-based technology.[43] The European Union (EU), in an initiative to improve its ATM system, has established the Single European Sky (SES) initiative backed by the Single European Sky ATM Research (SESAR) Program.[44] The SES is an "initiative of organising airspace into functional blocks, according to traffic flows rather than to national borders."[45] Another laudable initiative is Asia and South Pacific Initiative to Reduce Emissions (ASPIRE) created by Airservices Australia, Airways New Zealand, and the FAA,[46] and later joined by Japan Air Navigation Services, the Civil Aviation Authority of Singapore, and AeroThai.[47] ASPIRE "is designed to lessen the environmental impact of aviation across Asia and the South Pacific with each partner to focus on developing ideas that contribute to improved environmental standards and operational procedures in aviation."[48]

3.3 LEGAL BARRIERS TO ACHIEVING SUSTAINABLE FLIGHT MANAGEMENT

The concept of State sovereignty, the undisputed customary international law principle enshrined in the *Chicago Convention*,[49] is a stumbling block to achieving sustainable flight management. Article 1 of the *Chicago Convention* provides that each State has "complete and exclusive sovereignty over the airspace above its territory."[50] This principle is responsible for indirect or less-than-direct routings, and States' resistance to cross-border air navigation service (ANS) provisions.[51]

43 See US Federal Aviation Administration, "NextGen: Modernization of U.S. Airspace," www.faa.gov/nextgen/ last accessed October 17, 2017.

44 SESAR, "About: Discover SESAR," www.sesarju.eu/discover-sesar last accessed October 17, 2017.

45 EUROCONTROL, "Single European Sky," www.eurocontrol.int/dossiers/single-european-sky last accessed October 17, 2017.

46 ASPIRE: Asia and Pacific Initiative to Reduce Emissions, "About ASPIRE: What is ASPIRE?" www.aspire-green.com/about/default.asp last accessed October 17, 2017.

47 Ibid.

48 Ibid.

49 See *Convention on International Civil Aviation* (adopted December 7, 1944, entered into force April 4, 1947) 15 UNTS 295, Can TS 1944 No 36, ICAO Doc 7300/9. See e.g. Case C-366/10, *Air Transport Association of America and others* v. *Secretary of State for Energy and Climate Change* [2011] ECR I-13833 at I-13885–I-13886; I. Brownlie, *Principles of Public International Law*, 7th edn. (Oxford: Oxford University Press, 2008), 105.

50 *Chicago Convention, supra* Note 49, Art. 1.

51 See also P. P. Fitzgerald, "Europe's Emissions Trading System: Questioning its raison d'etre," *Issues in Aviation L & Policy*, 10 (2011), 189 at 216.

Due to this principle, States are reluctant to delegate their ANS provision to other States or any entity therein. Lack of cross-border ANS provisions is causing more GHG emissions in the EU. The expanding GHG emissions caused by the well-known inefficiencies of the EU air traffic control system are intimidating.[52] For example, the pilot of LOT flight 434 from Madrid to Warsaw[53] will speak to 45 different air traffic controllers during the 3:35 flight,[54] or a different air traffic controller every 4.7 minutes![55]

According to Article 68 of the *Chicago Convention*, Contracting States to the Convention possess the right to designate the international air routes and airports in their territory,[56] and, according to Annex 11 to the Convention, these States must determine, *inter alia*, those portions of the airspace over their territories where air traffic services will be provided.[57] In recognition of State sovereignty, Article 9 of the Convention authorizes Contracting States to uniformly restrict or prohibit national and foreign aircraft engaged in international scheduled airline services from flying over certain areas of its territory for military or public safety reasons.[58] Aircraft entering the restricted or prohibited areas may be required to promptly land at some designated airport within the State's territory.[59] Commercial flights must avoid those restricted or prohibited airspace to avoid forced landing and, hence, these flights often have to choose indirect or less-than-direct routings.[60] During the Cold War, "the need to avoid Russian restricted airspace resulted in indirect routings that made non-stop U.S.-China services commercially unviable and required en-route stops in Anchorage or Japan."[61]

In order to reduce fuel consumption, aircraft should fly more direct routings, and more cross-border ANS provisions are required.[62] In this regard,

52 Most airlines that service EU airports would like to see a revamp of Eurocontrol, the European Air Traffic Control system. See J. A. Lewis and A. Witkowsky, *Transforming Air Traffic Management beyond Evolution: A Report of the CSIS Technology and Public Policy Program* (Washington, DC: Center for Strategic and International Studies, 2004), 11.

53 The flying distance between them is 2,270 km or 1,410 miles.

54 H. Kleisny, "European airspace – Acting as one" (December 2, 2010), euroscientist.com/2010/12/european-airspace-%E2%80%93-acting-as-one/ last accessed October 17, 2017.

55 This is the 215 minutes duration of the flight divided by the number of Air Traffic Controllers contacted.

56 *Chicago Convention, supra* Note 49, Art. 68.

57 *Annex 11, supra* Note 24 at 2–1.

58 *Chicago Convention, supra* Note 49, Art. 9(a).

59 Ibid., Art. 9(c).

60 See also Fitzgerald, *supra* Note 51 at 217.

61 Ibid.

62 See e.g. ibid. at 216; A. Kotaite, "Is there a lessening of state sovereignty or a real will to co-operate globally?" *Air & Space L*, 20 (1995), 288 at 291. See also T. Barker et al., "Technical

States should either reduce the size of or grant civil aircraft additional access to those restricted areas or prohibited airspace at least during peak hours.[63] Additionally, States should opt for more cross-border ANS provision. Greater cooperation and coordination between civil and military authorities, and between States, which are largely based on notions of State sovereignty,[64] are required.[65] States need to recognize that the concept of State sovereignty is an evolving concept, influenced by dominant factors that are critical for the society at a given time and circumstance. Environmental impacts of aviation are a dominant concern now and, hence, may influence the notion of State sovereignty over the airspace above their territory.[66]

3.4 THE EVOLUTION OF THE CONCEPT OF STATE SOVEREIGNTY

The French philosopher Jean Bodin introduced the concept of State sovereignty to the Western world.[67] State sovereignty essentially means the right of a State within its territory to exercise its functions to the exclusion of other States.[68] This normative perspective of exclusivity of the notion of sovereignty commenced to turn to an approach accommodating globalization and democratization in the 1960s and 1970s, as viewed by legal scholars,[69] owing to "a

summary," in B. Metz et al. (eds.), *Climate Change 2007: Mitigation: Contribution of Working Group III to the Fourth Assessment Report of the Intergovernmental Panel on Climate Change* (Cambridge: Cambridge University Press, 2007), 25 at 51.

63 See also L. Merry Brown, "Operations: Impact of operational changes on global emission levels – Findings of the operational goals group," in ICAO, *ICAO Environmental Report 2013: Aviation and Climate Change* (ICAO, 2013), 119 at 121.

64 A. A. Cocca, "The Chicago Convention and technological development in air and space," *Ann Air & Sp L*, 19:2 (1994), 135 at 148.

65 González, *supra* Note 2 at 3.

66 Ahmad, *Climate*, *supra* Note 42 at 136.

67 J. Bodin, *Les six livres de la repvbliqve de I. Bodin Angeuin. A Monseignevr dv Favr, Seigneur de Pibrac, conseiller du Roy en son conseil priué* (Paris: Jacques du Puys, 1576). See also R. Abeyratne, *Convention on International Civil Aviation: A Commentary* (Cham: Springer International, 2014), 16; S. M. Shrewsbury, "September 11th and the Single European Sky: Developing concepts of airspace sovereignty," *J Air L & Com*, 68:1 (2003), 115 at 117.

68 See generally Bodin, *supra* Note 67 at 125; J. G. Starke, *Introduction to International Law*, 10th edn. (London: Butterworths, 1989) at 157; S. A. Williams and A. L. C. de Mestral, *An Introduction to International Law: Chiefly as Interpreted and Applied in Canada*, 2nd edn. (Toronto and Vancouver: Butterworths, 1987), 108; Abeyratne, *supra* Note 67 at 17. "The competence of states in respect of their territory is usually described in terms of sovereignty … The normal complement of state rights, the typical case of legal competence, is described commonly as 'sovereignty' … In brief, 'sovereignty' is legal shorthand for legal personality of a certain kind, that of statehood." Brownlie, *supra* Note 49 at 105–6.

69 See F. P. Schubert, "The creation of a Single European Sky: The shrinking concept of sovereignty," *Ann Air & Sp L*, **25** (2000), 239 at 246.

shift in focus of international law, later fuelled by the end of the Cold War."[70] Starke argues that "it is probably more accurate today to say that the sovereignty of a state means the *residuum* of power which it possesses within the confines laid down by international law."[71] Back in 1981, Professor Matte predicted that the notion of sovereignty "will be overtaken by ... a new international legal order," and "will evolve so that the order of importance, such as is presently drawn from conventions on aerial navigation will be changed, making State sovereignty conditional upon the freedom of international movement."[72] Matte's predictions are coming true.[73]

Two decades later, it was noted that "changes in the understanding and the characterizations of airspace sovereignty have marched on in steady fashion,"[74] and "the move towards a different kind of airspace sovereignty regime will continue as economic and other forces drive change."[75] Judge Manfred Lachs argues that the maxim *cujus est solum ejus usque ad coelum*, from which the concept of State sovereignty over airspace flows, is "not law."[76] Rather, to Lachs, the maxim "may only encapsulate a legal rule or indicate a direction."[77] In reality, "a thorough reading of the Chicago Convention would reveal that the Convention does not authorize unrestricted freedom to contracting States."[78] This is also apparent from Article 9, which, although it grants States the right to establish restricted or prohibited zones, requires, among other things, that "[s]uch prohibited areas shall be of reasonable extent and location so as not to interfere unnecessarily with air navigation."[79] Again, according to Article 22, Contracting States agree "to adopt all practicable measures, through the issuance of special regulations or otherwise, to facilitate

70 Abeyratne, *supra* Note 67 at 17.

71 Starke, *supra* Note 68 at 100 [emphasis in original]. Interestingly, Kelsen advises "not to use the *ambiguous* term 'sovereignty' at all in relation to the state." H. Kelsen, *Principles of International Law* (New York: Rinehart, 1952), 113 [emphasis added].

72 N. M. Matte, *Treatise on Air-Aeronautical Law* (Montreal: ICASL, McGill University, 1981), 79.

73 See Ahmad, *Climate, supra* Note 42 at 142.

74 Shrewsbury, *supra* Note 67 at 116.

75 Ibid. See also Schubert, *supra* Note 69 at 259.

76 M. Lachs, "Freedoms of the air – The way to outer space," in T. L. Masson-Zwaan and P. M .J. Mendes de Leon (eds.), *Air and Space Law: De Lege Ferenda: Essays in Honour of Henri A. Wassenbergh* (Leiden: Martinus Nijhoff, 1992), 241 at 241.

77 Ibid.

78 M. T. Ahmad, "Achieving global safety in civil aviation: A critical analysis of contemporary safety oversight mechanisms," *Ann Air & Sp L*, 37 (2012), 81 at 115. See also Cocca, *supra* Note 64 at 145; P. S. Dempsey, *Public International Air Law* (Montreal: McGill University, Institute and Centre for Research in Air & Space Law, 2008), 44.

79 *Chicago Convention, supra* Note 49, Art. 9(a).

and expedite navigation by aircraft between the territories of contracting States, and to prevent unnecessary delays to aircraft, crews, passengers and cargo."[80]

3.5 PROTECTION OF THE ENVIRONMENT: NEW FORCE IN THE EVOLUTION PROCESS

Environmental protection is one of the new forces and the concern over protection of the environment can, and should, drive change in the understanding and characterizations of sovereignty of airspace.[81] The issue of air pollution has already circumscribed the exercise of State sovereignty as is apparent from the famous *Trail Smelter* arbitration.[82] The arbitration gave birth to the established customary international law principle according to which States have sovereign right to exploit their own resources and simultaneous responsibility to ensure that activities within their jurisdiction or control do not cause damage to the environment of other States or of areas beyond the limits of national jurisdiction.[83] This principle is also recognized under various international legal instruments,[84] and "already forms the basis for"[85] the *Long-Range Transboundary Air Pollution Convention*,[86] the *Vienna Convention*,[87] and the *United Nations Convention on Climate Change*.[88] Concern over the protection of the environment will and has already commenced to bring a new way of exercising national sovereignty – "an *evolution*

80 Ibid., Art. 22.
81 A similar argument concerning right of overflight is made by Jae Woon Lee. Lee argues that "global environmental concern … demands universal freedom of overflight as an effective measure to mitigate climate change." J. W. Lee, "Revisiting freedom of overflight in international air law: Minimum multilateralism in international air transport," *Air & Space L*, 38:4/5 (2013), 351 at 367.
82 *Trail Smelter Arbitration (United States* v. *Canada)* [1938 & 194] 3 RIAA 1905 (Arbitrators: Charles Warren, Robert AE Greenshields, Jan Frans Hostie).
83 See e.g. M. Adam, "ICAO Assembly's resolution on climate change: A 'historic' agreement?," *Air & Space L*, 36:1 (2011), 23 at 28.
84 *Declaration of the United Nations Conference on the Human Environment* (June 16, 1972) 11 ILM 1416, Principle 21; *Rio Declaration on Environment and Development* (June 14, 1992) 31 ILM 874, Principle 2.
85 P. Birnie, A. Boyle, and C. Redgwell, *International Law and the Environment*, 3rd edn. (Oxford: Oxford University Press, 2009), 339.
86 *Convention on Long-Range Transboundary Air Pollution* (adopted November 13, 1979, entered into force March 16, 1983) 1302 UNTS 217, Can TS 1983 No 34.
87 *Vienna Convention for the Protection of the Ozone Layer* (adopted March 22, 1985, entered into force September 22, 1988) 1513 UNTS 293, Can TS 1988 No 23.
88 *United Nations Framework Convention on Climate Change* (adopted May 9, 1992, entered into force March 21, 1994) 1771 UNTS 107, Can TS 1994 No 7.

in the *exercise* of national sovereignty"[89] – that will accommodate environmental concerns.[90] The new understanding and characterization of airspace sovereignty, which should not negatively affect the substance of State sovereignty, is required to evade all the limitations that impede necessary operational improvements.[91]

Call for a new understanding of and a new way of exercising sovereignty to accelerate operational improvement is coming from the aviation industry as well. Roberto Kobeh González emphasized the need to "consider sovereignty within the context of the global, harmonized air navigation framework,"[92] and stated that "[s]overeignty must not be an obstacle to progress in making institutional the required changes for a more efficient management of the global air navigation system."[93] CANSO, which aspires to be the global voice of ATM in the transformation of the aviation system,[94] contends that, since "a global, seamless, and performance-based approach to management of airspace, rather than one based on national borders," is required for air navigation services, "all stakeholders need a fully developed understanding of the meaning of national sovereignty consistent with present and future political, economic and social realities."[95]

3.6 EFFORTS TO ENSURE SUSTAINABLE FLIGHT MANAGEMENT FROM A STATE OR GROUP OF STATES

The EU has taken various initiatives to ensure sustainable flight management, and these are facilitating a new understanding of sovereignty of airspace within the European airspace. Among those initiatives, the SES backed by the SESAR Program is a laudable step.[96] The EU has shown that "the basis of

89 P. Haanappel, "The transformation of sovereignty in the air," *Air & Space L*, 20:6 (1995), 311 at 317 [emphasis in original].

90 See e.g. Schubert, *supra* note 69 at 248, 259; Civil Air Navigation Services Organisation (CANSO), *Air Space Sovereignty*, ICAO Worldwide Air Transport Conference (ATCONF), 6th Mtg., Agenda Items 1, 1.1, Working Paper, Doc ATConf/6-WP/80 (March 4, 2013), www.icao.int/Meetings/atconf6/Documents/WorkingPapers/ATConf.6.WP.080.1.en.pdf last accessed October 17, 2017.

91 See Schubert, *supra* Note 69 at 259; Cocca, *supra* Note 64 at 148.

92 González, *supra* Note 2 at 3.

93 Ibid. at 4.

94 CANSO: Civil Air Navigation Services Organisation, "About CANSO," www.canso.org/about-canso last accessed October 17, 2017.

95 CANSO, *Air Space*, *supra* Note 90 at 1.

96 However, this is not the first time that the EU has ignored national borders for the advancement of aviation. "[R]egulation has been set at the Community level in the field of competition law, slot allocation, computerized reservation systems, harmonisation of safety

the Chicago Convention's complete and exclusive sovereignty can be overcome to the benefit of all players."[97] The creation of the SES exhibits that primarily economic factors, as distinct from State interests in maintaining sovereignty over airspace, are gradually "drawing states away from the Chicago Convention's absolute sovereignty formula."[98]

With regard to prohibited area, an admirable step has been taken by NAV Canada, a corporatized entity "that owns and operates Canada's civil air navigation service."[99] To ensure access of civil aircraft to a segment of airspace in eastern Quebec, which was historically reserved as a military flying area, NAV Canada finalized an arrangement with the Department of National Defence, 3 Wing, at Bagotville in spring 2012, under which civil aircraft would have access to that airspace when not required for military operations.[100] If required for military operations, 3 Wing will secure the airspace by NOTAM.[101] As a consequence of this arrangement, "on most days what had been approximately a six minute route diversion can be avoided, saving an estimated $2 million in fuel costs per year."[102]

Concerning cross-border ANS provisions, there exist a good number of examples in all regions of the world.[103] There is a mutual delegation of ANS authority between the United States and Canada; "Tonga and Samoa have a delegation to New Zealand; there are various delegations in Europe from and

rules, common rules for personnel licenses, aircraft noise, etc." K. H. Böckstiegel and P. M. Krämer, "Filling in the gaps of the Chicago Convention: Main features of the new legal framework for aviation in the European Community," *Ann Air & Sp L*, 19:1 (1994), 127 at 133.

97 Ibid. at 138.

98 Shrewsbury, *supra* Note 67 at 150.

99 NAV Canada, "About us," www.navcanada.ca/en/about-us/Pages/default.aspx last accessed October 17, 2017.

100 NAV Canada, *CIFER 2013: Collaborative initiatives for emissions reductions: Forward thinking for a smaller footprint* (2013), 7, www.navcanada.ca/EN/media/Publications/CIFER-Report-2013-EN.pdf last accessed October 17, 2017.

101 Ibid. "A NOTAM is a notice distributed by means of telecommunications containing information concerning the establishment, conditions or change in any aeronautical facility, service, procedure or hazard, the timely knowledge of which is essential to personnel concerned with flight operations." NAV Canada, *Canadian NOTAM procedures manual*, P-NOF-101 Version 11, 1, www.navcanada.ca/EN/media/Publications/NOTAM-Manual-EN.pdf last accessed October 17, 2017.

102 Ibid.

103 See CANSO, *Air Space*, *supra* Note 90 at 2. See generally N. Van Antwerpen, *Cross border provision of air navigation services with specific reference to Europe: Safeguarding transparent lines of responsibility and liability* (Alphen aan den Rijn: Wolters Kluwer Law & Business, 2008); Skybrary, "Delegation of Air Traffic Services," www.skybrary.aero/index.php/Delegation_of_Air_Traffic_Services last accessed October 17, 2017.

to Finland, France, Norway, Sweden and Switzerland."[104] It should be noted not only that all these provisions have been successfully operating since their inception, but also no question about the legal basis for these delegations ever arose.[105]

3.7 CONCLUSION

In 2008, Emirates Airlines negotiated with the governmental agencies in the United Arab Emirates, Russia, Iceland, Canada, and the United States to secure access to an "over the pole" route from Dubai to San Francisco.[106] As a result of the negotiations, the nonstop flight operates over a route that is not significantly longer than the 8,090 miles (13,000 kilometers) that separate the two cities and avoids congested airspace over the EU. Over the flight's nearly 16-hour duration,[107] pilots will talk to fewer than a dozen air traffic controllers. Were the flight to cover a similar distance in EU skies or territories of small countries with similar ATM policies, the route would not be as direct and nonstop service might not be possible.[108] Undoubtedly, its GHG footprint would be bigger. Indeed, Emirates' negotiations were predicated upon the concept that PBN and a specific over the pole route would allow the fuel savings that would make the flight viable, and consequently result in reduced aviation emissions. Emirates was able to succeed because three of the countries with whom it negotiated control most of the territory that the flight will overfly.

Emirates' negotiations were clearly in furtherance of a commercial objective, but they illustrate the potential of air traffic management to contribute to reducing aviation emissions. Where some observers might discount ATM's potential, Emirates clearly understood that even if one uses a very environmentally friendly plane (the Boeing 777–200 LR) and adopts environmentally conscious practices like using electrical power at the gate, taxiing on one engine, and using reduced thrust on landing, efficient ATM is still a precondition to an energy-efficient, sustainable Dubai–San Francisco flight. Absent these initiatives, Emirates argues that each flight would consume an

[104] CANSO, *Air Space, supra* Note 90 at 2.
[105] See ibid.
[106] See "Emirates Airline launches San Francisco service with world's longest green flight trial," *eTurboNews* (December 10, 2008), www.eturbonews.com/12961/emirates-airline-launches-san-francisco-service-worlds-longest-gr last accessed October 17, 2017.
[107] Ibid.
[108] See *supra* Notes 53–55, and accompanying text.

additional 2,000 gallons of fuel and produce 30,000 more pounds of carbon emissions than would otherwise be the case.[109]

Without the necessary efficiency in ATM system, Emirates' flight might not have been viable. Emirates operates worldwide, has considerable expertise in operating long distance flights, and has a very modern fuel-efficient fleet. That it saw the need to negotiate overflight rights with Canada, Iceland, Russia, and the United States confirms its recognition of the potential of ATM to help reduce emissions from aviation. Emirates is clearly the first to negotiate such a route with so many disparate countries but the precedent has been set, and other carriers such as Etihad, Qatar Airways, and Turkish Airlines will undoubtedly follow suit. It is hoped that their engagement, and perhaps even that of airlines from other regions of the world, will underscore ATM's potential in the campaign to reduce emissions from aviation and incite ATM to find ways to further reduce aviation emissions on routes long and short all over the world.

[109] Emirates, *News*, "Emirates Airline," *supra* Note 106.

4

Environmental Sustainability Measures for Airports

Maha Mousavi Sameh and Juliana Scavuzzi dos Santos

Airports are considered important contributors to local economy and employment. However, together with the socioeconomic benefits they offer, environmental impacts also result from the operation of airports. Some of the main environmental and sustainable development concerns raised with respect to the operation of airports are emissions, noise, land use by airports and energy consumption. When deciding on building or expanding an airport, the challenge ahead of airport operators is to find a balanced approach for maximizing the capacity of airports and potential for future growth on one hand, and minimizing the accompanying environmental impacts on the other hand. By having appropriate and effective environmental management that develops and implements approaches, and a mechanism to integrate airports and their activities into sustainable development plans, airport operators can accomplish the best possible results, which means reaching an optimum balance between the airport's growth and maximizing its social and economic benefits, as well as satisfying communities and regulators. Community involvement has a key role in facing the environmental concerns associated with operation and expansion plans of airports. Airport operators have a strong record of working together with their communities. Regarding regulatory initiatives for making airports more environmentally friendly and sustainable, a comprehensive and collaborative approach at international and national levels is needed, and therefore the role of international bodies like the ICAO in producing proper environmental standards for aircraft and environmental guidance to airports are highlighted. The ICAO is a global forum that works to realize the goals of the Chicago Convention of achieving uniformity in regulations, standards, procedures, and all other matters affecting international aviation; therefore this forum, by proactively addressing issues concerning aviation environmental impacts, can support national and local authorities with comprehensive guidelines for producing proper regulations.

4.1 INTRODUCTION

The facilities and services provided by airports are among the most important parts of the global infrastructure required for the regular operation of aircraft.[1] Airports also play a vital role in local and national economies, and can employ hundreds, thousands, or even tens of thousands of people.[2] Notwithstanding the obvious socioeconomic benefits provided by airports, however, there are environmental costs and impacts that are the result of airport operations. Moreover, the increasing international demand for both passenger and cargo air traffic will inevitably demand the construction of new airports and the expansion of those that already exist. This will in turn intensify the significance and complexity of environmental and sustainable development issues as they pertain to airports, including, *inter alia*, Greenhouse Gas (GHG) emissions, noise, land use by airports, and energy consumption.[3] One of the challenges facing airport owners and operators presently and in the future is to find a balanced approach for maximizing the capacity of airports and the possibilities and potential for sustainable growth while minimizing their impacts on the environment – the key to community permission to operate and grow at both global and local levels.

In addition, the economic and social benefits brought by airports to their communities are undeniable, but more often airport operators are incorporating into their sustainability programs the concept of sustainability of their own communities, understanding that airports are part of the community, and communities are also part of bigger societies; this means that everyone has their own contribution to sustainable development.

In response to community concerns and as part of their Corporate Social Responsibility (CSR), airport operators are attempting to devise new and various strategies and procedures to diminish the adverse effects that airport activities have on the environment. In addition, general growing public awareness of environmental issues related to aviation activities and regulatory measures employed by local authorities and governments designed to deal

1 Milan Janić, *Greening Airports: Advanced Technology and Operations* (Delft, Netherland: Springer, 2011) at 6, 12 [Janić, *Greening Airports*]. Another important component of this infrastructure is Air Traffic Control Services.

2 Michael B. Charles et al., "Airport futures: Towards a critique of the aerotropolis model," *Futures*, 39 (2007), 1009 at 1011; Milan Janić, "Modelling Operational, Economic and Environmental Performance of an Air Transport Network," *Transportation Research Part D*, 8 (2003), 415 at 415 [Janić, "Modelling"].

3 Energy consumption, wastage, and water contamination are among other problems. See Janić, *Greening Airports, supra* Note 1 at 20–21, 35.

with environmental issues have also demanded a more mature response from airports regarding their environmental protection programs. With the implementation of effective environmental management mechanisms, which integrate the activities of airports with the objectives of sustainable environmental development, airport operators aim to achieve an appropriate balance between airport growth and environmental protection.

This chapter will analyze the primary environmental impacts raised by the operation of airports, and will also discuss the importance of air traffic management, community engagement, and effective government regulation in devising and promoting future environmental sustainability measures for airports.

4.2 THE ENVIRONMENTAL IMPACTS AT AIRPORTS

4.2.1 *Emissions and Environmental Capacity*[4]

GHG and other emissions produced by the operation of aircraft, both on the ground and in the airspace, have numerous negative effects on air quality, the climate, and the ozone layer. In terms of airport operations, an additional adverse environmental effect resulting from aircraft emissions is the degradation of local air quality, which, in turn, could adversely impact human health.[5] Emissions created at the ground level and within the vicinity of airports also are not limited to aircraft emissions; ground vehicles and service equipment required to service aircraft contribute their own emissions.[6]

[4] Environmental capacity of an airport can be defined as: "the capacity of the receiving environment, both human and non-human, to tolerate the impacts of airport activity." See Paul Upham et al., "Environmental capacity and airport operations: Current issues and future prospects," *J Air Transport Management*, 9:3 (2003), 145 at 146.

[5] Rae Andre, *Take Back the Sky: Protecting Communities in the Path of Aviation Expansion* (London: Sierra Club Books, University of California Press, 2004) at 26; L. Q. Maurice and D. S. Lee, eds., *Assessing Current Scientific Knowledge, Uncertainties and Gaps in Quantifying Climate Change, Noise and Air Quality Aviation Impacts*, Final Report of the International Civil Aviation Organization (ICAO) Committee on Aviation and Environmental Protection (CAEP) Workshop (Washington, DC and Manchester: US Federal Aviation Administration and Manchester Metropolitan University, 2009) at iv, 7; ICAO, *ICAO Environmental Report 2010: Aviation and Climate Change* (Montreal: ICAO, 2010) at 18 [ICAO, *Environment Report*].

[6] This includes motor vehicles (e.g. cars and buses for airport operations, and passenger, employee, and rental agency vehicles), ground service equipment (GSE) (e.g. aircraft tugs, baggage and belt loaders, generators, lawn mowers, snow plows, loaders, tractors, air-conditioning units, and cargo moving equipment), and stationary sources (e.g. boilers, space heaters, emergency generators, incinerators, fire training facilities, aircraft engine testing facilities, painting operations, and solvent degreasers). See *Environmental Impacts of Airport*

To address the GHG emissions, and local air quality concerns raised by airport operations, several solutions have been implemented by airport operators, including utilization of procedures and technologies designed to reduce aircraft emissions at landing and take-off, the development of more environmentally friendly airport fleets, in order to increase aircraft efficiency on the ground, including the use of alternative fuel sources for ground support equipment and power heating, and investing in hybrid, electric, or gas-powered service vehicles.[7]

There are also environmental constraints that could be imposed by airport operators and/or government regulators that limit the number of air traffic movements of people and cargo in order to minimize the environmental impacts caused by airport operations, including emission caps and quotas for airports.[8]

It is important to note in this regard that strategies for minimizing emissions from sources owned or controlled by airport operators as well as emissions created by off-site producers of electricity purchased by airports are quite different from the strategies used to prevent acceleration of environmental impacts created by emissions from sources that are not owned or controlled by airport operators, such as emissions produced by aircraft, ground access vehicles, and public transport.[9] One, however, cannot ignore the fact that airport operators generally have to deal with the problem, often responding to their communities for emissions, including noise, that are not directly under their control. This demonstrates how complex the problem can be and why the need for coordination of actions among different stakeholders always seems like a good approach.

One popular initiative to reduce GHG emissions at airports is the implementation of solar installations.[10] Because solar energy systems do not release any emissions or store any hazardous materials, any potential environmental damage related to their use is limited to impacts associated with land development.[11] While the use of solar energy can provide clear benefits in terms of

Operations, Maintenance, and Expansion, CRS Report for Congress, April 5, 2007, at 10. See also Janić, *Greening Airports, supra* Note 1 at 55; Janić, "Modelling," *supra* Note 2 at 422.

7 Karen Thomas, "Airports and the Environment – A sustainable Approach," in Airports Council International, *Celebrating 20 Years – 1991–2011* (2011) at 103–4.

8 Janić, *Greening Airports, supra* Note 1 at 15, 60.

9 Xavier Oh, "Greenlight to Grow," *Airport World*, 17:1 (2012), 51.

10 Stephen Barrett, "Glare Factor: Solar Installations And Airports," *Solar Industry*, 6:5 (2013), online: www.faa.gov/airports/environmental/policy_guidance/media/airport-solar-guide.pdf.

11 "Technical Guidance for Evaluating Selected Solar Technologies on Airports" (November 2010) Federal Aviation Administration Office of Airports, Office of Airport Planning and Programming Airport Planning and Environmental Division (APP-400), online: Federal Aviation Administration http://www.faa.gov/airports/environmental/policy_guidance/media/airport-solar-guide.pdf.

producing clean energy, solar energy can also pose challenges for regular operations, such as interference with communication systems or reflectivity from solar panels.[12] They require, therefore, careful planning before implementation. More than 100 airports globally have installed solar energy systems, including Indianapolis International Airport, Fresno Yosemite Airport, Gatwick Airport, Birmingham Airport, Salzburg Airport, Athens International, Ancona Falconara Airport, and Denver International Airport.[13] Indeed, Cochin International Airport Limited, located in Kochi, Kerala (India), has become the first airport in the world to be powered entirely by solar power, and a reduction of 300,000 tons of carbon emissions is expected over the next twenty-five years as a result.[14]

Another environmental initiative is the implementation of Aircraft Ground Energy Systems at airports. When operating on the ground, aircraft require power for various uses, such as air conditioning, which has traditionally been derived from generators located on board the aircraft. Many airports are now utilizing ground-based systems to provide such energy. Consisting of a combined power and air-conditioning unit, these systems have been found, in some cases, to reduce fuel consumption by up to 90 percent compared with on-board aircraft generators.[15] Zurich Airport, for example, through implementation of its aircraft ground energy systems, has benefitted significantly in terms of reduced fuel consumption.[16]

Airports Council International (ACI),[17] the organization that represents airports worldwide and promotes airport excellence in safety, security, and the environment, has developed several guidelines, tools, and initiatives to

[12] Ibid.

[13] A. Kandt and R. Romero, "Implementing Solar Technologies at Airports" (July 2014) National Renewable Energy Laboratory (NREL), Department of Energy Office of Energy Efficiency & Renewable Energy, online: NREL www.nrel.gov/publications.

[14] Anand Upadhyay, "Cochin (India) – World's First Airport To Go 100% Solar," *Solar Love* (August 2015), online: Solar Love solarlove.org/cochin-india-worlds-first-airport-go-100-solar/.

[15] "IST-Edelstahl-Anlagenbau – Well-grounded with AGES," Future Airports, online: Future Airports www.futureairport.com/contractors/ground-support-equipment/ist-edelstahl-anlagenbau/.

[16] Emanuel Fleuti, "Aircraft Ground Energy Systems at Zurich Airport," Flughafen Zürich AG, online: www.flughafenzuerich.ch/~/media/FlughafenZH/Dokumente/Das_Unternehmen/Laerm_Politik_und_Umwelt/Luft/2013_ZRH_Aircraft-Ground-Energy-System.pdf.

[17] Airports Council International (ACI) is the international association of the world's airports. It is a nonprofit organization, the prime purpose of which is to foster cooperation among its member airports and with other partners in world aviation, including organizations representing governments, airlines, and aircraft manufacturers. See Airports Council International, *Policies and Recommended Practices Handbook*, 7th edn. (2009), online: ACI www.aci.aero/Media/aci/file/Publications/2009/ACI_Policies_and_Recommended_Practices_seventh_edition_FINAL_v2.pdf.

assist airports in limiting or reducing their environmental impacts while supporting their economic and social benefits. For instance, two important initiatives are worth mentioning: *Airport Carbon Accreditation*[18] and Airport Carbon and Emissions Reporting Tool (ACERT).[19] They both assist their member airports to manage their CO_2 emissions, and to measure progress made.[20] Airport operators can decide to use ACERT to start their carbon mapping/management or even to improve their actual program. Airport Carbon Accreditation is an independent program that starts with carbon mapping, passing through reducing emissions, engaging with third stakeholders, and eventually offsetting their remaining emissions and reaching carbon neutrality. As of September 2017, more than 38 percent of global air passenger traffic travels through 192 airports in more than 54 countries that are part of the program, demonstrating how robust is the commitment taken by airports to reduce their emissions.[21]

4.2.2 *Noise Issues*

While the reduction of GHG emissions is a priority for airports, this objective is not pursued in isolation from the environmental impacts posed by aircraft noise. Since the dawn of the aviation industry, aircraft noise has been one of the primary sources of noise caused by human activities. Two sources of aircraft noise are the engines, which include two major types – jet and piston – and noise produced from the aircraft frame.[22] In view of the fact that aircraft produce more noise during take-off and landing,[23] airports and the communities they serve are consequently affected by such noise. Indeed, for those communities located in close proximity to airports, airport operations can be a significant source of annoyance.[24] Moreover, noise generated by ground access systems located within the airport land area can worsen the noise created by aircraft.[25]

To address the problem of noise in the vicinity of airports, airport operators have been working to find ways to reduce aircraft noise, reduce the number of

[18] To learn more about Airport Carbon Accreditation, see online: www.airportcarbonaccreditation.org/.

[19] To learn more about Airport Carbon and Emissions Reporting Tool (ACERT), see online: www.aci.aero/About-ACI/Priorities/Environment/ACERT.

[20] ICAO, *ICAO Environmental Report 2013: Destination Green* (Montreal: ICAO, 2013) at 45.

[21] See online: www.airportcarbonaccreditation.org.

[22] Zeldine Niamh O'Brien, "Civil Subsonic Jet Aeroplane Noise: Its Impact, Regulation and Remedies," *Irish Students L Rev* 14 (2006), 156 at 158.

[23] Janić, *Greening Airports, supra* Note 1 at 42.

[24] Andre, *supra* Note 5 at 36. Allegedly, a third of complaints about airports concern acoustic issues. Thomas, *supra* Note 7 at 105.

[25] Janić, *Greening Airports, supra* Note 1 at 56.

people exposed to excessive noise levels, and include local communities within future airport plans and activities for growth, particularly as they pertain to land use.[26] Among the solutions devised by various airports and other aviation stakeholders are, *inter alia*, specific urban planning that takes into account the impact of noise on surrounding communities; the application of new aircraft technologies and designs that reduce the degree of noise produced; restricting the operation of particular types of aircraft that create more noise, reducing the overall number and frequency of flights (especially night-time flights), better planning and management of land use, and redistribution of noise by managing runways, especially take-off and landing routes.[27] According to the ICAO Balanced Approach, operation restrictions should be the last resort and should be considered only after the other elements have been considered: reduction of noise at source, land use planning and management, and operational improvements.[28] Therefore, operation restrictions, including curfews should always be the last resort, because they can lead to under-utilization of airport infrastructure, which has negative consequences regarding the growth and economic viability of airports and the communities they serve that generally are also dependent on the airport as a source of economic prosperity.

Finally, there are also trade-offs that must be considered when dealing with the problem of noise as opposed to other pollutants in airports. For example, although modern turbofan engines are increasingly designed to reduce the overall level of noise emitted, such reductions have only been made possible through the use of higher engine operating temperatures, which, in turn, result in increasing the production of nitrogen oxide emissions.[29] Accordingly, although an understanding of the interplay between noise and other pollutants is still developing,[30] balancing the trade-offs between noise and emissions should be always considered.

4.2.3 *Land Utilization, Waste, and Congestion*

The environmental impacts of airports are complex and not limited to GHG emissions and noise. Land use by airports together with waste and ground congestion are additional problems that need to be addressed.

[26] Oh, *supra* Note 9 at 51.

[27] ICAO, *Environment Report, supra* Note 5 at 4; Janić, *Greening Airports, supra* Note 1 at 44; Thomas, *supra* Note 7 at 105.

[28] ICAO Balanced Approach, Doc, see online: https://www.icao.int/environmental-protection/Documents/Publications/Guidance_BalancedApproach_Noise.pdf.

[29] Konstantinos Zografos, Giovanni Andreatta, and Amedeo Odoni, eds., *Modelling and Managing Airport Performance* (New York: John Wiley & Sons, 2013) at 6.2.1.3.

[30] Ibid. See also Andreas Schäfer, *Transportation in a Climate-Constrained World* (Cambridge, MA: MIT Press, 2009) at 94.

"Land use" or "land taking" refers to the utilization of land by airports for the purpose of building and operating structures that serve airport-related activities. The efficient and environmentally friendly use of airport land requires proper planning and management of water, waste, and wildlife. The creation of efficient public transit options is a vital component in the planning of any new or expanded airport construction, as public transit reduces emissions with respect to passenger connections between the airport and their respective urban service areas. In spite of ground transportation not being part of the airport's own emissions, airport operators should engage with government and other stakeholders to encourage the development of such efficient systems. For example, Line 8 of the Madrid Metro, a major infrastructure investment co-financed by the EU from the period 1997 to 2002, is an external radial line of the network that links the core business center of Madrid with Barajas International Airport.[31] Madrid is part of a growing list of major EU airports with subway or rail access to the city center. Outside the EU, over two dozen major international airports have rail or subway links to the downtown core and more airport–downtown rail links are planned.[32] Announced new rail links to serve Denver International Airport,[33] São Paulo–Guarulhos International Airport,[34] and Washington Dulles Airport[35] confirm the importance of providing rail access to international airports. These improvements in public rail transport services contribute to reducing congestion of the road networks surrounding airports, and this also has positive impacts on the environment through the reduction of air pollutants, emissions, and noise.[36]

Airport "waste" refers to the waste generated by an airport's operations. Such waste can be generated by passengers, tenants, airfield operations, and maintenance activities, and can also be caused by construction and

[31] "Madrid Metro Line – Access to Barajas Airport" (2012) CENIT, Centre for Innovation in Transport, Barcelona in Partnership with CSIL, Centre for Industrial Studies, Milan (prepared for European Commission Directorate-General Regional Policy, Policy Development Evaluation) at 1–2 ["Madrid Metro"].

[32] The list includes Atlanta, Bangkok, Beijing, Boston, Chicago O'Hare, Delhi, Dubai, Hong Kong, Istanbul, Kuala Lumpur, Mexico City, Miami, Minneapolis, Moscow Sheremetyevo, Newark, Philadelphia, Portland, St. Louis, San Francisco, Seattle, Seoul, Singapore, Sydney, Tokyo, Toronto, Vancouver, and Washington Reagan.

[33] "East Rail Line Facts," Regional Transportation District, online: www.rtd-denver.com/FF-EastLRT.shtml.

[34] "SP: trem para Cumbica deve começar a operar em 2015, diz CPTM," online: noticias.terra.com.br/brasil/cidades/sp-trem-para-cumbica-deve-comecar-a-operar-em-2015-diz-cptm,71f8921ac6d41410VgnVCM10000098cceb0aRCRD.html.

[35] Online: www.dullesmetro.com/.

[36] "Madrid Metro," *supra* Note 31 at 87.

demolition.[37] Water management at airports is another environmental concern. Pollutants used by aircraft and ground service equipment, including fuel, could cause environmental damage if not properly dealt with. For instance, airfield deicing and anti-icing, fuel storage and refueling, and aircraft and vehicle cleaning and maintenance can result in the discharge of pollutants into adjacent water sources, in turn posing a danger to aquatic life and human health.[38] An airport operator should therefore work with the local government to fulfill the requirement to protect adjacent water sources. It is axiomatic that the primary objective of any waste management efforts should be to reduce the total amount of waste generated by a given airport over a specific period of time.[39] Wildlife management is another environmental issue at an airport. In this case, safety concerns are also elemental. For instance, wildlife can cause serious incidents and accidents. Therefore airports have a wildlife hazard management plan in place to avoid such risks and to protect the local wildlife. Airports Council International (ACI) has published a "Wildlife Hazard Management Handbook" containing best practices to assist airports in this regard.[40]

Finally, airline and air passenger congestion and delays is another issue, which can result in greater levels of pollutants, as increasing numbers of planes wait for landing, discharging additional emissions as they do so. Potential remedies in this regard obviously would include optimum utilization of airport and runway capacity in a manner that can minimize the aforementioned congestion, including improving the use of the airspace, which will be discussed in the following section on air traffic management (ATM).

4.3 THE ROLE OF ATM IN REDUCING ENVIRONMENTAL IMPACTS

Ensuring the continued and more efficient use of the global airspace has been one of the strategies implemented to reduce the adverse effects of aviation on the environment. The development of more efficient air traffic management services is also one of the most effective fuel saving opportunities available. In fact, the implementation of ATM systems, which permit more direct aircraft routings, as well as the utilization of more efficient conditions such as optimum altitudes and speeds can significantly reduce

37 Oh, *supra* Note 9 at 50.

38 ICAO, *Environment Report, supra* Note 5 at 5.

39 Janić, *Greening Airports, supra* Note 1 at 56.

40 Online: www.aci.aero.

CO_2 emissions.[41] For instance, ATM can reduce overall aviation fuel burn by between 8 and 18 percent.[42] Increased fuel efficiency through the implementation of new ATM operational procedures, however, also requires that institutional and regulatory arrangements be applied at both the national and international levels.[43]

In May 2007, in recognition of the importance of air navigation services in mitigating the negative impacts of aviation-related activities on the environment, the Civil Air Navigation Services Organization (CANSO) adopted a voluntary code of conduct that establishes a framework within which air navigation service providers can seek to offset the environmental impacts of growth both through their own initiatives and in collaboration with other industry stakeholders.[44] These efforts, together with various ICAO initiatives for improving global ATM systems, are concrete steps toward enhancing the environmentally sustainable use of global airspace.

Finally, the development and implementation of more advanced operational procedures through Air Traffic Control and Air Traffic Management operations can result in more efficient and effective utilization of the available airport airside capacity, which, in turn, can mitigate the production of emissions and/or noise around airports.[45] For example, Through the Arrival and Departure Flow Management component of ATM, it is possible to optimize usage of an existing airport's runway capacity and/or the number of aircraft landing in the most efficient way by changing the time patterns of various flights.[46] In addition, advanced technologies can assist in maximizing runway landing capacity by reducing separation and increasing diversity of air traffic control separation rules.[47]

Another example of such approaches in air traffic management is Collaborative Decision Making (CDM), which initially was intended for other

[41] ICAO, *ICAO Environmental Report 2007* (Montreal: ICAO, 2007) at 108 [*Environmental Report 2007*].

[42] Intergovernmental Panel on Climate Change, *IPCC Special Report: Aviation and the Global Atmosphere* (1999) at 11.

[43] *Environmental Report 2007*, *supra* note 41 at 139. Improved ATM operational measures are also considered an effective and quantifiable means of minimizing aircraft emissions, with near-term results.

[44] Ibid., 138.

[45] This includes procedures such as ATC time-based instead of distance-based separation, prioritizing instead of the currently used FCFS (First-Come–First-Served) priority rules for landing aircraft, and steeper approach procedures for landings on closely spaced parallel runways. See Janić, *Greening Airports*, *supra* Note 1 at 43–44, 100.

[46] Ibid., 45.

[47] Applying ATC time-based instead of distance-based separation rules is considered an effective method for increasing runway capacity. Ibid., 100–3.

applications such as decreasing ground delays, and has led to environmental benefits for airports.

Collaborative Decision Making, initially implemented in the United States, concerns improving air traffic management and enhancing execution of ground delay programs (GDPs) through information exchange, procedural improvements, collaborative routing, performance monitoring and analysis, collaborative resource allocation mechanisms, and collaborative information collection and distribution.[48] CDM helps in fuel planning, diversion decisions, and management of flow into hubs. With CDM, fuel burn due to queues at the threshold can be reduced, and less noise and lower emissions of CO_2 and NO_X that affect climate change and local air quality will be released.[49]

4.4 COMMUNITY PARTICIPATION IN AIRPORT ACTIVITIES

Community opposition to airport plans for expansion and growth generally arise from concerns regarding pollution and noise, and can be so influential that even very important and economically critical plans for airport expansion could be compromised. For example, community opposition compelled London Heathrow to cancel plans for the construction of an additional runway.[50] Another example is the expansion of Hong Kong International Airport, which was proposed by constructing a third runway; however, this proposal has raised a great debate.[51] Indeed, it is usually environmental concerns that are the decisive factor in igniting local community opposition to airport growth. Such community opposition is generally caused by either lack of public awareness of proper environmental management at the airport or some limitations faced by the airport regarding their environmental program. In some cases, however, when a big hub is located in a densely populated area, growing to reach the level of demand for such airport will be a permanent challenge, even though a proper environmental program is in

48 Mo Ball et al., "Assessing the Benefits of Collaborative Decision Making in Air Traffic Management," in George L. Donohue, ed., *Air Transportation Systems Engineering* (Reston, VA: American Institute of Aeronautics and Astronautics, 2001) at 239.

49 For more information on the subject, see the special website that Eurocontrol has developed together with ACI Europe and IATA, online: www.euro-cdm.org.

50 "Heathrow runway plans scrapped by new government", *BBC News* (May 12, 2010), online: BBC News news.bbc.co.uk/2/hi/uk_news/england/london/8678282.stm.

51 Linna Li and Becky P. Y. Loo, "Impact analysis of airport infrastructure within a sustainability framework: Case studies on Hong Kong International Airport," *Intl J Sustainable Transportation*, 10:9 (2016), 781 at 786.

place, including a strong community engagement program. In any case, if the airport is not successful in its engagement with the communities it serves, demonstrating its concern to minimize environmental impact, understanding community needs, and showcasing its positive economic impact, community opposition could result in limiting the airport's use of its complete capacity and infrastructure. Therefore, the adoption of airport initiatives that include the environmental concerns of surrounding communities is essential. Creating and maintaining a relationship with local communities that is based on mutual trust can be influential in ensuring community acceptance of an airport's future plans for growth.[52] In this context, there are various steps that airports can adopt to secure local community acceptance of plans for such growth.

(i) The first step pertaining to greater community involvement in environmental management of airport activities is the carrying out of careful studies of the actual environmental burdens that could accompany an airport's activities and plans for further growth, the objective of which is to diminish the negative environmental impacts posed by airport growth and expansion to the greatest extent possible. The potential environmental problems at a given airport must first be identified, at which point the negative effects on each area, such as air quality, noise, waste, water contamination, and traffic congestion, can be measured and quantified. To achieve this goal, advanced modeling techniques and methodologies for precise quantification of such effects should be applied, with the evaluation methods and techniques updated regularly in order to obtain the most accurate results.[53]

(ii) Another important step involves carefully designing plans for controlling and diminishing potential environmental impacts through which environmental constraints in terms of noise and allowed emissions of pollutants are set in advance. This is done in order to protect the local population, air quality, and the overall environment from potential adverse environmental effects and to minimize the number of people affected. This requires development of both preventative and mitigation measures and the implementation thereof so they can meet defined targets and goals; community involvement in the preparation of such targets is a crucial element in the success of these plans.[54] Moreover,

[52] Oh, *supra* Note 9 at 52.

[53] B. Griefahn et al., "Protection Goals for Residents in the Vicinity of Civil Airports," *Noise & Health*, 6:24 (2004), 51 at 52.

[54] Upham et al., *supra* Note 4 at 149.

airport authorities must assure local communities that their concerns are being addressed, and this can be done through the implementation of community engagement programs in which citizens are actively involved in any process that involves the preparation of future airport environmental plans.[55] Vienna International Airport, for example, in its mediation process regarding environmental concerns, engaged various groups of stakeholders, including local communities, before issuing a final mediation agreement.[56]

(iii) Still another step in protecting communities from the potential negative impacts posed by operation of airports is the implementation of an ongoing and dynamic process that involves continuous monitoring of airport performance.[57] Such a process should include continuous transparent monitoring and assessments of airport performance with respect to environmental factors, and should also include an evaluation of disturbances such as emissions, noise, congestion, and wastage within a given period of time in order to determine whether the plans were implemented as intended, and whether such measures were effective. In this context, public access to the prepared reports should be ensured,[58] with the results of such reports and assessments being both transparent and easily accessible to members of the public in order to acquire and maintain the trust of communities.[59] By demonstrating a genuine commitment to the promotion of green initiatives, airports will improve their relationships with their local communities, and this can often eventually lead to less opposition to future expansion.[60] By way of example, in its Environment Strategy for 2010–2015, Sydney Airport provided up-to-date environmental information to the surrounding community, and made information regarding key environmental achievements readily available to the public.[61]

55 Thomas, *supra* Note 7 at 107; Oh, *supra* Note 9 at 52.

56 "Environment and Sustainability" (2015) Vienna International Airport, online: www.viennaairport.com/jart/prj3/va/main.jart?rel=en&content-id=1249344074276&reserve-mode=active.

57 Griefahn et al., *supra* Note 53 at 52.

58 Upham et al., *supra* Note 4 at 149.

59 Oh, *supra* Note 9 at 52.

60 Thomas, *supra* Note 7 at 105.

61 "The Sydney Airport Environment Strategy 2010–2015," online: www.sydneyairport.com.au/investors/~/media/files/corporate/environment%20plan/policy%20and%20strategy/envirostratgy102015.pdf.

Finally, in some cases, building airports far from urban areas is another initiative that has been taken by airport planners and aviation authorities in response to community concerns.[62]

4.5 GOVERNMENT REGULATION

Government regulation has always had a significant impact on the transportation industry, and issues related to the environment are not different.[63] Policymakers and regulators play a key role in ensuring that regulating the air transportation industry takes into account the interests of society generally, as well as of the communities located in the vicinity of airports. The positive economic impact of the aviation industry and airports in particular cannot be ignored. In addition, regulation should not impose such a burden that it would compromise the sustainable development of the industry. As an indispensable party in the policy planning process for transportation-related activities, governments must also protect people against the health hazards that may accompany such activities.[64] With respect to the aviation industry, this requires coordination between transportation, environmental, and health policymakers in developing policies at all stages, from the manufacturing of aircraft and building infrastructure to the actual operation of airports. If airports are owned or managed by the State or a private entity, it is important to secure compliance with the desired regulatory regime.

[62] A list of some airports that are built some distance away from heavily populated urban areas includes Montreal Mirabel (1976, built on expropriated land); Tokyo Narita (1978, built on farmland); San Salvador Comalapa (1980, built along the coast); São Paulo Guarulhos (1985, former Air Force base); Osaka Kansai (1994, constructed on a specially built artificial island); Denver International (1995, built on farmland); Shanghai Pudong (1999, built in a less populated area); Seoul Incheon (2001, built on reclaimed land); Dubai Al Maktoum (2010, built in the desert); and Mariscal Sucre International Airport (2013, built away from populated areas). Although building airports far from urban areas can reduce the impact of noise on populated areas, this also increases GHG emissions as a result of travelers and airport employees being forced to travel further between the airport and the community it serves. Often the construction of airports in remote locations coincides with the building of rail or subway access to the city center.

[63] Environmental issues are perceived to have a great impact on supply and demand. See Brian Graham and Claire Guyer, "Environmental Sustainability, Airport Capacity and European Air Transport Liberalization: Irreconcilable Goals?" *J Transport Geography*, 7:3 (1999), 165 at 172–73.

[64] The Preamble of the Charter on Transport published by the Environment and Health of World Health urges policymakers to ensure that community wellbeing be put first when preparing and making decisions regarding transport and infrastructure policies. *The World Health Organization 1999 Charter on Transport, the Environment and Health*, EUR/ICP/EHCO 02, 02 05/9 Rev.4. 09009 (1999), Preamble.

Both the excess and the absence of appropriate laws and regulations could become a problem. Governments should work in close collaboration with the industry to propose a regulatory regime that is sufficient to stabilize and/or diminish the negative environmental effects of aviation-related activities on the public, representing real incentives for airports, manufacturers, and airlines to control their environmental impacts. Achieving such a balance is not an easy challenge, but the international aviation community has already faced similar difficulties and has prevailed. For instance, the International Civil Aviation Organization (ICAO) has recently agreed to implement a Carbon Offsetting Scheme for International Aviation (CORSIA). Such a scheme was the outcome of many years of discussions and studies that involved ICAO member States and several aviation and environmental stakeholders that have finally found a compromise between the different interests at stake. Such a compromise was able to progress with the implementation of the scheme, the very first of its kind in any global industry. In this regard, the environment wins and the industry that is able to settle an agreement that does not compromise its future economic development wins, at least that is what is foreseen at the stage of this writing.

Airport operators, however, do face an additional challenge regarding regulatory compliance. Although airports seem very similar to many, they can indeed be very different from each other, depending on their location, their community, their size, their public or private nature, and so on. Such a complex framework requires flexibility to operate and also to minimize their environmental impacts that also vary, depending on the airport size and location. In this regard, although one can say that regulations, including permitting and licensing procedures, are necessary to compel airport operators to implement sustainability practices regarding the operations and/or expansion of airports,[65] keeping a degree of flexibility for the airport to adjust to its demands is essential. Many airports are already front runners among their communities regarding environmental protection. In such cases, it is not the imposition of regulation per se that accomplishes such a result, but a combination of corporate social responsibility with community demands and the entire society's understanding of what should be their concern.

Finally, it is important that any policies and regulations created by the government do not give rise to under-utilization of airport infrastructure and capacity; the social and economic benefits provided by a given airport's operation, and aviation activities in general, including due attention to the

[65] Kris Pauwels, "Road Map to Sustainability," *Airport World*, 17:1 (2012), 58.

possibilities and potential for future growth and the concomitant positive impact this can have on local communities and society generally, are arguably at least as important as giving due consideration to environmental issues. Thus, concerns regarding sustainability means considering not only the environmental issues surrounding airport development and management but also fully appreciating the social and economic impacts of airports, and the benefits they bring to local communities.[66]

It is the policymaker's responsibility to balance the often inherently opposing interests associated with aviation activities.[67] Building new airports or expanding those that already exist is a very long process. This can be due to the extensive local and national regulations governing such construction, which can often require a complex and time-consuming procedure that negatively affects the smooth operation of airports. Accordingly, sufficient, but not excessive, environmental constraints, which could impair the successful performance of airports, require consideration and balancing of different factors and variables, achieved primarily through the implementation of careful studies that evaluate the trade-offs between particular effects and benefits with the related impacts and costs through utilization of various policy instruments.[68] That being said, the importance of community perception of the environmental impacts posed by airport activities in this context once again becomes evident, because by securing the local community's acceptance of the operation or expansion of a given airport, the adoption and implementation of overly restrictive regulations can be avoided.[69]

In addition, the promulgation of international standards through international bodies such as the ICAO is a very important part of the regulatory process. Through the adoption and amendment of Standards and Recommended Practices (SARPs) that deal with a wide range of matters affecting the international air transport industry, the ICAO implements the goals of the Chicago Convention[70] for achieving uniformity in regulations, standards, procedures, and all other matters affecting international aviation, including issues pertaining to the environment. Specifically, the ICAO has addressed environmental concerns posed by aviation, particularly in terms of aircraft

[66] Thomas, *supra* Note 7 at 104.
[67] Janić, *Greening Airports*, *supra* Note 1 at 28.
[68] Ibid., 61.
[69] Oh, *supra* Note 9 at 52.
[70] *Convention on International Civil Aviation*, December 7, 1944, 15 UNTS 295 [*Chicago Convention*].

noise and GHG emissions, in Annex 16 to the Chicago Convention.[71] Because the ICAO is reliant on its Member States for implementation of its standards, States that are unable to comply with Annex 16 should notify the ICAO of any differences between their national regulations and practices and the SARPs promulgated within the Annex as required by Article 38 of the Chicago Convention.[72] Although Article 38 gives States the right to reject the application of the international Standards and Recommended Practices to their own aviation industry, there is great pressure from the international aviation community to comply, and as a result, the SARPs adopted by the ICAO normally enjoy widespread compliance.[73] Since ICAO SARPS on environmental protection are focused on the aircraft, the ICAO has also established useful and detailed manuals, such as *Airport Planning Manual*,[74] which set out different aspects of airport planning. ICAO *Airport Planning Manual*, Part II tries to create a balance between airport developments and ecological considerations.[75]

In 2016 and in its 39th triennial Assembly, the ICAO adopted Resolutions A39–1, A39–2, and A39–3, which constitute the consolidated statement of continuing ICAO policies and practices related to environmental protection, including general provisions, noise and local air quality, climate change, and the Global Market-based Measure (MBM) scheme. As mentioned in this

71 *Annex 16 to the Convention on International Civil Aviation, Environmental Protection*, International Standards and Recommended Practices adopted by International Civil Aviation Organization (ICAO) Vol. II (3rd edn., July 2008, Amendment 7) at v.

72 *Chicago Convention, supra* Note 70, art 38.

73 Heather L. Miller, "Civil Aircraft Emissions and International Treaty Law," *J Air L & Com*, 634 (1997–98), 697 at 729.

74 ICAO, *Airport Planning Manual*, ICAO Doc 9184, Parts 1 and 2, online: ICAO www.icao.int/environmental-protection/Pages/environment-publications.aspx. Other examples of manuals and guidance materials are: ICAO, *Guidance on the Balanced Approach to Aircraft Noise Management*, ICAO Doc 9829; ICAO, *Airport Air Quality Guidance Manual*, ICAO Doc 9889; ICAO, *Recommended Method for Computing Noise Contours around Airports*, ICAO Doc 9911 replacing Cir 205; ICAO, *Noise Abatement Procedures: Review of Research, Development and Implementation Projects – Discussion of Survey Results*, ICAO Doc 9888 (2010); ICAO, *Environmental Technical Manual Volume I – Procedures for the Noise Certification of Aircraft*, ICAO Doc 9501; ICAO, Environmental Technical Manual Volume II – Procedures for the Emissions Certification of Aircraft Engines, ICAO Doc 9501; ICAO, *Guidance on Aircraft Emission Charges Related to Local Air Quality*, ICAO Doc 9884; ICAO, *ICAO's Policies on Charges for Airports and Air Navigation Services*, ICAO Doc 9082; ICAO, Guidance on Environmental Assessment of Proposed Air Traffic Management Operational Changes, ICAO Doc 10031. For a complete list, see ICAO, "Environmental Publications," online: ICAO www.icao.int/environmental-protection/Pages/environment-publications.aspx.

75 Ruwantissa Abeyratne, *Law and Regulation of Aerodromes* (Cham: Springer Science & Business Media, 2014) at 19.

chapter, member states have now agreed to implement a global MBM scheme in the form of the Carbon Offsetting and Reduction Scheme for International Aviation (CORSIA) to address any annual increase in total CO_2 emissions from international civil aviation (i.e. civil aviation flights that depart in one country and arrive in a different country) above the 2020 levels, taking into account special circumstances and respective capabilities.[76] The ICAO and its Member States will strive to:

(a) limit or reduce the number of people affected by significant aircraft noise;
(b) limit or reduce the impact of aviation emissions on local air quality; and
(c) limit or reduce the impact of aviation greenhouse gas emissions on the global climate...[77]

The ICAO, through resolutions and numerous documents, guidance materials, and manuals, continues to demonstrate its leadership role in all international civil aviation matters, including the ones related to the environment.

Another useful guide for policymakers are the policies and recommended practices of ACI, which provides detailed actions and strategies that can help ensure growth that can be sustained in the longer term on noise, emissions and local air quality, greenhouse gas emissions and global climate change, sustainability and system methods, reporting and certification, environmental awareness, training, sharing information and communications, and stakeholder communications and understanding.[78]

Thus, while international standards and best practices have helped make aviation and airports more environmentally sustainable, because implementation of ICAO standards and internationally recognized best practices is generally performed at the national level, effective regulation and policymaking

[76] ICAO, "Carbon Offsetting and Reduction Scheme for International Aviation (CORSIA)," online: ICAO www.icao.int/environmental-protection/Pages/market-based-measures.aspx; In Resolution A39–2, the Assembly requested the Council to encourage States and stakeholders to develop air traffic management that optimizes environmental benefits, and promote and share best practices applied at airports. See ICAO Resolution A39–2: *Consolidated statement of continuing ICAO policies and practices related to environmental protection – Climate change*, at para 19(g), online: ICAO www.icao.int/environmental-protection/Documents/Resolution_A39_2.pdf.

[77] See ICAO Resolution A39–1: *Consolidated statement of continuing ICAO policies and practices related to environmental protection – General provisions, noise and local air quality*, online: ICAO www.icao.int/environmental-protection/Documents/Resolution_A39_1.PDF.

[78] The latest edition of this handbook is available online: ACI www.aci.aero/About-ACI/Policies-Practices.

regarding the environmental sustainability of aviation and airports, in particular, therefore require actions both at the international and national levels.

4.6 CONCLUSION

The exponential growth of aviation and the consequent increase of its environmental impacts is a constant challenge faced by airport operators. Because limiting airport growth through the imposition of environmental caps and quotas may pose additional negative economic consequences for local communities, decisions concerning the construction or expansion of airports must obviously involve considerations of the trade-offs regarding the positive and negative effects of environmental and economic factors, and their resulting impact on both local communities and society as a whole. In this regard, the role of government in appropriately addressing the environmental and sustainability considerations posed by airports must include an evaluation of economic and social factors.[79] While the growth of airports should be encouraged for the economic and social benefits they provide, such growth should optimally be a green growth in which increase in capacity is not achieved at the cost of negative impacts on the environment. Attaining a desirable balance between these objectives can be achieved only through the implementation of careful studies that assess both environmental capacities and constraints, as well as the active involvement of local communities in all stages of development and implementation of plans necessary for the effective environmental management of airports. Finally, effective public policy initiatives regarding environmental sustainability should proactively address such issues, with the ICAO and other international organizations such as ACI providing both national and local authorities with effective and comprehensive guidelines for implementation of best practices that promote environmental sustainability at airports, in turn contributing to the continued sustainable growth of the aviation industry in the future.

79 See Sgouris Sgouridis, Philippe A. Bonnefoy, and R. John Hansman, "Air Transportation in a Carbon Constrained World: Long-Term Dynamics of Policies and Strategies for Mitigating the Carbon Footprint of Commercial Aviation," *Transportation Research Part A*, 45:10 (2011), 1077 at 1078; Charles et al., *supra* Note 2 at 1011; Upham et al., *supra* Note 4 at 149; Thomas, *supra* Note 7 at 102.

PART II

Regional Aviation Issues

5

Sustainable Development and Emission Trading

The EU Perspective

Markus W. Gehring and Cairo Robb

This chapter aims to present the EU perspective on the controversial issue of carbon emission trading and aviation. The article analyses how the EU advanced to the concrete implementation of emissions trading in the aviation sector. It analyses why the EU first proposed and then introduced GHG emissions trading while at the same time seeking multilateral solutions to the issue of climate change contributions from the aviation sector. It highlights the technical issues at stake, the global resistance to what was perceived as a unilateral act by the EU, and how the fact that the EU had introduced the system influenced the 2016 ICAO climate decision to adopt the CORSIA carbon offsets scheme. The article documents how the EU system eventually influenced the global debate and the global compromise that arguably respected the most important sustainable development principles. It reviews ongoing EU policy respecting sustainable development and ends with an outlook on the unlikely scenario that the new ICAO mechanism could fail, in which case the EU's original scheme could be resurrected under EU law.

5.1 INTRODUCTION

The problem of aviation and climate change is simple – as more people travel, aviation grows and so do greenhouse gas (GHG) emissions. On the other hand, although figures vary, a report from the Intergovernmental Panel on Climate Change (IPCC) estimates that aircraft currently "contribute about 3.5 percent of the total radiative forcing (a measure of change in climate) by all human activities."[1]

[1] ICAO, "Aircraft engine emissions," www.icao.int/environmental-protection/Pages/aircraft-engine-emissions.aspx last accessed September 29, 2017. For the full report, see J. E. Penner

It is widely accepted that this figure will rise,[2] and the IPCC has predicted that it could rise to as much as 15 percent by 2050.[3] Carbon dioxide emissions from aviation were expected to grow by 176 percent between 1990 and 2050;[4] however, newer studies suggest growth in the order of 300 percent.[5]

The International Civil Aviation Organization (ICAO) was tasked under the 1997 Kyoto Protocol of the UN Framework Convention on Climate Change (UNFCC) with leading global action to reduce greenhouse gas emissions from the aviation industry. Unfortunately, progress in the ICAO had been excruciatingly slow until its decision to introduce its Carbon Offsetting and Reduction Scheme for International Aviation (CORSIA) at the 39th Triennial Assembly, which it is argued was strongly influenced by the EU's prior decisions.[6]

Continuing concerns over the increase in GHG emissions from aviation led the European Commission to propose their inclusion in the European Union (EU) Emission Trading Scheme (ETS) in 2008. The purpose, as stated in the preamble of Directive 2008/101/EC, is to try to prevent growth in aviation from undermining reductions in other sectors: "If the climate change impact of the aviation sector continues to grow at the current rate, it would significantly undermine reductions made by other sectors to combat climate change."[7] This prompted the Air Transport Association of America (ATAA), and individual US and Canadian airlines, to file a case before the European Court of Justice (CJEU), challenging the legality of the Directive on the basis of violation of international law. However, the CJEU, in its preliminary ruling,

et al., *Aviation and the Global Atmosphere: A Special Report of the Intergovernmental Panel on Climate Change* (Cambridge: Cambridge University Press, 1999).

2 R. C. N. Wit et al., *Giving Wings to Emissions Trading: Inclusion of Aviation under the European Emissions Trading System (ETS): Design and Impacts – Report for the European Commission* (CE, 2005) ec.europa.eu/clima/sites/clima/files/transport/aviation/docs/aviation_et_study_en.pdf last accessed September 29, 2017.

3 Penner et al., *Aviation and the Global Atmosphere, supra* Note 1, Executive Summary.

4 Centre for Clean Air Policy (2004).

5 European Commission DG Climate Action, "Reducing emissions from aviation," ec.europa.eu/clima/policies/transport/aviation_en last accessed September 29, 2017.

6 ICAO, "Draft text for the report on agenda item 22: Section on global market-based measure scheme," A39-WP/462 (October 5, 2016) www.icao.int/Meetings/a39/Documents/WP/wp_462_en.pdf last accessed September 29, 2017.

7 Directive 2008/101/EC of the European Parliament and of the Council of 19 November 2008, amending Directive 2003/87/EC so as to include aviation activities in the scheme for greenhouse gas emission allowance trading within the Community, OJ 2009 L 8, p. 3, recital 11.

upheld the legality of the Directive in including the aviation sector in the EU-ETS.[8]

Less than a year from the CJEU decision, or in July 2012, some form of movement was observed for the first time since the Kyoto Protocol entered into force in 2005. The ICAO Council's Committee on Aviation Environmental Protection (CAEP) adopted an Aircraft Carbon Dioxide (CO_2) Emissions calculation system as the first building block toward adopting a global standard.[9] Further, on November 9, 2012, the ICAO Council announced it was forming a special High-level Group (HGCC) to provide near-term recommendations on a series of policy issues that have arisen in the course of the ICAO's ongoing research into the feasibility of a global market-based measure (MBM) scheme appropriate to international aviation (i.e. global MBM feasibility). It would also examine the ICAO's development of a policy framework to guide the general application of any proposed MBM measures to international air transport activity (i.e. framework for national and regional MBMs).[10] These renewed signals from the ICAO triggered the EU to propose the suspension of the application of its ETS to international flights on November 12, 2012, otherwise known as the "stop the clock" decision.

During the 38th ICAO Assembly in October 2013, Member States agreed to develop a global market-based scheme to reduce the environmental effects of civil aviation, among other measures. The scheme was finalized in 2016, and is set to be implemented by 2020.[11]

In order to facilitate this compromise, the EU had deferred the full implementation of the EU-ETS for the period from 2013 to 2016. Hence, only emissions from flights within the European Economic Area (EEA) fall within

[8] Case C-366/10 *Air Transport Association of America, American Airlines Inc., Continental Airlines Inc., United Airlines Inc.* v. *Secretary of State for Energy and Climate Change* [2011] OJ C 260/9 . The principal EU institutions, together with interveners, including the United Kingdom and ten other EU Member States, as well as Iceland and Norway as ETS non-EU participants, defended the legality of the measure.

[9] ICAO Fact Sheet, "Aircraft CO2 emissions standard metric system," www.icao.int/Newsroom/Documents/CO2%20Metric%20System%20%20Information%20Sheet_FINAL.PDF last accessed September 29, 2017.

[10] The 37th Session of the ICAO Assembly in 2010 instructed the UN aviation body to prepare and deliver both the MBM Framework and Feasibility Report for consideration by its next triennial Assembly in October 2013. ICAO Press Release, "New ICAO Council high-level group to focus on environmental policy changes," COM 20/12 (November 15, 2012) www.icao.int/Newsroom/Pages/new-ICAO-council-high-level-group-to-focus-on-environmental-policy-challenges.aspx last accessed September 29, 2017.

[11] ICAO Res A38–17 (2013) Doc 10022.

its application.[12] The European Commission is required to provide a full report to the European Parliament and Council on the outcome of the 2016 ICAO Assembly. The full report should take into account international developments and propose on the scope for coverage of emissions from flights located outside the EEA. No final decision has been taken to date, as the details for the ICAO CORSIA are being developed, but in February 2017 the Commission proposed legislation that would convert CORSIA into EU law as all EU Member States have committed to participate in the new ICAO system.[13] The current proposed amendment institutes a duty for the Commission to report on international progress, also made by other ICAO states, while indefinitely suspending the application of the ETS to international flights.[14]

In December 2015, the Paris Agreement was adopted during the 21st Conference of the Parties of the UNFCCC.[15] The Agreement seeks to hold the increase in the global average temperature steady. In order to achieve this, "Parties aim to reach global peaking of greenhouse gas emissions as soon as possible." The participation of the Parties in the Agreement starts with the preparation, communication, and maintenance of "nationally determined contributions." There is no concrete form of enforcement under the Agreement but the publication and monitoring of the nationally determined contributions may deter Parties from not fulfilling their commitment.

It is noteworthy that the developed States Parties are expected to undertake economy-wide absolute emission reduction targets. Moreover, developing States Parties are expected to continue their mitigation efforts but are encouraged to move toward economy-wide emission reduction or limitation targets. These can be used to justify the position of the EU in including the aviation sector in the EU-ETS given the expected contribution of aviation in GHG emissions.

[12] Regulation (EU) No 421/2014 of the European Parliament and of the Council of 16 April 2014 amending Directive 2003/87/EC establishing a scheme for greenhouse gas emission allowance trading within the Community, in view of an implementation by 2020 of the international agreement applying a single market-based measure to international aviation emissions, OJ L 129/1.

[13] European Commission DG Climate Action, "EU global scheme to offset emissions," ec.europa.eu/clima/policies/transport/aviation_en last accessed September 29, 2017.

[14] European Commission, "Proposal for a Regulation of the European Parliament and of the Council amending Directive 2003/87/EC to continue current limitations of scope for aviation activities and to prepare to implement a global market-based measure from 2021," COM (2017) 54 final (February 3, 2017) eur-lex.europa.eu/legal-content/EN/TXT/PDF/?uri=CELEX:52017PC0054&from=EN last accessed September 29, 2017.

[15] UNFCCC, "Adoption of the Paris Agreement: Proposal by the President," UNFCCC/CP/2015/L.9 (December 12, 2015) unfccc.int/resource/docs/2015/cop21/eng/l09.pdf last accessed September 29, 2017.

5.2 EU LEGAL BACKGROUND

Under the Lisbon Treaty, combating climate change is a Treaty objective for the EU, both with regard to the Union's external relations and its internal environmental laws.[16]

After advocating for and preferring carbon taxes in the 1990s, the European Commission shifted its approach in line with the Kyoto Protocol, and now considers emissions trading the best way to address GHG emissions from diverse sources, given the less significant impacts on economic growth. Emissions trading is widely recognized as an important policy and regulatory instrument in the transition to a greener economy.[17]

The EU-ETS is a cornerstone of the EU's efforts to curb GHGs and combat climate change. It was established in Directive 2003/87/EC, which set up a scheme for greenhouse gas emission allowance trading within the Union.[18] The Directive promotes "reductions of greenhouse gas emissions in a cost-effective and economically efficient manner."[19] The EU-ETS has a cap that is reduced every year. It is expected to deliver an overall 21 percent reduction in industrial GHGs by 2020.[20]

In 2008, the EU-ETS was expanded to include emissions from the aviation sector.[21] Flights were from that point on considered a source, and each airline company received an operation permit specifying that the airline had to report verified emissions data each year, and surrender a number of allowances equal to the amount of GHGs emitted in relation to passenger miles. The reasons for the expansion of the EU-ETS were explained in the Directive: "The Sixth Community Environment Action Programme … provided for the Community to identify and undertake specific actions to reduce greenhouse gas emissions from aviation if no such action were agreed within the ICAO by

[16] *Consolidated version of Treaty on European Union* (December 13, 2007) Art. 21(1)(f) [*TEU*]; *Consolidated version of the Treaty on the Functioning of the European Union* (13 December 2007) Art. 192(1) [*TFEU*].

[17] For an economic analysis see for example, Sustainable Prosperity, *White paper towards a green economy in Canada* (June 2012) www.sustainableprosperity.ca/dl864&display last accessed September 29, 2017.

[18] Directive 2003/87/EC of the European Parliament and of the Council of 13 October 2003 establishing a scheme for greenhouse gas emission allowance trading within the Community and amending Council Directive 96/61/EC, OJ 2003 L 275, p. 32.

[19] Ibid. Article 1 Subject matter.

[20] EU press release, "Climate change: European Union notifies EU emission reduction targets following Copenhagen Accord," IP/10/97 (January 28, 2010) europa.eu/rapid/pressReleasesAction.do?reference=IP/10/97 last accessed September 29, 2017.

[21] European Commission, "Reducing emissions," *supra* Note 5.

2002," and "[I]f the climate change impact of the aviation sector continues to grow at the current rate, it would significantly undermine reductions made by other sectors to combat climate change."[22] What this meant at the time was that as of 2012, the number of allowances necessary for each flight to, or from, the EU, were to be calculated on the basis of the entire flight. Thus, on a flight from Los Angeles to Heathrow, the airline would have to surrender allowances for their voyage over US and Canadian territory and the high seas – not just over UK airspace.[23]

While the extension of the EU-ETS to cover aviation emissions was controversial within the EU,[24] it was greeted with a unique level of hostility from many other parts of the world. Few other policies have united countries as diverse as China, Russia, the United States, Canada, India, and Saudi Arabia in their opposition to a measure. Some argued even at the time that the EU was actually aiming for a global approach and as such it can be said to have sparked a debate that eventually led to movement within the ICAO and its adoption of the CORSIA.

5.3 AVIATION AND THE EU EMISSIONS TRADING SCHEME

In a preliminary ruling on *Air Transport Association of America (ATAA) v. Energy Secretary* the European Court of Justice (CJEU) delivered a

[22] Ibid., Recitals 10 and 11.

[23] A Los Angeles–London flight covers 8,769 km or 5,449 miles. When the plane has travelled roughly 5,000 km (3,100 miles) the Canadian airport of Goose Bay (YYR) is overflown; thus fully 57 percent of the flightpath occurs over US or Canadian territory.

[24] It is difficult to summarize the reactions within the EU. The lobbying at the Union level was intense, whereby the EU airline industry sent letters to EU leaders, including Chancellor Merkel and Prime Minister Cameron, warning of severe economic consequences if the inclusion of aviation was maintained. Given the suspension of the inclusion, it can only be assumed that this lobbying at the highest level was successful. The problem that ETS participation only for the EU industry is not exactly increasing the competitiveness of that industry can be forgotten in the debate. Financial Times, "Delay EU carbon levy, says air industry," www.ft.com/cms/s/0/3362d176-6b9c-11e1-8337-00144feab49a.html#axzz2CWgAcuP6 last accessed October 29, 2017. The signatories, which included Airbus, Lufthansa, Swiss, Iberia, British Airways, and Virgin Atlantic among others, argued that the pollution levy threatens 2,000 jobs and trade. They were concerned about trade-related retaliation by countries not complying with the Emissions Trading Scheme (ETS). The industry executives also said they expect "suspensions, cancellations and punitive actions" by other countries to grow "as other important markets continue to oppose the extension of ETS", according to the FT article, citing the letter. See Reuters, "Aviation calls on EU leaders to fix carbon tax" (March 11, 2012) www.reuters.com/article/2012/03/12/us-aviation-tax-eu-idUSBRE82B01020120312 last accessed September 29, 2017 .

groundbreaking decision.[25] The case was concerned with the legality of the inclusion of the aviation sector in the EU emissions trading scheme (ETS). As such, it discussed many interesting legal questions from EU external relations and EU environmental law points of view but ultimately what the case represented was a resounding victory for the EU and its Member States in confirming the legality of the inclusion of aviation in the EU-ETS.

Directive 2003/87/EC established a scheme for greenhouse gas emissions allowance trading within the Union. The EU-ETS has a cap that is reduced every year. It is expected that there will be an overall 21 percent reduction in industrial greenhouse gases (GHGs) by 2020.[26] The Directive promoted "reductions of greenhouse gas emissions in a cost-effective and economically efficient manner."[27] The EU-ETS was and is a cornerstone of the EU's efforts to curb dangerous greenhouse gases and combat climate change. It should be mentioned that following the Lisbon Treaty, combating climate change is also a Treaty objective both with regard to the Union's international relations and its stipulation of internal environmental laws.[28]

The applicants challenged the United Kingdom's implementation of Directive 2008/101/EC on the grounds of extra-territoriality as well as the allegations of illegal charges contrary to the 1944 *Chicago Convention*, US–EU Open Skies Agreement, and principles of customary international law. The CJEU, largely following the opinion of the Advocate General, decided that the EU had not overstepped any jurisdictional principle in applying the EU-ETS to entire international flights. The Court thus reasserted full territorial jurisdiction over aircraft landing or starting in the EU and pointed out that overflying aircraft do not have to comply with the ETS as they can choose whether or not to have the EU as a destination.

Building on its findings in *Ahlstroem* and *Commune de Mesquer* cases, the CJEU opened further regulatory space beyond EU borders for climate change. More precisely, it adopted a new legal standard:[29]

> [t]he fact that, in the context of applying European Union environmental legislation, certain matters contributing to the pollution of the air, sea or land territory of the Member States originate in an event which occurs partly

[25] This part shares thoughts with Markus Gehring's case note in RECIEL; M. Gehring, "Air Transport Association of America v. Energy Secretary: Clarifying direct effect and providing guidance for future instrument design for a green economy in the European Union," *Review of European Community & International Environmental Law*, 21:2 (2012), 149.

[26] EU press release, "Climate change," *supra* Note 21.

[27] Directive 2003/87/EC, *supra* Note 18, Art. 1.

[28] See Articles 21(1)(f) TEU and 192(1) TFEU, respectively.

[29] Case C-366/10, *supra* Note 8, para. 129.

> outside that territory is not such as to call into question, in the light of the principles of customary international law capable of being relied upon in the main proceedings, the full applicability of European Union law in that territory.

This conclusion is particularly important for the future development of EU environmental law, sustainable development, and the green economy in Europe. Many environmental problems do not stop at national or even regional borders and so this interpretation of the limits of the EU's jurisdiction in the international sphere arguably expands the EU's regulatory space to address environmental challenges of a transnational nature, especially climate change, which is a global challenge.

The Court also concluded that the EU-ETS was not a tax, a charge, or a customs duty on fuel in violation of the EU–US Open Skies Agreement. Distinguishing the decision in *Braathens*, and relying on its findings in *Arcelor*, the Court examined the EU-ETS as an instrument design, differentiating its "economic logic" from a "tax, fee or charge" as defined by the *Chicago Convention*. The main arguments brought forward by the Court include that, unlike a duty, tax, fee, or charge on fuel consumption, the scheme, "apart from the fact that it is not intended to generate revenue for the public authorities, does not in any way enable the establishment, applying a basis of assessment and a rate defined in advance, of an amount that must be payable per tonne of fuel consumed for all the flights carried out in a calendar year."[30]

International law was thus not found to be violated by the inclusion of the aviation sector in the EU-ETS.

This decision remains important for the future design of economic instruments to internalize environmental costs. It demonstrated that there was greater flexibility for the Union to introduce or expand emissions trading schemes. While simple fuel consumption taxes might be easier to administer, they might run counter to international obligations, such as the *Chicago Convention*.[31] This lesson was important because it allowed for further expansion of the EU-ETS, such as the currently discussed inclusion of shipping in the EU-ETS, or new trading schemes such as wetland or riparian pollution trading (as practiced in some US states).

[30] Ibid., paras. 140 and 143.

[31] See also V. M. Tunteng, ed., "Legal analysis on the inclusion of civil aviation on the European Union Emissions Trading System," CISDL Legal Brief (2012) www.cisdl.org/public/docs/news/CISDL_EU_ETS_Expansion_Legal_Brief.pdf last accessed September 29, 2017.

The case, however, begs for review of legality of the measure before the World Trade Organization (WTO), or indeed from the WTO law perspective. There may be some open questions,[32] since all obstacles to international transport (including air transport) could constitute an illegal discrimination of foreign traders. If, indeed, such discrimination was found, a possible defense might be to argue that the EU-ETS was a case of reverse discrimination since EU traders also had to pay to comply with the EU-ETS for internal EU flights. Alternatively, the EU-ETS could arguably be justified under the general GATT exception, and more precisely under Article XX – if protection of plant, animal, and human life and health are interpreted broadly or the global climate is defined as an exhaustible natural resource.

There may be a valid argument to say that the expansion of the EU-ETS might be a violation of the principle of common but differentiated responsibility,[33] which is an argument that the CJEU did not examine. However, properly understood, the application of the principle must mean that smaller airlines with less than a couple of flights per week should be excluded, and not developing country carriers, which are actively competing on lucrative routes.[34]

5.3.1 *European Aviation Environmental Report 2016*

In 2016 the European Commission, the European Aviation Safety Agency (EASA), the European Environmental Agency, and EUROCONTROL released a paper that aimed to monitor, promote, and strengthen the sustainability of the European aviation sector.[35]

It found that between 1990 and 2005, air traffic and emissions of CO_2 had both increased by 80 percent.[36] Due to improvements in the technology, fleet

[32] L. Bartels, "The inclusion of aviation in the EU ETS. WTO law considerations," ICTSD Trade and Sustainable Energy Series, No 6 (2011) www.ictsd.org/bridges-news/biores/news/the-inclusion-of-aviation-in-the-eu's-ets-wto-law-considerations last accessed September 29, 2017.

[33] J. Scott and L. Rajamani, "EU climate change unilateralism: International aviation in the European Emissions Trading Scheme," *European Journal of International Law*, **23**:2 (2011), 469.

[34] Directive 2008/101/EC, *supra* Note 7, para. 18.

[35] European Commission, "European Aviation Environmental Report" (2016) https://ec.europa.eu/transport/sites/transport/files/european-aviation-environmental-report-2016-72dpi.pdf last accessed September 29, 2017.

[36] Part of this explosive growth was the result of the subsidization by regional airports within the EU of new routes by low cost airlines such as Ryanair. See generally, P. Fitzgerald, "Europe's emissions trading system: Questioning its raison d'être," *Issues of Aviation L. & Pol'y*, 10 (2011), 189 at 208.

renewal, or increased air traffic management efficiency, and the 2008 economic downturn, emissions levels in 2014 were the same as those of 2005. Still, improvements in reducing emissions would not be enough to prevent the overall growth in emissions for the next twenty years.

In order to address the sustainability of aviation, the EU has adopted the following measures: technological improvements, air traffic management and operations, the Airport Carbon Accreditation program, market-based measures, sustainable alternative fuels, and adaptation to the changing climate. With respect to market-based measures, specifically the EU-ETS, the estimated amount of emissions it will reduce for every year from 2013 to 2016 is around 16 million tonnes, partly within the aviation sector or in other sectors through the purchase by airlines of units. From this point, it can be inferred that the EU, given its experience with the application of EU-ETS in the aviation sector, has a clear commitment to pursuing a global market-based measure as a primary scheme to address GHG emissions.

5.4 EU SUSPENSION OF ETS APPLICABILITY TO INTERNATIONAL FLIGHTS

In deference to its preference for a multilaterally agreed solution, and despite its victory in the *AATA* case, the EU Commissioner for Climate Action responded to what she viewed as recent positive developments within the ICAO by announcing a suspension of the applicability of the EU-ETS scheme to international flights in order to "create a positive atmosphere" and "[pave] the way for strong decisions to be taken by the next ICAO General Assembly" taking place in September/October 2013.[37]

The Commissioner was explicit however that "If this exercise does not deliver ... then needless to say we are back to where we are ... with the *EU ETS*. Automatically."[38]

The reasons why the EU was more hopeful that the ICAO might be the right forum for climate and aviation were principally two-fold. First, there were now very concrete discussions about an ICAO framework for market-based measures (with a focus on national and regional) with technical discussions as to how to implement them. The EU hoped that the ICAO would adopt guidance on how to treat international flights, and favored the departing

[37] EU press release, "Stopping the clock of ETS and aviation emissions following last week's International Civil Aviation Organisation's (ICAO) Council" (November 12, 2012) http://europa.eu/rapid/press-release_MEMO-12-854_en.htm last accessed September 29, 2017.

[38] Ibid.

flight approach. There was also the opportunity for at least agreement in principle on a global MBM. Second, the EU was also hopeful that other measures could be adopted: "There exist several technological and operational measures (e.g. state action plans, CO2 aircraft standards) to reduce the climate impacts of aviation. The EU is in favour of these measures and supports such action. However, the EU considers that these measures are on their own insufficient to deliver the necessary emission reductions."[39] With the adoption of CORSIA in October 2016, the ETS remains suspended for the foreseeable future. There may be slim possibilities that CORSIA might still fail to deliver on its promises if the detailed rules for its operation are not promoting the integrity of the system but no automatic "revival" of the EU-ETS for international flights is possible in that case. It would require an explicit legislative decision by the EU.

5.5 LEGAL AND POLICY REACTIONS FROM THE REST OF THE WORLD

As noted previously, countries that are important for global GHG emission reduction efforts, including China, India, and the United States, disagreed with the EU's steps, including the Court's decision as to EU jurisdiction. The opposition was expressed in the various declarations issued by the BASIC coalition (Brazil, South Africa, India, and China),[40] India, and Russia,[41] alleging violations of various instruments and principles of international law and calling for the suspension of the EU ETS for aviation. Moreover, China and the United States[42] adopted legislation explicitly prohibiting their domestic airlines from complying with the EU-ETS. In addition, Russia, joined by

39 EU Council Document 7066/13 of 8 March 2013 containing an "Update on ICAO negotiations and 'Stopping-the-clock' Information note by the Commission," p. 3.

40 "Joint statement issued at the conclusion of the 10th BASIC Ministerial Meeting on Climate Change" (February 13–14, 2012) envfor.nic.in/downloads/public-information/10th-BASIC-Meeting-Delhi-Joint-Statement.pdf last accessed September 29, 2017 (New Delhi Joint Statement).

41 "Joint declaration of the Moscow meeting on inclusion of international civil aviation in the EU-ETS" (February 21–22, 2012) www.ruaviation.com/docs/1/2012/2/22/50/ last accessed September 29, 2017 (Moscow Declaration).

42 Public Law 112–200 November 27, 2012 126 STAT.1477. See also N. Purvis and S. Grausz, "Air supremacy: The surprisingly important dogfight over climate pollution from international aviation," Policy Brief (The German Marshall Fund of the United States, 2012), www.gmfus.org/publications/air-supremacy-surprisingly-important-dogfight-over-climate-pollution-international last accessed October 29, 2017; and C. Voigt, "Up in the air – Aviation, the EU Emissions Trading Scheme and the question of jurisdiction," *Cambridge Yearbook of European Legal Studies*, 14 (2012), 475.

twenty-six other nations in the Moscow Declaration, introduced a basket of retaliatory measures in reaction to the EU-ETS targeting the EU carriers.[43]

5.6 INTERNATIONAL POLITICS OF ICAO AND GHG EMISSION REDUCTION ACTIONS

ICAO was tasked, under the Kyoto Protocol, to lead global action to reduce greenhouse gas emissions from the aviation industry.[44] While it asserted that it could play a leading role in tackling the environmental impact of air transport, the ICAO faced various challenges in the adoption of effective climate change measures.

5.6.1 *ICAO Mandate under the Kyoto Protocol*

In the negotiations leading to the Kyoto Protocol, States Party to the UNFCCC discussed how to include emissions from the international aviation sector in a global climate change agreement.[45] These discussions focused on how to allocate international aviation GHG emissions among Contracting States.[46] Various options were debated, including a division of emissions between the countries of origin and destination, or assigning allowances based on the countries that purchased or sold jet fuel, or assigning allowances based on the nationality of aircraft.[47] No agreement on this issue was reached. Although States Party to the Kyoto Protocol must report emissions from the international aviation sector in their national greenhouse gas inventories, these emissions are not included in the calculation of developed countries'

[43] C. Alcock, "Russia escalates European Union emissions trading row," AINonline (June 18, 2012) www.ainonline.com/aviation-news/ain-air-transport-perspective/2012-06-18/russia-escalates-european-union-emissions-trading-row last accessed September 29, 2017. Russia withheld approval of certain flights until the very last minute and China refused the operation of a Lufthansa Airbus A380 to Shanghai, J. Flottau, "India, Russia mounting retaliation against European Emission Trading System," *Aviation Daily* (March 22, 2012).

[44] This part shares thoughts with the CISDL working paper on Climate Change and Aviation, see Tunteng, ed., "Legal Analysis," *supra* Note 32.

[45] E. Haites, "Linking emissions trading schemes for international aviation and shipping emissions," *Climate Policy*, 9 (2009), 415 at 417.

[46] S. Oberthür, 'Institutional interaction to address greenhouse gas emissions from international transport: ICAO, IMO and Kyoto Protocol," *Climate Policy*, 3 (2003), 191 at 196.

[47] D. McCollum, G. Gould, and D. Greene, "Greenhouse gas emissions from aviation and marine transportation: Mitigation potential and policies," Pew Center on Global Climate Change: Solutions White Paper Series (2009), 26–27.

emission reduction commitments.[48] As a compromise, Article 2.2 was inserted into the Kyoto Protocol, with the aim of promoting continued dialogue:

> The Parties included in Annex I shall pursue limitation or reduction of emissions of greenhouse gases not controlled by the Montreal Protocol from aviation and marine bunker fuels, working through the International Civil Aviation Organization and the International Maritime Organization, respectively.[49]

As such, the Parties are to pursue emissions reductions from aviation, working through the ICAO. The *Chicago Convention*[50] does not address GHG emissions from the aviation sector. However, the ICAO has developed binding international standards and regulations on environmental issues.[51] At the 37th ICAO Assembly held in Montreal in November 2010, the ICAO maintained that it holds a leading role in tackling the environmental impact of aviation and acknowledged its responsibility in this area.[52]

5.6.2 *The ICAO's Progress on GHG Emissions*

Since the ICAO was delegated responsibility in 1997 to regulate and limit international aviation emissions, various commentators have characterized its progress as slow.[53] In 2004, the ICAO adopted three major environmental goals, one of which was "to limit or reduce the impact of aviation greenhouse gas emissions on the global climate."[54] At the 37th ICAO Assembly Resolution A37–19 was adopted. Member States committed to a global annual average

48 K. Kulovesi, "Make your own special song, even if nobody else sings along: International aviation emissions and the EU emissions trading scheme," *Climate Policy*, 2 (2011), 4 at 3.

49 *Kyoto Protocol to the United Nations Framework Convention on Climate Change* (adopted March 16, 1998, entered into force February 16, 2005) 37 ILM 22 [*Kyoto Protocol*] Art. 2.2.

50 *Convention on International Civil Aviation* (adopted December 1, 1944, entered into force March 5, 1947) 15 UNTS 295 [*Chicago Convention*] Art. 43.

51 International Civil Aviation Organization, "ICAO in brief" (2011) www.icao.int last accessed November 30, 2011.

52 International Civil Aviation Organization, "Resolutions Adopted by the Assembly at its 37th Session" (September 28–October 8, 2010), A37–18: Consolidated statement of continuing ICAO policies and practices related to environmental protection: General provisions, noise and local air quality and A37–19: Consolidated statement of continuing ICAO policies and practices related to environmental protection – Climate Change.

53 *See inter alia* Haites, "Linking emission trading schemes," *supra* Note 46 at 418; Oberthür, "Institutional interaction," *supra* Note 47 at 192; A. Macintosh and L. Wallace, "International aviation emissions to 2025: Can emissions be stabilised without restricting demand?" *Energy Policy*, 37:1 (2009), 264 at 265.

54 International Civil Aviation Organization, "Environment branch" (2011) www.icao.int/env/ last accessed October 29, 2017.

fuel efficiency improvement of 2 percent through to 2020, and an aspirational goal of a global fuel efficiency improvement rate of 2 percent per annum from 2021 to 2050.[55] In addition, Member States adopted a collective medium-term global aspirational goal (from 2020) of maintaining global net carbon dioxide (CO_2) emissions from international aviation at 2020 levels.[56]

The ICAO invited Member States to submit voluntary national action plans outlining their CO_2-reduction policies and activities by June 2012,[57] and received voluntary action plans from at least fifty-three members representing 75 percent of global international air traffic.[58] There was agreement in principle between ICAO Member States that the most desirable policy design was a market-based mechanism that would include emissions trading.[59] A set of "guiding principles" for the development and design of market-based mechanisms by Member States, either bilaterally, or multilaterally, was considered.[60] One of the guiding principles is that participation in any domestic mechanism should be on the basis of the mutual consent of the countries involved.[61] Forty-two European countries made a reservation to this guideline, due to the potential conflict with the inclusion of aviation in the EU-ETS.[62] Resolution A37–19 called on the Council to develop a framework for MBMs, and to continue to explore the feasibility of a global MBM scheme for consideration by the 38th Assembly in 2013.[63] The 2015 Paris Agreement did not contain a provision similar to the Kyoto Protocol. It thus raised the possibility of regulating aviation emissions also in the UNFCCC. While this appeared to be a last resort measure, it could not be completely disregarded as a legal possibility.[64]

55 ICAO, "Resolution A37–19," *supra* Note 53, para. 4; also submitted to the UNFCCC as part of FCCC/SBSTA/2010/MISC.14.

56 Ibid., para. 6.

57 Ibid., paras. 9–10.

58 Some national action plans are publicly available on the ICAO website – ICAO, "Climate change: Action plan," www.icao.int/environmental-Protection/Pages/action-plan.aspx last accessed September 30, 2017.

59 Haites, "Linking emissions trading schemes," *supra* Note 46 at 418; B. F. Havel and G. S. Sanchez, "Toward an international aviation emissions agreement," *Harv Envtl L Rev*, 36 (2012), 351.

60 ICAO, "Resolution A37–19," *supra* Note 53, para. 14 and Annex.

61 Ibid.

62 McCollum, Gould, and Greene, "Greenhouse gas emissions," *supra* Note 48 at 27.

63 ICAO, "Resolution A37–19," *supra* Note 53.

64 S. Maciunas, "Will ICAO do its part to meet the climate change challenge?" CIGI Commentary (September 28, 2016) www.cigionline.org/publications/will-icao-do-its-part-meet-climate-change-challenge last accessed September 30, 2017.

The aspirational targets and guiding principles noted in this section are the result of more than a decade of work by the ICAO on the regulation of aviation GHG emissions. A previous ICAO High-level Group stated that its action so far was no more than a "first step to address greenhouse gas emissions from international aviation."[65] After two more years of negotiations, the ICAO finally agreed upon the CORSIA in October 2016, though many details still remain to be worked out.

5.6.3 *ICAO Working Paper and Resolution*

In response to the EU actions, an ICAO working paper adopted on November 2, 2011 invited the ICAO Council to urge the EU and its Member States to refrain from including flights by non-EU carriers to and from airports located in the territory of EU Member States in the ETS.[66] The paper was backed by twenty-six of the thirty-six Member States on the ICAO Council – including China, Japan, Russia, and the United States. Besides the eight EU Member States that opposed the adoption, Australia and Canada were absent at the vote. Although the paper was not legally binding for the Council or any ICAO member it reflected the strong opposition to the inclusion of aviation in the ETS by the majority of ICAO member countries.[67]

The ICAO working paper claimed that the unilateral measure of including civil aviation in the EU-ETS contravenes international law, and that implementation of the EU-ETS without the ICAO's concurrence would undermine the ICAO's leading role in matters related to aviation and the environment and in particular preempt and negate ICAO Assembly

[65] International Civil Aviation Organization, "Programme of action: Declaration by the High-level Meeting on International Aviation and Climate Change," HLM-ENV/09 (2009).

[66] International Civil Aviation Organization, "Working paper, Council – 194th Session, 17 October 2011, Subject No 50: Questions related to the environment: Inclusion of International Civil Aviation in the European Union Emissions Trading Scheme (EU ETS) and its impact (presented by Argentina, Brazil, Burkina Faso, Cameroon, China, Colombia, Cuba, Egypt, Guatemala, India, Japan, Malaysia, Mexico, Morocco, Nigeria, Paraguay, Peru, Republic of Korea, Russian Federation, Saudi Arabia, Singapore, South Africa, Swaziland, Uganda, the United Arab Emirates, and the United States)," C-WP/13790 (October 17, 2017) http://www.greenaironline.com/photos/ICAO_C.194.WP.13790.EN.pdf last accessed September 30, 2017.

[67] Compare; International Centre for Trade and Sustainable Development, "EU Emissions Trading Scheme faces pushback from UN Civil Aviation Body," *Bridges Weekly Trade News Digest*, 15 (November 9, 2011), 38 ictsd.org/i/news/bridgesweekly/117954/ last accessed October 1, 2017; Greenair, "States opposed to Europe's emissions trading scheme win ICAO Council backing but EU remains defiant," Greenair online.com (November 3, 2011) www.greenaironline.com/news.php?viewStory=1366 last accessed October 1, 2017.

Resolution A37–19,[68] which was also supported by EU Member States. As mentioned previously in this chapter, the Resolution called on the Council to develop a framework for market-based mechanisms for consideration at the 38th ICAO Assembly.[69] It also reaffirmed the declaration that the ICAO is the most appropriate forum for future discussions on solutions to international aviation emissions including marked-based mechanisms.[70] It finally adopted CORSIA in October 2017, and while the concrete implementation rules are currently being developed, CORSIA signifies a sea change for aviation and climate change. It is the first global climate mechanism covering aviation, and while it has been criticized by environmental groups as not being ambitious enough, the mere adoption of the mechanism is quite revolutionary for an organization with such a diverse membership as the ICAO.

5.6.4 *Political Drivers and Paris Agreement*

The drivers of deadlock did not disappear overnight, but it is clear that the adoption of the Paris Agreement in 2015 and its anticipated entry into force in November 2016 played a crucial role for progress also at the global ICAO level. Given the participation and commitments of all states in the Paris Agreement, the argument based on historical contributions to the problem of climate change that developing countries have a right to increase their GHG emissions while requesting stronger reductions by developed countries was also overcome in the ICAO. In light of the slightly amended application of the principle of common but differentiated responsibility (CBDR) in the Paris Agreement, which denied the claim that developing countries should not take any mitigation measures, this argument also lost significant traction in the ICAO.[71] CBDR "recognises that developed countries are principally

[68] International Civil Aviation Organization, "Consolidated statement of continuing ICAO policies and practices related to environmental protection – Climate change," Res A37–19, ICAO Doc A37–2P/402,P/66 (October 7, 2010) www.icao.int/environmental-protection/37thAssembly/A37_Res19_en.pdf last accessed October 1, 2017.

[69] Ibid., para. 13ff; ICAO, "Working paper," *supra* Note 67, paras. (2.1)–(2.4), (4.2).

[70] ICAO Resolution A37–19, *supra* Note 68; International Civil Aviation Organization Assembly, "Consolidated statement of continuing ICAO policies and practices related to environmental protection," ICAO Res A36–22 (September 2007); M. Adam, "ICAO Assembly's resolution on climate change: A 'historic' agreement?" *Air Space L*, 36 (2011), 23 at 24; Havel and Sanchez, "Towards an international emissions agreement," *supra* Note 60 at 10, 11; S. Truxal, "The ICAO Assembly resolutions on aviation and climate change: An historic agreement, a breakthrough deal and the Cancun effect," *Air and Space Law*, 37:2 (2011), 217 at 224.

[71] Scott and Rajamani, "EU climate change unilateralism," *supra* Note 34 at 469–94.

historically responsible for the current high levels of greenhouse gas emissions in the atmosphere."[72] Consequently, the burden for reducing greenhouse gas emissions is to be placed primarily on developed nations, which is reflected in CORSIA by excluding least developed and landlocked developing states. At the same time, the principle of nondiscrimination under the *Chicago Convention* states that all regulations, standards, and rules are to apply equally to aircraft of all countries, without distinction as to nationality.[73] However, the voluntary participation of all countries provides significant opportunities to also buy offsets from least developed and landlocked developing countries.

Aviation is of high political importance. In an increasingly globalized world, new middle classes in Asia, Africa, and Latin America are rightly demanding increased international travel, while travel continues to grow in developed countries as well. Some countries were concerned that the EU-ETS would suppress aviation growth.[74] Moreover, they regarded the actions by the EU as being distinctly to the EU's advantage as it "is the global leader in aviation emission reduction technologies. The collection of carbon tax is useful to drive the demand of countries for green and low-carbon materials and relevant products, thus the EU can foster new economic growth point by exporting its green technology and equipment."[75] With the CORSIA system, which focusses on offsets rather than just emission reductions, some of these competitiveness concerns have been addressed internationally.

At the same time, there is a fear in developing countries in which tourism is the major industry that any plans to curb emissions from aviation, for which the costs will most likely be added to ticket prices, will affect their national tourism sector as well as their development goals.[76] On the one hand, tourism

[72] *Kyoto Protocol, supra* Note 50.

[73] *Chicago Convention, supra* Note 51, Art. 11.

[74] DNAIndia, "India tells Asia-Pacific nations: Oppose EU's airline emissions tax" (October 8, 2012) www.dnaindia.com/india/report_india-tells-asia-pacific-nations-oppose-eu-s-airline-emissions-tax_1750233 last accessed October 1, 2017. BASIC equally condemned the EU measures following its meeting in Beijing which ended on November 20, 2012; M. Xinxang, "BASIC issues joint statement on climate change," China.org.cn (November 21, 2012) www.china.org.cn/environment/2012-11/21/content_27183689.htm last accessed October 1, 2017.

[75] Third World Network, "EU carbon tax on maritime transport the next controversy?" (March 16, 2012) http://www.twn.my/title2/climate/info.service/2012/climate20120301.htm last accessed October 1, 2017.

[76] S. Gössling, P. Peeters, and D. Scott, "Consequences of climate policy for international tourists arrival in developing countries," *Third World Quarterly*, **29** (2008), 873 at 874. The study shows, however, that the tourist sectors in the selected island nations that rely heavily on air traffic will grow despite the ETS. The study suggests that although there might be a decrease of tourists from ETS countries, there will be an increase from non-ETS countries, Ibid. at 884–85, 890.

is a major industry in many developing countries and civil aviation is therefore essential for the development of these countries. The emerging infrastructure around airports consisting of carriers and feeder plants also contributes to the economic development of a country. Fast connections are essential for the export of perishable goods that constitute a large part of many developing countries' economies in contrast to the more service-based economies in industrialized countries. On the other hand, they reinforce reliance on fossil fuels and possibly carbon-intensive tourism.[77] It is necessary to develop approaches that are truly comprehensive and take into account of all these intrinsic and interwoven aspects.

The aviation industry, as represented by the IATA, although preferring a multilateral approach, nonetheless saw the EU as "pushing for environmental mitigation and making it a primary concern for the aviation industry," but they are opposed to coexisting competing regional solutions that would force airlines to pay several times for the same emissions. It expressed the hope that the subsequent ICAO Assembly in September/October 2013 would lead to a global solution.[78] There are nuances within the community of aviation companies. State-owned companies obviously reflect their government's stance, whereas other airlines may be more likely to accept any form of regulation. Some airlines such as Qantas already have their own, although voluntarily, carbon-offsetting mechanisms in place and generally there seems to be an increasing knowledge, awareness, and acceptance in public opinion toward possibilities and mechanisms to offset carbon footprints.[79] Public opinion, though, seems to favor a global and comprehensive solution. IATA itself welcomed the adoption of CORSIA and expressed its commitment to work with the governments in its successful implementation.[80]

In this context it should be acknowledged that the European Union did consult with other governments, international organizations, and other players throughout the development of the ETS inclusion of aviation, as the first part

[77] E. Carter, "Ecotourism in the third world: Problems for sustainable tourism development," *Tourism Management*, 14 (1993), 85 at 86.

[78] IATA, "EU Emission Trading Scheme – A world of difference" (June 1, 2012) airlines.iata.org/analysis/eu-emissions-trading-scheme-a-world-of-difference last accessed October 1, 2017.

[79] Various private initiatives, companies and NGOS now inform about offsetting possibilities and offer opportunities to do so, i.e. by planting trees: Carbon Footprint, "UK tree planting," www.carbonfootprint.com/plantingtrees.html last accessed October 1, 2017; also climatecare, "Calculate and offset your carbon footprint," www.climatecare.org/home.aspx last accessed October 1, 2017.

[80] IATA, "Governments need to support production of sustainable aviation fuels" (June 5, 2017) www.iata.org/pressroom/pr/Pages/2017-06-05-04.aspx last accessed October 2, 2017.

of a broader objective to include the transport sector in the ETS.[81] Also, as mentioned already, several non-EU countries did consider adopting national legislation linking in with EU-ETS.

The EU claimed to have made a major contribution to the October 2016 ICAO CORSIA decision. It announced in February 2017: "The European Union is a leading advocate for addressing fast-growing emissions from aviation. At the 2016 ICAO Assembly, the European Union and its Member States played an instrumental role in securing a deal on a global market-based measure to stabilize international aviation emissions. The system will require airlines to monitor and report their annual CO2 emissions on international routes and offset those exceeding 2020 levels."[82] It is difficult to precisely measure the importance of EU states on the CORSIA decision but there is some evidence to suggest that the mere suspension of the application of the ETS had some impact on enabling the compromise at the Ministerial Conference in 2016.[83]

5.7 EU IMPLEMENTATION OF THE ICAO CORSIA

The EU has accepted the ICAO compromise and the Commission has proposed legislation to monitor international progress and implement internationally agreed rules at the earliest. In their proposal, the Commission proposes to closely monitor international progress. The proposed amendment of Article 28b of Directive 2003/87/EC contains a reporting obligation by the Commission on the implementation of the ICAO's global market-based measure. It says:

> 1. The Commission shall report to the European Parliament and the Council on the relevant ICAO standards or other legal instruments as well as on domestic measures taken by third countries to implement the global market-based measure to be applied to emissions from 2021, and on other relevant international developments.
>
> 2. The report should consider ways for those ICAO instruments to be implemented in Union law through a revision of this Directive. The report

[81] A. Anger and J. Köhler, "Including aviation emissions in the EU ETS: Much ado about nothing?" *Transport Policy*, 17 (2010), 38 at 39.

[82] EU Press Release, "The EU tackles growing aviation emissions" (February 3, 2017) ec.europa.eu/clima/news/eu-tackles-growing-aviation-emissions_en last accessed October 1, 2017.

[83] J. Beard, "A global climate deal for aviation! So what next?" (October 11, 2017) www.climatechangenews.com/2016/10/11/a-global-climate-deal-for-aviation-so-what-next/ last accessed October 1, 2017.

> shall also consider the rules applicable in respect of flights within the European Economic Area (EEA) as appropriate.
>
> 3. The report may be accompanied by proposals, as appropriate to the European Parliament and the Council to amend, delete, extend or replace the derogations provided for in Article 28a [suspension of the ETS to non EEA flights], consistent with the Union economy-wide greenhouse gas emission reduction commitment for 2030.

This provision clearly signals that the EU aims to fully participate in the new ICAO CORSIA system while maintaining an option whereby the EU might still attempt to reapply its initial ETS proposal if global progress on detailed rules is not achieved. The Commission is tasked with proposing implementation legislation, which in turn depends on the ICAO rules that are being developed at the global level.

The EU Parliament expressed its views on the Commission's proposal though its Environment, Public Health and Food Safety Committee. In her draft report on amendment of the Directive 2003/87/EC, the rapporteur Julie Grimming largely agrees with the Commission proposal.[84] Hence, the draft report supports maintaining the derogation in the EU-ETS regime and its continuous applicability only to the intra-EU routes, favoring the global measures adopted by the ICAO. In the implementation of the ICAO-based measures, the report calls on the Commission to provide regular updates to the Parliament and the Council on the measures adopted by the ICAO. In implementing the ICAO measures, the draft report tasks the Commission to come up with a legislative proposal within six months from its initial report, to be submitted by January 1, 2019. The report, however, also considers the situation where the ICAO measures are "insufficient to achieve the Union's climate objectives," whereas, in such case, "other carbon mitigation options should also be explored."

Therefore, no major changes were proposed by the Parliament's rapporteur to the Commission's initial proposal for maintaining the EU-ETS derogation and implementing the ICAO-based global measures. Nonetheless, it is obvious that the Parliament expects a level of certainty and implementation in a timely manner as evidenced by the proposed concrete deadlines and timelines to be inserted in the Directive 2003/87/EC amendment. Indeed, Parliament's

[84] European Parliament, "Draft report on the proposal for regulation of the European Parliament and of the Council amending Directive 2003/87/EC to continue limitations of scope for aviation activities and to prepare to implement a global market-based measure from 2021," 2017/0017(COD) (May 8, 2017) www.europarl.europa.eu/sides/getDoc.do?pubRef=-//EP//NONSGML+COMPARL+PE-602.955+01+DOC+PDF+V0//EN&language=EN last accessed October 1, 2017.

interest in this field is not novel, as documented by its earlier 2016 resolution calling on the implementation of the Paris Agreement[85] or its support for the global market-based measures in its 2015 aviation resolution.[86]

Moreover, the Council also approved the negotiating position to both "extend existing provisions covering aviation activities" and "to prepare for the implementation of a global market-based measure as of 2021."[87] In its position, the Council welcomes the adoption of CORSIA and pledges the support and participation of all EU Member States in the program's initial, voluntary, phase. The Council is also on board with the Commission's proposal to extend the derogation for non–intra-EEA flights from the EU-ETS regime. The Council also points out that the new legislation, amending the Directive 2003/87/EC, needs to be adopted by the end of the year to avoid the legislative gap as the current derogation is about to expire.

Indeed, as it is still not yet clear what the actual content of CORSIA measures will be, the policy adopted by the European Union is rather vague. Nonetheless, by pledging to implement the carbon-offsetting scheme as proposed by the ICAO and to voluntarily participate already in the program's pilot phase, the EU seems to uphold its commitments to the global solution of aviation emissions. Furthermore, agreeing to further derogate from the application of the EU-ETS regime to the non–intra-EEA flights can be interpreted as the EU's satisfaction with the global measures and its belief that these measures have the potential to be effective.

Nevertheless, the ICAO's CORSIA, and the EU's participation, still raises a number of serious questions. Unlike the EU-ETS, CORSIA is not an emissions-trading scheme but rather a system of offsetting measures. Hence, it remains to be seen whether the efficiency of the measures will mirror the numbers projected had the EU's carbon trading scheme been in place. What will happen if this is not the case? Will the EU retract the non–intra-EEA derogation? What will be the reaction of the international community in such

85 European Parliament, "Resolution of 6 October 2016 on the implementation of the Paris Agreement and the 2016 UN Climate Change Conference in Marrakesh, Morocco (COP22)," 2016/2814(RSP) (October 6, 2016) www.europarl.europa.eu/sides/getDoc.do?type=TA&language=EN&reference=P8-TA-2016-0383 last accessed October 1, 2017.

86 European Parliament, "Resolution of 11 November 2015 on aviation," 2015/2933(RSP) (November 11, 2015) www.europarl.europa.eu/sides/getDoc.do?type=TA&language=EN&reference=P8-TA-2015-0394 last accessed October 1, 2017.

87 EU Press Release, "ETS aviation: Ensuring legal certainty on emission reductions beyond 2016" (June 21, 2017) http://www.consilium.europa.eu/en/press/press-releases/2017/06/21/ets-aviation/ last accessed October 1, 2017.

case? All of these questions remain to be answered as the ICAO unveils the first concrete CORSIA measures.

Moreover, it ought to be noted that the developments on the world stage after CORSIA's adoption also give reasons for doubt. As the administration in the United States changed so did the approach toward the issues of environmental protection. The proactive approach toward resolving the threats of climate change has been replaced by denial of this problem of global importance. With President Trump announcing the intention to withdraw from the 2016 Paris Agreement,[88] there is yet again a risk of a setback in these global efforts due to nonparticipation of the key players. How this attitude of the United States reflects on the field of aviation has yet to be seen. Currently, the initial full commitment promised by the Obama administration is "under review."[89] If the earlier commitment is revised, CORSIA's initial goals might become unattainable. What will be the reaction of the EU in such case? Some answers to these questions can be derived from the EU's general policy on sustainable development and, more particularly, the policy and measures concerning air pollution. Sustainable development has been an overarching policy of the EU since its explicit mention in the Amsterdam Treaty. Currently, the *Treaty on European Union* (TEU)[90] refers to the sustainable development in its preamble, as well as in its text as a guiding principle in both intra-EU policies and in the Union's external action. Moreover, the *Treaty on the Functioning of the European Union* (TFEU)[91] provides explicitly that environmental protection and sustainable development "must be integrated into the definition and implementation of the Union's policies and activities." Hence, the EU has been historically a firm advocate of sustainable development policies, playing key roles in international negotiations and adopting a wide range of stringent domestic measures aiming to implement the international policies and protect the EU's environment.

Currently, the sustainable development principle is being channeled into EU policy and legislation mainly through the so-called EU Sustainable Development Strategy, published by the Commission in 2001, which, among other serious issues, identified emissions of GHG as one of the main threats to

[88] White House, "Statement by President Trump on the Paris Climate Accord" (June 1, 2017) www.whitehouse.gov/the-press-office/2017/06/01/statement-president-trump-paris-climate-accord last accessed October 1, 2017.

[89] A. Karp, "Trump administration reviewing ICAO aviation emissions agreement" (June 9, 2017) atwonline.com/eco-aviation/trump-administration-reviewing-icao-aviation-emissions-agreement last accessed October 1, 2017.

[90] *TEU*, *supra* Note 17, Arts. 3 and 21.

[91] *TFEU*, *supra* Note 17, Art. 11.

sustainable development.[92] Moreover, the Strategy explicitly mentions transportation as an area where emissions need to be tackled, with emphasis on more eco-friendly means of transport.

The implementation of the strategy has been monitored by the progress reports being published regularly since 2007. The latest report from 2015 discusses progress in achieving sustainable development goals in numerous areas, including, among others, climate change and energy, sustainable transport, or global partnerships.[93] As to the first area, GHG emissions, the report refers to the goals set in another strategic policy document adopted by the Commission in 2010 – "Europe 2020: A European Strategy for Smart, Sustainable and Inclusive Growth"[94] – under which, with the Kyoto targets in mind, the overall goal is a 20 percent reduction of GHG emissions by 2020 as compared with 1990. The report notes that this goal is to be attained and welcomes adoption by the Council of new targets of further reduction of GHG emissions by 40 percent until 2030 in comparison with 1990. The 2015 Report notes that in 2012 the overall reduction of GHG emissions was 17.9 percent, well on track to meet the 2020 20 percent reduction target. This number also included emissions from aviation. The Report also points out a rapid reduction specifically in the international aviation sector as of 2007.

Thus, it appears from the 2015 Sustainable Development Report as well as the 2016 Aviation Environmental Report that the basket of measures, including the EU-ETS as its integral and important part, remains significant for achieving the sustainable development goals of the EU, in particular GHG emissions reductions. With even more ambitious goals set for 2030, there seems to be a general perception within the EU that the policies and measures in place are performing as envisaged. Consequently, respecting civil aviation, one may reasonably expect the EU to remain faithful to its original objectives, including the ETS for non–intra-EEA flights, should the ICAO CORSIA prove to be unsatisfactory.

[92] Communication from the Commission, "A sustainable Europe for a better world: A European Union Strategy for Sustainable Development" (May 15, 2001) eur-lex.europa.eu/legal-content/EN/TXT/PDF/?uri=CELEX:52001DC0264&from=EN last accessed October 1, 2017.

[93] "Sustainable development in the European Union: 2015 Monitoring report of the EU Sustainable Development Strategy" (2015) http://ec.europa.eu/eurostat/documents/3217494/6975281/KS-GT-15-001-EN-N.pdf last accessed October 1, 2017.

[94] European Commission, "Europe 2020: A European strategy for smart, sustainable and inclusive growth" (March 3, 2010) ec.europa.eu/eu2020/pdf/COMPLET%20EN%20BARROSO%20%20%20007%20-%20Europe%202020%20-%20EN%20version.pdf last accessed October 1, 2017.

Though a matter of speculation, a question arises as to what the relaunch of the EU-ETS non-EEA flights might look like. Would it involve the controversial applicability of the scheme to the entirety of an international flight departing or landing in EU territory? Perhaps some readjustments could be made in this regard – for instance, only calculating the emissions from the section of a flight within the Union's airspace. Another matter is the reallocation of the emissions allowances. Since its launch, the ETS has entered into its third stage, in which most allowances are no longer allocated freely but instead are being auctioned.[95] Would there still be free initial allocation for the air carriers operating international flights to and from the EU? Lastly, but perhaps most importantly, what would be the reaction of the industry and the international community to such EU-ETS relaunch, even if readjusted? Would there be another backlash by the international community and aviation industry against the EU approach or, accepting the failure of global measures, would other countries follow the EU's lead and introduce their own national or regional measures aiming at reduction of aviation GHG emissions?

These questions will only be answered in the, hopefully, unlikely scenario of CORSIA's failure. Until such a situation arises, it is extremely difficult to predict any concrete actions by the EU. It is also problematic to derive some hints from the Union's approach toward emissions in other international transport fields. Maritime transport remains to be the most likely point of reference, with the EU being similarly concerned about reduction of its GHG emissions and calling for global action under the auspices of IMO.[96] However, even intra-European maritime transport does not currently fall under the EU-ETS. Consequently, should the EU-ETS be relaunched for non-EEA flights, a *sui generis* solution is to be expected.

5.8 CONCLUSIONS

The Paris Agreement has been an important milestone in addressing the climate challenge. The EU rightly assumes that it will not go unnoticed in carbon-intensive industries such as the aviation industry. While it is clear that the EU is willing to compromise, it is important to bear in mind that the EU does possess the domestic regulatory authority necessary to regulate aviation

95 European Commission DG Climate Action, "The EU Emissions Trading System (EU ETS)," ec.europa.eu/clima/policies/ets_en last accessed October 2, 2017.

96 European Commission DG Climate Action, "Reducing emissions from the shipping sector," ec.europa.eu/clima/policies/transport/shipping_en last accessed October 2, 2017.

GHG emissions for all flights connected to Europe. This result of the ATAA decision and the relative international backlash against any form of unilateral action in this sector constitute important lessons for both the EU and the rest of the world. If there were to be a real danger that ICAO CORSIA would not be implemented in full, given the US's new climate change-sceptic administration, the EU Commission is certain to revisit the question of unilateral EU action in the future. For the time being, the EU rightly hopes that with the Paris Agreement and ICAO CORSIA in place and certainty as to the "direction of travel" on climate change, more partner countries in the aviation industry will support market-based mechanisms, and renewed conflict will be avoided.

6

Exporting Environmental Values through Open Skies

The Case of the European Union

Kuan-Wei (David) Chen

The growth of the aviation sector has been coupled with significant increases in emissions that cause environmental damage. In contrast to the slow international efforts to curb aviation emissions, the European Union (EU) has over the past two decades promulgated policies and regulations that foster the idea of "sustainable aviation." These policies and regulations do not only govern the EU's internal aviation market, but they have also been exported in the EU's external policies and activities. This chapter provides an overview of the EU's approach to sustainable development and aviation and turns to analyze how these policies and regulations have been integrated into the EU's aviation policy and air transport agreements with other countries.

6.1 INTRODUCTION

Globally, aviation is the most rapidly growing mode of transportation. Attached to such rapid growth in the aviation sector is the negative externality of pollution that has in the past three decades attracted attention worldwide.[1] Aircraft do not only create noise: The most pressing form of pollution comes

[1] While aviation accounts for around 2 percent of global Carbon Dioxide (CO_2) emissions – the proven cause of the greenhouse gas effect and global warming – emissions from aviation are increasing rapidly due to the rapid growth of the industry. If no measures are taken to mitigate and reduce aviation emissions, with the growth of air traffic worldwide, emissions are forecast to grow by 290 percent by 2050 (based on 2006 levels): see ATAG, "Aviation and climate change," aviationbenefits.org/environmental-efficiency/aviation-and-climate-change last accessed October 27, 2017; European Commission, "Commission Staff Working Document Accompanying the Document Communication from the Commission to the European Parliament, the Council, the European Economic and Social Committee and the Committee of Regions, An Aviation Strategy for Europe" (December 7, 2015), COM(2015) 598 final at 71,

from the burning of aviation fuels, which release gasses and particles that can alter atmospheric greenhouse gases and trigger global warming.[2] Various international and national initiatives have been undertaken to address how the aviation sector can sustain its growth while minimizing the impact that this vital economic force has on the environment. At the multilateral level, the International Civil Aviation Organization (ICAO) has been mandated to formulate and implement measures to limit or reduce the emission of anthropogenic gases derived from the aviation sector.[3] However, for almost two decades, the ICAO had only embraced an "aspirational goal" of fuel efficiency improvements of 2 percent annually until 2050[4] – aspirations that appear to have only been concretized in early 2017 with the adoption of CORSIA, the global Carbon Offsetting and Reduction Scheme for International Aviation.[5] Only time will tell whether the international aviation community, and the ICAO, the foremost intergovernmental body in charge

eur-lex.europa.eu/legal-content/EN/TXT/PDF/?uri=CELEX:52015SC0261&from=EN last accessed October 28, 2017. [*An Aviation Strategy for Europe Staff Working Document*].

2 See generally IPCC, "IPCC special report: Aviation and the global atmosphere," (1999), www.ipcc.ch/pdf/special-reports/spm/av-en.pdf last accessed October 28, 2017.

3 *Kyoto Protocol to the United Nations Framework Convention on Climate Change* (adopted December 11, 1997, entered into force February 16, 2005), UN Doc FCCC/CP/1997/7/Add.1, 37 ILM 22 (1998), Art. 2(2) [*Kyoto Protocol*]. Though the Paris Agreement of 2015 (*Framework Convention on Climate Change* [adopted December 12, 2015, entered into force November 4, 2016], UN Doc FCC/CP/2015/L9 [2015]) refrained from any mention of aviation, the ICAO Council did issue a declaration that affirmed its "continuous leadership ... on environmental issues relating to international civil aviation, including greenhouse gas (GHG) emissions": see UNFCCC, Information relevant to emissions from fuel used for international aviation and maritime transport, "ICAO council declaration on international aviation and climate change," (November 18, 2015), App. A, unfccc.int/resource/docs/2015/sbsta/eng/misc05.pdf last accessed October 27, 2017.; See also "Omission of international aviation from Paris climate agreement a vote of confidence, says ICAO President," *GreenAir Online* (December 16, 2015), www.greenaironline.com/news.php?viewStory=2173 last accessed October 27, 2017.

4 ICAO, "Consolidated statement of continuing ICAO policies and practices related to environmental protection – Climate change," ICAO Res A38–18, para. 5, www.icao.int/Meetings/a38/Documents/Resolutions/a38_res_prov_en.pdf last accessed October 27, 2017. [*ICAO Res* A38–18]. Indeed, these "aspirational goals" explicitly do *not* "attribute specific obligations to individual States": ibid., para. 6.

5 See ICAO, "Consolidated statement of continuing ICAO policies and practices related to environmental protection – Global Market-based Measure (MBM) scheme," Res A39–3, www.icao.int/environmental-protection/Documents/Resolution_A39_3.pdf last accessed October 27, 2017. In order to accommodate the "special circumstances and respective capabilities of States," there are three phases of participation in CORSIA:

- Pilot phase, from 2021–2023, that applies to States that volunteer to participate in the scheme;
- First phase, from 2024–2026, that applies to States that volunteered to participate in the pilot phase and those that volunteer to participate in this phase;

of global aviation governance, will be able to realize the lofty goals to reduce aviation emissions that have been set.

In contrast, for decades, the European Union (EU) has proactively pursued policies and regulations to address aviation pollution. These policies do not only apply internally between Member States, but they have also, by virtue of the Union's external competences and activities, become integral parts of treaty obligations *vis-à-vis* third parties. In relation to aviation, the EU has entered into air transport agreements that encompass provisions committing parties to adopt measures to address the environmental impacts of air transport. The discussion that follows will outline the EU's policies and regulations protecting the environment and how these have been "exported" through air transport agreements.

6.2 SUSTAINABLE DEVELOPMENT AND AVIATION: EU POLICIES AND REGULATIONS

Comprised of twenty-eight Member States, the EU is the largest single market in the world, and, naturally, as a collective, it is also one of the most important players in international aviation.[6] With an annual growth rate of up to 4 percent,[7] air transport is by far the fastest growing mode of transport in

– Second phase, from 2027–2035, that is applicable to all States that have an individual share of international aviation activities in Revenue Tonnes Kilometres (RTKs) in 2018 that is above 0.5% of total RTKs.

See ibid., para. 9. CORSIA's coverage extends between international flights on routes between States that are participating in the Scheme (ibid., para. 10); even States that are exempt from CORSIA must take part in the implementation of a global monitoring, reporting, and verification (MRV) system and must ensure their aircraft operators compile emissions data that is to be transmitted to the ICAO. As of April 21, 2017, sixty-seven States, which represent over 87.5 percent of international aviation, have expressed their intention to voluntarily participate in the initial phase of the global MBM scheme: ICAO, "Carbon offsetting and reduction scheme for international aviation," www.icao.int/environmental-protection/Pages/market-based-measures.aspx last accessed October 27, 2017. See also ICAO, "On board a sustainable future," www.icao.int/environmental-protection/Documents/ICAOEnvironmental_Brochure-1UP_Final.pdf last accessed October 27, 2017.

6 European Commission, "Communication from the Commission on the consequences of the Court judgements of 5 November 2002 for European air transport policy," (November 19, 2002), COM(2002) 649 final, para. 40, eur-lex.europa.eu/legal-content/EN/TXT/?uri=CELEX:52002DC0649 last accessed October 27, 2017.

7 EEA, "A closer look at urban transport – TERM 2013: Transport indicators tracking progress towards environmental targets in Europe," EEA Report No 11/2013 at 33 [*A closer look at urban transport 2013*], www.eea.europa.eu/publications/term-2013/at_download/file last accessed October 28, 2017.

the EU.[8] Though emissions from the aviation sector make up very little of the EU's total emissions,[9] between 1990 and 2011, the increase in the aviation sector's greenhouse gas emissions, at over 94 percent, was the steepest percentage increase of all sectors in the EU.[10] Aspiring to be the aviation "frontrunner in the use of low-carbon fuels" and to reach its emissions reduction target in 2050,[11] the EU has over the last decade alone adopted a wide range of policies and measures to reduce the impact and amount of aviation externalities, in particular aviation emissions.[12] Indeed, in its latest comprehensive aviation policy, the Union committed to be "a leading player in international aviation

8 European Commission, "White Paper on European Transport Policy for 2010: Time to decide," (September 12, 2011), COM(2001) 370 final at 35, ec.europa.eu/transport/themes/strategies/doc/2001_white_paper/lb_com_2001_0370_en.pdf last accessed October 28, 2017. [*White Paper on European Transport Policy*].

9 EU-wide, international and national aviation contributed to around 4 percent of NO_X emissions, and less than 1 percent of SO_2 emissions, and CO_2 emissions in 2010: see EEA, "The contribution of transport to air quality – TERM 2012: Transport indicators tracking progress towards environmental targets in Europe," EEA Report No 10/2012 at 53, www.eea.europa.eu/publications/transport-and-air-quality-term-2012/at_download/file last accessed October 26, 2017.

10 International aviation and shipping contributes to approximately 6 percent of the EU's total greenhouse gas emissions: *A closer look at urban transport 2013*, *supra* Note 7 at 18. See also European Commission, Mobility and Transport, "All facts and figures," ec.europa.eu/transport/strategies/facts-and-figures/all-themes/index_en.htm last accessed October 28, 2017.

11 European Commission, "Roadmap to a single European transport area – Towards a competitive and resource efficient transport system" (March 28, 2011), COM(2011) 144 final, para. 28 [*Roadmap to a Single European Transport Area*], eur-lex.europa.eu/LexUriServ/LexUriServ.do?uri=COM:2011:0144:FIN:en:PDF last accessed October 29, 2017

12 These include noise mitigation measures (e.g. European Commission, Directive 2002/30/EC of the European Parliament and of the Council of March 26, 2002 on the establishment of rules and procedures with regard to the introduction of noise-related operating restrictions at Community airports, OJ 2009 No L 85/40), environmental certification of aircraft equipment (e.g. Commission Regulation (EC) No 1702/2003 of September 24, 2003 laying down implementing rules for the airworthiness and environmental certification of aircraft and related products, parts and appliances, as well as for the certification of design and production organizations OJ 2003 No L 243/6), and a "Clean Sky" initiative to develop technologies for "a clean, innovative and competitive" air transport system (Council Regulation (EC) No 71/2007 of December 20, 2007 setting up the Clean Sky Joint Undertaking OJ 2008 No L 30/1). Further, there is the ambitious scheme to increase the operational efficiency of air traffic management (ATM) in the crowded airspace above Europe with the introduction of the Single European Sky. An integrated pan-European ATM system will enhance the safety and security of air traffic while simultaneously "reduce the aviation environmental footprint": see European Commission, "Single European sky," ec.europa.eu/transport/modes/air/single_european_sky_en last accessed October 29, 2017. See also "Declaration of Madrid: Conclusions of the high-level conference on the roadmap towards implementing the single European sky," February 25 and 26, 2010, skybrary.aero/bookshelf/books/1074.pdf last accessed October 28, 2017. See also "European aviation environmental report 2016," ec.europa.eu/transport/sites/transport/files/european-aviation-environmental-report-2016–72dpi.pdf last accessed October 29, 2017.

and a global model for sustainable aviation, with a high level of service and ambitious EU standards."[13]

6.2.1 *Outline of the EU's Legal Framework*

The Treaty on European Union (TEU), which describes the foundations of the pillar structure of the EU and gave the Union international legal personality, established that Europe prioritized the concept of sustainable development based on "a high level of protection and improvement of the quality of the environment."[14] In short, sustainable development denotes the ability to meet the needs of the present generation without compromising how future generations meet their needs, and is the "overarching objective" of *all* EU policies and activities.[15]

Vis-à-vis the world, the EU acts on behalf of its Member States in the pursuit of, among others, common foreign actions and policies that "ensure sustainable development," aimed at preserving and improving the quality of the environment.[16] The Treaty on the Function of the European Union (TFEU), which details the policies of the EU, stipulates that environmental protection measures must be an integral part of the "definition and implementation of the [EU's] policies and activities,"[17] while the EU committed itself to preserve, protect, and improve the quality of the environment within the Union *and* at the international level.[18] Clearly expressed, the EU's

[13] Communication from the Commission to the European Parliament, the Council, the European Economic and Social Committee and the Committee of the Regions, "An aviation strategy for Europe," (December 7, 2015), SWD(2015) 261 final at 2 [*An Aviation Strategy for Europe*], eur-lex.europa.eu/legal-content/EN/TXT/PDF/?uri=CELEX:52015DC0598&from=EN last accessed October 28, 2017.

[14] *Consolidated version of the Treaty on European Union*, OJ 2012 C 326/13 [*TEU*], Art. 3(3).

[15] Council of the European Union, "Review of the EU Sustainable Development Strategy (EU SDS) – Renewed Strategy (June 26, 2006), 10917/06 at 1 [*EU SDS Review*], register.consilium.europa.eu/doc/srv?l=EN&f=ST%2010917%202006%20INIT last accessed October 27, 2017. This objective was first elaborated in 1988: see European Council in Rhodes (December 2–3, 1988), Ann. I: *Declaration on the Environment*, para. 1, www.europarl.europa.eu/summits/rhodes/rh2_en.pdf last accessed October 29, 2017.

[16] *TEU*, *supra* Note 14, Art. 21(2)(f). see also G. M. Duran, "The role of the EU in shaping the trade and environment regulatory nexus: Multilateral and regional approaches," in B. V. Vooren, S. Blockmans, and J. Wouters (eds.), *The EU's Role in Global Governance: The Legal Dimension* (Oxford: Oxford University Press, 2013), 224–40 at 228.

[17] *Consolidated version of the Treaty on the Functioning of the European Union*, OJ 2012 C 326/47 [*TFEU*], Art. 11; *Charter of Fundamental Rights of the European Union*, OJ 2012 C 326/391, Art. 37. See also *EU SDS Review*, *supra* Note 15 at 2.

[18] *TFEU*, *supra* Note 17, Art. 191(1).

environment policy is grounded in the "precautionary principle" and the belief that environmental damage should first "be rectified at source and that the polluter should pay."[19]

In playing a "leading role" in protecting the environment,[20] the EU's Sustainable Development Strategy (SDS) recognized economic growth and environmental protection as being "mutually supporting."[21] To reduce the "carbon intensity" of the economy and prevent "dangerous anthropogenic interference" with the climate system,[22] market-based measures were identified as the most "cost-effective and economically efficient"[23] means of combatting emissions and halting the speed of climate change. In 2003, an emissions trading scheme (ETS) was instituted across the EU,[24] and all sectors of the economy were obliged to partake in offsetting their emissions.

6.2.2 "*Sustainable Aviation*"

The EU's transportation policy specifically integrates its commitment to environmental protection as laid out in its founding treaties.[25] Already in 1999, the EU began looking into using emissions trading as a possible market-based measure to combat the impact of aviation on climate change.[26] In its 2001 White Paper on European Transport Policy, the European Commission underlined the introduction of measures to combat noise and gaseous emissions as a *sine qua non* for striking a balance between growth in air transport and protecting the environment.[27] In short, this arguably laid the

19 Ibid. Art. 191(2).

20 European Council, "Declaration on the Environment," *supra* Note 15, para. 4.

21 European Commission, "Mainstreaming sustainable development into EU policies: 2009 Review of the European Union Strategy for Sustainable Development," (July 24, 2009), COM(2009) 400 final at 2, eur-lex.europa.eu/legal-content/EN/TXT/PDF/?uri=CELEX:52009DC0400&from=EN last accessed October 28, 2017.

22 Brussels European Council, March 8–9, 2007, Presidency Conclusions, 7224/1/07 REV1 (May 2, 2007), www.consilium.europa.eu/ueDocs/cms_Data/docs/pressData/en/ec/93135.pdf last accessed October 28, 2017, para. 27.

23 European Commission, Directive 2003/87/EC of October 13, 2003 on Establishing a Scheme for Greenhouse Gas Emission Allowance Trading within the Community and amending Council Directive 96/61/EC, OJ 2003 No L 275/32 [*EU ETS*], Art. 1.

24 Ibid.

25 *White Paper on European Transport Policy*, *supra* Note 8 at 9–10.

26 European Commission, "Air transport and the environment, towards meeting the challenges of sustainable development" (December 1, 1999), COM(1999) 640 final (December 1, 1999), paras. 33–38, eur-lex.europa.eu/LexUriServ/LexUriServ.do?uri=COM:1999:0640:FIN:EN:PDF last accessed October 28, 2017.

27 *White Paper on European Transport Policy*, *supra* Note 8 at 39.

hallmarks of the concept of "sustainable aviation" – a notion that was concretized in the most recent aviation strategy.[28]

Months after the Kyoto Protocol came into effect in 2005,[29] the European Commission announced a series of possible measures to mitigate the climate impact of aviation.[30] Alongside dedicating more research into cleaner air transport[31] and improving air traffic management,[32] the Commission noted emissions trading is "a fundamental design feature of the Kyoto Protocol and is a key component of the EU's future climate change strategy,"[33] and is as such economically and environmentally speaking the "best way forward" to combat climate change.[34] In the face of global inaction in combating emissions from aviation, particularly due to apparent procrastination on the part of the ICAO, the international body saddled with the legal mandate to tackle the issue of global aviation emissions,[35] in 2008 Directive 2008/101/EC legally incorporated international aviation into the EU emissions trading scheme (ETS).[36]

28 *An Aviation Strategy for Europe, supra* Note 13 at 2.

29 The application of the Kyoto Protocol to the EU was laid out in *Council Decision of 25 April 2002 concerning the approval, on behalf of the European Community, of the Kyoto Protocol to the United Nations Framework Convention on Climate Change and the joint fulfilment of commitments thereunder*, OJ 2002, No L 130/1.

30 European Commission, "Reducing the climate change impact of aviation" (September 27, 2005), COM(2005) 459 final, eur-lex.europa.eu/legal-content/EN/TXT/HTML/?uri=CELEX:52005DC0459&from=EN [*Reducing the Climate Change Impact of Aviation*].

31 See "Clean Sky" Joint Undertaking, *supra* Note 12.

32 For example, the Single European Sky is expected to dramatically improve the efficient use of European air space by threefold while cutting emissions per flight by up to 10%: European Commission, "Greening transport" (July 8, 2008), COM(2008) 433 final at 9, eur-lex.europa.eu/LexUriServ/LexUriServ.do?uri=COM:2008:0433:FIN:EN:PDF last accessed October 27, 2017; "Single European Sky," *supra* Note 12.

33 *Reducing the Climate Change Impact of Aviation, supra* Note 30, sect 6.3.

34 Ibid., sect 9.

35 See *Kyoto Protocol, supra* Note 3. See also J. Scott, "Contingent unilateralism – International aviation in the European emissions trading scheme," 209–23 in Vooren, Blockmans, and Wouters (2013), *supra* Note 16 at 210. See also *Reducing the Climate Change Impact of Aviation, supra* Note 30, sect 4.2.

36 European Commission, Directive 2008/101/EC of the European Parliament and of the Council of November 19, 2008 amending Directive 2003/87/EC so as to include aviation activities in the scheme for greenhouse gas emission allowance trading within the Community, OJ 2009 No L 8/3 [*Directive 2008/101/EC*]. By virtue of European Economic Area (EEA) Joint Committee Decisions 6/2011 and 43/2011, the EU-ETS was also extended to Iceland, Lichtenstein, and Norway. Switzerland and the EU are currently still discussing the possibility of incorporating aviation emissions into the EU-ETS system: Swiss Federal Office for the Environment, "Fifth round of Swiss-EU negotiations on linking their emissions trading systems" (December 12, 2013), https://www.bafu.admin.ch/bafu/en/home/topics/climate/news-releases.msg-id-51350.html last accessed October 27, 2017.

6.2.3 *EU-ETS and Aviation: Attempt at Global Environmental Leadership*

Directive 2008/101/EC was an "ambitious"[37] measure to combat aircraft emissions and an excellent demonstration of the Union's commitment to environmental protection and vying for global environmental leadership in this domain.[38] Initially entered into force on January 1, 2012, the Directive applied the emissions trading scheme to all flights "which depart from or arrive in an aerodrome situated in the territory of a Member State to which the Treaty."[39] Effectively, this would have covered and impacted all carriers with operations within, flying out of, or flying into the EU-zone.[40]

Though the impact of the European directive would be proportionally greater on EU carriers than non-EU carriers, internationally, States were vehemently against the adoption and application of EU-ETS to aviation.[41] A subsequent ICAO Assembly resolution urged that the implementation of an aviation emissions trading system only be based on mutual agreement

[37] J. Scott and L. Rajamani, "EU climate change unilateralism," *EJIL*, **23** (2012), 469 at 493.

[38] The EU has managed to shape global dialogue and action on environmental issues by proposing so-called win-win solutions to the environmental discourse, i.e. advocating that a climate policy has environmental benefits and does not have to come at the expense of economic development: see R. S. Dimitrov, "Environmental diplomacy: International conferences and negotiations," in P. G. Harris, *Routledge Handbook of Global Environmental Politics* (London: Routledge, 2014), 259–71 particularly at 266–67. Indeed, the EU held the potential to be a "norm entrepreneur" with respect to the climate change issue: see A. P. Valdés, "Greenhouse gas emissions from international aviation: Legal and policy challenges," in M. Benkö (ed.), *Essential Air and Space Law* (Utrecht: Eleven International Publishing, 2015), vol. 14, particularly at 279–82.

[39] Directive 2008/101/EC, *supra* Note 36, Annex. Member States denotes not only those of the EU but also the EEA, thus including Norway, Iceland, and Lichtenstein, though the latter has neither an airport nor an air carrier: see European Parliament, "The European Economic Area (EEA), Switzerland and the North," www.europarl.europa.eu/atyourservice/en/displayFtu.html?ftuId=FTU_6.5.3.html last accessed October 29, 2017.

[40] Only certain flights, such as transporting heads of State or military flights, are exempted. Intended to exonerate developing countries from the scheme, an air carrier that operates less than 243 flights or emits less than 10,000 tonnes of CO_2 over a period of a year is also excluded. See Ibid. *Annex, 'Aviation,'* (a), (b) and (j).

[41] See e.g. *Joint Declaration of the Moscow Meeting on Inclusion of International Civil Aviation in the EU-ETS* (February 22, 2012); and *Proposals by India for inclusion of additional agenda items in the provisional agenda of the seventeenth session of the Conference of the Parties*, FCCC/CP/2011/INF.2/Add.1 at 6. Some argue that the EU-ETS would distort competition in the aviation market and have very limited impact on reducing aviation emissions: A. Anger and J. Koehler, "Including aviation emissions in the EU ETS: Much ado about nothing? A review," *Transport Policy*, 17(2010) 38 at 43–44.

between States.[42] Other than allegations that the EU's aviation ETS directive is extraterritorial and unilateral,[43] critics also cite that it failed to take into account the concept of common but differentiate responsibility that holds much influence in environment circles, particularly in emerging economies.[44]

Directive 2008/101/EC was much criticized and legally challenged by a coalition of aviation-related trade organizations and airlines. In the *ATA* case,[45] the (then) European Court of Justice (ECJ) ultimately held the EU directive as being legal and consistent with the EU's various international obligations.[46] Despite the affirmative ruling of the EU's highest court and the firm belief that the inclusion of aviation in the EU-ETS may very well "serve as a model for the use of emissions trading worldwide,"[47] in the face of fierce

[42] ICAO "Consolidated statement of continuing ICAO policies and practices related to environmental protection," Res A36–22, Doc 9902, App. L, para. 1(b), http://europa.eu/rapid/press-release_MEMO-07-391_en.htm last accessed October 28, 2017.

In response, the forty-two Member States of the (then) European Community and the European Civil Aviation Conference (ECAC), which endorsed the EU-ETS's application to aviation as being fully consistent with international law, filed a reservation to the ICAO resolution. See European Commission, "Written statement of reservation on behalf of the member states of the European Community (EC) and the other states members of the European Civil Aviation (ECAC)," Memo/07/391 (October 2, 2007), http://europa.eu/rapid/press-release_MEMO-07–391_en.htm last accessed October 28, 2017.

"Whilst being ready and willing to continue to take part in ICAO activities aimed at promoting the reduction of aviation emissions, the forty-two States of the European Community and ECAC must also express in the strongest terms their great disappointment with the lack of ambition and concrete actions in the resolutions tackling greenhouse gas emissions being adopted by this Assembly."

[43] See e.g. B. F. Havel and J. Q. Mulligan, "The triumph of politics: Reflections on the judgment of the court of justice of the European union validating the inclusion of Non-EU airlines in the emissions trading scheme," *Air and Space Law*, **37**(2012) 3; M. T. Ahmad, "The CJEU's radical ETS judgment: Destabilizing the Chicago Convention system," *Issues in Aviation Law and Policy*, **13** (2013) 139. See also P. S. Dempsey, *Public International Air Law* (2nd edn.) (Montreal: Centre for Research in Air and Space Law, 2017) at 596ff. Ironically, in its 2001 White Paper on European Transport Policy, the EU did underline that "account must be taken of the international commitments entered into by the Member States within [ICAO]: *White Paper on European Transport Policy*," *supra* Note 8 at 39.

[44] See Scott and Rajamani, *supra* Note 37 at 476; "The principle of common but differentiated responsibilities: Origins and scope," CISDL, "A CISDL legal brief for the world summit on sustainable development," (August 26, 2002), cisdl.org/public/docs/news/brief_common.pdf.

[45] Case c-366/10, *Air Transport Association of America and Others* v. *Secretary of State for Energy and Climate Change*, [2011] ECR I-13755 [ATA].

[46] Ibid., para. 79 *et seq*. Professor Dempsey succinctly underlines how the EU-ETS scheme is at odds with the EU-United States Open Skies Agreement, customary international law and several provisions of the Chicago Convention – the latter matter of which a matter was completely sidelined by the ECJ: Dempsey, *supra* Note 43 at 596ff.

[47] Directive 2008/101/EC, *supra* Note 36, recital 17.

international opposition[48] and reluctance to adhere to the scheme,[49] in 2013 the EU temporarily suspended the application of the EU-ETS to flights originating from or to non-European countries.[50] In 2014, the EU scaled back the implementation of the EU-ETS to cover only emissions from flights departing from and arriving at EU airports (thus covering only intra-EU flights).[51] The application of the reduced scope of aviation within the EU-ETS would continue until 2016, the year the ICAO was expected to clarify the mechanism for global emissions mitigation.[52]

48 See European Commission, "Proposal for a Directive of the European Parliament and of the Council amending Directive 2003/87/EC establishing a scheme for greenhouse gas emission allowance trading within the Community, in view of the implementation by 2020 of an international agreement applying a single global market-based measure to international aviation emissions" (October 16, 2016), COM/2013/0722at 2 [COM/2013/0722], eur-lex.europa.eu/LexUriServ/LexUriServ.do?uri=COM:2013:0722:FIN:EN:PDF last accessed October 29, 2017.

49 The United States adopted a "blocking legislation" preventing US-based airlines from participating in the EU scheme: US, *European Union Emissions Trading Scheme Prohibition Act 2011*, HR 2494, October 24, 2011.

50 Decision No 377/2013/EU of the European Parliament and of the Council of 24 April 2013 derogating temporarily from Directive 2003/87/EC establishing a scheme for greenhouse gas emission allowance trading within the Community, OJ 2013 L 113/1. This is commonly referred to as the "Stop the Clock" initiative: European Commission, "Commission proposes to 'stop the clock' on international aviation in the EU ETS pending 2013 ICAO General Assembly" (November 12, 2012), online: European Commission, ec.europa.eu/clima/news/articles/news_2012111202_en.

51 Regulation (EU) No 421/2014 of the European Parliament and of the Council of 16 April 2014 amending Directive 2003/87/EC establishing a scheme for greenhouse gas emission allowance trading within the Community, in view of the implementation by 2020 of an international agreement applying a single global market-based measure to international aviation emissions, OJ 2014 L 129/1. See also European Aviation Environmental Report 2016, *supra* Note 12 at 63–64. Again, here the EU also includes Member States of the EEA, thus it includes Norway and Iceland: *supra* Note 39. With regard to Switzerland, the EU and Switzerland have been negotiating linking their emissions trading systems with each other, which would also include emissions from aviation. Though the Linking Agreement was concluded in January 2016, the Agreement has not yet entered into effect at the time of writing: see "EU and Switzerland to link carbon markets after talks conclude," *Carbon Pulse* (January 25, 2016), carbon-pulse.com/14646/ last accessed October 27, 2017; Swiss Federal Office for the Environment (BAFU), "Linking the Swiss and EU emissions trading schemes," www.bafu.admin.ch/bafu/en/home/topics/climate/info-specialists/climate-policy/emissions-trading/linking-the-swiss-and-eu-emissions-trading-schemes.html last accessed October 28, 2017; and European Commission, "International carbon market," ec.europa.eu/clima/policies/ets/markets_en last accessed October 28, 2017.

52 Regulation (EU) No 421/2014, *supra* Note 50, Preamble, recitals 3 and 14. European Aviation Environmental Report 2016, *supra* Note 12 at 63.

With the ICAO's adoption of a global market-based measure in the form of CORSIA, the EU intends to prolong the reduced scope of the EU-ETS until 2020.[53] In the meantime, the European Commission has proposed to amend the EU-ETS to ensure that it is consistent with future emissions reduction objectives.[54] While the ICAO has finally moved forward in respect to tackling aviation emissions,[55] the EU actively continues to assume the role of "a leading advocate for addressing fast-growing emissions from aviation."[56]

6.3 SUSTAINABLE AVIATION AND AIR TRANSPORT AGREEMENTS

Having outlined the policies and intricacies relating to the EU's commitment to sustainable development and sustainable aviation, it is of interest to turn to the EU's external policies and activities *vis-à-vis* third countries. In this vein, environmental provisions in the EU's air transport agreements are most enlightening and provide evidence of the EU's laudable attempts to export its environmental values globally.

[53] See European Commission, "Reducing emissions from aviation," ec.europa.eu/clima/policies/transport/aviation_en last accessed October 29, 2017; European Commission, "Memo: 39th Assembly of the international civil aviation organization" (October 7, 2016) Fact Sheet MEMO-16–3332, http://europa.eu/rapid/press-release_MEMO-16-3332_en.htm last accessed October 29, 2017; and "ICAO negotiations on CORSIA scheme challenging, European climate chief tells EU environment ministers," *GreenAir Online* (March 2, 2017), www.greenaironline.com/news.php?viewStory=2345 last accessed October 29, 2017.

[54] See European Commission, "Proposal for a Regulation of the European Parliament and of the Council amending Directive 2003/87/EC to continue current limitations of scope for aviation activities and to prepare to implement a global market-based measure from 2021," COM(2017) 54 final, data.consilium.europa.eu/doc/document/ST-5968–2017-INIT/en/pdf, last accessed October 29, 2017. As the Commission noted:

While both are market-based measures addressing aviation emissions, there are some important differences between them. For instance, the EU-ETS is a "cap and trade" scheme, which means that emissions cannot increase beyond a certain amount (cap). The GMBM on the other hand is an "offsetting scheme," where emissions can grow without limit as far as they are compensated with offsets. The level of ambition (climate objective and associated baseline) and the type of units are other relevant differences.

European Commission, "Memo: 39th Assembly of the International civil aviation organization," Fact Sheet MEMO-16–3332 (October 7, 2016), europa.eu/rapid/press-release_MEMO-16–3332_en.htm, last accessed October 29, 2017.

[55] At the time of writing, the latest action by the ICAO is the adoption of new CO_2 standards for aircraft engines that will come into effect in January 2018: see ICAO, "ICAO Council adopts new CO_2 emissions standard for aircraft" (News Releases, March 6, 2017), www.icao.int/Newsroom/Pages/ICAO-Council-adopts-new-CO2-emissions-standard-for-aircraft.aspx last accessed October 29, 2017 .

[56] European Commission, "The EU tackles growing aviation emissions" (Press Release IP-17–189, February 3, 2017), http://europa.eu/rapid/press-release_IP-17-189_en.htm last accessed October 29, 2017.

6.3.1 *The Chicago Convention and Air Transport Agreements*

The Chicago Convention[57] laid the foundation whereby States could grant or restrict commercial access under the air transport agreements. Article 1 of the Chicago Convention provides that every State has complete and exclusive sovereignty over the airspace above its territory. Article 11 stipulates that laws and regulations relating to the admission/departure of an aircraft engaged in international air navigation to/from the territory of a contracting State shall be applied "without distinction as to nationality, and shall be complied with by such aircraft upon entering or departing from or while within the territory of that State." Charges for the use of airports and air navigation facilities by the aircraft of any other State must be levied under uniform conditions and cannot discriminate based on nationality.[58] Article 6 of the Chicago Convention provides that scheduled international air service over or into the territory of a contracting State must obtain permission or other authorization of the State, and must be compliant with the terms of such permission or authorization. These provisions are pertinent to the air transport agreements discussed in the next section, provisions of which stipulate that States must adhere to technical, operational, or environmental standards to be granted access to the EU's aviation market.

6.3.2 *Aviation Single Market and External Aviation Policy*

Much of the growth of the EU aviation sector can be attributed to the liberalization of the aviation sector,[59] which began internally among Member States of the Union and the members of the European Economic Area (EEA) and Switzerland.[60] Since the 1990s, the EU has adopted a series of legislative

57 *Convention on International Civil Aviation* (adopted December 7, 1944, entered into force April 4, 1947) 15 UNTS 295, ICAO Doc 7300/6 [*Chicago Convention*].

58 Ibid. Art. 15.

59 S. Kallas, "Speech: Aviation in Europe: Contributor to growth and competitiveness?" SPEECH/14/185 (March 6, 2014), http://europa.eu/rapid/press-release_SPEECH-14-185_en.htm last accessed October 20, 2017.

60 Norway, Iceland, and Lichtenstein (though it has neither an airport nor an air carrier) are already part of the single market by virtue of the European Economic Area (EEA), whereas Switzerland signed an agreement with the Union whereby air transport has been liberalized on the same basis as EU legislation: see *Agreement between the European Community and the Swiss Confederation on Air Transport – Final Act*, OJ 2002 L 114/73; see also COM(2002) 649 final, *supra* Note 6, paras. 18–19.

packages to create a single market in the air transport sector[61] and apply common rules governing aviation safety, security, and environmental matters.[62]According to the legal principle of parallelism between internal and external powers,[63] once the Union has promulgated measures related to the single market in a particular policy area (in this case the aviation sector), in its external relations the EU retains the exclusive competence to act on behalf of Member States to conclude agreements with third parties pertaining to that policy area.[64] The ECJ's "Open Skies judgments"[65] confirmed the Union's exclusive competence to act in the pursuit of a common aviation policy,[66] and paved the way for a common external aviation policy.[67]

In order to align earlier aviation bilaterals with Union rules and policies, the Commission undertook to pursue so-called horizontal agreements with third States.[68] Core to these agreements were provisions aimed at liberalizing the

[61] Known as the "Third Package" of measures adopted in 1992, principles of the single market applied to the aviation industry and guaranteed equal access to all air carriers of Member States, thereby establishing "Community air carriers" with equal market access rights and subject to common standards of safety, environmental, and passenger protection: see COM (2002) 649 final, *supra* Note 6, paras. 4–7. See also B. F. Havel, *Beyond open Skies: A New Regime for International Aviation* (Alphen aan den Rijn: Kluwer Law International, 2009) at 401–2.

[62] Regulation (EC) No 1008/2008 of the European Parliament and of the Council of September 24, 2008 establishing common rules for the operation of air services in the Community, OJ 2008 L 293/3.

[63] Case 22/70, *Commission of the European Communities* v. *Council of the European Communities (European Agreement on Road Transport)*, [1971] ECR 263, para. 17 [*AETR*]. See also "Glossary: European Powers," europa.eu/legislation_summaries/glossary/community_powers_en.htm last accessed October 29, 2017.

[64] See "Opinion of the Court of 15 November 1994 – Competence of the Community to conclude international agreements concerning services and the protection of intellectual property – Article 228 (6) of the EC Treaty," Opinion 1/94, [1994] ECR I-05267, para. 77.

[65] *Commission* v. *United Kingdom, Denmark, Sweden, Finland, Belgium, Luxembourg, Austria, Germany*, [2012] Cases C-466/98, C-467/98, C-468/98, C-469/98, C-471/98, C-472/98, C-475/98 and C-476/98. In the Commission's perspective, open skies agreements between e.g. the Netherlands and the United States are still "traditional bilateral agreements in that they reserve traffic rights strictly to the airlines from the two parties to the agreement," COM(2002) 649 final, *supra* Note 6, para. 14.

[66] *AETR*, *supra* Note 63. This principle was applied to various "open skies judgments", see e.g. Case 469/98, *Commission* v. *Finland*, [2002] ECR I-9627, para. 67; Case 467/98, *Commission* v. *Denmark*, [2002] ECR I- 9528, para. 66; Case 471/98, *Commission* v. *Belgium*, [2002] ECR I-9681, para. 77. See also COM(2002) 649 final, *supra* Note 6, paras. 29–30.

[67] European Commission, "Developing the agenda for the Community's external aviation policy, agenda for the Community's external aviation policy" (March 11, 2005) [*Agenda for the Community's external aviation policy*], eur-lex.europa.eu/legal-content/EN/TXT/HTML/?uri=CELEX:52005DC0079&from=EN last accessed October 29, 2017.

[68] See European Commission, "Communication from the Commission on relations between the Community and third countries in the field of air transport" (February 26, 2003), COM(2003)

aviation market, but also promoting sustainable aviation.[69] Explicitly, the Commission underlined the importance of acting with a single voice so as to best "counter the negative effects on the environment of the growth of the aviation sector, notably in terms of climate change."[70]

Immediately surrounding the EU, the Commission's external aviation policy is centered on the signing of comprehensive air services agreements with the EU's neighboring States to the south and to the east.[71] The creation of a European Common Aviation Area (ECAA)[72] would operate according to the same market and regulatory rules as the EU's internal market,[73] and domains such as aviation safety, security, air traffic management, and the environment would be subject to "common rules."[74] Further afield, the external aviation policy actively pursues the conclusion of air services

94 final (February 26, 2003), eur-lex.europa.eu/legal-content/EN/TXT/?uri=CELEX:52003 DC0094 last accessed October 29, 2017.

69 *Agenda for the Community's external aviation policy, supra* Note 67, sect I, para. 2.

70 Ibid., sect I, para. 3. See also European Commission, "Common Aviation Area with the Neighboring Countries by 2010 – Progress Report," COM(2008) 596 final (October 1, 2008), online: EUR Lex eur-lex.europa.eu/legal-content/EN/TXT/?uri=CELEX:52008DC0596, paras. 35–37; and "The EU's external aviation policy – Addressing future challenges" (September 27, 2012), COM(2012) 556 final, paras. 45–46 [*EU's External Aviation Policy* 2012].

71 The ECAA forms part of the EU's broader European Neighborhood Policy (ENP), which aims to promote stability and sustainable development in the region. Agreements were to be first concluded with Romania and Bulgaria, at the time still pre-accession States, and with Western Balkan States and Morocco. For an overview of the States deemed by the EU as key aviation partners, see European Commission, "External Aviation Maps – European neighborhood and key partners," http://europa.eu/rapid/press-release_MEMO-12-714_en.htm, last accessed October 29, 2017.

Though the objective was to conclude aviation agreements with neighboring countries like Azerbaijan, Egypt, Tunisia, Turkey, and Ukraine, political instability in some of these countries and impasse have delayed the conclusion of such agreements: European Commission, "EU External Aviation Policy Package," MEMO 12 714 (September 27, 2012), http://europa.eu/rapid/press-release_MEMO-12–714_en.htm last accessed October 29, 2017.

72 See generally *Agenda for the Community's external aviation policy, supra* Note 67; "Common aviation area with the neighboring countries by 2010 – Progress report," COM(2008) 596 final, paras. 18–23; European Commission, "The EU and its neighboring regions: A renewed approach to transport cooperation" (July 7, 2011), COM(2011) 415 final at 3–4, eur-lex.europa.eu/legal-content/EN/TXT/HTML/?uri=CELEX:52005DC0079&from=EN last accessed October 29, 2017.

73 *Agenda for the Community's external aviation policy, supra* Note 67, sect II, para. 2.1.

74 *Multilateral Agreement between the European Community and its Member States, the Republic of Albania, Bosnia and Herzegovina, the Republic of Bulgaria, the Republic of Croatia, the former Yugoslav Republic of Macedonia, the Republic of Iceland, the Republic of Montenegro, the Kingdom of Norway, Romania, the Republic of Serbia and the United Nations Interim Administration Mission in Kosovo on the establishment of a European Common Aviation Area*, OJ 2006 L 285/3, Art. 1.

agreements with key aviation players such as China and Russia and third countries in the Asia-Pacific and the Americas.[75]

To date, the EU has negotiated comprehensive air transport agreements with the United States, Canada, Morocco, the Western Balkan countries, Jordan, Georgia, Moldova, and Israel, with more agreements to be concluded in years to come.[76] In early 2014, the EU took steps to establish an Open Skies Agreement with the Association of Southeast Asian Nations (ASEAN),[77] which if eventually implemented would form the "world's first comprehensive region-to-region aviation agreement."[78] The following air transport agreements demonstrate the EU's commitment to incorporate environmental provisions and promote the notion of sustainable aviation.

6.3.3 *EU–US Air Transport Agreement*

The conclusion of a comprehensive air transport agreement with the United States sealed "the integration of the two largest aviation markets" and paved the way for a "new regulatory framework for international civil aviation."[79] The first stage of the EU–US "Open Skies" Agreement[80] was signed on April 30, 2007, and entered into force on March 30, 2008. It provided for the liberalization of air traffic and removed restrictions on air fares on either side

[75] *EU's External Aviation Policy*, *supra* Note 70 at paras. 51–53.

[76] Ibid. at para. 6. The EU had negotiated a comprehensive air transport agreement with Brazil, which was initialed in 2011 but still pending signature: European Commission, "International aviation: Brazil," ec.europa.eu/transport/modes/air/international_aviation/country_index/brazil_en last accessed October 29, 2017. Though signature from the Brazilian side is still pending. See European Cockpit Association "EU & Brazil re-start open skies negotiation" (February 6, 2014), https://www.eurocockpit.be/news/eu-brazil-re-start-open-skies-negotiation last accessed October 29, 2017. At the time of writing, the EU and Armenia began a Comprehensive Air Transport Agreement on the Common Aviation Area between the two sides: EEAS, "EU-Armenia talks on comprehensive air transport agreement kick off in Yerevan" (Press release, April 27, 2017), eeas.europa.eu/headquarters/headquarters-homepage/25160/eu-armenia-talks-comprehensive-air-transport-agreement-kick-yerevan_en last accessed October 29, 2017. The Commission also began negotiations for comprehensive air transport agreements with Qatar, the United Arab Emirates, and Turkey: see "Comprehensive EU air transport agreements: Council adopts mandates" (Press release 313/16, June 7, 2016), www.consilium.europa.eu/en/press/press-releases/2016/06/07-comprehensive-eu-air-transport-agreements last accessed October 29, 2017.

[77] *Joint Declaration on EU-ASEAN Aviation Cooperation* (February 12, 2014), http://asean.org/storage/images/Statement/2014/Feb/jd-eaas-final.pdf last accessed October 29, 2017.

[78] Kallas, "Speech: Aviation in Europe: Contributor to growth and competitiveness?"

[79] *Agenda for the Community's external aviation policy*, *supra* Note 67, sect II.

[80] *Air Transport Agreement between the European Community and its Member States, on the one hand, and the United States of America, on the other hand* OJ 2007 L 134/4 [*EU-US Agreement*].

of the Atlantic.[81] Overall, the comprehensive air transport agreement between the EU's Member States[82] and the United States aimed to create more harmonization in the policies between the United States and EU States.

Under the EU–US Agreement, no party can unilaterally limit the "volume of traffic, frequency or regularity of service, or the aircraft type or types operated by the airlines of the other Party."[83] The only derogation from this general free access to the market is an exception based on technical, operational, or environmental reasons.[84]

The original Article 15 reflects the positions of the EU and the United States with regard to the environment. Both parties recognize the importance of protecting the environment.[85] Any proposed environmental measures must consider "possible adverse effects" on the rights of either party contained in the Agreement.[86] Article 15(3) stipulates "except where differences have been filed," environmental measures adopted by either parties must follow standards adopted by the ICAO.[87] This provision would be most pertinent to the application of EU-ETS to aviation, for which the Member States of the EU have filed a reservation to the ICAO standard.[88] Further, environmental measures must be applied in a nondiscriminatory manner in accordance with the "fair and equal opportunity" clause.[89]

The Memorandum of Consultations following the EU–US Agreement "noted the *intention* " of either side to enhance technical cooperation that "will enhance safety, improve fuel efficiency, and reduce emissions in air transport."[90] Expressly, both sides underlined the provisions of the Agreement do not restrict "in any way [the parties'] respective legal and policy positions on various aviation-related environmental issues."[91]

81 For a summary, see European Commission, "Informationnote: Air transport agreement between the EU and US" (March 6, 2007), ec.europa.eu/transport/modes/air/international_aviation/country_index/doc/2007_03_05_us_information_note.pdf last accessed October 29, 2017.

82 Iceland and Norway also acceded to the EU–US Air Transport Agreement in 2009, with the agreement taking effect on June 21, 2011: "Iceland and Norway join EU-US Air Transport Agreement" (Press release IP/09/1962, December 17, 2009) https://www.norwegianamerican.com/featured/iceland-and-norway-join-eu-us-air-transport-agreement/ last accessed October 29, 2017.

83 *EU-US Agreement, supra* Note 80, Recital 11 and Art. 3(4).

84 Ibid.

85 *EU-US Agreement, supra* Note 80, Art. 15(1).

86 Ibid. 15(2).

87 See also *ATA, supra* Note 45, paras. 7, 34, and 40.

88 The EU has indeed done this in regard to ICAO Res A36 22, App. I.; see *supra* Note 42.

89 *EU-US Agreement, supra* Note 80, Art. 2. See also *ATA, supra* Note 45, para. 99.

90 *EU-US Agreement, supra* Note 80, *Memorandum of Consultations*, para. 36 [emphasis added].

91 Ibid., para. 54.

However, the planned implementation of the EU-ETS and *ATA* reference to the EJC[92] changed the dynamic of the open skies negotiations across the Atlantic. The second stage EU–US Agreement, which appeared in the form of an amendment protocol,[93] went into effect on June 24, 2010 and addressed various market access opportunities and regulation in areas including aviation safety and security and the environmental impact of aviation. Severe disagreements over the application of the EU-ETS to all flights entering or leaving the EU led to the complete scrapping and replacement of the environment provision with a much watered-down provision, and the EU and United States issued a statement that underlined the commitment of both sides to address the environmental impact of aviation through multilateral forums like the ICAO.[94]

It can be safely presumed that any environmental measures adopted by either side must continue to be applied in a nondiscriminatory manner in accordance with the "fair and equal opportunity" clause.[95] To address aircraft noise, the Amended Protocol adopted the "balanced approach principle"[96] coined by the ICAO as the "environmentally responsive and economically responsible" manner to alleviate noise at the source.[97] New to the Amendment Protocol, parties expressed their intention to "work together to limit or reduce, in an economically reasonable manner, the impact of international aviation on the environment."[98] The adverse effects on the rights of the other party contained in the Agreement must be evaluated when adopting an environmental measure, and the Amendment Protocol inserted a clause that allows any party to have a description of mitigation measures to be implemented.[99] The parties only endorsed "exchange information and regular dialogue" aimed at

[92] Proceedings were brought on December 16, 2009, and a reference to the ECJ was made on May 28, 2010, a month before the Amended Protocol came into effect: see R *(Air Transport Association of America Inc etc.)* v. *Secretary of State For Energy And Climate Change* [2010] EWHC 1554 (Admin); see also *ATA*, *supra* Note 45, paras. 43–44.

[93] *Protocol to amend the Air Transport Agreement between the European Community and its Member States, of the one part, and the United States of America, of the other part*, OJ 2010 L 223/3 [*Amendment Protocol*].

[94] *Joint Statement on the Environment*, ec.europa.eu/transport/modes/air/international_aviation/country_index/doc/2010_03_25_joint_state_env_attach_c.pdf last accessed October 29, 2017.

[95] *EU-US Agreement*, *supra* Note 76, Art. 2. See also *ATA*, *supra* Note 45, para. 99.

[96] *Amendment Protocol*, *supra* Note 93, Arts. 15(4)–15(5); see also *EU-US Agreement*, *Memorandum of Understanding*, para. 35.

[97] ICAO Res 35–5, "Consolidated statement of continuing ICAO policies and practices related to environmental protection, Appendix C; ICAO, Guidance on the Balanced Approach to Aircraft Noise Management," ICAO Doc 9829 (2008), sect 1.2.

[98] *Amendment Protocol*, *supra* Note 93, amended Art. 15(1).

[99] Ibid. amended Art. 15(2).

enhancing cooperation in finding solutions to the environmental impact of aviation.[100] Such exchanges could center on the development of environmentally friendly technology and coordinating "views on issues and options in international fora" to deal with the environmental effects of aviation.[101] With regard to the ability of either party to adopt market-based measures to mitigate emissions, in the case of a dispute regarding the interpretation or application of the Agreement,[102] parties can request a meeting of the Joint Committee "to consider the issue and develop appropriate responses to concerns found to be legitimate."[103]

6.3.4 *EU–Canada Air Transport Agreement*

Following the agreement between the EU and the United States, the EU–Canada Air Transport Agreement,[104] signed on December 17–18, 2009, is deemed the "most ambitious" of the EU's air transport agreements.[105] The EU–Canada Air Transport Agreement places no limitation on the frequency and capacity of air services either party offers.[106] Again, derogation from this general free access to the market is an exception based on technical, operational, or environmental reasons.[107] Article 15, on air traffic management, has a general reference to the parties cooperating to ensure the efficient and economic enhancement of air navigation systems in a way, where possible, that reduces the environmental impact of aviation.

Article 18 of the EU–Canada Agreement specifically deals with the environment.[108] Interestingly, the original EU–US Agreement provisions governing the environment[109] did not disappear when it was repealed and replaced with the watered-down provisions contained in the Amendment Protocol. Instead, the same text governing the environment reappeared in the EU–Canada

[100] Ibid. amended Art. 15(6).
[101] Ibid. amended Art. 15(6)(c).
[102] *EU-US Agreement, supra* Note 80, Art. 18(2).
[103] Ibid. Art. 18(4)(b).
[104] *Agreement on Air Transport between Canada and the European Community and its Member States*, OJ 2010 L 207/32 [*EU-Canada Agreement*].
[105] European Commission, "International Aviation: Canada," ec.europa.eu/transport/modes/air/international_aviation/country_index/canada_en.htm last accessed October 29, 2017.
[106] *EU-Canada Agreement, supra* Note 104, Art. 13(2).
[107] Ibid.
[108] Provisions dealing with the environment were labelled as a "groundbreaking element" of the Agreement: European Commission, "The EU-Canada aviation agreements – Q&A," MEMO/09/218 (May 6, 2009), http://europa.eu/rapid/press-release_MEMO-09-218_en.htm last accessed October 29, 2017.
[109] *EU-US Agreement, supra* Note 80, Art. 15.

Agreement. Here, the EU and Canada reiterated the importance of protecting the environment in developing and implementing international aviation policy,[110] and both sides reserve the right to "take and apply the appropriate measures to address the environmental impacts of air transport" *within its own sovereign jurisdiction*.[111] Such measures must not prejudice the rights and obligations of the parties under international law (and the Chicago Convention) and must be applied "without distinction as to nationality."[112] While recognizing the importance of working together to mitigate the effects of aviation on the environment, any environmental measures undertaken must be consistent with the objectives of the Agreement[113] and should follow ICAO standards.[114] The Agreement also provides for a party to differ from international standards provided that the party has filed the difference with the ICAO.[115] Perhaps taking account of the critical voices against the unilateral implementation of the EU-ETS at the time, the EU–Canada Agreement explicitly cautions that when adopting environmental measures, "possible adverse effects on the exercise of rights" must be considered and that steps must be taken to mitigate these adverse effects.[116] Article 18(6) provides for the possibility of engaging in consultation to discuss measures that aim to protect the environment that may have "a significant effect on the international air services."

6.3.5 *EU–Israel Air Transport Agreement*

The EU–Israel Air Transport Agreement, signed in 2013, also includes a provision with regard to the protection of the environment.[117] Similar to the EU–Canada Agreement, the agreement with Israel stipulates that both parties

[110] *EU-Canada Agreement, supra* Note 104, recital 11 and Art. 18(1). The EU and Canada share the commitment to a low-carbon economy and a market for achieving emissions reduction: see *EU-Canada Summit Declaration*, 9547/09 (May 6, 2009), http://europa.eu/rapid/press-release_PRES-09-120_en.htm last accessed October 29, 2017.

[111] *EU-Canada Agreement, supra* Note 104, Art. 18(2). Indeed, prior to negotiations, the Commission was adamant the Agreement must be consistent with commitments to sustainable development and not hamper the EU's ability to "apply regulatory or economic instruments to mitigate" side-effects of aviation: see European Commission "Developing a Community civil aviation policy towards Canada," COM(2006) 871 final, para. 5.3.

[112] *EU-Canada Agreement, supra* Note 104, Art. 18(2).

[113] Ibid. Art. 18(4).

[114] Ibid. Art. 18(5).

[115] Ibid. Art. 18(5). *Chicago Convention, supra* Note 57, Art. 38.

[116] Ibid. Art. 18(3).

[117] *Euro-Mediterranean Aviation Agreement between the European Union and its Member States, of the one part and the government of the State of Israel*, of the other part (August 2, 2013) OJ 2013 L 208/3 [*EU-Israel Agreement*].

can take "all appropriate measures," so long as they do not discriminate on the basis of nationality, to address the environmental impact of air transport.[118] Similarly, during negotiations the Commission underlined the need to incorporate sustainable development into any aviation agreement with Israel and noted that any agreement must not hamper the EU's ability to establish "regulatory or economic instruments to mitigate unwanted side-effects of growth in air traffic."[119]

6.3.6 *Future Air Transport Agreement with the United Kingdom*

With the results of a June 2016 referendum in the United Kingdom narrowly favoring the Member State to leave the Union, the UK Government and the Commission have been negotiating the terms of "BREXIT."[120] Among the multitude of economic, social, and political issues to be discussed and agreed upon with the United Kingdom's exit from the Union, and the associated single market, will no doubt be a new air transport agreement for EU carriers to fly into and from the United Kingdom.[121] Though the exact terms of such an air transport agreement remain largely a matter of speculation, the United Kingdom may remain part of the European Common Aviation Area or perhaps negotiate an open skies type bilateral agreement, in order to minimize disruption.[122]

Leaving the Union means that the United Kingdom's carriers will no longer be subject to the EU-ETS, which is applicable to EU-based carriers. Would the United Kingdom follow in the footsteps of Switzerland and negotiate a

[118] Ibid. Art. 16(4).

[119] European Commission, "Developing a common aviation area with Israel," COM/2007/691 final at 7, eur-lex.europa.eu/legal-content/EN/TXT/PDF/?uri=CELEX:52007DC0691&from=EN last accessed October 29, 2017.

[120] After much speculation and many legal challenges, the Great Britain's exit from the EU is definite: see "Theresa May's Brexit speech in full," *The Daily Telegraph* (January 17, 2017), www.telegraph.co.uk/news/2017/01/17/theresa-mays-brexit-speech-full/ last accessed October 29, 2017.

[121] There is much fear of disruptions and uncertainty for civil aviation: see D. Donald, "Legal experts fear major Brexit disruption for aviation," *AIN Publications* (March 4, 2017), www.ainonline.com/aviation-news/business-aviation/2017-03-04/legal-experts-fear-major-brexit-disruption-aviation last accessed October 29, 2017. See also D. Elliott, "Brexit – over & out," *Airport Business* (October 17, 2016), www.airport-business.com/2016/10/brexit/ last accessed October 29, 2017.

[122] IATA, "The impact of 'BREXIT' on UK Air Transport"(June 2016), www.iata.org/publications/economic-briefings/impact-of-brexit.pdf last accessed October 29, 2017. See also P. McClean and A. Barker, "Will Brexit complicate landing rights for UK flights," *Financial Times* (February 12, 2017), www.ft.com/content/57c0c01c-ef9c-11e6-930f-061b01e23655 last accessed October 29, 2017.

similar deal to link their emissions trading systems with each other that also covers emissions from civil aviation? Speculation aside, what is clear is that as with other air transport agreements, acceptance of and adherence to the EU's environmental standards with regard to aviation will no doubt be a part of the air transport agreement framework to facilitate continued flight operations into/out of the EU zone.

6.4 IMPACT OF THE EU'S ENVIRONMENTAL POLICIES AND VALUES ON THE CHICAGO CONVENTION

The judgment and reasoning of the ECJ in *ATA*, as well as the environmental provisions inserted into the EU's bilaterals with countries around the world, are of great interest, not only as evidence of how the EU wishes to be a global leader in dealing with aviation emissions but also for the implementation of the Chicago Convention.

As has been alluded to, the EU's air transport bilaterals, which are in fact signed by all Member States of the Union with third States, make repeated references to the Chicago Convention. In *ATA* the ECJ held, perhaps controversially,[123] that the EU is not bound by the Chicago Convention because it is not a party to the Convention.[124] However, the judgment and references made to provisions of the Chicago Convention in fact reinforce the status of that instrument as the principal source of international air law.[125]

Article 82 of the Chicago Convention specifically prohibits any "obligations and understandings" that are inconsistent with its terms.[126] As the ECJ reasoned, though the EU itself is not a party to the Convention or the ICAO, the EU aviation ETS relates to "the objective of improving environmental protection"[127] and is therefore perfectly consistent with the ICAO's guiding principles for the design and implementation of market-based measures for

123 Centre for International Sustainable Development Law, "Legal analysis on the inclusion of civil aviation in the European Union emissions trading scheme" (May 2012) at 6, cisdl.org/public/docs/news/CISDL_EU_ETS_Expansion_Legal_Brief.pdf last accessed October 29, 2017.

124 *ATA*, *supra* Note 45, paras. 3, 60, and 71. In rejecting the applicability of the Chicago Convention, Benoît Mayer writes the ECJ embarked on a path of "isolationism," which is dangerous for the integrity of international law: see B. Mayer, "Case C-366/10, *Air Transport Association of America and Others* v. *Secretary of State for Energy and Climate Change*, Judgment of the Court of Justice (Grand Chamber) of 21 December 2011," CMLR, 49 (2012), 1113, especially at 1123–25.

125 M. Milde, "International air law and ICAO," in M. Benkö (ed.), *Essential Air and Space Law* (Utrecht: Eleven International Publishing, 2008), vol. 4 at 17.

126 *Chicago Convention*, *supra* Note 57, Art. 82. See also Milde, *supra* Note 125 at 18.

127 *ATA*, *supra* Note 45, para. 138.

international aviation.[128] An aircraft operator wishing to land or take off at an EU airport simply must comply with the high standard of environmental protection the EU has set for itself and is required by the EU legislator.[129] Though such EU standards are higher than those required by the ICAO, they are valid as long as they are applied in a nondiscriminatory manner,[130] and as long as they are not duplicative in nature.[131]

In less than twenty years, the matter of the environment has been propelled from a mere passing mention[132] to become one of the most pressing concerns of global aviation governance.[133] The fact that environmental matters are now a core objective of the ICAO can perhaps be attributed to the EU's ambitious efforts in this regard, though often much to the chagrin of other States. In referring to the provisions of the Chicago Convention, despite repeated denial of its application to the Union as an entity, the European court in fact affirms the obligations and rights of States, individually and collectively, contained in the primary source of international aviation law.

Though the Chicago Convention does not explicitly mention, let alone deal with, environmental matters of aviation, the text of the Convention, perhaps due to the astute foresight of the drafters, does contain enough leeway to allow the ICAO to adopt measures to deal with "all aspects of international civil aeronautics."[134] This "capture" phrase can and should be continually used by the ICAO to adopt concrete measures and policies to address aviation emissions.[135] For the longest time, impasse and the inability to achieve the

[128] Ibid., paras. 149–50; see also ICAO Res A37–19, "Consolidated statement of continuing ICAO policies and practices related to environmental protection," – Climate Change, Ann. b) and f), respectively, www.icao.int/environmental-protection/37thAssembly/A37_Res19_en.pdf last accessed October 29, 2017.

[129] *ATA*, *supra* Note 45, para. 128. For compliance with laws and regulations relating to the admission to or departure from its territory of aircraft engaged in international air navigation, see *Chicago Convention*, *supra* Note 57, Art. 11.

[130] *ATA*, *supra* Note 45, paras. 154–55. See also Directive 2008/101/EC, *supra* Note 36, Preamble, recitals 17, 21.

[131] *ATA*, *supra* Note 45, paras. 150–51.

[132] ICAO, "Strategy: Guiding international civil aviation into the 21st century," www.icao.int/Documents/strategic-objectives/sap1997_en.pdf last accessed October 29, 2017. The ICAO report noted "as for the environment there is a *perception* that the aviation sector may be contributing unduly to both existing and emerging problems": ibid. at 7 [emphasis added].

[133] Environmental protection is now one of the ICAO's Strategic Objectives, alongside safety, capacity and efficiency, security and facilitation, and economic development: ICAO, www.icao.int/Pages/default.aspx.

[134] *Chicago Convention*, *supra* Note 57, Art. 44(i).

[135] A. de Mestral and M. T. Ahmad, "A pre-analysis of Canada–EU aviation relations post-ICAO assembly meeting concerning emissions trading system" (produced for the Canada-Europe Transatlantic Dialogue, Carleton University, Centre for European Studies, April 2013) at 7,

necessary consensus on the issue of environmental protection resulted in the ICAO being unable to adopting measures to address aviation emissions. Until the ICAO took concerted action in the adoption of the CORSIA plan in 2016, the European Union's internal legislation, air transport agreements that form part of its engagement with external partners, and even the jurisprudence of its highest court, serve to remind us that it takes someone to challenge global inaction and spearhead change.

6.5 CONCLUSION

The benefits, as well as detrimental effects, of civil aviation in an interconnected world are by nature internationally felt and shared. In order to effectively address emissions from international aviation in a manner that is sustainable, economically viable, and enjoys the support of all stakeholders, it is necessary to secure international agreement and concerted efforts to that effect.

Though the contribution of aviation to climate change accounts around 2–3 percent of all CO_2 emissions, the rapid growth of the industry will certainly mean that, if unchecked, emissions will increase to unmanageable proportions.[136] Aviation remains the "least climate friendly" mode of transport.[137] In 2013, the reaching of an ICAO agreement on market-based measures was cited as "an historic milestone for air transport and for the role of multilateralism in addressing global climate challenges."[138] In 2016, the

labs.carleton.ca/canadaeurope/2013/a-pre-analysis-of-canada-eu-aviation-relations-post-icao-assembly-meeting-concerning-emissions-trading-system/ last accessed October 29, 2017. See also M. T. Ahmad, "Environmental effectiveness of ICAO's basket of mitigation measures to arrest emissions from international civil aviation," *Annals of Air and Space Law* (2014), 75 at 82.

136 See ICAO, "ICAO environment report 2016: On board a sustainable future," at 50, www.icao.int/environmental-protection/Documents/ICAO Environmental Report 2016.pdf last accessed October 29, 2017. See also "Sustainable development in the European Union: 2013 monitoring report of the EU sustainable development strategy," at 13 and 185, http://ec.europa.eu/eurostat/documents/3217494/5760249/KS-02-13-237-EN.PDF/f652a97e-e646-456a-82fc-34949bbff956 last accessed October 29, 2013.

Emissions from aviation and maritime transport increased by a staggering 66 percent since 1990.

137 See European Parliament, "Report on the Proposal for a Directive of the European Parliament and of the Council amending Directive 2003/87/EC establishing a scheme for greenhouse gas emission allowance trading within the Community, in view of the implementation by 2020 of an international agreement applying a single global market-based measure to international aviation emissions," COM(2013)0722–C70374/2013–2013/0344(COD), A7–0079/2014 (January 31, 2014) at 22 [*EP Report*], www.europarl.europa.eu/sides/getDoc.do?pubRef=-//EP//NONSGML+REPORT+A7-2014-0079+0+DOC+PDF+V0//EN last accessed October 29, 2017.

138 ICAO, "Dramatic MBM agreement and solid global plan endorsements help deliver landmark ICAO 38th Assembly" (News Release, October 4, 2013), www.icao.int/Newsroom/News%20Doc%202013/COM.36.13.A38.Closing.EN.pdf last accessed October 29, 2017.

adoption of CORSIA was hailed as "historic" as well.[139] Only time will tell whether these historic moments in time will be remembered as moments when the world just spoke about taking action or actually did begin to take action to address the environmental impact of a mode of transportation that is integral to the global economy, mobility, and connectivity. The hope is that States, and the airline industry, will have the resolve, resources, and capacity to ensure the successful implementation of CORSIA and reduce emissions from aviation to the agreed upon levels.

The EU, on the other hand, is on target to reach its goals to reduce greenhouse gas emissions by 20 percent compared to 1990 levels by 2020.[140] As it attempts to be a "global aviation hub,"[141] the EU has projected itself as "a new heavyweight player"[142] in the field of aviation and as a leader in combating emissions.[143] This is not just out of conviction and commitment to mitigating the effects of growth and development on the environment in general, but also due to the fact that some 42 percent of all flights worldwide originate in or are bound for the EU zone.[144]

Indeed, the EU has repeatedly underlined its "continued willingness" to adhere to a global approach to tackling the issue of environmental protection and ensure the sustainable development of the aviation industry.[145] Internally, the EU's founding principles empower policies and regulations that place the importance of economic development on par with protecting the environment. These principles and policies have infused applicable regulations that ensure "sustainable aviation" in the internal market. At times, the EU has

139 ATAG, "Historic aviation climate agreement reached at ICAO" (October 6, 2016), aviationbenefits.org/newswire/2016/10/historic-aviation-climate-agreement-reached-at-icao/ last accessed October 29, 2017.

140 By 2012, the EU already achieved the target of an 18 percent reduction compared to 1990 levels of greenhouse gas emissions, and is projected to over-achieve the target by reaching a reduction of 24 percent compared to 1990s levels in 2020. See European Commission, "Taking stock of the Europe 2020 strategy for smart, sustainable and inclusive growth," COM(2014) 130 final/2 (March 19, 2014) at 12–13, ec.europa.eu/europe2020/pdf/europe2020stocktaking_en.pdf last accessed October 28, 2017.

141 *Roadmap to a Single European Transport Area*, *supra* Note 11, para. 28.

142 *Agenda for the Community's external aviation policy*, *supra* Note 67, sect I, para. 1.

143 S. Oberthür and C. R. Kelly, "EU leadership in international climate policy: Achievements and challenges," *International Spectator*, 4 (2008) 35.

144 European Commission, "Address by transport commissioner Violeta Bulc before the Council of the international civil aviation organization (ICAO)" (Press Release SPEECH/16/461, February 29, 2016), http://europa.eu/rapid/press-release_SPEECH-16-461_en.htm last accessed October 28, 2017.

145 *EU's External Aviation Policy*, *supra* Note 70 at para. 9.

engaged in unilateral action as a means to prompt greater multilateral action[146] – much to other States' chagrin – of which the adoption of the EU aviation ETS is a prime example. Alternatively, and this is commendable, in its external relations and in the air transport agreements with third countries, the EU has succeeded in infusing the value of environmental protections and its commitment to "decarbonizing the economy."[147] The future of the world, and the future of succeeding generations, needs more idealists and champions of global interests and values like the European Union.

[146] See E. Morgera, "Ambition, complexity, and legitimacy of pursuing mutual supportiveness through the EU's external environmental action," 195–208 in Vooren, Blockmans, and Wouters (2013), *supra* Note 16 at 197–98. Indeed, the *Lisbon Treaty*, under Art. 21(2)(h), mandates the Union to "promote an international system based on stronger multilateral cooperation." See also COM/2013/0722, *supra* Note 48 at 2. Mayer, *supra* Note 124 at 1138, notes that:

"It is not a secret that the EU was built at least partly as a way to ensure that European States maintain a say in international matters in a decolonized world. Thus, it is not surprising for the EU to press for international efforts, and such actions may not be illegitimate, provided they are compatible with international law and global interests."

[147] *EU's External Aviation Policy*, *supra* Note 70 at para. 9. See also An Aviation Strategy for Europe Staff Working Document, *supra* Note 1, c 4.

7

Aviation and Sustainable Development

Some Perspectives from the Asia-Pacific

Jae Woon Lee, Benoît Mayer, and Joseph Wheeler

The rapid growth of passenger and freight traffic in the Asia-Pacific region has come in hand with greater environmental concerns. Affirming its growing influence, the Asia-Pacific has widely contributed to recent ICAO actions to develop multilateral bases for market-based environmental measures in international aviation as an avenue to mitigate greenhouse gas (GHG) emissions. States in the Asia-Pacific regions also have engaged in some laws and policies aimed at contributing to climate change mitigation, in particular by reducing GHG emissions. Yet, there is no broad consistency in the measures undertaken, or a particular focus on international aviation. Individual states in the Asia-Pacific region have approached the objective of mitigating aviation impacts very differently, from countries that have only adopted embryonic climate laws to countries with fully operational carbon-pricing schemes. Given the spirit of the Chicago Convention 1944, it is principally important to make every effort to come up with a global approach through the ICAO. However, alternative approaches should also be considered. The alternatives may well stem from the "bottom-up" collective linkages being created between regional or single-state ETSs, such as the bilateral trade link that will be forged between the EU and Australia. This model of cooperation could be an alternative to stalling multilateral negotiations on a global regime.

7.1 INTRODUCTION

The Asia-Pacific region is witnessing rapid growth in civil aviation activities.[1] The International Civil Aviation Organization (ICAO) notes that the

[1] See for example the presentation given by the Director General of the Association of Asia Pacific Airlines (AAPA) in 2015, which reported that the region accounts for 35 percent of the value of global trade, and is home to 56 percent of the world's population, See AAPA,

Asia-Pacific region was the world's largest air transport market in 2012, accounting for a 30 percent share of the world's revenue passenger kilometers (RPKs).[2] It also foresaw that airlines of the Asia-Pacific region will experience the highest growth in passenger traffic at 5.8 percent per year until 2025.[3] Since 2009, the profit margin of Asia-Pacific air carriers has been significantly higher than in any other region.[4] The number of passenger kilometers completed in the Asia-Pacific in recent years has only been outshone by the Middle East.[5] This sectoral development reflects the "rise of Asia" – with two-digit growth figures in several countries of the region despite a context of global economic downturn. Yet, the rapid growth of passenger and freight traffic in the Asia-Pacific region has been accompanied by greater environmental concerns. Affirming its growing influence, the Asia-Pacific has widely contributed to recent ICAO actions to develop multilateral bases for market-based environmental measures in international aviation as an avenue to mitigate greenhouse gas (GHG) emissions. This chapter submits that, as a significant driver of air transport demand and capacity, the Asia-Pacific region's particular characteristics have become a necessary reference for the development of sustainable aviation policies and regulations in the coming years.

The Asia-Pacific is, admittedly, a vast region with stark contrasts. "Asia" itself arguably stands for little more than what lies east of Europe. The Asia-Pacific region contains roughly half of the world's population, and spans more than half of the Earth's surface. There are evident contrasts between the states of the region, in cultural, political, economic, or developmental terms, among others. The rise of Asia is driven by the four "Asian Tigers" (Hong Kong, Singapore, South Korea, and Taiwan) and Japan, as well as by two mastodons (China and India). It is supported by international trade but also by growing endogenous demand, in particular in China, India, and Southeast Asian nations. Other countries of the region, however, are among the world's least developed countries (e.g. Afghanistan, Bangladesh, Cambodia, Nepal, and

www.aapairlines.org/resource_centre/AAPA_SP_AP59_DG_Presentation_13Nov15.pdf last accessed October 29, 2017.

2 ICAO, "Forecasts of scheduled passenger traffic: Medium-term passenger and freight traffic forecasts," https://www.icao.int/sustainability/pages/eap_fp_forecastmed.aspx last accessed October 29, 2017.

3 ICAO, "Forecasts of scheduled passenger traffic: Long-term traffic and aircraft movement forecasts," www.icao.int/sustainability/pages/eap_fp_forecast_longterm.aspx last accessed October 29, 2017.

4 IATA, "Financial forecast: Better structure offsets weak economy" (December 2012).

5 See ICAO, "Forecasts of scheduled passenger traffic: Medium-term passenger and freight traffic forecasts," www.icao.int/sustainability/pages/eap_fp_forecastmed.aspx last accessed October 27, 2017.

several island states of the Pacific). The political regimes range from well-established liberal democracies all the way to some of the world's grimmest regimes. In spite of this heterogeneity, however, the eastern hemisphere has been seen as animated by a vague unity, linked precisely from its not-being Europe: a "will to differ,"[6] as a regional observer called it in Southeast Asia, or a quest for (quite controversial) "Asian values."[7] At the subregional level, the Association of Southeast Asian Nations (ASEAN) and the South Asian Association for Regional Cooperation (SAARC) have promoted regional rapprochement. Economic cooperation has also been promoted at the regional scale, for instance through the Asia-Pacific Economic Cooperation (APEC), the ASEAN +3 (i.e. China, Japan, and Korea) initiative, and the ASEAN regional forum.

This context of regional identity-building by opposition to Europe impacts the Asia-Pacific region's perspectives on aviation and sustainable development. Asia's "takeoff" must be approached as possibly something other than just a historical addendum to the aviation growth and development of the West, or just seen as emulating Western development. In aviation, as in other sectors, growth has been highly unequally distributed – and most of the growth of Asian aviation can be attributed to just a few states in the region, whose upwardly economically mobile populations have supported the increase in traffic: China, India, Japan, Malaysia, Singapore, South Korea, and Taiwan.[8] This highly contrasting picture is in itself a significant difference from Europe or North America – one which may have significant consequences in the position that Asia-Pacific states have taken with regard to sustainable aviation policies. With regard to sustainable development, the region's efforts have frequently been pushed by extraneous actors such as trade partners, aid donors, international organizations, or nongovernmental organizations. Yet, in the climate negotiations, the region contributed significantly in the emergence of the principle of a common but differentiated responsibility, according to which those states that have greater historical responsibilities for climate change or a higher financial capacity should take the lead in efforts to mitigate GHG emissions and support other states in adapting to the unavoidable consequences of climate change. In accordance with this principle, Australia, Japan, New Zealand, and Russia[9]

6 S. Tay, "Human rights, culture, and the Singapore example," *McGill Law Journal*, 41 (1995), 743 at 768.

7 See in particular J. Donnelly, *Universal Human Rights in Theory and Practice* (Ithaca, NY: Cornell University Press, 2003) at 108.

8 See IATA, "Air passenger forecasts global report," www.iata.org/events/agm/2015/Documents/air-pax-forecasts-executive-summary.pdf last accessed October 29, 2017.

9 Russia is not traditionally considered part of Asia, but the majority of its land mass is east of the Urals and is therefore situated in Asia.

were the only countries of the region listed in Annex B of the Kyoto Protocol specifying binding mitigation goals.

The following sections briefly describe the particular Asia-Pacific complexion of opposition to the unilateral imposition of the European Union (EU) Emissions Trading Scheme (ETS) to foreign air carriers, outline legal and policy measures intended to address aviation's effects on the climate, and, where relevant and in the absence of aviation-specific measures, describe the diverse climate-related efforts of states in the region. It will be seen that the region may hold the key to a potential global solution for market-based measures in reducing international aviation emissions, and that this key is not a new element of public international air law relations.

7.2 OPPOSITION TO THE EU-ETS

States of the Asia-Pacific region have played an important role in contesting the application of the EU-ETS to foreign air carriers. Opposition has manifested in different ways throughout the region. Russia, for instance, retaliated by delaying approvals on certain European air carrier traffic rights,[10] and has considered imposing fees on European air carriers that overfly Siberia and capping numbers of flights that traverse Siberian airspace.[11] Similarly, in a clear trade-based retaliation, China cancelled significant aircraft orders from the European manufacturer Airbus and banned compliance with the EU-ETS by air carriers based in China.[12] At the Council of the ICAO, India, China, Malaysia, Russia, Singapore, and South Korea (among other non-European states) sponsored the "Delhi declaration" that "oppose[d] the EU's plan to include all flights by non-EU carriers to/from an airport in the territory of an EU Member State in its emissions trading system (EU Directive 2008/101/EC), which is inconsistent with applicable international law."[13] A few months later, the same states backed the strong words of the Moscow declaration – denouncing the "unilateral" action of the EU and affirming a

[10] K. Hofmann, "Russian opposition to ETS delays Lufthansa Cargo's traffic rights approval," *Air Transport World* (March 22, 2012), atwonline.com/international-aviation-regulation/news/russian-opposition-ets-delays-lufthansa-cargo-s-traffic-right last accessed October 28, 2017.

[11] P. Samant and S. Goligorsky, "Non-EU countries oppose inclusion of emissions from airlines in EU ETS", *National Law Review* (March 8, 2012), www.natlawreview.com/article/non-eu-countries-oppose-inclusion-emissions-airlines-eu-ets last accessed October 28, 2017.

[12] K. Cantle, "Chinese carriers shun EU ETS rules warning; signals retaliation," *Air Transport World* (May 16, 2012), atwonline.com/aeropolitics/chinese-carriers-shun-eu-ets-rules-warning-signals-retaliation last accessed October 28, 2017.

[13] ICAO, Council Declaration 194/2 (November 2, 2011).

"unanimous position that the EU and its Member States must cease application" of this legislation.

By contrast to the United States or Canada's mostly economic concerns, the Asia-Pacific regional opposition to the EU-ETS was often phrased in more political terms. When presenting what would become the "Delhi declaration," an Indian representative argued for instance that "the paper was about affirming and re-affirming the *sovereignty* of ICAO Member States in accordance with the Chicago Convention."[14] Likewise, the representative of Singapore put the emphasis on the issue of applying EU law beyond Europe.[15] These positions elaborated on a critical, "post-colonial" discourse widespread throughout Asia. Beside the purely economic stakes, Asian states were keen to highlight the unacceptable principle that decisions taken in Brussels could be imposed on foreign actors without territorial connection – recalling the time when European metropolises ruled over most of the world. If not uniquely Asian, the postcolonial perspective that Asian states took participated in an effort at framing Asia (or part of it) as the leader of an emancipated "third world."

To this extent, attention should be given to an article on "EU Climate Change Unilateralism" that Lavanya Rajamani of the Center for Policy Research in New Delhi coauthored with Joanne Scott of University College London.[16] Unlike the position of many Asian authors and virtually all Asian states, the European-Indian tandem "do[es] not take issue with [the EU's] unilateral *means*."[17] Referring to Keohane and Victor's theory of a "regime complex for climate change,"[18] where many different forms of regulations are used to make up for insufficient centralized governance,[19] they consider that "the EU may be thought to be acting as a 'norm entrepreneur', using (the threat of) unilateral action to stimulate climate action elsewhere."[20] Political influence through trade is, after all, current practice, and such an influence is quite widely accepted as long as it does not breach any specific legal obligation.

14 ICAO Council, 194th Sess., "Summary minutes of the second meeting," C-MIN 194/2, 18/11/11, at para. 10 (emphasis added).

15 Ibid. para. 83.

16 J. Scott and L. Rajamani, "EU climate change unilateralism," *European Journal of International Law*, **23** (2012) 469.

17 Ibid. at 469 (emphasis added).

18 See R. O. Keohane and D. G. Victor, "The regime complex for climate change," *The Harvard Project on International Climate Agreements* (January 2010), belfercenter.ksg.harvard.edu/files/Keohane_Victor_Final_2.pdf last accessed October 28, 2017.

19 Ibid. at 470. See also R. O. Keohane and D. G. Victor, "The regime complex for climate change," *Perspectives on Politics*, 9 (2011), 7.

20 Scott and Rajamani, *supra* Note 16 at 472–73.

If not the *means*, what seems to disturb Scott and Rajamani is the *outcomes* of such contingent unilateralism: the consequences of unilateral exercise of power on the substance of the regime complex for climate change. In the course of multilateral negotiations on an emissions reduction scheme, developing countries would have a strong claim for certain derogations in consideration of their lower past and current emissions and of their lower financial capacities. These claims are reflected by the notion that states have common but differentiated responsibilities for climate change.[21] Yet, Scott and Rajamani argue, the EU-ETS is rooted in the EU's principle of *equal* treatment, not in the international climate law principle of common but differentiated responsibility.[22] This reflects the critical dimension of the choice of forum in the regime complex for climate change. Scott and Rajamani conclude that the "EU Climate Change unilateralism is likely to disregard important aspects of the recognized ethics of international relations."[23]

Asian nations and their allies have exhibited strong opinions in relation to emissions reduction. The Association of Asia Pacific Airlines[24] resolved in 2009 to call on governments to adopt a global sectoral approach to aviation emissions developed through the ICAO.[25] More recently, a powerful group containing two Asian powerhouse nations ("BASIC," which consists of Brazil, South Africa, India, and China) has reinstated their similar commitments, including voluntary participation, multilateralism, and a focus on the entire "basket" of measures available to mitigate climate change from emissions, including non–market-based measures. Following the 14th BASIC Ministerial Meeting on Climate Change, in Chennai, India) a joint statement concluded:[26]

> The discussion on market based measures in ICAO, even if these market based measures are undertaken within the national jurisdiction, should be

[21] See in particular United Nations Framework Convention on Climate Change, May 9, 1992, Art. 3(1) and 4. See generally L. Rajamani, *Differential Treatment in International Environmental Law* (Oxford: Oxford University Press, 2006).

[22] Scott and Rajamnit, *supra* Note 16, at 493.

[23] Ibid.

[24] AAPA is a forum for the expression of views on matters of mutual interest to the aviation industry in the Asia-Pacific region and has fifteen member airlines, including flag carriers and some privately owned carriers, like Bangkok Airways.

[25] AAPA, Resolution No 7 of 2009, www.aapairlines.org/resource_centre/AAPA_53AP_Res007_Environment_20Nov09.pdf last accessed October 27, 2017.

[26] See "Joint statement issued at the Conclusion of the 14th BASIC Ministerial Meeting on Climate Change" (February 16, 2013). A copy of the full statement is available at www.scribd.com/doc/126015048/XIV-BASIC-Joint-Statement-Final last accessed October 27, 2017.

based on the principles of the UNFCCC, environmental integrity, voluntary participation and not prejudge the outcome of the negotiations in the UNFCCC.[27]

Yet this attitude of the Asian nations and groups thereof, for example the views of BASIC set out in this section, do not bode well for a sectoral approach through the ICAO, unless a final proposal settled on a way to satisfy the perceived inequities that would arise for these nations if a mandatory multilateral aviation market-based measure was considered. BASIC nations argue that developing countries are protected somewhat by the climate law principle, which ensures climate action is proportionate to each state's ability to respond and their responsibility for historical emissions.

7.3 MITIGATION EFFORTS IN THE ASIA-PACIFIC REGION

States in the Asia-Pacific region have engaged in some laws and policies aimed at contributing to climate change mitigation, in particular by reducing GHG emissions. Yet, there is no broad consistency in the measures undertaken, or a particular focus on international aviation. This is especially so if one considers the dramatic policy efforts of the EU, described in the previous section of this chapter and elsewhere in this treatise.

7.3.1 *The Advocacy of Small Island Developing States (SIDS) and Others*

Extraneous pressure, in particular from Europe, has anecdotally played an instrumental role in putting climate change mitigation and adaptation on political agendas in the Asia-Pacific region. However, some countries in the region have also been particularly vocal in calling for international efforts. This is particularly the case of SIDS of the Pacific and Indian Oceans,[28] which are particularly vulnerable to the effects of global climate change. These islands are indeed highly vulnerable to some of the consequences of climate change – most obviously, sea level rise, but also increases in the frequency and intensity of cyclones and storm surges, drought, acidification of the oceans

[27] Ibid. See also J. Parnell, "BASIC countries threaten to block aviation emissions deal," *Climate Change News* (February 19, 2013), www.climatechangenews.com/2013/02/19/basic-countries-threaten-to-block-aviation-emissions-deal/ last accessed October 28, 2017.

[28] These include, in the Pacific Ocean, Cook Islands, Fiji, Federated States of Micronesia, Kiribati, Marshall Islands, Nauru, Niue, Palau, Papua New Guinea, Samoa, Solomon Islands, Tonga, Tuvalu, and Vanuatu, and, in the Indian Ocean, Comoros, the Maldives, Mauritius, and Seychelles.

(damaging the coral reefs), and an increase in temperature. Some of them – the Maldives, Tuvalu, and Kiribati – might even become uninhabitable in the decades to come. Yet, given the size of these countries, their own contribution to global GHG emissions is marginal.

Most of these countries are represented in the Alliance of Small Island States (AOSIS). Through AOSIS or individual initiatives, small island states have represented an influential lobby in the international climate negotiations, calling for radical mitigation efforts and larger North–South adaptation funding. At the 17th Conference of the Parties (COP 17) to the UN Framework Convention on Climate Change (UNFCCC), Samoa's ambassador to the United States, Aliioaiga Feturi Elisaia, noted "[w]e are at the frontline of the impacts of climate change in the Pacific, so for us it is not something that is theoretical."[29] Yet, given their geography, and the role aviation plays in fostering connectivity between island states and the home countries of tourists and diaspora communities, SIDS have a particularly strong reliance on aviation.

7.3.2 *Technical Cooperation*

Notably for the region, there have been broad technical cooperative measures seeking to reduce the impact of aviation emissions. Typically, these seek to promote best practice through more efficient and effective operational procedures by Air Navigation Service Providers (ANSPs) and airlines. In particular, the Asia and South Pacific Initiative to Reduce Emissions (ASPIRE) agreement was signed in Singapore on February 18, 2008 by the ANSPs of Australia and New-Zealand, soon to be expanded to their Japanese, Singaporean, and Thai counterparts.[30] The strategic plan of the partnership notes:[31]

> In order to meet the growing regional demand for air transportation, while maintaining the industry's leadership position, it is essential for Asia and Pacific aviation partners to collaborate on environmental stewardship.[32]

[29] See Pacific Islands Forum Secretariat, "Pacific in Durban: Updates from COP17," https://www.forumsec.org/pacific-in-durban-updates-from-cop17-2/ last accessed October 27, 2017.

[30] The original signatories were Airservices Australia, Airways New Zealand, Federal Aviation Administration. Japan Civil Aviation Bureau (JCAB) joined in October 2009. The Civil Aviation Authority of Singapore (CAAS) joined in 2010. AeroThai joined in 2011. See ASPIRE, "What is ASPIRE," www.aspire-green.com/about/default.asp last accessed October 28, 2017.

[31] See ASPIRE, "Asia and Pacific initiative to reduce emissions: Strategic plan," www.aspire-green.com/mediapub/docs/strategic_plan_2011.pdf last accessed October 27, 2017.

[32] Ibid. at 4.

7.3.3 *Three Models of National Approaches to Mitigating Aviation Impacts*

Individual states in the Asia-Pacific region have approached the objective of mitigating aviation impacts very differently, depending in particular on their obligations under the international climate regime and other national circumstances. States can be situated on a long continuum between mere inaction and strong engagement. It is beyond the scope of this chapter to canvas every climate change initiative in any of the states of the Asia-Pacific region. However, some commonalities can be recognized among these countries, and some call for more attention.

Thus, the next three sections will discuss three different models on this continuum. At one extreme, most least-developed or developing countries (mostly most low-income and lower-middle-income ones) of the region have only adopted some weak policies on climate change, with general goals and only a few constraining measures, and without significant impact on the aviation sector. In the middle of the continuum, some upper-middle-income or high-income countries are starting to establish a carbon-pricing mechanism, with little provisions for aviation as yet. At the other edge of the continuum, some other upper-middle-income or high-income countries have developed a full-fledged legal regime to mitigate climate change through a full-fledged carbon-pricing (in particular market-based) mechanism that may apply to the aviation sector

7.4 COUNTRIES WITH EMBRYONIC CLIMATE LAWS

In many developing countries of the region (as certainly elsewhere), climate change policies are usually very general, and rarely followed by strict implementation measures. They put a relatively large emphasis on adaptation to climate change, although they may also contain some principled statements or limited concrete policies on mitigation. Such efforts are often carried out by coordinating agencies or subnational authorities rather than driven by a centralized body. This is largely due to the nature of adaptation, extending to many different sectors (from land-use to constructions, from education to industrial policies), and the limited specificity of such policies.

For example, the Climate Change Act 2009[33] in the Philippines mandates that local governments draft local Climate Change Action Plans and, in Pakistan, a special Provincial Climate Change Policy Implementation

[33] Republic Act No 9729, Climate Change Act of 2009, www.lawphil.net/statutes/repacts/ra2009/ra_9729_2009.html last accessed October 29, 2017.

Committee has been established.[34] Similarly, Bangladesh has, through its Ministry of Environment and Forests, published a Climate Change Strategy and Action Plan (2008),[35] and passed the Sustainable and Renewable Energy Development Authority Act, which is designed to promote the production and use of green energy. As a country with only 49 percent of citizens having access to electricity, renewable forms of energy are pursued to complementarily contribute to the provision of enhanced and secure energy supply, while also reducing fossil fuel use.[36]

Malaysia has passed the Sustainable Energy Development Authority Act 2011, which establishes an authority to provide for functions under sustainable energy laws, such as advising the Government on matters relating to sustainable energy, implementing national policy objectives for renewable energy, and conducting other research and assessments as needed to enhance investment and public participation and awareness on matters relating to sustainable energy.[37]

Some significant steps have, however, been taken. India, in particular, has initiated a levy on coal, with the revenue raised being used to fund clean energy research. It also published its twelfth Five-Year Plan as approved by the National Development Council in December 2012.[38] While this is not legislation, the Plan sets the aspirational strategic direction of the economy, and includes recommendations put forward by the Low Carbon Expert Group, including measures to promote and diversify domestic sources of energy and reduce the energy intensity of production processes.[39]

34 Government of Pakistan, Ministry of Climate Change, "National climate change policy" (September 2012), http://www.gcisc.org.pk/National_Climate_Change_Policy_2012.pdf last accessed October 28, 2017.

35 Ministry of Environment and Forests, Government of the People's Republic of Bangladesh, "Bangladesh climate change strategy and action plan 2008," www.sdnbd.org/moef.pdf last accessed October 28, 2017.

36 Islam et al. "Renewable energy: The key to achieving sustainable development of rural Bangladesh," *Journal of Chemical Engineering*, ChE 26 (2011).

37 See *Sustainable Energy Development Authority Act 2011* (Malaysia), Act No 726, Laws of Malaysia.

38 See "National development council approves 12th five year plan," *The Indian Express* (December 27, 2012), archive.indianexpress.com/news/national-development-council-approves-12th-five-year-plan/1051012/ The Twelfth Plan is for 2012–17 last accessed October 27, 2017.

39 These include "increasing green cover by one million hectare every year and adding 30,000 MW of renewable energy generation capacity in the Plan period" and reducing "emission intensity of the GDP in line with the target of 20–25 reduction by 2020 over 2005 levels"; see ibid.

Vietnam approved its national United Nations Reducing Emissions from Deforestation and forest Degradation (REDD+) Action Programme in June 2012.[40] This is designed to reduce emissions by setting up a legal framework for pilot REDD+ programs and activities. It includes a target to reduce emissions from the agricultural sector by 20 percent and to increase natural forest cover to 44–45 percent, both by 2020.[41]

In Mongolia, the Ministry of Nature, Environment and Tourism released the Mongolia Second National Communication Under the UNFCCC in 2010 summarizing its government policy and strategies to solve climate change challenges, and the key findings and results of climate change research and studies conducted in Mongolia.[42] More recently, a Mongolian law has been introduced that regulates air pollution and introduces measures for reduction and monitoring of emissions of air pollutants.[43] Yet, this legislation aims at combatting atmospheric pollution in the valley of Ulaanbaatar rather than at mitigating climate change, and it might have a relatively low impact on GHG emissions.

Singapore's National Climate Change Strategy of 2012 gives an indication of the city-state's priorities with regard to mitigation "[t]hrough fuel taxes, controlling vehicle ownership and usage, energy efficiency incentives and other policies, Singapore has proactively reduced the growth of carbon emissions."[44] The Strategy emphasizes technology and highlights their low capacity to develop renewable energy for lack of territory (despite the promises of tidal power in the Singapore Strait). Singapore, as a major regional hub, also participates in ASPIRE (as discussed in this section) and the Airport Carbon Accreditation Programme, an initiative by the Airports Council International (Asia Pacific), which is supported by the ICAO. Under this initiative, the Changi Airport Group will work toward reducing its carbon emissions to eventually achieve carbon neutrality.

[40] The United Nations REDD Global Programme supports REDD+ national readiness efforts in forty-six countries in Africa, Asia-Pacific, and Latin America; see UN REDD, http://www.un-redd.org last accessed October 27, 2017.

[41] See "The global climate legislation study 2015," Globe International, https://globelegislators.org/publications/legislation/climate-2015 last accessed October 28, 2017.

[42] See Mongolia Second National Communication under the United Nations Framework Convention on Climate Change, unfccc.int/resource/docs/natc/mongnc2.pdf last accessed October 27, 2017.

[43] *Mongolian law on Air*, May 17, 2012, Art. 1.

[44] National Climate Change Strategy of 2012 at 13.

7.5 COUNTRIES WITH CARBON-PRICING MECHANISMS BUT LITTLE PRESENT APPLICATION TO AVIATION

The last few years have witnessed a significant move toward pricing carbon, primarily through carbon trading but also using carbon taxes, as a tool with which to tackle GHG emissions. Many of these regimes and frameworks have been entered into but not pursued to implementation for various local political reasons. The global hesitations as to the post-2012 regime (until the last-minute agreement to some prolongation at COP 18 in December 2012) may also have discouraged some developed countries like Japan and South Korea.

7.5.1 *Japan*

The 1998 Law Concerning the Promotion of the Measures to Address Global Warming[45] is the centerpiece of Japanese climate policy, even though it does not set legally binding national targets.[46] Under this Law, Japan has operated a voluntary emissions trading scheme since 2005 that covers carbon dioxide emissions from fuel consumption, electricity and heat, waste management, and industrial process from over 300 companies, of which six are aviation companies.[47] Although Article 22 of the Law provides that designated transportation companies and cargo owners have obligations to report their emissions annually, air transportation is not included.

Japan, the world's fifth-biggest greenhouse gas emitter, had been expected to launch a trading scheme that would curb companies' emissions from 2013.[48] However, after witnessing uncertainty over a global climate framework beyond 2012 in the 16th session of the Conference of the Parties of the UNFCCC (COP 16) in Cancun, and strong opposition by powerful Japanese business groups that warned of job losses as they compete against overseas

45 Japan, *Law Concerning the Promotion of the Measures to Cope with Global Warming*, Law No 117 of 1998 (effective October 9, 1998), www.env.go.jp/en/laws/global/warming.html last accessed October 28, 2017.

46 Y. Takamura, "Chapter 9 Japan," in R. Lord, et al. (eds.), *Climate Change Liability – Transnational Law and Practice* (Cambridge: Cambridge University Press, 2012) at 210.

47 See Japan's Voluntary Emissions Trading Scheme (JVETS) March 19, 2009, presentation by the Office of Market Mechanisms, Climate Change Policy Division, Global Environment Bureau, Ministry of the Environment, Japan, www.env.go.jp/en/earth/ets/jvets090319.pdf last accessed October 28, 2017.

48 R. Maeda, "Japan shelves carbon emissions trading scheme," *Reuters* (December 28, 2010), www.reuters.com/article/2010/12/28/us-climate-japan-idUSTRE6BR06120101228 last accessed October 28, 2017.

rivals facing fewer emissions regulations, Japan shelved their plan.[49] While there is a possibility of reviving the carbon trading discussion,[50] nothing has been confirmed at the time of writing.

7.5.2 *Indonesia*

The first Indonesian domestic carbon market, or Skema Karbon Nusantara, is being considered by the National Council on Climate Change of Indonesia.[51] The goals of this voluntary mechanism are to raise awareness before implementing a mandatory scheme. Raising awareness is a major issue, as Indonesia has been cited as the world's third largest producer of greenhouse gas emissions (from, often illegal, deforestation). Forests are sought to be protected through government categorization as village forests rather than participation in programs such as "Reducing Emissions from Deforestation and Forest Degradation" (REDD), in which developed countries can offset their carbon emissions by paying developing nations to protect their forests.[52]

The ICAO has made moves to assist Indonesia with the creation of appropriate mechanisms.[53] The ICAO's press release on the initiative[54] notes the agreed objectives include:

> a Master Plan for Indonesian legislative improvements on emissions, Green Flights and Green Airports operational programs, more efficient airspace design utilizing Performance-based Navigation guidelines, advice on appropriate market-based measures, as well as initiatives relating to alternative fuels and the development of a comprehensive emissions inventory.

49 Ibid.

50 C. Watanabe, "Japan may revive carbon trading discussion after election," *Bloomberg* (March 10, 2013), www.bloomberg.com/news/2013-03-10/japan-may-revive-carbon-trading-discussion-after-election.html last accessed October 28, 2017.

51 See for example, D. E. Hindarto, "Indoenisa's perspectives on future Carbon market," www.iges.or.jp/jp/archive/cdm/pdf/indonesia/20120216/DNPI_Dicky_NMM.pdf last accessed October 27, 2017.

52 A. Dewan, "Indonesian forest community rejects emissions trading," *Voice of America* (July 21, 2010), www.voanews.com/content/ndonesian-forest-community-rejects-emissions-trading-99010114/122414.html last accessed October 28, 2017.

53 ICAO, "ICAO to assist Indonesia with new aviation emissions reduction initiatives" (Press Release, March 27, 2013), www.icao.int/Newsroom/Pages/ICAO-to-assist-Indonesia-with-new-aviation-emissions-reduction-initiatives.aspx last accessed October 26, 2017.

54 Ibid. per Indonesia's Vice Minister of Transportation, Dr. Bambang Susantono.

7.5.3 *China*

China is yet to enact a dedicated law on climate change.[55] Only policy-level plans and a white paper have been issued. The National Plan for Addressing Climate Change in 2007 is the first overall policy document addressing climate change.[56] In 2008, China also issued a White Paper on China's Policies and Actions on Addressing Climate Change, which discusses the impact of climate change on the country and its responses to the threat.[57]

Recently, there has been an interesting development in emission trading systems. China has proceeded with the development of pilot emissions trading systems in seven municipalities and provinces, due to begin in 2013, with a view to a national scheme before 2020, and, in 2012, Shenzhen was one of seven designated areas in which the central government plans to roll out experimental carbon trading programs.[58] The trading scheme will cover 638 companies that are responsible for 38 percent of the city's total emissions and eventually expand to include transportation.[59] However, it is doubtful if the scheme will include air transportation.

7.5.4 *South Korea*

"Low Carbon, Green Growth" was one of the guiding principles of the former President Lee Myung-bak's administration. Accordingly, the Presidential Committee on Green Growth was established in January 2009 and the Framework Act on Low Carbon, Green Growth was enacted in December 2009. The foremost reason for the enactment of the Framework Act on Low Carbon, Green Growth is to implement measures to effectively address climate change and energy issues and promote sustainable development.[60] With regard to the transportation field, Article 53 (Establishment of

[55] D. Haifeng, "Chapter 6 China," in R. Lord, et al. (eds.), *Climate Change Liability – Transnational Law and Practice*, 117.

[56] Ibid.

[57] Ibid.

[58] J. Kaiman, "China unveils details of pilot carbo-trading programme", *The Guardian* (May 22, 2013), www.guardian.co.uk/environment/2013/may/22/china-carbon-trading-shenzhen last accessed October 28, 2017.

[59] Ibid.

[60] Ground for the enactment.

Low-Carbon Traffic Systems) of the Act set out the principle,[61] and Article 41 of the Enforcement Decree of the Framework Act on Low Carbon, Green Growth provides an obligation of implementing targets.[62] However, air transportation is not included.

As to emissions trading, the Act on Allocation and Trading of Greenhouse Gas Emissions Allowances was passed by the Korean parliament in May 2012 with bipartisan support for the legislation, and the Act was followed by a presidential decree that set out the detailed rules governing the scheme. In November 2012, the presidential decree implementing Korea's emissions trading scheme received official approval, which paves the way for the commencement of the ETS in 2015.[63] Although it is confirmed that a sectoral approach will be applied to the ETS, the question as to whether air transportation will be included has not been discussed.

More recently, the Global Green Growth Institute (GGGI) was formed – an international organization dedicated to supporting and promoting sustainable economic growth in developing countries and emerging economies. The GGGI was formed in 2012, at the Rio+20 United Nations Conference on Sustainable Development.

According to GGGI,

> in contrast to conventional development models that rely on the unsustainable depletion and destruction of natural resources, green growth is a coordinated advancement of economic growth, environmental sustainability,

[61] Art. 53 (1) The Government shall set and manage goals, etc. for the reduction of greenhouse gases, as prescribed by Presidential Decree, in order to develop the environment for reducing greenhouse gases in the traffic sector and to manage emission of greenhouse gases and energy efficiently.

[62] Art. 41 (Targets for Greenhouse Gas Reduction in Traffic Sector)

According to Art. 53 (1) of the Act, the Minister of Land, Transport and Maritime Affairs shall establish and implement targets for greenhouse gas reduction, energy saving, and energy efficiency in the traffic sector including each of the following, based on consultation with the heads of the central administrative agencies concerned:

1. Status of greenhouse gases emission and the rate of energy consumption by each means of transportation including automobiles, trains, airplanes, and vessels;
2. Status of greenhouse gases emitted by type of energy;
3. Five-year targets for greenhouse gas reduction, energy saving, and energy efficiency and the implementation plans; and
4. Annual targets for greenhouse gas reduction, energy saving, and energy efficiency and the implementation plans.

[63] "Next steps for Korea's emissions trading scheme," *Law 360* (January 2, 2013), www.law360.com/articles/403793/next-steps-for-korea-s-emission-trading-scheme last accessed October 27, 2017.

> poverty reduction and social inclusion driven by the sustainable development and use of global resources.
>
> GGGI is an interdisciplinary, multi-stakeholder organization that believes economic growth and environmental sustainability are not merely compatible objectives; their integration is essential for the future of humankind.[64]

GGGI is headquartered in Seoul.

7.6 FULLY OPERATIONAL CARBON-PRICING SCHEMES

Only two countries in the Asia-Pacific region can be said to have developed a full-fledged carbon-pricing mechanism with possible implications for the aviation sector: Australia and New Zealand.

7.6.1 *New Zealand*

New Zealand's ETS has been in operation since 2008 and was established by the Climate Change Response (Emissions Trading) Amendment Act 2008, which amended the Climate Change Response Act 2002.[65] The mandatory NZ ETS currently covers emissions from forestry, stationary energy, industrial processes, and liquid fossil fuels, which are collectively responsible for roughly 50 percent of New Zealand's emissions. Similar to the well-understood EU-ETS, the purpose of the scheme is to create a financial incentive for emitters of carbon to reduce their emissions. It operates by way of some organizations surrendering carbon credits[66] to account for their direct emissions or those associated with their products. NZUs may be earned or granted by the Government in certain cases.

The NZ ETS addresses emissions from the use of all liquid fossil fuels used in New Zealand such as petrol, diesel, aviation gasoline, jet kerosene, light fuel oil, and heavy fuel oil. Consistent with New Zealand's international obligations under the UNFCCC and the Kyoto Protocol,[67] emissions from

64 See Global Green Growth Institute, "Council," http://gggi.org/about/the-council/ last accessed October 27, 2017.

65 *Climate Change Response (Emissions Trading) Amendment Act 2008*, Parliamentary Counsel Office, New Zealand, www.legislation.govt.nz/act/public/2008/0085/latest/whole.html#DLM1130933 last accessed October 28, 2017.

66 Known as New Zealand Units (NZUs). One NZU is equivalent to one tonne of carbon dioxide equivalent emissions. Other units can be traded: Ministry for the Environment, www.climatechange.govt.nz/emissions-trading-scheme/obligations/surrendering-units.html last accessed October 27, 2017.

67 *Kyoto Protocol to the United Nations Framework Convention on Climate Change* (adopted March 16, 1998, entered into force February 16, 2005) 2303 UNTS 148 [*Kyoto Protocol*].

international aviation and marine transport are excluded from the scheme, but emissions from domestic flights are covered by the ETS regardless of the carrier that purchases the fuel.[68] The importance of domestic aviation in New Zealand should not be understated, even though it is a (relatively) small nation, with a population of only just above 4 million. A 2011 report indicated over 200,000 domestic flights make over 13 million seats annually available to passengers.[69]

7.6.2 *Australia*

Australia passed legislation in 2011 to develop a national ETS.[70] The scheme commenced operation on July 1, 2012 and involves a carbon-pricing mechanism fixed for the first three years (2012–15), which will rise at 2.5 percent in real terms per year. It applies to emissions from domestic aviation, domestic shipping, rail transport, and nontransport use of fuels, but does not apply to household transport fuels, light vehicle business transport, and off-road fuel use by the agriculture, forestry, and fishing industries. The price is fixed each year for 2012–15, starting at $23 a tonne in 2012–13. From 2015–16 the price was to be set by the market. In place now, following a change in federal government, is a legislative safeguard mechanism that uses historical information on those companies that produce the most greenhouse gas emissions, to in effect cap them.[71] Under the present Government's policy, emissions must be kept under a government-mandated limit, and those companies can then pay for credits to pay for emissions that exceed the cap.

Australia's (then) Department of Infrastructure and Transport noted this measure would fully capture domestic aviation emissions from July 1, 2012,

[68] These are called "obligation fuels" under Regulation 4 of the *Climate Change (Liquid Fossil Fuels) Regulations 2008*, Parliamentary Counsel Office, New Zealand, www.legislation.govt.nz/regulation/public/2008/0356/latest/DLM1635601.html last accessed October 27, 2017.

[69] See the Oxford Economics Report, "Economic benefits from air transport in New Zealand," www.benefitsofaviation.aero/Documents/Benefits-of-Aviation-New-Zealand-2011.pdf last accessed October 27, 2017.

[70] See *Clean Energy Act 2011; Clean Energy (Consequential Amendments) Act 2011; Climate Change Authority Act 2011; Clean Energy (Unit Shortfall Charge – General) Act 2011; Clean Energy (Unit Issue Charge – Fixed Charge) Act 2011; Clean Energy (Unit Issue Charge – Auctions) Act 2011; Clean Energy (Charges – Excise) Act 2011; Ozone Protection and Synthetic Greenhouse Gas (Manufacture Levy) Amendment Act 2011; Carbon Credits (Carbon Farming Initiative) Act 2011; Clean Energy Regulations 2011; Australian National Registry of Emissions Units Regulations 2011.*

[71] See Australia, *National Greenhouse and Energy Reporting Act 2007*, www.environment.gov.au/system/files/pages/dbabd13c-f8f1-49cd-ab40-621f056de35a/files/es-safeguard-rule.pdf last accessed October 27, 2017.

and on the international level "discussions are continuing within ICAO on the development of a market-based measures framework for international aviation ... through ICAO."[72]

The carbon price was expected to transition to a flexible price cap and trade emissions trading scheme from July 1, 2015, but due to a change in government policy a new Emissions Reduction Fund, part of the Government's Direct Action Plan to cut greenhouse gas emissions to 5 percent below 2000 levels by 2020 and to 26–28 percent below 2005 levels by 2030, was developed and was in consultation at the time of writing. It comprises "a fund to purchase emissions reductions and a safeguard mechanism to ensure that these reductions are not displaced by a significant rise in emissions above business-as-usual levels elsewhere in the economy."[73]

Legislation for the Emissions Reduction Fund was passed in November 2014. This established the framework for the safeguard mechanism in the National Greenhouse and Energy Reporting Act 2007. The entity with operational control of a designated large facility will be responsible for meeting safeguard requirements, including that the facility must keep net emissions at or below certain baseline emissions levels. The safeguard mechanism will commence on July 1, 2016.

On August 28, 2012, the Australian Minister for Climate Change and Energy Efficiency, and the European Commissioner for Climate Action, announced Australia and the EU will link their ETSs by no later than July 1, 2018,[74] an initiative that has not been retracted, and which would, if pursued, increase the prospect of an intercontinental carbon price in the medium term. This linking of ETSs, as the EU puts it, will form the basis of "bottom-up" linking of compatible emissions trading systems.[75] The benefits advanced by the EU include "reducing the cost of cutting emissions, increasing market liquidity, making the carbon price more stable, leveling

[72] *Managing the Carbon Footprint of Australian Aviation*, Australia's Action Plan developed in response to the ICAO 2010 Assembly Resolution A37–10, November 2012.

[73] The Exposure Draft Explanatory Statement sets out the policy behind the reform, and is available at Department of the Environment and Energy, www.environment.gov.au/system/files/pages/dbabd13c-f8f1-49cd-ab40-621f056de35a/files/es-safeguard-rule.pdf last accessed October 28, 2017.

[74] See http://www.cleanenergyregulator.gov.au last accessed October 28, 2017 and European Commission, "Australia and European Commission agree on pathway towards fully linking emissions trading systems" (August 28, 2012), ec.europa.eu/clima/news/articles/news_2012082801_en.htm last accessed October 28, 2017.

[75] European Commission, "International carbon market (policies on emissions trading system)," https://ec.europa.eu/clima/policies/ets/markets_en#tab-0-0 last accessed October 27, 2018.

the international playing field and supporting global cooperation on climate change."[76] Both Australia and the EU are considering further bilateral links with compatible or "credible international schemes."[77] The EU-ETS was also extended to several EU neighbors and negotiations are ongoing for a bilateral EU–Switzerland agreement.[78]

The Australian legislation, at present, contains some flexibility to allow Australian domestic airlines to better manage their carbon-cost liability, somewhat similarly to the way they hedge against fuel prices. Thus, Associate Professor David Hodgkinson notes airlines may opt-in[79] to the Australian ETS from mid-2013 through an arrangement provided for in the Clean Energy Act 2011 rather than pay a carbon price through amendments to fuel tax credit and excise schemes.[80]

7.7 POTENTIAL LESSONS FROM THE REGION GOING FORWARD

The outlook for the international legal resolution of a market-based measure for aviation emissions reduction is bleak. But perhaps it is this pessimism that needs to be acknowledged and accepted, to encourage and secure the kind of cooperation needed within the ICAO to reach a workable solution.[81]

The alternatives may well stem from the "bottom-up" collective linkages being created between regional or single-state ETSs, such as the bilateral trade link that will be forged between the EU and Australia. This model of cooperation could be an alternative to stalling multilateral negotiations on a global regime.[82] The repetition of bilateral agreements could develop a "minilateral" regime over the shorter term.[83] In such a "minilateral" regime, umbrella global agreements would only need to define how these national or regional

[76] Ibid.

[77] See *supra*, Note 27.

[78] Ibid. see also European Commission, "International carbon market," ec.europa.eu/clima/policies/ets/markets/index_en.htm last accessed October 27, 2017.

[79] See "See you in court: Solving aviation emissions is an international mess," *The Conversation* (February 7, 2012), theconversation.com/see-you-in-court-solving-aviation-emissions-is-an-international-mess-5183 last accessed October 28, 2017.

[80] *Clean Energy Act 2011*, part 3, div.7; *Clean Energy Regulations 2011*.

[81] See comments by Associate Professor David Hodgkinson at *The Conversation*, theconversation.com/not-even-nobel-prize-winners-can-fix-aviation-emissions-13266 last accessed October 28, 2017.

[82] See D. Hodgkinson, "Airlines, climate change and carbon pricing," Clayton UTZ www.claytonutz.com.au/publications/edition/08_december_2011/20111208/airlines_climate_change_and_carbon_pricing.page.

[83] K. Kulovesi, "Addressing sectoral emissions outside the United Nations Framework Convention on Climate Change: What roles for multilateralism, minilateralism and

regimes interact with each other in relation to, for example, the controversial charging of aviation emissions over the high seas. Whereas the "minilateral" regime on ETS could be cross-sectoral, global agreements may be more efficiently negotiated where they seek to address international aviation emissions, within the auspices of specialized organizations such as, with regard to aviation, the ICAO.

With regard to aviation at least, a "minilateral" approach could most practically be fostered through the auspices of international organizations, whereas a purely multilateral approach on the market-based measures themselves, and their multilateral harmonization, would necessitate considerable aero-political wrangling. If the regional clusters of ETSs produce and accede to their own acceptable regional aviation market-based measures (minus international aviation emissions), then the ICAO need only broker a deal among the regional clusters to agree on how those clusters will deal with each other in terms of *international* emissions (e.g. each region bilaterally and reciprocally agrees to include provisions for 50 percent of the emissions over the high seas for flights between both regional clusters, to avoid double imposition [or payments] by carriers of all the relevant states). Such proposals may find favor with airlines.[84]

A further advantage of a bilateral approach is that, while it is not the most elegant or logically satisfying of solutions, bilateralism and regionalism has a strong history of *actually working* in public international, and public international *aviation*, relations. The complex patchwork of air services agreements in place around the world was arguably brought about by the failure of the International Civil Aviation Conference of 1944[85] to accomplish a multilateral exchange of traffic rights (except in a limited sense, as a side agreement).[86] However, that system has been a workable and productive means of ensuring the growth of international air transport, and has ensured its economic sustainability since the ICAO's inception. Notably, not a single multilateral

unilateralism?" *Review of European Community and International Environmental Law*, **21** (2012) 193.

84 Airlines typically need certainty of regulation on which to base their operations, and it is on their shoulders (and on their customers' shoulders) that costs from market-based measures will ultimately fall.

85 The conference resulted in the adoption of the Convention on International Civil Aviation signed in Chicago.

86 P. S. Dempsey, *Public International Air Law* (Montreal: Centre for Research in Air and Space Law, 2008) at 43.

agreement on the commercial aspects of international air transport has been successfully implemented thus far."[87]

7.8 CONCLUSION

At its 39th Session in 2016, the ICAO Assembly adopted Resolution A39–3, titled *Consolidated statement of continuing ICAO policies and practices related to environmental protection – Global Market-based Measure (MBM) scheme*. The crux of this resolution is the decision to implement a global market-based measure scheme in the form of the Carbon Offsetting and Reduction Scheme for International Aviation (CORSIA). It is too early to declare that CORSIA is a success story. The success of CORSIA will depend on its implementation and enforcement. Although it is challenging, it is important to make every effort to implement CORSIA through the ICAO. If, however, CORSIA does not work, contrary to the high expectations, alternative approaches should be considered.

Whether the EU–Australia approach, or others like it, will succeed and thereby prompt the kind of "minilateralism" discussed herein, remains to be seen. The authors consider the Asia-Pacific region may hold the conceptual key to a potential global solution for market-based measures in reducing international aviation emissions, in the potential experimental joining of the Australian and EU carbon markets. As with the current state of play with air services agreements, which has taken over sixty years to develop, it may be a considerable time before such an approach (without further guidance from the ICAO) results in the newly emerging Australia–EU type arrangement spawning further partners in the region, and thereafter stimulating expansion of such clusters elsewhere. However, it is clear that the needs of the region demand acceleration of international emissions mitigation regulatory progress.

[87] For example, in 2001 the United States signed the Multilateral Agreement on the Liberalization of International Air Transportation (MALIAT) with Brunei, Chile, New Zealand, and Singapore. Likewise, there is the EU–US Open Skies Agreement, signed in 2007, which became effective March 30, 2008, and the ASEAN Multilateral Agreement on Air Services adopted on November 12, 2010.

8

Sustainable Aviation and the Transfer of Environmentally Sound Technologies to Africa

Paradoxes, Barriers, and Prospects

Damilola S. Olawuyi

Sustainable aviation is often propounded as a pathway for promoting efficiency within the aviation sector, while reducing the emission of greenhouse gases from aircraft and other aviation facilities. Attaining sustainable aviation in practice requires large-scale investment in environmentally sound technologies (ESTs) that reduce pollution, use resources in a sustainable manner, utilize renewable sources of energy, and handle all residual waste in a more environmentally acceptable way. Most important are "cleaner" and energy-efficient aircraft, improved facilities for air traffic control and management, and alternative/renewable fuel options.

Current realities, however, show that the availability, affordability, and accessibility of new and cleaner technologies that could promote sustainable aviation remain a huge concern in many African countries. Transferring the requisite ESTs to Africa is often not the most straightforward endeavor. This is mainly due to legal, institutional, and bureaucratic hurdles that make the process challenging and daunting.

This chapter takes a look at the legal and institutional barriers to sustainable aviation in Africa. Drawing examples from Nigeria, South Africa, and Ethiopia, it discusses how legal and governance questions may continue to derail opportunities and efforts to facilitate the transfer of aviation technologies into Africa. Even though some of the legal barriers are preexisting and are not specific to aviation technologies, they must be addressed with respect to aviation, considering the large infrastructural development and technologies required for sustainable aviation projects.

8.1 INTRODUCTION

The central focus of this chapter is to highlight and discuss legal and institutional barriers to the transfer of sustainable aviation technologies to Africa.

The International Civil Aviation Organization (ICAO) has been at the forefront of promoting drastic cuts in greenhouse gas (GHG) emissions from aviation. According to the ICAO, a transition from dirty aviation to a more sustainable aviation future would require technological and operational measures; state action plans; sustainable alternative fuels; Market-based Measures (MBMs); and global aspirational goals to promote cleaner and more efficient technologies in the aviation sector.[1] Reducing emissions from aviation would, to a large extent, depend on the availability, accessibility, and affordability of environmentally sound technologies (ESTs) that aid the transition from old, inefficient, and environmentally unsound technologies and aviation facilities to cleaner and energy-efficient ones.[2]

Furthermore, chapter 34 of Agenda 21 emphasizes that ESTs protect the environment, are less polluting, leverage aviation resources in a more sustainable manner, recycle waste and by-products, and handle residual wastes in a more acceptable manner than the technologies for which they substitute.[3] ESTs in the aviation sector would result in a drastic cut in emissions associated with flying. Through fleet upgrades and renewals; "cleaner" and energy efficient aircrafts, improved facilities for air traffic control and management, and alternative/renewable fuel options, and robust technological infrastructure that would support the migration to more sustainable aviation practices, countries could begin to make progress in adopting cleaner methods of aviation. To attain these objectives, a number of countries have put together voluntary national action plans to reduce CO_2 emissions from international civil aviation and to promote sustainable and carbon neutral aviation.[4]

1 ICAO, "Consolidated statement of continuing ICAO policies and practices related to environmental protection – Climate change," Res A37–1 (2010).

2 Ibid. See also International Transport Forum, "Reducing transport GHG emissions: Opportunities and Costs," http://admin.indiaenvironmentportal.org.in/files/GHGsum.pdf last accessed March 14, 2016.

3 United Nations, "Agenda 21 – Chapter 34, transfer of environmentally sound technology, cooperation and capacity-building" (United Nations Conference on Environment and Development, Rio de Janeiro, Brazil, June 3–14, 1992).

4 Currently twenty-five countries/regional groups have submitted to the ICAO their respective Action Plans aimed at reducing greenhouse gas emissions from aviation. They include Australia, Austria, Brazil, Canada, Central American States, China, Denmark, Finland, France, Germany, Greece, Hungary, Iceland, Ireland, Italy, Nepal, Norway, Slovak Republic, Sri Lanka, Sweden, Switzerland, Thailand, Trinidad and Tobago, United Kingdom, and United States. Notably, no African country has submitted an Action Plan on emissions reduction. See for example "Canada's action plan to reduce green-house gas emissions from aviation," www.icao.int/environmental-protection/Documents/ActionPlan/AviationGHGActionPan_En.pdf last accessed October 29, 2017; See also Action Plan of Central America to Reduce Emissions from International Civil Aviation (CAAPER); and

Despite increased global awareness of and drives for sustainable aviation, African countries continue to grapple unsuccessfully with the concept. A major challenge facing the continent is that cleaner and more efficient technologies that are required to foster sustainable aviation are either unavailable, or, where they are available, there is a dearth of human capacity to maintain or optimally utilize them. This concern is not new; it was in fact envisaged by climate change negotiators as far back as 1992 when the United Nations Framework Convention on Climate Change (UNFCCC) was adopted. Article 4(1) (c) of the UNFCCC therefore enjoins industrialized countries to promote and cooperate in the transfer of technologies, practices, and processes that control, reduce, or prevent anthropogenic emissions of greenhouse gases in the transport sector.[5] Article 4 (5) also provides that developed countries shall promote, facilitate, and finance, as appropriate, the transfer of, or access to, environmentally sound technologies and know-how needed by the developing country parties to meet the targets of emission reductions. Developed countries therefore have general obligations to facilitate the transfer of ESTs to developing countries in order to foster emission reduction in key sectors and sub-sectors, such as transportation and aviation.

However, the extent to which these ambitious provisions of the UNFCCC have resulted in the transfer of ESTs to African countries remains doubtful. While technologies and measures that promote sustainable aviation, such as the use of alternative fuels, have increasingly become available in many industrialized states, a number of African countries are still unable to access, deploy, and utilize these newer technologies.[6] Arguably, this is mainly due to a number of regulatory and institutional barriers that hinder the transfer of advanced biofuel technologies, technology enhancements, engineering/infrastructural improvements, and improved air traffic control gadgets that could reduce emissions in Africa's aviation sector.

For African countries to attract robust renewal of aviation infrastructure and benefit from technology transfer provisions of the UNFCCC, the appropriate starting point is to create a legal framework that defines sustainable aviation priorities and then removes institutional, regulatory, and bureaucratic barriers

Brazil's *Flight path to Aviation Biofuels in Brazil: Action Plan*, www.fapesp.br/publicacoes/flightpath-to-aviation-biofuels-in-brazil-action-plan.pdf last accessed April 16, 2018.

5 *United Nations Framework Convention on Climate Change* (adopted January 20, 1994) A/RES/48/189.

6 Le Grange and Buys, for example, document how several legal, bureaucratic, and regulatory barriers hinder the transfer of aviation technologies to South Africa. See L. Le Grange and A. J. Buys, "The management of maintenance technology transfer in the South African aviation industry," *South African Journal of Industrial Engineering*, **13** (2002), 81–99.

to the smooth transfer of ESTs that could aid sustainable aviation. This chapter unpacks some of the legal and institutional barriers that stifle the transfer of aviation technologies into Africa. These barriers include the absence of comprehensive aviation action plans on sustainable aviation, archaic laws on technology transfer, inadequate legal protection for intellectual property rights, lack of intergovernmental cooperation of technology transfer, the absence of a coordinated focal point or institution on technology transfer, and the hectic bureaucratic process in securing governmental permits for technology transfer. While some of these barriers are preexisting and are not peculiar to the aviation sector alone, this chapter demonstrates how they particularly hinder the capacity of African countries to attain any meaningful progress in the global quest for sustainable aviation.

This chapter is divided into four sections. Following this introductory section, Section 8.2 analyzes the meaning of sustainable aviation within a developing country context. Efforts to propagate the sustainable aviation message in low income countries in Africa would only be tenable if it spearheads a radical transformation of existing aviation technologies, opens the door to newer jobs for local communities, reduces the cost of aviation to make it accessible to the poor, and promotes sustained economic growth. Section 8.2 will highlight the absence of adequate technologies to move this idea of "sustainable aviation" from the realm of theory to practice in many African countries. Section 8.3 identifies legal and institutional barriers to technology transfer in Africa. It discusses preexisting and unique concerns to the transfer of aviation technologies that hinder progress in efforts to achieve sustainable aviation in Africa. Section 8.4 discusses how legal and institutional frameworks on aviation in African states can be revitalized to remove barriers to the transfer of aviation technologies.

8.2 SUSTAINABLE AVIATION: A DEVELOPING COUNTRY PERSPECTIVE

The concept of sustainable aviation draws heavily from general notions of sustainability and sustainable development, concepts that have been heavily theorized under public international law. The most commonly cited definition of sustainable development is the definition provided by the Brundtland Commission: "development that meets the needs of the present without compromising the ability of future generations to meet their own needs."[7]

7 The United Nations World Commission on Environment and Development Report (the Brundtland Report), "Our common future" (Oxford: Oxford University Press, 1987). See also M. C. C. Segger and A. Khalfan, *Sustainable Development Law: Principles, Practices and*

Article 3(1) of the 2002 Convention for Cooperation in the Protection and Sustainable Development of the Marine and Coastal Environment of the Northeast Pacific also defines sustainable development in terms of economic growth with social equity through the transformation of production methods and consumption patterns, sustained by the ecological balance and life support systems of the region.[8] Sustainability emphasizes the need to protect the environment while pursuing economic growth and development. As the International Court of Justice (ICJ) noted in the *Gabcikovo–Nagymaros* case, the need to reconcile economic development with the protection of the environment is aptly expressed in the concept of sustainable development.[9] Furthermore, the Rio+20 United Nations World Summit on Sustainable Development, held in 2012, specifically identifies the three mutually reinforcing pillars of sustainable development as economic development, social development, and environmental development.[10]

In the context of aviation, the 2010 ICAO Assembly adopted *Resolution* A37–19, which promotes a suite of measures aimed at achieving a balance among the three pillars of sustainability – social, economic, and environmental.[11] The ICAO advocates for technological and operational measures, state action plans; sustainable alternative fuels; Market-based Measures (MBMs); and global aspirational goals to ensure the long-term sustainability of aviation.[12] This predominantly requires the use of alternative fuels such as biofuels; use of low-carbon technology, environmentally friendly materials, new aircraft systems, and sustainable energy sources; reducing the impact of air transport operations on noise and local air quality around airports; and reducing GHG emissions from aircraft through aircraft that are more fuel-efficient and quieter. There is already increased progress in ensuring that

Prospects (Oxford: Oxford University Press, 2004) 45–50; D. French, *International Law and Policy of Sustainable Development* (Manchester: Manchester University Press, 2005) 51.

8 United Nations Environment Program (UNEP), 2002 *Convention for Cooperation in the Protection and Sustainable Development of the Marine and Coastal Environment of the Northeast Pacific* (adopted February 18, 2002), https://wedocs.unep.org/bitstream/handle/20.500.11822/11135/nep_convention_en.pdf?sequence=1&isAllowed=y last accessed April 16, 2018. [*Antigua Convention*]

9 Case Concerning the Gabcikovo–Nagymaros Dam *(Hungary* v. *Slovakia)* [1998] ICJ Rep. 7, 37 ILM 162 (1998).

10 UN, 2012A/CONF.216/L.1 (Rio de Janeiro, Brazil, June 20–22). For a description of economic development, social development, and environmental protection as interdependent and mutually reinforcing pillars of sustainable development see UNGA, Res A/RES/64/236, https://undocs.org/A/RES/64/236 last accessed April 16, 2018.

11 ICAO, "Consolidated statement of continuing ICAO policies and practices related to environmental protection – Climate change," Res A37–19.

12 Ibid.

aviation does not produce environmental pollution or irreversible social impacts. For example, a number of airlines in Europe and North America now run on jatropha, camelina, animal fats, and used cooking oils to reduce GHG emissions from conventional energy sources.[13] The ICAO has also developed a CO_2 emissions calculator for passenger flights; a fuel savings estimation tool (IFSET); and a green meetings calculator as toolkits for achieving these low GHG emissions in air travel.[14]

Despite this renewed awareness and progress, however, global efforts aimed at promoting sustainable aviation are often faced with the realization of the intricate social dynamics of the wholesale upgrade of airport facilities in many African countries, where the requisite technologies are either unavailable, or, where they are available, there is a dearth of human capacity to maintain them or to properly put them to use.[15] As Biru notes, while commenting on the lack of training facilities and human capacity in Ethiopia's aviation sector, Africa as a whole has a huge deficit and need when it comes to aviation training and capacity development.[16] Lack of the requisite skilled, reliable, and experienced workforce needed to implement the precepts of sustainable aviation remains a fundamental impediment facing the African continent.[17]

[13] On October 6, 2011, Thomson Airways became the first commercial flight in Europe to fly using biofuels. The Boeing 757–200 carried 232 passengers from Birmingham Airport, United Kingdom, to Arrecife using a sustainable biofuel blend in one engine. From 2011, the Dutch airline KLM says it has used 50 percent biokerosene derived from recycled cooking oil (collected in the EU and refined in the United States) on 200 flights between Paris and Amsterdam. In 2012, The European Commission, in coordination with Airbus, leading European airlines such as Lufthansa, Air France/KLM, and British Airways, and key European biofuel producers (Neste Oil, Biomass Technology Group and UOP), launched an initiative to speed up the commercialization of aviation biofuels in Europe. See European Technology and Innovation Platform, www.etipbioenergy.eu last accessed April 16, 2018; also EIA, "The potential and role of biofuel in commercial air transport", https://advancedbiofuelsusa.info/the-potential-role-of-biofuels-in-commercial-air-transport-biojetfuel/ last accessed April 16, 2018.

[14] See ICAO, "ICAO Carbon emissions calculator" (2012).

[15] I. Biru, "The need and challenges of harmonizing CAA trainings in Africa" (ICAO, Aviation Panel 3).

[16] Ibid.

[17] See the 2012 *Abuja Declaration on Aviation Safety in Africa* (adopted on July 20, 2012, in Abuja, Nigeria), www.afcac.org/en/documents/conferences/october2012/15wp4c.pdf last accessed March 10, 2016, which decries the "insufficient number of competent/skilled aviation professionals for ensuring aviation safety in Africa." See also African Union, "African civil aviation policy" (2nd session of the African Union Conference of Ministers Responsible for Transport, November 21–25, 2011, Luanda, Angola) stating that "there is a growing insufficiency in qualified personnel that is worsened by attrition to other markets commonly referred to as 'brain drain' and high turnover of middle and senior managers particularly in government owned institutions" para. 1.2.7.

Furthermore, in a number of African countries, current aviation infrastructure is dilapidated, unsafe, and outdated. While African countries such as South Africa, Morocco, Egypt, and Tunisia have fared comparably well in aviation infrastructure and safety, there remains a desperate need in several African countries, especially in sub-Saharan Africa, to upgrade and modernize aviation facilities to catch up with international standards. Due to poor infrastructure and inadequate regulatory emphasis on safety, aviation fatalities in Africa remain over twelve times greater than the global average.[18] For example, in Nigeria, Africa's most populous nation, many years of corruption, neglect, and inadequate maintenance have resulted in a largely dysfunctional aviation sector, which has been bedeviled by fatal crashes, unprecedented inefficiency, and infrastructural decay. These problems have seen a number of international aircraft operating in or passing through Nigeria being faced with incessant cases of power outages at airports, herds of cows on a runway, obsolete safety facilities, dysfunctional information and communication systems, and potholes in runways.[19] Where facilities are available, they are often antiquated, mainly due to many years of zero upgrades or the consistent proliferation of cheap and disused aviation facilities into Nigeria by unscrupulous state authorities.[20] For example, Nigeria is currently one of the most consistent locations for old and disused airplanes. A number of airlines run on ageing but meticulously refurbished and repainted airplanes, which were not designed to use alternative fuels, while a number of designated international airports in Nigeria are surviving on ancient imported air traffic control and communication technologies and equipment that barely work.

Mauritania, Mali, Niger, Chad, Uganda, Central African Republic, and the Republic of the Congo all present even more worrisome situations in which

[18] See International Air Transport Association (IATA) Safety Performance Results for 2011–2015 at www.iata.org/pressroom/pr/pages/2011-02-23-01.aspx last accessed March 10, 2016.

As of January 2016, only twenty-one African States had accomplished at least 60 percent implementation of the ICAO's safety-related standards and recommended practices (SARPS), see www.iata.org/pressroom/pr/Pages/2016-02-15-01.aspx last accessed March 10, 2016.

[19] "Plane hits cows on Nigeria runway," *BBC News* (2005), news.bbc.co.uk/2/hi/africa/4659281.stm last accessed April 16, 2018. See generally C. Eze, "Nigeria: Impediments, challenges to aviation sector growth" (All Africa Report, 2012). Also A. Amwe and D. Jonathan, "An appraisal of Nigerian transport sector: Evidence from the railway and aviation subsectors," *Journal of Economics and Sustainable Development*, 4 (2013), 6–9.

[20] G. Odidi, "Challenges facing the aviation industry in Nigeria," *The Nigerian Voice* (June 5, 2012).

radio communication and radar coverage, GPS and performance-based navigation (PBN), precision approaches, near-real-time weather and good airports gadgets, are at worst, nonexistent, or at best archaic and unreliable.[21] To speak of sustainable aviation under such models may therefore be an illusion.[22] In many of these referenced countries, environmental objectives, such as switching to aircraft that utilize Sustainable Alternative Fuels (SUSTAF), utilizing a CO_2 emissions calculator for passenger flights, adopting a fuel savings estimation tool (IFSET), and leveraging a green meetings calculator, are simply relegated to the background due to several preexisting infrastructural deficits in the aviation sector.[23]

Considering current infrastructure, capacity, and technology gaps in aviation sector governance in many African states, global action plans to reinforce sustainable aviation practices must, to be effective, deliver coherent economic, environmental, and social outcomes. From an economic and financial perspective, a key question is how international climate finance mechanisms under the international climate can *facilitate and assist* developing countries to access financial resources, technology transfer, and capacity building required for low-carbon and cheaper aviation.[24] The international legal regime must ensure a systemic and coherent commitment to the

[21] See "Assessing Africa's aviation infrastructure," *Aviation Week*, aviationweek.com/bca/assessing-africa-s-aviation-infrastructure last accessed October 28, 2017, stating that the best infrastructure in Africa can be found in the arid north (Morocco and Egypt), sub-Saharan west (Senegal, Guinea, Ivory Coast, and Ghana), in some states along the eastern coast (Kenya, Rwanda, and Tanzania) and in the extreme south (Republic of South Africa, which is the cream of the crop).

[22] The European Union has gone as far as banning several African airlines from flying in Europe due to their inability to comply with safety and technical upgrade standards. Thirteen of the seventeen countries affected by the EU ban are from Africa, with a total of 111 African airlines blacklisted. See EC, Commission Regulation (EC) No 474/2006 of March 22, 2006 establishing the Community list of air carriers that are subject to an operating ban within the Community referred to in Chapter II of Regulation (EC) No 2111/2005 of the European Parliament and of the Council, OJ 2006, L 84/14, as amended. See further European Union, "List of airlines banned within the EU," ec.europa.eu/transport/modes/air/safety/air-ban/search_en.htm last accessed October 27, 2017.

[23] See African Union, *African Civil Aviation Policy, supra* Note 17, at paras. 1.2.4 and 12, which note that due to inadequate financing for aviation infrastructure, human resource development, and airline capitalization, Africa continues to lag behind the rest of the world in the quest for a sustainable and environmentally friendly civil aviation industry.

[24] African Union, *African Civil Aviation Policy*, ibid.; the ICAO High Level Meeting (see HLM-ENV/09) in October 2009 agreed on, "further elaboration on measures to assist developing States and to facilitate access to financial resources, technology transfer and capacity building"; also, the Abuja Declaration, which decries the inadequacy of financial resources to ensure aviation safety in Africa.

TABLE 8.1 *Sustainable development matrix*

Social dimensions	Economic dimensions	Environmental dimensions
Improved quality of life due to less pollution and noise from airports	Sustained in-flow of infrastructural investments in the aviation sector	Reduction of GHG emissions and the use of fossil fuels; reduced air and water pollution
	Carbon neutral growth in the aviation sector	Reduced aircraft noise
Poverty alleviation through increased employment opportunities in the aviation sector	Financial returns to local aviation companies; creation of new growth opportunities	Reduced pressure on local environments and improved local air quality
	Availability of flights at affordable rates (new technologies should not result in higher fares)	Harmonization of routes to reduce environmental impacts
Improved stakeholder engagement in the design of aviation policies; capacity-building opportunities for stakeholders in the aviation sector	Transfer of environmentally sound technologies (ESTs) to replace old and dirty technologies	Meeting local renewable energy portfolio standards and other environmental standards

founding principle and need to "promote, facilitate and finance the transfer of, or access to, environmentally sound technologies and know-how needed by the developing country parties to meet the targets of emission reductions."[25]

As indicated in Table 8.1, sustainable aviation in the African context, arguably, goes above and beyond shifting to low carbon fuels or practices in the aviation sector. Achieving sustainable aviation in Africa requires technology transfer, capacity development, and financial assistance to address several preexisting infrastructural deficits. The international drive for sustainable aviation will only be meaningful and successful in the Africa context if underpinned by the transfer of ESTs that could facilitate renewal and upgrade of aircrafts, foster a holistic revamp of current infrastructure to first of all bring them to speed, and then a near 100 percent replacement with newer and more efficient technology. This would be followed by capacity development to train stakeholders in the aviation sector on how to properly utilize these new technologies.

[25] *United Nations Framework Convention on Climate Change, supra* Note 5, Art. 4 (1).

Furthermore, there is need for sustainable aviation technology and measures that impose minimal financial or economic pressure on fragile economies in several African states. For example, how will costs of airport and flight upgrades be allocated in many African countries where air travel costs are already considered to be exorbitant and the exclusive preserve of the rich? This question of allocating costs of aircraft technology improvements and upgrades is a key contributor to the continued use of old and dilapidated aviation infrastructure in many African states.[26] As airlines strive for profitability, and members of the public protest against marginal increases in airfares, issues of safety, technology upgrades, aircraft efficiency, low-carbon aviation, and proper aircraft maintenance have taken a back seat. To facilitate sustainable aviation in Africa, tailored mechanisms, such as the UN Technology Mechanism, must be enhanced and implemented to provide developing countries with requisite aviation-specific technology and high-performance aviation infrastructure at low to moderate costs.[27] Without tailored aviation technology deployment mechanisms, many African countries will simply not be willing, or able, to afford the cost of shifting to sustainable and low carbon aviation.

Despite this reality, technology transfer to many African states has not been the easiest endeavor. The international climate regime, through the Technology Executive Committee (TEC), has therefore increasingly recognized the need for national systems innovations (NSI) to address and remove barriers to climate technology development and transfer in developing countries.[28] The next section examines key barriers to technology deployment and transfer that must be addressed in African states to foster the transfer of sustainable aviation technology.

[26] See The Infrastructure Consortium for Africa, "Opening up aviation services in Africa" (African Development Bank) para. 35–66, www.icafrica.org/fileadmin/documents/Publications/Opening_up_Aviation_Services_in_Africa_-_Phase_1_Review_Report.pdf last accessed March 10, 2016, discussing high operational costs and pressure to reduce fare price as some of the key barriers to the development of aviation in Africa.

[27] The Conference of the Parties (COP), by decision 1/CP.16, established a Technology Mechanism comprising a Technology Executive Committee (TEC) and a Climate Technology Centre and Network (CTCN) to facilitate the implementation of enhanced action on technology development and transfer to support action on mitigation and adaptation. For example, the Joint report of the Technology Mechanism, released in 2015, fails to discuss aviation or measures aimed at enhancing sustainable aviation technology development and transfer. Conference of the Parties on its sixteenth session, held in Cancun from November 29 to December 10, 2010.

[28] See UNFCCC, Decision 12/CP.21, "Enhancing climate technology development and transfer through the technology mechanism" (Conference of the Parties Twenty-first session Paris, November 30 to December 11, 2015).

8.3 LEGAL BARRIERS TO TECHNOLOGY TRANSFER

Technology transfer is the dissemination of know-how, experience, and equipment among different stakeholders such as governments, private sector entities, financial institutions, NGOs, and research education institutions.[29] With respect to sustainable aviation, it includes the movement of cleaner aviation facilities and technologies from countries where they are readily available for use in other countries where they are not. Despite the prevailing rhetoric on the transfer of sustainable aviation technologies into Africa, the practical reality is that not a lot has been achieved. For example, although the international climate regime has established a Technology Mechanism that will assist developing countries to assess and meet their climate technology needs, much of the work of the mechanism has failed to focus on aviation.[30] This lack of a coherent and system integration of international efforts to promote the transfer of ESTs in the aviation sector, coupled with local barriers to technology deployment and transfer, continue to stifle the abilities of developing countries in Africa to access the required technology needed to revitalize aviation infrastructure.[31] This section highlights and discusses some preexisting legal and institutional concerns that generally stifle and frustrate the transfer and proliferation of sustainable aviation technologies in Africa's aviation sector.

8.3.1 *Absence of Comprehensive Sustainable Aviation Action Plans*

As earlier noted, a number of countries have, in response to the ICAO's call, come up with voluntary sustainable aviation action plans to reduce GHG emissions from domestic and international civil aviation.[32] Such action plans

29 See Intergovernmental Panel on Climate Change (IPCC), *Climate Change 2001: Synthesis Report. A Contribution of Working Groups I, II, and III to the First Assessment Report of the Intergovernmental Panel on Climate Change* (Cambridge University Press, 2001). See also Draft International Code on the Transfers of Technology, 1985.

30 The Conference of the Parties (COP), by decision 1/CP.16, established a Technology Mechanism comprising a Technology Executive Committee (TEC) and a Climate Technology Centre and Network (CTCN) to facilitate the implementation of enhanced action on technology development and transfer to support action on mitigation and adaptation. For example, the Joint report of the Technology Mechanism, released in 2015, fails to discuss aviation or measures aimed at enhancing sustainable aviation technology development and transfer.

31 Decision 12/CP.21 "Enhancing climate technology development and transfer through the Technology Mechanism," *supra* Note 28.

32 *Supra* Note 4.

describe the series of proposed strategies, measures, and programs that States aim to voluntarily adopt to reduce emissions from flights and to enhance environmental protection in general. It also provides robust descriptions of how sustainable aviation is conceptualized in a country and how the nation intends to attain its desired level of sustainability. According to the ICAO, the action plans will allow a State to showcase the specific voluntary measures they intend to take in order to improve efficiency and thereby contribute to the global environmental aspirational goals established by the Assembly.[33]

Apart from providing concrete legal frameworks, they spell out the technologies and approaches that must be adopted to reach carbon neutral growth. For example, one of the key features of Brazil's action plan is to establish a new biofuels industry to replace jet fuels.[34] This gives an idea on the question of "how," i.e. the mechanisms to be adopted by the country to achieve its ambitious sustainable aviation goals. Such action plans also highlight institutional strengthening strategies, infrastructure modernization, operational improvements, fiscal incentives, research development and investigation, and compensation programs that could bring about sustainable aviation within the country. Furthermore, such action plans would clearly identify technology deficiencies, needs, and areas where international collaboration, technical assistance and financial support is needed.[35] The Action Plan therefore serves as a statement of intent by the government of a country to pursue sustainable aviation, invest in aviation technologies, and welcome foreign collaboration in respect of the set objectives.

Many African countries are, however, yet to come up with such comprehensive action plans. A survey of the ICAO compilation of national action plans shows that no African country has submitted an action plan to the ICAO. In fact, only Lesotho has established something comparable.[36] Nigeria, South Africa, Ethiopia, Kenya, and a number of other African countries have yet to put in place such robust action plans that could have helped the ICAO identify areas where they require technical and technological collaboration. This is in spite of the fact that the ICAO has repeatedly offered, and has

33 ICAO, "Action plans on emissions reduction," www.icao.int/environmental-protection/Pages/action-plan.aspx last accessed April 16, 2018.

34 See "Flight path to aviation biofuels in Brazil: Action plan," www.fapesp.br/publicacoes/flightpath-to-aviation-biofuels-in-brazil-action-plan.pdf last accessed April 16, 2018.

35 ICAO, "Action plans on emissions reduction," www.icao.int/environmental-protection/Pages/action-plan.aspx last accessed April 16, 2018.

36 See ICAO, "Action plan for Lesotho," www.icao.int/safety/scan/PlansOfAction/ICAO%20Plan%20of%20Action%20for%20Lesotho%20(Accepted).pdf last accessed April 16, 2018.

conducted, regional training aimed at assisting States to prepare their action plans.[37]

There is a need for African countries to develop robust action plans on sustainable aviation. To be comprehensive, an inclusive plan must be put together with the active participation and involvement of key stakeholders in the aviation sector such as heads of airlines, airport management authorities, air navigation service providers, airport and air traffic navigation staff, fuel suppliers, and aircraft manufacturers.[38] The action plan would be comprehensively designed after a holistic national assessment of the technological, economic, and sustainability challenges and opportunities associated with the development and commercialization of sustainable aviation fuels, practices, and approaches in the country. The resultant document would be able to highlight the technology needs of every respective country, thereby opening the door for technical and financial support from private sector participants, foreign companies, and international agencies such as the ICAO, the World Bank, and the African Development Bank.

8.3.2 *Deficient or Archaic Laws on Technology Transfer at National Levels*

Technology transfer into Africa is often stifled by laws that tend to protract and complicate technology transfer processes. In a number of surveyed African countries, technology transfer laws are either absent, or, when present, are archaic, overzealous, anachronistic, and complex.[39] For example, in Nigeria, the National Office for Technology Acquisition and Promotion Act (NOTAPA) established a licensing and permit system, which includes the registration of contracts and agreements for virtually all technologies coming into Nigeria.[40] NOTAP is also empowered to examine the quality of imported technology with a view to determining price, ensure compliance with

37 For example, the ICAO worked with the Government of Lesotho to design an action plan, ibid.

38 The actions plans can build on some of the core strategic action points already identified by the African Union in *African Civil Aviation Policy*, *supra* Note 17.

39 See J. De Beer, et al., "Innovation, intellectual property and development narratives in Africa," in J. De Beer, et al., *Innovation & Intellectual Property Collaborative Dynamics in Africa* (Cape Town: University of Cape Town Press, 2014) 2–5, discussing how administrative bottleneck, systemic inefficiencies, and overzealous IP protection regimes raise the costs of future innovations in Africa and may, therefore, discourage potential innovators and creators who cannot afford high up-front investment.

40 *National Office for Technology Acquisition and Promotion Act* (NOTAPA) Cap. N 62, Laws of the Federation of Nigeria 2004.

intellectual property requirements, and register contracts/agreements that deal with the transfer and acquisition of foreign technology and grant permits for their importation into Nigeria. In order to prevent the transfer of obsolete technology, the Director of NOTAP may refuse to register any contract/agreement that in his opinion may result in price distortion, monopoly, or violation of intellectual property laws.[41]

While these are very necessary and important mandates, the process of obtaining approvals and registrations from NOTAP is most often not straightforward. Due to bureaucratic delays in processing permit applications, institutional corruption, and lack of institutional coordination with other relevant regulatory agencies, obtaining relevant documentation and clearance for technology transfer to Nigeria is often herculean and frustrating.[42] The situation is the same in many other African countries where administrative inefficiency and lack of transparency often frustrate registration and regulatory approval processes for ESTs, thereby reducing the ease of doing business.[43] Le Grange and Buys also document how several legal, bureaucratic, and regulatory barriers hinder the transfer of aviation technologies to South Africa.[44]

Similarly, technology transfer laws in Africa have lagged in terms of establishing financial and policy incentive mechanisms that would stimulate private sector participation in technology development and transfer in Africa. For example, India and China have been able to attract foreign transfer of technology through a web of tax incentives and fiscal measures that make their markets very attractive to investors.[45] In order for African markets to

41 Ibid., Sec. 6 (2),

42 See T. Akande, *NOTAPA and technology transfer in Nigeria* (Nigerian Institute of Social and Economic Research, NISER Joint ICTSD/FES, December 2, 2002) at 2.

43 In the 2015 World Bank's "Ease of Doing Business" rankings, by which the World Bank gauges the intricacies of running a company in different countries, including the ease of obtaining regulatory approvals, African countries rank very low. Mauritius is the highest ranked African country at 28 out of 189 nations surveyed, followed by South Africa (43) Rwanda (48), Morocco (71); while Kenya (136), Nigeria (170), Libya (188), Eritrea (189) and several other African countries all dominate the very poor layer of the list. See http://www.doingbusiness.org/rankings last accessed March 10, 2016.

44 See Le Grange and Buys, 81–99.

45 Article 66.2 of the Agreement on Trade-Related Aspects of Intellectual Property Rights (TRIPS), signed at Marrakesh on April 15, 1994, recognizes the importance of incentives in promoting technology transfer. It requires developed country WTO Members to "provide incentives to enterprises and institutions in their territories for the purpose of promoting and encouraging technology transfer to least-developed country Members."

favorably compete with other countries in attracting the required technologies required to improve the aviation sector, there is a need for established technology transfer laws to include fiscal incentives and measures such as custom and duties waivers, tax breaks and technology bonuses, or incentives for foreign investors. This will aid the competitiveness and attractiveness of African countries to favorably attract ESTs into the aviation sector.

There is a need to address the gap in laws and policies on technology transfer by establishing comprehensive and updated laws that simplify technology transfer processes, establish less cumbersome methods of screening technologies, and also provide financial and policy incentives on transferred technologies.

8.3.3 *Inadequate Legal Protection for Intellectual Property Rights (IPRs)*

One of the key barriers to the transfer of technology to many developing countries, especially African countries, is the inadequate level of protection accorded to intellectual property rights (IPR). Generally, innovators want to be sure that their innovations and technological advancements are not abused, or deployed without adequate permission or protection under national regimes of the country to which the technology is transferred. Generally, countries that do not have in place adequate and efficient intellectual property rights systems to protect innovation struggle to attract aviation technology. As Article 7 of the Trade Related Aspects of Intellectual Property Rights (TRIPS) Agreements notes, the objective of the protection and enforcement of IP should be to contribute "to the promotion of technological innovation and to the transfer and dissemination of technology, to the mutual advantage of producers and users of technological knowledge and in a manner conducive to social and economic welfare." Article 8 also recognizes that measures "may be needed to prevent the abuse of intellectual property rights by right holders or the resort to practices which … adversely affect the international transfer of technology." Although many African countries are parties to the TRIPS regime, legal and policy frameworks have not been robustly implemented to strengthen IPR protection.[46]

Concerns over inadequate protection of IPR in Africa manifest in two broad ways. One is the wide exclusion of certain technologies from patentability. A patent is usually a grant made by relevant government authorities within a country that confers upon an inventor the right to exclude others from the

[46] D. Foray, *Technology Transfer in the TRIPS Age: The Need for New Types of Partnerships between the Least Developed and Most Advanced Economies* (Geneva: ICTSD, 2008).

commercial exploitation of a particular invention.[47] It is simply a form of market monopoly granted to inventors as an incentive to invent or innovate. Prior to the TRIPS Agreement, countries could exclude inventions of certain types or in certain areas of technology from patentability, based on their development priorities and strategies. However, Article 27.1 of the TRIPS Agreement now requires WTO Members to grant patents to all types of inventions in all fields of technology, as long as these inventions meet certain basic criteria of novelty, inventive step, and industrial applicability.[48] However, patent laws in many African states still maintain and apply rigid and exclusionary definitions of patents and inventions, which exclude certain technologies from patentability. As Mgbeoji rightly argues, most of the legal approaches to patenting in Africa are still based on colonial antecedents, with only a few countries reflecting modest improvements on the status quo since the colonial era.[49]

For example, section 1 of the Nigerian Patents and Design Act (PDA) discusses circumstances in which an invention could be considered patentable. Under the section, an invention is patentable if: (i) it is new, results from inventive activity and is capable of industrial application, or, (ii) it constitutes an improvement upon a patented invention, and also, is new, results from inventive activity, and is capable of industrial application. However, under the PDA, scientific principles and discoveries are not classified as inventions for purposes of a patent application and grant. Furthermore, under section 1(4)(a) and (b) of the PDA, patents cannot validly be granted or obtained in respect of plant or animal varieties, or essentially biological processes for the production of plants or animals (other than microbiological processes and their products; or for inventions the publication of or exploitation of which would be contrary to public order or morality). Section 1 (4) has created uncertainty as to whether biofuel innovations or low-carbon fuels from agricultural products such as coconuts, jatropha, and sugar cane can be patented in Nigeria. Concerns about legal barriers to biofuel patenting, have also been raised in

47 See Sec. 2(1) of the Nigeria's Patents and Designs Act (PDA) Cap. P2 Laws of the Federation of Nigeria 2004, stating that a patentee is thereby granted a right in law to prevent others from making, using or dealing in his invention whether by sale, importation or hire. See also W. Cornish and D. Llewelyn, *Intellectual Property: Patents, Copyright, Trade Mark, and Allied Marks* (London: Sweet & Maxwell, 2003) 112.

48 Cap. P2 Laws of the Federation of Nigeria 2004.

49 I. Mgeboji, "African patent offices not fit for purpose," in J. De Beer, et al., *Innovation & Intellectual Property Collaborative Dynamics in Africa* (Cape Town: University of Cape Town Press, 2014) 234.

Mozambique and Egypt.[50] Furthermore, the PDA does not define the benchmark for determining inventions that would be contrary to public order or morality in Nigeria. This vagueness has operated as a master key that can be deployed at any time by governments to deny any innovation patentability. The excessive and arbitrary power to deny patentability on undefined public policy or morality grounds, coupled with the fear of autocratic regimes in African states, results in uncertainty and has remained a disincentive for innovators to transfer needed technology to African states.

A second paradox in IPR protection laws in surveyed African countries is the application of expanded compulsory license provisions that allow the use of a patented product or process without authorization or compensation to the patent rights holder. Compulsory license provisions, as recognized under articles 30 and 31 of TRIPS, allow an administrative or judicial authority to grant to a third party rights to exploit or use a patented invention without consent of the patent for overriding public policy or emergency reasons.[51] A person that has been granted a compulsory license has all the rights of a patentee. Article 31 of the TRIPS Agreement, however, provides some safeguards, including the requirements that the proposed user should have made good faith efforts to obtain authorization from the patent holder, the use will be for domestic supply only, that the patent holder shall be granted adequate remuneration, and that there be an established review process for considering the application for compulsory licenses. In many of the surveyed African regimes, several of the procedural safeguards under TRIPS are not replicated.[52] In Nigeria, for example, not only does the PDA not codify these safeguards, it in fact provides that once a compulsory license has been granted, the licensee is insulated from making any payment to the patentee in the form of royalty or any other manner described. Similarly, the Nigerian law authorizes federal, and even state, authorities to utilize or obtain a patented product for the service of the government agency in Nigeria for public interests. This excessive power to leverage innovations for "public interest" again raises concerns on the adequacy of legal protection available, in practical terms, to IPRs in African regimes.

[50] B. Awad and P. A. Zeid, "Reflections on the lack of biofuel innovation in Egypt," ibid. at 267; see also F. dos Santos and S. Pelembe, "The State of biofuel innovation in Mozambique," ibid. at 248, stating that despite the clear articulation of biofuel policies in Mozambique's National Policy and Strategy on Biofuels (NPSB) of 2009, patenting and IPR protection are not adequately addressed in Mozambique's biofuel strategy.

[51] PDA, Note 47.

[52] See for example ss. 55 and 56 of South Africa's *Patents Act* No 57 of 1978.

In a continent in dire need of ESTs, over-zealous legal provisions and policies that narrow or weaken IPR protection must be addressed and removed. The level of protection accorded to IPR must not only be strengthened, but appropriate institutions and regulatory structures must also be revitalized or put in place to instill confidence in inventors that transferred ESTs will be protected from arbitrary confiscation or abuse.

8.4 INSTITUTIONAL BARRIERS TO TECHNOLOGY TRANSFER

A number of institutional gaps also frustrate technology transfer processes into African countries. Some of the most critical include:

8.4.1 *Lack of Intergovernmental Coordination and Linkages*

One chief concern with technology transfer laws in Africa are the multiple licensing and permit systems that investors may have to face when trying to bring in ESTs. In Nigeria, for example, investors have been faced with the herculean task of obtaining permits and licenses from multiple agencies, departments, and parastatals at the federal, state, and local government levels when bringing in new technologies. Apart from registration with NOTAP, other allied organizations may have statutory oversight roles and functions: for example, the Nigeria Custom Service, which is often the first point of scrutiny before importation; the Standard Organization of Nigeria (SON), which is empowered to ensure that all equipment or tools are not obsolete of fake; the Ministry of Finance, which must approve importations exceeding certain financial benchmarks; the Ministry of Environment; and the Ministry of Commerce and Industry to mention but a few. While these standards are required, the processes of navigating through each bureaucratic agency are often daunting and frustrating.

Countries in Eastern Europe have increasingly adopted a "one stop shop approach," which allows one agency to coordinate all required approvals,[53] so that investors do not have to deal with multiple licensing agencies. This approach streamlines the process of technology transfer, reduces administrative bottlenecks, and ultimately reduces the frustration and stress involved in registering technology transfer agreements.

There is a need for African countries to streamline technology transfer processes and ensure the coordination of governmental ministries, agencies,

[53] See World Bank, "Doing business 2011: Making a difference for entrepreneurs" (World Bank, 2011).

and departments involved in technology transfer. In this way, the process of importing the required aviation tools, facilities, and technology required to transform the aviation sectors would be more encouraging and less daunting.

8.4.2 *Limited Capacity*

To promote sustainable aviation, there is a need for a large pool of officers and staff trained and skilled in utilizing the newer and cleaner technology options. This is one area that requires more work in Africa. Importation or availability of new technologies is not enough; without the required human capacity, such facilities may rot away without use or may be suboptimally deployed. Governments must therefore, as priority, identify the training needs of regulators, airport management agencies, and airport officials and then endeavor to provide adequate and updated knowledge for them in essential areas.

Relevant air force institutions in many African countries lack updated training resources, funding, and technology to foster improvement in aviation practices. For example, the Nigerian College of Aviation Technology, set up to train aviation professionals such as Pilots, Air Traffic Controllers, Aircraft Maintenance Engineers, Aeronautical Telecommunications Engineers, Flight Dispatchers, Cabin Crew, and Avionics Engineers, among others, has often been reported as lacking adequate operational and top-level training facilities and management personnel.[54] As the ICAO notes, a considerable number of institutions in Africa that have been training pilots, air traffic controllers, and mechanics for decades now do not possess the critical mass of resources to meet an increasing demand.[55] Biru also noted the lack of training capacity in a broad range of disciplines at the Ethiopian Aviation Academy.[56] Despite efforts and initiatives by regional bodies, such as the African Civil Aviation Commission, in spearheading safety training courses for aviation personnel in Africa, overall success has been too little and too slow due to financial constraints, lack of political will, and lack of adequate

54 See A. Amwe and D. Jonathan, "An appraisal of Nigerian transport sector: Evidence from the railway and aviation subsectors," *Journal of Economics and Sustainable Development*, 10 (2013), 6–9; also G. Odidi, "Challenges facing the aviation industry in Nigeria" *The Nigerian Voice* (June 5, 2012).

55 Ibid.

56 See I. Biru, "The need and challenges of harmonizing CAA trainings in Africa" (ICAO, Aviation Panel 3).

capacity and resources to meet the overwhelming need and demand in various African states.[57]

Concerted regulatory and institutional change is therefore necessary if Africa is to shift to sustainable aviation. There is a need for collaborative efforts between the international community, the private sector, and African governments to remove barriers to the transfer of aviation-specific ESTs, and to provide increased financing for aviation training institutions such that they can be abreast of new technologies, facilities, and best practices in aviation. There is also a need to provide continuous learning opportunities for key stakeholders in the aviation sector to learn of new trends in sustainable aviation, this could be through foreign exchange programs, capacity development conferences, and short courses. The International Airline Training Fund (IATF), which is supported by the International Air Transport Association (IATA), already provides a number of laudable training programs on safety oversight for aviation authorities and professionals in Africa.[58] These training programs will even deliver more value if training centers are brought closer to African countries where training is urgently required. Currently, many of IATA's training centers are located in Europe and the American region, with no training center in Africa. This logistical challenge makes it more expensive and difficult for aviation professionals in Africa to access IATA's training programs.

8.5 CONCLUSION

Despite the increased awareness of the need for countries to adopt a basket of measures aimed at reducing emissions from civil aviation, African countries are often hindered by the fact that ESTs required to transform the aviation sector to a cleaner and carbon neutral one are often not readily available on the continent. Technology transfer is therefore key for Africa to transit to an era of sustainable aviation. Even though Article 4(1) (c) of the UNFCCC enjoins industrialized countries to promote and cooperate in the transfer of technologies, practices, and processes that control, reduce, or prevent

[57] For a discussion of the many practical and logistical constraints facing aviation training in Africa, see African Civil Aviation Commission, "Efforts and commitment towards the provision of sustainable aviation training in Africa," www.icao.int/safety/afiplan/documents/aato%20assembly,%20abuja,%20nigeria,%20april%202013/presentations/presentation%20by%20afcac.pdf last accessed March 10, 2016.

[58] A comprehensive list of tailored courses is available at http://www.iata.org/about/Pages/index.aspx last accessed October 27, 2017.

anthropogenic emissions of greenhouse gases in transport, transferring technologies to Africa has often not been the most straightforward endeavor.

Stakeholders and investors have perennially been faced with inherent legal and institutional barriers that stifle technology transfer and frustrate foreign and private investments in Africa's aviation sector. Drawing examples from Nigeria, Ethiopia, and South Africa, this chapter has discussed some of the key barriers to the smooth transfer of technology to Africa, specifically the lack of coherent national action plans on sustainable aviation; deficient technology transfer laws; lack of institutional coordination; and the lack of human capacity to optimally utilize relevant clean technologies.

To attain the goals of sustainable aviation in the African context there is a need to remove all the identified barriers to the transfer of environmentally sustainable aviation technologies. African policy leaders must address and remove these identified barriers to technology transfer through proactive law-making and institutional rearrangements that would make the transfer of aviation technologies into Africa less cumbersome. Doing so would not only signify Africa's readiness to contribute to the global goals of sustainable aviation, it could also deliver local social, environmental, and economic benefits that would solve some of the perennial sustainability challenges facing Africa as a whole.

9

Sustainable Tourism and the Impact of Climate Change on the Caribbean

Nicole Gonzales

Tourism is an essential source of revenue and employment in the Caribbean region. The impact of climate change on the Caribbean tourism sector is therefore of great importance to these island States, as the effects of climate change on the climate-sensitive ecosystems of the Caribbean will affect the islands socially and economically. Nevertheless, the tourism sector itself produces a considerable amount of CO_2 emissions, which in turn have a deleterious effect on the climate.

Climate change mitigation measures imposed on the international aviation sector pose an indirect threat to the Caribbean's tourist sector. Air transport is a vital service, not just for transporting tourists to and from the islands but also with regard to the imports necessary to cater to these tourists. Climate change mitigation or greenhouse gas reduction measures imposed on international flights, such as the UK APD and the EU-ETS, can indirectly impact the Caribbean economy by causing an increase in ticket prices, placing the islands at a competitive disadvantage with other nearby tourist destinations or reducing arrival numbers and therefore tourist expenditure.

This chapter further expands on the two-way relationship between tourism and climate change and the Caribbean's path toward sustainable tourism. Subsequently, the impact of international aviation measures on the Caribbean tourism sector as well as the importance of the ICAO's Global Market-Based Measure Scheme for the international aviation industry are examined, followed by recommendations on how to further strengthen the Caribbean's position within the global climate change framework of the UNFCCC.

9.1 INTRODUCTION

The developing States in the Caribbean, Small Island Developing States (SIDS), Southeast Asia, and Africa have been identified as being most at-risk with regard to the anticipated effects of climate change.[1] Additionally, the Caribbean region is also one of the most highly tourist-reliant regions in the world.[2] The dependence of the tourism sector on the Caribbean's climate-sensitive ecosystem means that climate change will have a substantial impact on tourism. At the same time, greenhouse gas (GHG) emissions resulting from tourist activities will have a deleterious effect on the climate, which in turn will affect tourism. Because of this strong two-way relationship between the tourism sector and climate change, policies and measures directed at mitigating the negative effects of climate change may in turn have a negative impact on tourism as well.

The social, economic, and environmental impacts of climate change on tourism are predicted to be of considerable magnitude in the long term. The degree of these impacts will further depend on the extent to which the world can mitigate greenhouse gas emissions on a global basis and the Caribbean region can adapt its tourism sector to the changing climate conditions.

This chapter aims to elucidate the relation between sustainable tourism and climate change, the importance of aviation to the Caribbean tourism sector, and the impact of climate change mitigating measures on Caribbean Island States. Furthermore, it proposes a few ways to create a stronger position for Caribbean Island States against climate change and mitigating measures through the United Nations Framework Convention on Climate Change ("UNFCCC") framework.

9.2 THE IMPORTANCE OF TOURISM TO CARIBBEAN ISLAND STATE ECONOMIES

Tourism is an extremely significant global source of revenue and employment, worldwide indirectly creating one out of every eleven jobs and

[1] S. Gössling, C. M. Hall, and D. Scott, "The challenges of tourism as a development strategy in an era of global climate change," in Eija Palosuo (ed.), *Rethinking Development in a Carbon Constrained World: Development Coorporation and Climate Change* (Finland: Ministry of Foreign Affairs, 2009) at 100.

[2] UNWTO, "From Davos to Copenhagen and beyond: Advancing tourism's response to climate change," WTO bckground paper (2009), sdt.unwto.org/sites/all/files/docpdf/fromdavostocopenhagenbeyondunwtopaperelectronicversion.pdf last accessed October 15, 2017.

contributing 5 percent of global GDP and US$ 1.260 billion in international tourism receipts.[3] The United Nations World Tourism Organization (UNWTO) estimates that international tourist arrivals worldwide will reach 1.8 billion by 2030 at an increase of 3.3 percent per year from 2010 to 2030.[4]

However, to Caribbean Island State economies, tourism is even more crucial as it significantly contributes through both direct and indirect earnings via the development of craft industry, infrastructure, and hotels, and the creation of jobs in tourism-related sectors such as transportation, construction, and security.[5] In 2015, the direct contribution[6] of tourism to the Caribbean region's GDP was US$ 16.8 billion, 4.7 percent of the region's total GDP, and tourism directly supported 709,000 jobs. The total contribution[7] of tourism amounted to US$ 53.1 billion, 14.8 percent of the total GDP of the Caribbean and directly and indirectly supported 2.255 million jobs.[8]

The direct contribution of travel and tourism to the Caribbean's GDP is expected to grow annually by 3.4 percent from 2016 to 2026, which amounts to US$ 24.1 billion. Its total contribution of travel and tourism is also expected to grow annually by 3.4 percent from 2016 to 2026, which amounts to US$ 76.2 billion.[9]

As most tourists arrive in the Caribbean region by air, air transport is an essential contributor to the continuous growth of tourism in the region. Furthermore, air transport is essential to the import of products necessary to accommodate the higher standard and quality of living demanded by tourists, such as food and drink, entertainment, shopping, and other services and goods. The relationship between air transport and tourism is also mutually reinforced and interdependent as tourism provides passengers, and thereby creates new and increased business to the air transport sector.[10]

3 UNWTO, "Tourism highlights 2016" (2016).
4 UNWTO, "Tourism towards 2030, global overview" (2011).
5 CARICOM, "The CARICOM environment in figures" (2009).
6 The direct contribution of travel and tourism to GDP includes visitor exports, domestic expenditure, and purchases by tourism providers (including imported goods).
7 The total contribution of travel and tourism to GDP includes the domestic contribution, the domestic supply chain, capital investment, government collective spending, imported goods from indirect spending, and induced impacts.
8 World Travel & Tourism Council, "Economic impact 2016, Caribbean" (2016).
9 Ibid.
10 J. Orozco, "Caribbean airlift and Caribbean tourism," *Caribbean Journal*, www.caribjournal.com/2014/08/08/caribbean-airlift-and-caribbean-tourism last accessed October 13, 2017.

Most Caribbean Island States have been defined by the UN Statistics Division[11] as "Small Island Developing States," and one island (Haiti) has been classified as a "Least Developed Country." The importance of tourism is therefore not only related to its direct or indirect contribution to an island's economic development but also to its potential to reduce poverty, as tourism is a labor-intensive activity with a low entry barrier that the region's poor can take advantage of. However, in order for tourism to have such an alleviating effect, tourism jobs must be properly remunerated, and its employees given opportunities for advancement.[12]

9.3 CLIMATE CHANGE AND TOURISM IN CARIBBEAN ISLAND STATES

The tourism sector is unlike many other sectors, as the consumer of tourism (the tourist) travels to the producer and the product (in this case, the Caribbean Island) as opposed to the other way around. The dependency of Caribbean tourism on the island's environment, such as its beaches, forests, reefs, and local communities, is indisputable.[13] Considering this dependency, the impact of global climate change on the environment of the Caribbean Islands is of vital importance for the continuation and further development of their tourism sector. In turn (increased) tourism is a burden on an island's environment, producing increased amounts of waste and using scarce resources such as land, water, and energy.[14] It is expected that both the direct environmental impact of tourism and global climate change will have a broad range of environmental, economic, and social impacts on Caribbean Island States and the tourism sector.

Tourism's CO_2 emissions are expected to grow substantially in absolute terms and, through this, considerably contribute to climate change.[15] The

[11] UN Statistic Division, "Composition of macro geographical (continental) regions, geographical sub-regions, and selected economic and other groupings," unstats.un.org/unsd/methods/m49/m49regin.htm last accessed October 15, 2017.

[12] UN Environmental Programme, "Making tourism more sustainable: A guide for policy makers" (2005), 13.

[13] "Climate not only determines the length and quality of the tourism season, it is also an important driver of tourism demand to some regions, because it affects the natural environment in ways that can either attract or deter visitors." M. Simpson, D. Scott, and U. Trotz, "Climate change's impact on the Caribbean's ability to sustain tourism, natural assets, and livelihood" (Inter-American Development Bank, 2011), 1.

[14] CARICOM, "The CARICOM environment in figures."

[15] C. M. Hall, D. Scott, and S. Gössling, "The primacy of climate change for sustainable international tourism," *Sustainable Development*, **21** (2013), 115.

CO_2 emissions from tourism may grow by about 135 percent to 2035, totaling approximately 3059 Mt, based on a Business As Usual scenario for 2035, which would make tourism an increasing source of greenhouse gas emissions in the medium- to long-term future.[16]

The direct environmental impact of climate change to the Caribbean may include such phenomena as a rise in sea levels, an increase of frequency, and intensity of extreme storms, warmer temperatures, and changes in marine biodiversity.[17] As most of the tourism-related infrastructure lies in the islands' coastal zones, the rising of the sea level and the increase of frequency and intensity of extreme storms will affect the islands' beaches, coral reefs, waterfronts, and sea defenses. More resources will have to be put into the protection and maintenance of these coastal areas. Second, a prolonged and more violent hurricane season may put tourists off from visiting the islands during that period of time. The warmer temperatures may cause extra cooling costs, changes in plant, wildlife, and insect population and distribution, and an altered seasonality that may negatively impact the agreeable temperatures that draw tourists to the islands. Furthermore, the warming of the sea surface temperature will lead to coral reef bleaching and changes in marine biodiversity, thereby affecting snorkeling and diving tourism.

Indirectly, the environmental changes will impact the islands on an economic and social level as well. Beach loss will have a negative effect on resort attractiveness, room rates, and property value.[18] Prolonged hurricane seasons may cause longer interruptions to businesses and higher insurance premiums. More violent hurricanes will threaten the properties of the local population, which can cause social unrest, and money that could have gone to poverty alleviation may have to be invested in recovering the damages of climate change.[19] The altered tourism demand will cause a decrease in visitor arrivals and expenditure, resulting in less foreign exchange income, less jobs, and higher local unemployment.[20]

[16] D. Scott et al., *Climate Change and Tourism: Responding to Global Challenges* (UNWTO, 2008).

[17] Simpson, Scott, and Trotz, "Climate change's impact on the Caribbean's ability to sustain tourism, natural assets, and livelihood," 2; D. Scott et al., "Climate change and tourism: Responding to global challenges."; ibid.

[18] D. Scott, S. Gössling, and C. M. Hall, "International tourism and climate change," *Wiley Interdisciplinary Reviews: Climate Change*, 3 (2012), at 220.

[19] R. Bueno et al., *The Caribbean and Climate Change, the Costs of Inaction* (Stockholm: Stockholm Environment Institute, 2008) at 8–9.

[20] "A case for compensation for climate change destruction," *Jamaica Observer* (January 5, 2014), www.jamaicaobserver.com/columns/A-case-for-compensation-for-climate-change-destruction_15733479 last accessed October 15, 2017.

9.4 SUSTAINABLE TOURISM TO BALANCE OUT CLIMATE CHANGE

Caribbean tourism is of a climate-sensitive nature. It is therefore of the utmost importance that the effects of climate change be taken into account for the further development of the tourism sector. Tourism, however, is also one of the contributors to climate change. The UNWTO estimated that greenhouse gas emissions contributed by tourism transport, accommodation, and activities combined amounted to 5 percent of global CO_2 in 2005, of which most was accounted for by air transport (40 percent).[21] Given that much of the tourism to the Caribbean is in the form of one to two-week package holidays sold in North American and European markets, the vast majority of visitors to Caribbean Island States arrive by air. The continued growth of tourism by 3.3 percent to 2030 will therefore increase the absolute CO_2 emissions in the sector substantially.[22] Therefore, in order to conserve the environment that the tourism sector depends on and to balance out climate change and tourism while still remaining profitable, the tourism sector should strive to become sustainable.

9.4.1 *Definition of Sustainable Tourism*

In 1987, the World Commission on Environment and Development described sustainable development as "a process to meet the needs of the present without compromising the ability of future generations to meet their own needs." This concept has since evolved and expanded into the three dimensions of sustainable development, namely economic, social, and environmental stability. With regard to sustainable tourism, the United Nations Environmental Programme (UNEP) currently defines this as "tourism that takes full account of its current and future economic, social and environmental impacts, addressing the needs of the visitors, the industry, the environment and host communities."[23]

The UNWTO has subsequently developed guidelines and management practices to all forms of tourism in all types of destinations in order to promote (more) sustainable tourism. A suitable balance of the economic, social, and environmental aspects of tourism is necessary to establish sustainability.

[21] Scott, et al., "Climate change and tourism: Responding to global challenges."
[22] Scott, Hall, and Gossling, "The primacy of climate change for sustainable international tourism," at 118.
[23] UN Environmental Programme, "Making tourism more sustainable: A guide for policy makers," 12.

However, it is also argued that tourism may never be totally sustainable, but that the "sustainable development of tourism is a continuous process of improvement."[24] The continuous path to sustainability requires, on the one hand, a high level of tourist satisfaction to create a meaningful experience for the tourist while continuously remaining aware of the ongoing sustainability issues. On the other hand, strong political leadership is necessary to build consensus and ensure participation by all relevant stakeholders.

On a global level, a multi-stakeholder conference in 2007 on the complex relationship between the tourism and travel sector and climate change resulted in the Davos Declaration.[25] The Davos Declaration contains global guidelines for sustainable tourism. Brought forth by the Declaration are the four key areas that require action from the tourism sector:

(i) Mitigate the GHG emissions derived especially from transport and accommodation activities;
(ii) Adapt tourism businesses and destinations to changing climate conditions;
(iii) Apply existing and new technology to improve energy efficiency; and
(iv) Secure financial resources to help poor regions and countries.[26]

9.4.2 *Sustainable Tourism Projects and Organizations in the Caribbean*

The Caribbean region has seen a number of sustainable tourism projects and organizations in the last decade. The Caribbean Challenge Initiative (CCI) is a collaboration between nine Caribbean Island States[27] that aims to provide leadership for the sustainable use, conservation, and effective management of the marine and coastal environment across the Caribbean. The CCI plans to conserve at least 20 percent of their near-shore marine and coastal environments in national marine protected area systems by 2020, and to create the National Conservation Trust Funds dedicated solely to park management.[28] Since its initiation in 2008, the CCI states have declared fifty new marine and

[24] Ibid.

[25] The Second International Conference on Climate Change and Tourism was organized by the UNWTO together with the UN Environment Programme (UNEP) and the World Meteorological Organization (WMO), and was supported by the World Economic Forum (WEF) and the Swiss Government, in Davos, Switzerland, October 1–3, 2007.

[26] UNWTO, "From Davos to Copenhagen and beyond," at 11.

[27] The island States currently participating in the Caribbean Challenge Initiative are Bahamas, British Virgin Islands, Dominican Republic, Grenada, Jamaica, Puerto Rico, St. Kitts & Nevis, St. Lucia, and St. Vincent and the Grenadines.

[28] Caribbean Challenge Initiative, "Caribbean challenge initiative," www.nature.org/ourinitiatives/regions/caribbean/caribbean-challenge.xml last accessed October 15, 2017.

coastal protected areas. Furthermore, in May 2013, the CCI organized the Summit of Caribbean Political and Business Leaders to launch phase two of the CCI; the largest coordinated, multinational conservation initiative in the region. The Summit committed US$ 64 million from business and political leaders worldwide to the conservation of the Caribbean.

At the UN Conference on Small Island Developing States, 2014 was proclaimed to be the International Year of Small Island Developing States. The Conference celebrated the contributions made to the world by SIDS, the challenges faced by them, and the efforts made to address sustainable development and global issues.[29] It also noted the "sustainable development of Small Island Developing States through genuine and durable partnerships," wherein the CCI was highlighted as one of these important partnerships.[30]

The Agro and Culinary Tourism Product Development is also a great balance between economic, social, and environmental development for the Caribbean. This project recently started with an agro and culinary-tourism workshop in Barbados in 2011 and another workshop during the 13th Annual Caribbean Conference on Sustainable Tourism Development in 2012 in Guyana.[31] The project combines the participation of the local community with the promotion of local agriculture and rural revenue sources, while maintaining national heritage, tradition, and culinary techniques. Gastronomical tourism further helps enrich the tourist experience and their involvement with the locals and the island.

Another such project is the Caribbean Hotel Energy Efficiency Action Programme.[32] The objective of this project is "to drive the Caribbean hotels to implement energy efficient practices and to generate their own renewable energy" in order to improve the competitiveness of Caribbean hotels through their improved energy use. This 24-month project uses Barbados as a case study for the design and preparation of an energy efficiency program and institutional strengthening. The case study involved detailed energy audits in order to gather an understanding of the energy consumption patterns among

[29] United Nations, "International year of small island developing states," www.un.org/en/events/islands2014/#&panel1-2 last accessed October 15, 2017.

[30] Caribbean Challenge Initiative, "UN Conference on small islanddeveloping states," www.caribbeanchallengeinitiative.org/index.php?option=com_content&view=article&id=72:un-conference-on-small-island-developing-states&catid=14:upcoming-events&Itemid=293#.V5KouegrKhd last accessed October 15, 2017.

[31] As demonstrated by the Food Tourism Benefits listed by the World Food Travel Association, see World Food Travel Association, "What is food tourism: Food tourism benefits," www.worldfoodtravel.org/cpages/what-is-food-tourism last accessed October 15, 2017.

[32] Caribbean Alliance for Sustainable Tourism, "Caribbean alliance for sustainable tourism," www.caribbeanhotelandtourism.com/cast last accessed October 15, 2017.

Caribbean hotels. The goal of this project is both to achieve higher energy efficiency for Caribbean hotels as well as obtain carbon credits for reducing CO_2 emissions through the UNFCCC's Clean Development Mechanism.

An important organization in, and to, the Caribbean is the Caribbean Community and Common Market (CARICOM), established by the Treaty of Chaguaramas in 1973.[33] The organization has fifteen member states, five associate members, and eight observers.[34] Most, but not all, CARICOM member states are islands in the Caribbean, such as Suriname and Guyana. The objectives of the organization are, among others, to improve economic development and convergence, to achieve a greater measure of economic leverage and effectiveness in trade relations with third States, and to enhance the coordination of foreign and economic policies between member states. The organization also operates as a regional single market (the CARICOM Single Market and Economy[35]), which allows for free movement of goods, services, people, and capital within the CARICOM. Furthermore, CARICOM strives to formulate proposals for sustainable tourism development.[36]

In February 2009, CARICOM launched the Caribbean Aviation Safety and Security Oversight System (CASSOS), which is an institution of CARICOM. Its main objectives are compliance with the standards and recommended practices established by the ICAO, to facilitate the growth and development in aviation within the Caribbean region through training, the sharing of technical resources, the harmonization of regulatory processes, and the minimization of safety and security risks.[37] CASSOS is also a Regional Safety Oversight Organization.

By combining CARICOM's sustainable tourism development with CASSOS' facilitation of the development of the aviation sector within the

33 *Revised treaty of Chaguaramas establishing the Caribbean Community including the CARICOM single market and economy* (signed July 5, 2001, entered into force February 4, 2002), 2259 UNTS 40269, https://treaties.un.org/Pages/showDetails.aspx?objid=0800000280075f53 last accessed October 15, 2017.

34 CARICOM member states are Antigua and Barbuda, Bahamas, Barbados, Belize, Dominica, Grenada, Guyana, Haiti, Jamaica, Montserrat, Saint Kitts and Nevis, Saint Lucia, Saint Vincent and the Grenadines, Suriname, and Trinidad and Tobago. The CARICOM associate members are Anguilla, Bermuda, British Virgin Islands, Cayman Islands, and Turks and Caicos Islands. The CARICOM observers are Aruba, Colombia, Curacao, Dominican Republic, Mexico, Puerto Rico, Sint Maarten, and Venezuela.

35 CARICOM, "Single market and economy," http://csmeonline.org/ last accessed October 15, 2017.

36 CARICOM, "Revised treaty of Chaguaramas" (2001), Art. 55.

37 CASSOS, "About us," http://cassos.org/home/index.php/about-us?showall=&start=2 last accessed October 15, 2017; CASSOS, http://cassos.org/home/ last accessed October 15, 2017.

Caribbean region, CARICOM has the tools to continue the economic development of the region while conserving its cultural and natural resources and maintaining a balance between a healthy ecology and economic development.[38]

In June 2011, CASSOS presented a proposal for the establishment of a "Single Caribbean Airspace."[39] Like the Single European Sky,[40] it intends to "reduce fragmentation and complexity, increase air traffic control capacity, reduce delays, facilitate introduction of new technology and increase harmonization and cooperation."[41] This initiative could organize Caribbean airspace in case of increased air traffic flows, and reduce the environmental impact of aircraft by improving flight efficiency.

The Caribbean region should continue to develop and participate in these projects and organizations to mitigate or reduce the industry's GHG emissions, and adapt and expand their tourism business while keeping in mind the economic, social, and environmental aspects of the islands for a more sustainable tourism.

In order to further sustainable development in the region, cooperation and participation is necessary on a regional level to share expertise, resources, and data. The regional reach of CARICOM, both in an economic sense and in relation to aviation through CASSOS, is a good example of how Caribbean Island States could combine their efforts to further their regional development. Caribbean Island States should be encouraged to seek membership of such organizations and actively participate in the region's development.

9.5 THE IMPORTANCE OF AVIATION TO THE CARIBBEAN TOURISM SECTOR

In 2015, 54 percent of all international inbound tourists worldwide arrived at their destination by air. For the Caribbean, this amounted to a total of 23.9 million international tourist arrivals in 2015.[42] Considering the geographical location of the Caribbean islands, the common ways for international tourists

[38] *Revised treaty of Chaguaramas*, Art. 55.

[39] CASSOS, "Feasibility of the establishment of a 'single sirspace' within the Caribbean" (2011), www.onecaribbean.org/content/files/SingleCaricomAirspaceJune2011.pdf last accessed October 15, 2017.

[40] EC, "Single European sky," http://ec.europa.eu/transport/modes/air/single_european_sky/index_en.htm last accessed October 15, 2017.

[41] CASSOS, "Feasibility of the establishment of a 'single airspace' within the Caribbean."

[42] UNWTO, "Tourism highlights 2016" www.e-unwto.org/doi/pdf/10.18111/9789284418145 last accesed October 15, 2017.

to reach the islands are by air or by sea, which makes air transport an essential player in the tourism sector of the Caribbean. Air transport is the fastest and most flexible means of access to and from the islands.[43]

The Dominican Republic, which is the most popular Caribbean tourist destination for Canada[44] in 2013 and the United States[45] in 2015, received approximately 529,000 Canadian and 447,000 American visitors in 2013. In that year, it is estimated that the Canadian visitors spent C$560 million during their visit. An important historical aspect of this success is that the Dominican Republic has concluded bilateral air transport agreements with Canada and the United States in, respectively, 2008[46] and 1986.[47]

Bilateral air transport agreements facilitate the passenger traffic between countries, and in order to facilitate and further develop this traffic, island State governments should invest in further facilitating the air transport and tourist arrivals between the Caribbean and its (biggest) tourist markets.

Further travel facilitation can be provided by the removal of the requirements for travel visas.[48] A "visa openness" study by the UNWTO and the World Travel and Tourism Council showed that though the Caribbean is one of the most "visa open" regions in the world, it still requires 55 percent of the world population to obtain a visa before arrival.[49]

Air transport is not only important for the flow of tourists, but also with regard to imports necessary to cater to these tourists. However, an uncontrolled influx of mass tourism may negatively affect the fragile environmental and social equilibrium of an island if it is not met with a strategy for sustainable tourism. An increase in air traffic may also have an impact on the islands' environment and infrastructure as the creation and development of airports to handle an increased number of tourists generally takes place near the coast,

43 UNWTO, "Challenges and opportunities for tourism development in small island developing states" (2012).

44 Statistics Canada, "Travel by Canadians to foreign countries, top 15 countries visited," www.statcan.gc.ca/tables-tableaux/sum-som/l01/cst01/arts37a-eng.htm last accessed October 15, 2017.

45 US DOT, "US international air passenger and freight statistics June 2015" (2016).

46 Agreement on Air Transport (Canada – Domincon Republic) (September 5, 2008), https://otc-cta.gc.ca/eng/transport-agreement/dominican-republic last accessed October 15, 2017.

47 Air Transport Agreement (US-Dominican Republic) (June 22, 1986), www.state.gov/documents/organization/155527.pdf last accessed October 15, 2017.

48 UNWTO, "Facilitation of tourist travel," http://rcm.unwto.org/content/facilitation-tourist-travel last accessed October 15, 2017.

49 UNWTO, "Visa openness report 2015" (January 2016), www.e-unwto.org/doi/pdf/10.18111/9789284417384 last accessed October 15, 2017.

and may affect the equilibrium of coastal ecosystems, including beaches or mangrove forests.[50]

9.5.1 *The Impact of International Aviation Measures on the Caribbean Tourism Sector*

International climate change mitigation measures pose one of the most immediate economic risks to the Caribbean tourism sector by impacting areas that the sector depends on.[51] Because of aviation's crucial role in the Caribbean tourism sector, international climate change mitigation measures imposed on foreign airlines can directly impact the Caribbean economy. Government taxation at the point of origin or point of destination, and other climate change mitigation measures, can have an impact on ticket prices and therefore on competition between Caribbean Island States and other destinations.[52] Two examples hereof are the United Kingdom Air Passenger Duty (UK APD)[53] and the European Union's Carbon Emissions Trading Scheme (EU-ETS).[54]

The importance of the UK APD and the EU-ETS lies in the dependency of Caribbean Island States on European tourists. Due to the historical link between the Caribbean and Europe, the large number of Caribbean immigrants living in the European mother country, their common language, and shared cultural aspects, the average EU market share within the Caribbean is 21.2 percent, of which the United Kingdom represents almost 25 percent.[55] Considering its sizeable market share, any reduction in European or UK tourists will have a significant negative effect on the Caribbean Island States.

Further importance should be attached to the relationship between the EU and CARICOM. In October 2008, the CARICOM and the EU signed the

[50] UNWTO, Challenges and opportunities for tourism development in small island developing states, at 49.

[51] Simpson, Scott, and Trotz, "Climate change's impact on the Caribbean's ability to sustain tourism, natural assets, and livelihood," at 5.

[52] UNWTO, "Challenges and opportunities for tourism development in Small Island Developing States," 56.

[53] Air Passenger Duty Regulations 1994, SI 1994/1738.

[54] European Commission, "Proposal for a directive of the European Parliament and of the Council amending directive 2003/87/EC so as to include aviation activities in the scheme for greenhouse gas emission allowance trading within the Community" (January 23, 2008) COM (2008) 30 final, eur-lex.europa.eu/legal-content/EN/TXT/?uri=COM:2008:0016:FIN last accessed October 15, 2017.

[55] World Travel & Tourism Council, "Travel and tourism's economic impact 2011" (2011).

CARIFORUM–EU Economic Partnership Agreement, which creates a platform to simplify trade and investment between the two regions. The agreement covers goods, services, and "trade in its widest sense."[56] This agreement, however, does not cover aviation measures, air transport agreements, or international climate measures related to aviation, such as the EU-ETS. Considering that any negative impact on the tourism sector of the Caribbean will be disadvantageous to the Caribbean region and the investments made there, these far-reaching international measures could also be considered in the application of the Agreement.

9.5.1.1 The UK APD

The UK APD is an excise tax that amounts to a standard rate per person per flight on a national or international flight departing from UK airports. Introduced in 1993, the tax came into effect on November 1, 1994.[57] The UK APD is generally viewed as a "green" tax.[58] However, John Healey, Chancellor of the Exchequer, noted in 2003 that the "[a]ir passenger duty (APD) was introduced in 1994 as a measure whose principal purpose was to raise revenue from the aviation industry but with the anticipation that there would be environmental benefits through its effect on air traffic volumes."[59]

Before April 1, 2015, the UK APD was structured into four "bands," which set rates based on the distance between London and the capital of the point of destination. Each band was split into "reduced," "standard," and "higher" bands, and linked with an associated rate.[60]

Until March 31, 2015, the rates were shown in Table 9.1.[61]

56 European Commission, "Factsheet: How the EU is putting the EPA into practice" (April 2012), www.eesc.europa.eu/resources/docs/factsheet-how-the-eu-is-putting-the-epa-into-practice.pdf last accessed October 15, 2017.

57 Air Passenger Duty Regulations 1994.

58 "Air passenger duty undermined public confidence in green taxes, say MPs," *The Journal* (July 7, 2011), www.journallive.co.uk/north-east-news/todays-news/2011/07/07/air-passenger-duty-undermined-public-confidence-in-green-taxes-say-mps-61634-29008906/ last accessed October 15, 2017.

59 See HC Deb 15 July 2003, col 207W, www.publications.parliament.uk/pa/cm200203/cmhansrd/vo030715/text/30715w18.htm#30715w18.html_sbhd5 last accessed October 15, 2017.

60 From April 1, 2013, the UK APD has applied to all flights on aircraft of 5.7 tonnes or more. The reduced rate applies to the lowest class of travel available on a flight. The standard rate applies to any class of travel that provides seating in excess of 1.016 meters/40 inches, or any other class of travel but the lowest. The higher rate applies to flights aboard aircraft of 20 tonnes or more with fewer than 19 seats.

61 HM Revenue and Customs, "Rates of air passenger duty (APD)" (2014), www.hmrc.gov.uk/rates/apd.htm last accessed October 15, 2017.

TABLE 9.1 *HM Revenue & Customs: Air passenger duty rates (March 2015)*

Band – From April 1, 2014	Reduced rate	Standard rate	Higher rate
Band A (0–2,000 miles)	£ 13 (US$ 16)	£ 26 (US$ 33)	£ 52 (US$ 66)
Band B (2,001–4,000 miles)	£ 69 (US$ 87)	£ 138 (US$ 174)	£ 276 (US$ 348)
Band C (4,001–6,000 miles)	£ 85 (US$ 107)	£ 170 (US$ 214)	£ 340 (US$ 428)
Band D (Over 6,000 miles)	£ 97 (US$ 122)	£ 194 (US$ 244)	£ 388 (US$ 489)[62]

In line with the banding system, Caribbean Island States fell into Band C because their capitals fall between 4,001 and 6,000 miles from London. However, competing tourist locations such as Hawaii, Florida, and California fell into Band B, because the distance between London and Washington DC is approximately 3,670 miles, whereas the factual location of these destinations is far beyond that. Based on this fact, Caribbean governments had protested that the UK APD is "unjust" and "discriminatory."[63]

A Caribbean study showed that "when the [UK APD] fares are raised progressively, there is a sharp negative reaction after reaching £500 in the UK market."[64] Their statement is further supported by British Airways, which announced cuts in flights and capacity on their Caribbean routes because of the sharp rise of APD charges.[65] "It is no coincidence that our reduction in the number of services to the Caribbean is accompanied by a rise in services to Florida – a destination that is taxed at a rate 20 per cent less than the Caribbean," explained chief executive Keith Williams.[66]

62 Conversion from British Pound to US dollar calculated by www.xe.com on January 25, 2017 at a rate of 1 GBP is 1.26 USD.

63 Caribbean Tourism Organization, "Caribbean response to the UK Government's consultation on reform of air passenger duty" (June 2011), www.onecaribbean.org/content/files/CaribbeanResponseAPDBriefingDocJune2011.pdf last accessed October 15, 2017.

64 Caribbean Tourism Organization OneCaribbean, "Caribbean Tourism Overview, 2009" (2009).

65 "British Airways chief executive Keith Williams blames APD for Caribbean cuts," *Breaking Travel News* (September 19, 2011), www.breakingtravelnews.com/news/article/british-airways-plans-to-cut-caribbean-routes/ last accessed October 15, 2017 and R. Doherty, "Over-taxed: BA cuts flights to Caribbean over high APD rates," *Daily Mail* (September 20, 2011), www.dailymail.co.uk/travel/article-2039113/BA-cuts-flights-Caribbean-high-APD-tax-rates.html last accessed October 15, 2017.

66 "BA cuts flights to Caribbean over APD tax levels," *TravelMole* (2011), http://www.travelmole.com/news_feature.php?news_id=1149404&c=setreg&region=2 last accessed October 15, 2017.

TABLE 9.2 *HM Revenue & Customs: Air passenger duty rates (April 2017)*

Band – From April 1, 2016	Reduced rate	Standard rate	Higher rate
Band A (0–2,000 miles)	£ 13 (US$ 16)	£ 26 (US$ 33)	£ 78 (US$ 98)
Band B (over 2,000 miles)	£ 75 (US$ 95)	£ 150 (US$ 189)	£ 450 (US$ 567)[69]

Since April 1, 2015, the UK APD has been structured into two "bands," split into "reduced," "standard," and "higher" bands, and linked with an associated rate.[67]

The rates as of April 1, 2017, are shown in Table 9.2.[68]

This change brought the Caribbean Island States and their competing United States tourist locations within the same UK APD band. However, though the Caribbean is no longer at a competitive disadvantage in relation to the United States because of the UK APD tax, it remains to be seen if this will cause a favorable change in UK passenger behavior toward the region.[70]

9.5.1.2 The EU-ETS

The global aviation industry has been forecast to grow at an average of 4.8 percent per year through the year 2036. Aviation emissions account for a modest 2–3 percent of total global CO_2 emissions, of which international flights are responsible for 62 percent of these emissions.[71] The European Commission (EC) felt that the growth of the aviation sector, whose international emissions had as of then gone unmitigated, would threaten to cancel out the efforts done to mitigate carbon emissions by other sectors. The EC

67 From April 1, 2016, the UK APD will apply to the carriage, from a UK airport, of chargeable passengers on chargeable aircraft. The reduced rate applies to the lowest class of travel available on a flight unless the seat pitch exceeds 1.016 metres (40 inches). The standard rate applies to any class of travel that provides seating in excess of 1.016 metres/40 inches, or any other class of travel but the lowest. The higher rate applies to flights aboard aircraft of 20 tonnes or more with fewer than nineteen seats.

68 Customs, "Rates of air passenger duty (APD)."

69 Conversion from British Pound to US dollar calculated by www.xe.com on January 25, 2017, at a rate of 1 GBP is 1.26 USD.

70 UK CAA, "UK Airport Data, International Passenger Traffic to and from Reporting Airports (in Thousands) by Country 2005–2015" (2016). The current available data on international passenger traffic from the United Kingdom to the Caribbean is only available for the years 2015 and 2016. It is therefore not possible to conclude whether there has been a significant increase in flights from the United Kingdom to the Caribbean, and whether this increase is caused by the amendment in UK APD bands for the United States.

71 ICAO, "ICAO environmental report 2010: Aviation and climate change" (2010) at 18, 31, 38.

therefore announced that it intended to introduce international aviation emissions into the EU-ETS.[72]

Since the initial introduction of aviation into the EU-ETS by means of EU Directive 2008/101/EC,[73] the scheme has been through numerous stages of applicability and international uproar, which resulted in such events as the court case brought forth by Air Transport Association of America, American Airlines, Continental Airlines, and United Air Lines against the Secretary of State for Energy and Climate Change of the United Kingdom in 2009,[74] and the Delhi Declaration.[75] In November 2012, the EC announced a "Stop the Clock" on the international implementation of the scheme for the period of 2013 to 2016 as a gesture of goodwill encouraging development toward a global market-based scheme to regulate greenhouse gases from the aviation industry. Following the 38th General Assembly of the ICAO in the Fall of 2013, the EC amended the remaining EU portion of the EU-ETS so that only the portion of the flight that takes place within EU airspace would be covered by the EU-ETS, a move widely applauded by the aviation industry.[76] After the ICAO's 39th Assembly and the adoption of the global market-based measure for international aviation named CORSIA, the EU Parliament still has to decide on how to adapt the EU-ETS to the new global MBM.[77]

[72] European Commission, "Proposal for amending Directive 2003/87/EC."

[73] Directive 2008/101/EC of the European Parliament and of the Council of November 19, 2008, amending Directive 2003/87/EC so as to include aviation activities in the scheme for greenhouse gas emission allowance trading within the Community, OJ 2009 No. L8/3 Art. 3 (b)(r).

[74] Case c-366/10, *Air Transport Association of America* v. *Secretary of State for Energy and Climate Change*. [2012] OJ C49/7; [2012] 2 CMLR 4; the claimants sought annulment of the measurements implementing Directive 2008/101 in the United Kingdom, and argued that the inclusion of international aviation, and in particular transatlantic flights, into the EU-ETS by Directive 2008 was in breach of a number of principles of customary international law and of several international agreements. The issue was sent to the Court of Justice of the European Union, which decided that the EU-ETS did not infringe customary international law, or the relevant articles of the EU–US Open Skies Agreement.

[75] The Delhi Declaration, drawn up in September 2011, recognized the need "to address the long-term growth of greenhouse gas emissions," condemning the EU's plan to include international flights into the ETS. It called upon States to work through the ICAO in developing a global scheme "that will reduce aviation emissions while at the same time avoiding adverse impacts on air transport." The Declaration was included as an appendix to working paper C-WP/13790 for the 194th ICAO Council session and presented to the Council by the Secretary General.

[76] European Commission, "Commission proposes limiting EU ETS to European regional airspace," http://ec.europa.eu/clima/policies/transport/aviation/index_en.htm last accessed October 15, 2017.

[77] Greenair, "European Parliament's environment committee agrees to tighten screw on aviation under reformed EU ETS," www.greenaironline.com/news.php?viewStory=2318 last accesed October 15, 2017.

A study by L. Pentelow and D. Scott shows that, until mitigation measures require deeper emission cuts and higher carbon costs as were the case in 2011, "there will be no meaningful impact on the growth of arrival numbers to the Caribbean."[78] An insignificant decrease in passenger demand makes it unlikely for an airline to drop any routes unless demand has reduced enough to reduce the number of flights on a route and make it unprofitable. However, any reduction in arrival numbers, and therefore tourist expenditure, is disadvantageous to the Caribbean region. Caribbean Island States must therefore remain vigilant about the evolution of global climate change mitigation measures and their subsequent impact on the Caribbean and its tourism sector.[79]

9.5.2 *The Caribbean's Vulnerability in International Aviation Mitigation Measures*

Both Caribbean and non-Caribbean governments must not underestimate the impact that a mitigating measure, tax, or fee, such as the UK APD and the EU-ETS, imposed on the international aviation industry, can have on the vulnerable economies of Caribbean Island States. The vulnerability of small island States to both the long-term effects of global climate change and the short-term impacts of climate change mitigation has been explicitly recognized and safeguarded by the UNFCCC.[80] The impact of the implementation of climate change measures on small island States must be considered during the implementation of UNFCCC commitments by all Parties. Most importantly, the UNFCCC and the Paris Agreement[81] both include the principle of "common but differentiated responsibilities and respective capabilities" to balance out historical and current emission responsibilities with the developed or developing country's capabilities.

78 L. Pentelow and D. J. Scott, "Aviation's inclusion in international climate policy regimes: Implications for the Caribbean tourism industry," *Journal of Air Transport Management*, 17 (2011).

79 Ibid., 204.

80 The UNFCCC was negotiated at the UN Conference on Environment and Development in Rio de Janeiro during the "Earth Summit" in June 1992. The Convention entered into force on March 21, 1994, and has currently been ratified by 195 Parties (194 States and 1 regional economic integration organization).

81 UNFCCC, "Adoption of the Paris Agreement: Proposal by the president" (December 12, 2015) UNFCCC/CP/2015/L.9 unfccc.int/resource/docs/2015/cop21/eng/l09.pdf last accessed October 15, 2017.

The Agreement entered into force on November 4, 2016, and has currently been ratified by 127 Parties.

However, none of these protective measures have found their way into such a GHG mitigation measure as the EU-ETS. Even so, only twelve of the thirty-one Caribbean Island States have ratified the UNFCCC and the Paris Agreement.[82] Therefore, even if these protective measures had been in place, it may not have benefited all the islands it would affect. Because half of the Caribbean Island States are not Party to the UNFCCC and Paris Agreement, the Caribbean tourism sector of these islands would be dependent on developed States taking into account their vulnerability to climate change mitigation measures.

Similarly, the implementation of a Caribbean mitigating measure, tax, or fee, such as the UK APD, could be a double-edged sword. Adding such a tax to passenger tickets would bring in additional revenue for the region, but it may also put the Caribbean at a competitive disadvantage with its neighbor tourist destinations, which do not have such an added tax, and cause the region to receive fewer visitor arrivals and less expenditure, resulting in less foreign exchange income.

9.5.2.1 One Global MBM Scheme to Rule Them All

An important event for the Caribbean tourism sector, as well as the entire aviation sector, is the creation of a global market-based measure by the ICAO, as per ICAO Assembly Resolution A37–19.[83] The creation of this global MBM benefits the Caribbean by it not having to participate in a patchwork of national or regional MBMs, not having to create its own regional MBM, and not having to deal with a new administrative burden.

In May 2016, the ICAO High-Level Meeting on a Global Market-Based Measure (MBM) Scheme reviewed the draft Assembly Resolution text on a global MBM scheme for international aviation, made recommendation to the draft text, and presented a paper with outstanding issues to the draft text that had not reached consensus during the meeting.[84] The recommendation from the High-Level Meeting was presented to the 208th Session of the ICAO

[82] The Caribbean Island States that have ratified the UNFCCC and Paris Agreement are Antigua-and-Barbuda, Bahamas, Barbados, Cuba, Dominica, Grenada, Guadeloupe, Martinique, Saint Kitts-and-Nevis, Saint Lucia, Saint Martin, and Saint Vincent-and-the-Grenadines. The Caribbean Island States that are signatories to the Paris Agreement but have not yet ratified it are the Dominican Republic, Haiti, Jamaica, and Trinidad-and-Tobago.

[83] ICAO, "Assembly resolutions in force as of 4 October 2013" (2014) Doc 10022, www.icao.int/publications/Documents/10022_en.pdf last accessed October 15, 2017.

[84] ICAO, "ICAO high-level meeting on a Global Market-Based Measure (MBM) Scheme," www.icao.int/Meetings/HLM-MBM/Pages/default.aspx last accessed October 15, 2017.

Council, in preparation for the 39th Session of the ICAO Assembly. Within the draft text as amended by the High-Level Meeting, article 7 sub c states that the global MBM "does not apply to States which are classified as the Least Developed Countries (LDCs), Small Island Developing States (SIDS) or Landlocked Developing Countries (LLDCs)."[85] Almost all Caribbean islands are considered SIDS, and Haiti is defined as an LDC.[86]

At the 39th Session of the ICAO Assembly, held from September 27 to October 7, 2016, the "Consolidated statement of continuing ICAO policies and practices related to environmental protection – Global Market-based Measure (MBM) scheme" was adopted in Assembly Resolution A39–3 (the Resolution).[87] The Resolution sets out the framework of the Carbon Offsetting and Reduction Scheme for International Aviation (CORSIA).

Within the framework of the CORSIA, LDCs, SIDS, and LLDCs are exempted from mandatory participation.[88] This exemption takes into account the Caribbean Island States' status as SIDS, developing states, and historically small emitters. However, the exempted states are encouraged to voluntarily participate in the scheme.

Even though the Caribbean Island States and their operators are exempted from active participation in the scheme, the states should take into account that "all States with aircraft operators undertaking international flights are requested to compile and transmit aggregated emissions information of their

85 ICAO, High-Level Meeting on a Global MBM Scheme, " Draft assembly resolution text on a global market-based measure (GMBM) scheme" (May 15, 2016) HLM-GMBM-Flimsy No. 2, / www.icao.int/Meetings/HLM-MBM/Documents/HLM_GMBM_Flimsy_2.pdf.

86 UN, "Who are the small island developing states?" www.un.org/en/events/islands2014/smallislands.shtml last accessed October 15, 2017; UNSD, "Composition of macro geographical (continental) regions, geographical sub regions, and selected economic and other groupings" (2008).

87 ICAO, "Provisional edition of resolutions adopted by the 39th session of the assembly" (October 2016).

88 ICAO Res A39–3, para 9 (e) states:

> 9. Decides the use of a phased implementation for the CORSIA to accommodate the special circumstances and respective capabilities of States, in particular developing States, while minimizing market distortion, as follows:
>
> e) Second phase applies from 2027 through 2035 to all States that have an individual share of international aviation activities in RTKs in year 2018 above 0.5 per cent of total RTKs or whose cumulative share in the list of States from the highest to the lowest amount of RTKs reaches 90 per cent of total RTKs, except Least Developed Countries (LDCs), Small Island Developing States (SIDS) and Landlocked Developing Countries (LLDCs) unless they volunteer to participate in this phase;

operators to ICAO, as part of the activities included in the States' implementation of a monitoring, reporting and verification (MRV) system."[89]

With support and assistance from the ICAO, the Caribbean Island States could implement a regional MRV system through the sharing of technical data, expertise, and resources, as encouraged by paragraph 22 of the Resolution, under the auspices of CASSOS. Furthermore, CASSOS' mandate could also support the facilitation of a regional Registry if various Caribbean Island States decide to join the CORSIA. Through this regional cooperation, the administrative burden and corresponding costs of setting up and maintaining an MRV system and Registry could be divided between the CARICOM member states instead of falling on each individual Caribbean Island State.

9.6 CONCLUSION

Because of the importance of tourism, and indirectly air transport, to the Caribbean Island States, any climate change mitigation or greenhouse gas reduction measures should be formulated and implemented in such a way as to not disadvantage these developing countries, or at least reduce the negative impact these measures would have.[90] The vulnerability of small island States to the long term effects of climate change and the short term impacts of climate change mitigation, as recognized and safeguarded by the UNFCCC, must be considered during the implementation of such mitigating measures. However, this is not always the case. The direct impact of aviation policies is illustrated by the UK APD, whereas the impact of a climate change mitigating measure is shown through the EU-ETS.

Unlike the UK APD and the EU-ETS, the ICAO's CORSIA has exempted LDCs, SIDS, and LLDCs from mandatory participation in its global MBM. This exemption provides Caribbean Island States the freedom to join the scheme when their developing economies allow it. However, all States, including those exempted from the scheme, are requested to compile and transmit aggregated emissions information of their operators to the ICAO as part of the activities included in the States' implementation of an MRV system. A regional approach through CASSOS to set up and maintain this MRV system as requested by the ICAO by sharing expertise, resources, and data could alleviate the administrative burden on each individual Caribbean

89 ICAO, "2. What is CORSIA and how does it work?" www.icao.int/environmental-protection/Pages/A39_CORSIA_FAQ2.aspx last accessed October 15, 2017.

90 UNWTO, "From Davos to Copenhagen and beyond."

island State and further encourage cooperation within the region on other aspects as well.

Further to any climate change mitigation measures based on the UNFCCC, and in order not to be further dependent on such climate change-related decisions of other States, the most direct and controllable solution to the Caribbean Island States should include that the remaining non-party Caribbean Island States become party to the UNFCCC and the Paris Agreement in order to be able to rely on the safeguards and protections provided by these treaties. In this way, the Caribbean Island States can create a stronger and more independent position for themselves within the global climate change framework of the UNFCCC, and establish a sustainable tourism sector that can balance out climate change while remaining profitable.

Furthermore, all Caribbean Island States should work together to create a sustainable tourism sector based on the guidelines and management practices of the UNWTO and Davos Declaration. Creating a common climate change mitigation strategy, the Caribbean Island States could achieve improved environmental practices without suffering from a competitive disadvantage to other Caribbean Island States.

Additionally, in creating national or Caribbean-regional projects that could obtain carbon credits for reducing CO_2 emissions through the UNFCCC's Clean Development Mechanism, such as the Caribbean Hotel Energy Efficiency Action Programme, the Caribbean islands can benefit anew from the UNFCCC system by selling their Certified Emission Reduction units to developed states in need of such units in order to meet their emission reduction commitments under the Paris Agreement.

PART III

Dispute Settlement

10

Settlement of Disputes at the ICAO and Sustainable Development

Armand de Mestral*

This article aims to present the dispute settlement mechanism established in Chapter XVIII of the Chicago Convention. To this end, the article will analyze how the Council could resolve a potential dispute involving a defense of sustainable development. For this exercise, purely hypothetical cases will be analyzed, in which the European Union (EU) decides to unilaterally implement its emissions trading scheme in the field of aviation or in which the EU or a major aviation state applies the GHS emissions scheme mandated by the ICAO Assembly in 2016 to a state that considers it should be exempted. These cases will serve as hypotheticals to consider whether the dispute settlement mechanism set out at Article 84 of the Chicago Convention could serve to resolve such a dispute. The ICAO dispute settlement mechanism has been criticized many times in the ICAO's history. In fact, the five disputes brought under the present article have each been resolved through diplomatic channels, involving the good offices of the President of the ICAO Council. Therefore, despite the difficulties presented by the procedure and the peculiarity of the EU representation at the ICAO, this chapter seeks to demonstrate that a potential dispute with respect to sustainable development will most likely be resolved the same way as has been done previously.

10.1 INTRODUCTION

This chapter seeks to determine whether the mechanism and the procedure for the settlement of disputes within the *Chicago Convention*[1] could be

* The author wishes to thank Mr. Mathieu Vaugeois, who was an LLM candidate within the Institute of Air and Space Law, McGill University, at the time this Chapter was written.

1 *Convention on International Civil Aviation* (adopted December 7, 1944, entered into force March 5, 1947), 15 UNTS 295, 61 Stat 1180 [*Chicago Convention*].

adapted to address potential disputes involving issues of sustainable development and environmental protection, if the ICAO's Member States are not able to implement global Market Based Measures (MBM) pursuant to Resolution A39–3 of the 39th Session of the Assembly.[2] For this purpose, we consider a potential scenario under which the European Union (EU) decides to reimpose unilaterally its Emission Trading Scheme (ETS) as of January 1, 2020 following the failure of the ICAO Council to adopt an effective scheme pursuant to Resolution A39–3. Any such scenario is at present purely hypothetical. Nevertheless, the analysis may serve as a framework in order to demonstrate how the *Chicago Convention* might potentially allow for the resolution of disputes of this nature.

This article examines the provisions of the *Chicago Convention* with respect to the settlement of disputes, the procedures currently in force regarding the presentation of an application before the Council, the scope of the jurisdiction of the ICAO Council for the settlement of disputes, and the previous cases brought before the Council. This chapter also considers the type of legal proceedings certain States could initiate against the EU in relation to the scenarios mentioned in this introduction. Moreover, it must be noted that the ambiguous status of the EU at the ICAO may well lead to uncertainty with respect to the parties involved in a potential application.

10.2 *CHICAGO CONVENTION* PROVISIONS FOR THE SETTLEMENT OF DISPUTES

The dispute settlement provisions are set out in Chapter XVIII (Articles 84–88) of the *Chicago Convention*.[3] Article 84 provides that if any disagreement arises between two or more contracting States relating to the interpretation or application of this Convention and its Annexes it shall, on the application of any State concerned in the disagreement, be decided by the Council. This provision also stipulates that no member of the Council shall vote in the

[2] ICAO Res A39–3 (October 6, 2016)

[3] On the subject of dispute settlement under Chapter XVIII of the *Chicago Convention* see B. Cheng, *The Law of International Air Transport* (London: Stevens, 1962), 101 ff; T. Buergenthal, *Law Making in the International Civil Aviation Organization* (New York: Syracuse University Press, 1969), 123f; M. Milde, *International Air Law and ICAO*, 2nd edn. (The Hague: Eleven International Publishing, 2012), 194; P. S. Dempsey, *Public International Air Law* (Montreal: Institute and Center for Research in Air and Space Law McGill University, 2008), 700; R. H. Mankiewicz, "Pouvoir judiciaire du conseil et réglement pour la solution des différends," *AFDI*, 3 (1957), 383 and R. C. Hingorani, "Dispute settlement in international civil aviation," *Arb J* 14 (1959), 14.

consideration by the Council of any dispute to which it is a party. Unusually for a UN specialized agency, a party to a dispute can appeal a decision taken by the ICAO Council directly to the International Court of Justice (ICJ). Article 85 provides for the situation that a State party to a dispute that wishes to appeal a decision of the Council is not a party to the ICJ Statute.[4] For certain authors, this provision seems to be no longer relevant since all 191 ICAO Member States are also members of the United Nations and therefore parties to the UN Charter and have accepted *de facto* the Statute of the ICJ.[5] Moreover, Article 86 stipulates that any decision of the Council on whether an international airline is operating in conformity with the provisions of the *Chicago Convention* shall remain in effect unless reversed on appeal and that the decisions of the Council, if appealed, shall be suspended until the appeal is decided. The decisions of the ICJ or an arbitral tribunal shall be final and binding.

In order to ensure compliance with decisions under Chapter XVIII, the *Chicago Convention* sets out two distinct types of sanctions: one for individual airlines and the other for States. The first is set out by Article 87, which provides that each contracting State undertakes not to allow the operation of an airline of a contracting State through its airspace if the Council has decided that the airline concerned is not conforming to a final decision rendered in accordance with Article 86. With respect to the sanction for States, Article 88 stipulates that the ICAO Assembly shall suspend the voting rights in the Assembly and in the Council of any contracting State that is found in default under the provision of this chapter. These sanctions have encountered a certain number of critics over the years. For example, Professor Milde has pointed out that in order to enforce the sanction of Article 88, a majority of States of the Assembly have to be in favor of such measure and would be "undoubtedly motivated by many policy considerations."[6]

10.3 THE RULES OF PROCEDURES FOR THE SETTLEMENT OF DIFFERENCES

The provisions of the *Chicago Convention* with respect to disputes are supplemented by the Rules of Procedure for the Settlement of Differences[7] (the

4 N. Mateesco-Matte, *Traité de droit aérien-aéronautique*, 2nd edn. (Paris: A Pedone, 1964), 221–22.
5 Cheng, *supra* Note 3 at 104; Milde, *supra* Note 3 at 194.
6 Ibid. at 199.
7 ICAO, "Rules for the Settlement of Differences," Doc 7782/2 (adopted 1957, revised 1975). [*Rules*]

Rules) adopted by the Council. These Rules set out the procedures for a State to introduce an application to the Council. Under these Rules, the Council, which is made up of the representatives of thirty-six member states, functions as a judicial body. The Council takes its decisions on the basis of the submission of written documents by the parties (memorials and counter memorials) as well as on the basis of oral hearings. Another important aspect of the Rules is the importance given to mediation and conciliation either before or during the proceedings.[8] For instance, it is provided at Article 2(g) of the Rules that any contracting State submitting a disagreement to the Council for settlement shall demonstrate that negotiations to settle the disagreement have taken place between the parties but were not successful.[9] Also, at any stage of the proceedings, the Council may invite the parties in dispute to engage in direct negotiations in order to settle the dispute or to narrow the issues.[10] Moreover, in order to facilitate the negotiations, the Council may designate an individual or a group of individuals to act as conciliators between the parties.[11] According to Professor Milde, this clearly departs from judicial functions because it promotes mediation and conciliation by the Council as well as allowing for the good offices of the President.[12] Therefore, as argued by Professor Buergenthal, the main task of the Council under article 84 of the *Chicago Convention* is "to assist in settling rather than in adjudicating disputes."[13]

Another interesting aspect of the Rules is the fact that they are closely aligned to the Rules of the Court of International Justice. This similarity may to some extent create certain problems,[14] as the ICJ is a judicial body and operates strictly as a tribunal. Therefore, the Rules adopted by the Council may be more adapted for a political body that does not operate according to the traditions of a court of justice.[15] The Rules were first adopted in 1957 and subsequently amended in 1975, but have not been modified since then. To this end, some have recently argued in favor of a review of these

[8] Hingorani, *supra* Note 3 at 24.
[9] *Rules*, Art. 2 (g).
[10] *Rules*, Art. 14 (1).
[11] *Rules*, Art. 14 (3).
[12] M. Milde, "Dispute settlement in the framework of the International Civil Aviation Organization (ICAO)," in K. H. Böckstiegel (ed.), *Settlement of Space Law Disputes: The Present State of the Law and Perspectives of Further Development: Proceedings of an International Colloquium, Munich, 13 and 14 September 1979* (Cologne: Heymann, 1980), 87–89.
[13] Buergenthal, *supra* Note 3 at 136.
[14] Milde, *supra* Note 3 at 197.
[15] Ibid.

Rules by the Council, which could potentially be a good opportunity to take into account the political specificity of this organ.[16]

10.4 JURISDICTION OF THE ICAO COUNCIL OVER THE SETTLEMENT OF DISPUTES

The Council can adjudicate legal disputes concerning the interpretation and the application of the *Chicago Convention*. Since the entry into force of the *Chicago Convention*, there have been five disputes under Article 84. Apart from its mandate for the settlement of disputes, the Council, by virtue of Article 66 of the *Chicago Convention*, also has jurisdiction over the settlement of disputes under the International Air Services Transit Agreement[17] and the International Air Transport Agreement.[18] Moreover, the Council has been empowered by the Assembly, during its First Session in 1947, to act as an arbitral body for disputes arising among contracting States relating to international civil aviation matters, when expressly requested to do so by all parties to such dispute.[19] A number of early bilateral agreements designated the ICAO Council as their dispute settlement body in case of any infringement by a party to such agreement.[20] Today, bilateral air agreements have largely abandoned any reference to the ICAO Council in its capacity of adjudicatory forum.[21] Most disputes under bilateral agreements are now resolved through arbitration.[22] The Council also has the duty to report to the Assembly any violation of the *Chicago Convention* as well as to consider any matter relating to the Convention that any contracting State refers to it.[23] Finally, at the request of any contracting State, the Council may investigate any situation

16 See for example J. Bae, "Review of the ICAO dispute settlement mechanism," *Journal of International Dispute Settlement*, 4 (2013), 65–81.

17 *International Air Services Transit Agreement* (adopted December 7, 1944, entered into force January 30, 1945) 84 UNTS 389, 59 Stat 1693, TIAS No 487.

18 *International Air Transport Agreement* (adopted December 7, 1944, entered into force February 8, 1945)171 UNTS 387, 59 Stat 1701, TIAS No 488.

19 ICAO Res A1–23. Nevertheless, we should note that since the entry into force of the *Chicago Convention*, no dispute was ever referred to the Council for arbitration under the terms of such resolution. *See* Milde, *supra* Note 3 at 197.

20 Dempsey, *supra* Note 3 at 702–3.

21 Ibid. at 702. Also, we should mention that certain States even proposed at the 6th Air Transport Conference electronic arbitration as a means of dispute settlement for bilateral agreements (*see* ATConf/6-WP/12).

22 To this end, certain agreements could designate the President of the ICAO Council to assist for the designation of arbitrator.

23 *Chicago Convention*, Art. 54 (j).

that may appear to present avoidable obstacles to the development of international air navigation.[24]

10.5 CASES REFERRED TO THE ICAO COUNCIL

Five cases have been brought to the attention of the Council under Article 84 of the *Chicago Convention*.[25] The first dispute occurred in 1952 and was between India and Pakistan with respect to the interpretation and application of the *Chicago Convention*.[26] India made an application before the Council, but the dispute was eventually settled by negotiation between the parties. The second dispute between the United Kingdom and Spain took place in 1967 and dealt with the Spanish ban on overflight of the approaches to Gibraltar.[27] The case was brought to the Council but the parties subsequently requested the Council in 1969 to defer the dispute *sine die*.[28] The third case arose in 1971 and involved Pakistan and India again following the suspension by India of all overflight of Indian territory by Pakistani aircraft.[29] India submitted preliminary objections to the Council denying its jurisdiction. Following their rejection by the Council, India lodged an appeal to the ICJ, which confirmed the Council's decision. This case was finally settled in 1976 following a joint statement by the parties announcing the discontinuance of the proceedings.[30] The fourth case was brought to the Council in 1996.[31] At that time, the United States denied Cuban aircraft the right to fly over its

[24] *Chicago Convention*, Art. 55 (e).

[25] For a summary of each of the cases see Milde, *supra* Note 3 at 200 ff and Dempsey, *supra* Note 3 at 703 ff. For the list of the Council documents with respect to each case see L. Weber, *International Civil Aviation Organization* (The Netherlands: Kluwer, 2012), 53–54.

[26] Cheng, *supra* Note 3 at 101ff; Buergenthal, *supra* Note 3 at 137; Frederick Tymms, "Le différend Inde-Pakistan" (1953) *Rev Gen Air*, **16** 207.

[27] Milde, *supra* Note 3 at 201–2; Weber, *supra* Note 25 at 53.

[28] ICAO, "Annual Report of the Council to the Assembly for 1969" (P/2 June 1970), Doc 8869 A18.

[29] G. F. Fitzgerald, "The Judgement of the International Court of Justice in the appeal relating to the jurisdiction of the ICAO council," *Can YB Int'l L*, **12** (1974) 153; T. L. Albertson, "Appellate jurisdiction of the international court of justice – Jurisdiction of the council of the international civil aviation organization," *Harv Int'l LJ*, **14** (1973), 612; K. Hailbronner, "Jurisdiction of the ICAO council case," in R. Bernhardt (ed.), *Encyclopedia of International Law* (Amsterdam: North Holland, 1981), vol 2, 161; P. M. Eisemann, "L'arrêt du 18 août 1972 en l'affaire de l'appel concernant la competence du Conseil de l'OACI (Inde c. Pakistan)," *AFDI*, **18** (1972), 284; A. Manin, "Appel concernant la compétence du conseil de l'OACI," *AFDI*, **19** (1973), 290; J. Huntzinger, "L'affaire de l'appel concernant la compétence du conseil de l'OACI devant la cour international de Justice (arrêt du 18 août 1972)," *RGDIP*, 78 (1974), 975.

[30] Milde, *supra* Note 3 at 203.

[31] Ibid. at 203–4; Dempsey, *supra* Note 3 at 709–10.

territory toward Canada. After the hearings of the parties, the President of the Council acted as Conciliator and the parties reached an agreement.[32] The most recent dispute brought to the Council occurred in 2000 and was between the United States and fifteen EU member States.[33] The issue related to the application of an EU Directive on the noise of aircraft engines, also known as the "hushkit Regulation." The application of this regulation would have had the consequence of denying almost all US carriers the right to fly their older aircraft into the EU.[34] The fifteen EU States submitted a preliminary objection concerning the jurisdiction of the Council.[35] This objection was rejected by the Council and the parties proceeded with the hearing on the substance.[36] The Council then decided to appoint the President as a Conciliator, and the case was finally settled when the EU repealed its initial regulation and adopted a directive that satisfied both Parties.[37]

The Council has never issued a decision on the merits of a case.[38] It seems that on every occasion, mediation as well as the use of the good offices of the President of the Council contributed to resolving the dispute.[39] The fact that the machinery set out in Chapter XVIII of the *Chicago Convention* has not been able to produce over the years a decision on the merits is certainly one of the main reasons why many authors believe that this mechanism is a "failure."[40] On the contrary, other authors believe that the incapacity of the Council ever to render a final adjudication does not necessarily indicate that the machinery under Chapter XVIII of the *Chicago Convention* is inefficient.[41] According to these authors the inability for the Council to render decisions on the merits demonstrates that States prefer to settle their aviation

32 Ibid.

33 Milde, *supra* Note 3 at 204; Dempsey, *supra* Note 3 at 711; B. A. Claes, "Aircraft noise regulation in the European Union: the Hushkit problem," *J Air L & Com*, 65 (2000), 329; K. E. Brown, "The International Civil Aviation Organization is the appropriate jurisdiction to settle hushkit dispute between the United States and the European Union," *Penn St Int'l L Rev*, 20 (2000), 465; "Report on economic law on 'the admissibility of U.S.-EU 'hushkits dispute' before the ICAO," *Am J Int'l L*, 95 (2001), 410.

34 Milde, *supra* Note 3 at 205.

35 Ibid.

36 Ibid.

37 Weber, *supra* Note 25 at 53.

38 Milde, *supra* Note 3 at 200.

39 Dempsey, *supra* Note 3 at 736–37.

40 Milde, *supra* Note 3 at 200. See also G. S. Sanchez, "The impotence of the Chicago Convention dispute settlement provisions," *Issues Aviation L & Policy*, 10 (2010), 27.

41 R. N. Gariepy and D. L. Botsford, "The effectiveness of the International Civil Aviation Organization's adjudicatory machinery," *J Air L & Com*, 42 (1976), 357–58.

disputes through the channel of diplomacy rather than adjudication.[42] In fact, it is probably more advantageous for States to settle their dispute through negotiation rather than letting the Council decide for them.[43] Also, except for the "hushkit case," the disputes brought to the Council under Article 84 of the *Chicago Convention* were bilateral in nature and concerned rights of overflight in restricted areas. Moreover, as pointed out by Professor Milde, even if those disputes were related to overflight rights, their "center of gravity" was in fact political in nature and their nature was often external to aviation.[44] In fact, the "hushkit case" was the only one clearly dealing with environmental protection and is the only one that may provide guidance on how the ICAO Council would deal with a comparable dispute arising in the future.

10.6 THE PERFORMANCE OF QUASI-JUDICIAL FUNCTIONS BY THE ICAO COUNCIL

In theory, when the Council is performing the duties set out under Chapter XVIII of the *Chicago Convention*, it "must consider itself an international judicial organ and act in accordance with rules of international law governing judicial proceedings. Thus, *inter alia*, members of the Council, even though they may be national representatives nominated by Governments must . . . act in an impartial and judicial capacity."[45] However, it seems that, in practice, the Council does not act as impartially and judicially as the statement suggests. Since the signature of the *Chicago Convention* in 1944, a number of authors have raised concerns with respect to the judicial functions of the ICAO Council.[46] These concerns are related to the fact that Council Members are neither necessarily independent nor always qualified in order to perform a judicial duty. The Council is composed of thirty-six sovereign States elected by the Assembly.[47] The Representatives are nominated by their States as diplomatic agents rather than independent experts – unlike the Air Navigation Commissioners.[48] Therefore, Council Members are not independent

[42] Ibid. at 358.
[43] Sanchez, *supra* Note 40 at 31.
[44] Milde, *supra* Note 3 at 203.
[45] Cheng, *supra* Note 3 at 101.
[46] See also D. Goedhuis, "Question of public international air law," *Rec des Cours*, 81 (1952), 201 at 223–24.
[47] *Chicago Convention*, Art. 50 (a).
[48] The Air Navigation Commission is the technical organ of the ICAO. Its principal function under Art. 57 of the *Chicago Convention* is to consider amendments or modifications to the

per se.[49] In opposition to ICJ judges, who are bound by their oath of office to act independently, the Council Members, decide disputes on the basis of the interests of their own State and most likely following precise instructions.[50] For example, during the hearing of the second case, *Pakistan* v. *India* (1971), a number of Representatives requested the postponement of a vote in order to seek instructions from their respective administrations.[51] Council Members are appointed by their governments based on their expertise in the field of civil aviation.[52] The *Chicago Convention* itself only stipulates that no Representative shall be actively associated with the operation of an international air service or have any financial interest in such service.[53] Consequently, the academic and professional background of the representatives is diverse and most of them are not necessarily lawyers by trade and have not exercised any judicial functions prior to their appointment. The ability of the Members of the Council to fully assume their judicial functions and render proper decisions based on the applicable law is therefore questionable.[54]

Nevertheless, we should mention that despite its apparent lack of independence, the Council has not faced any serious criticism caused by its absence of judicial capacity over the years.[55] One explanation given by an author is that most cases brought before the Council were very specific, localized, and concerned bilateral disputes.[56] Consequently, the Council was able to be seen as neutral and, to a certain extent, able to preserve its independence. Finally, considering the appeal mechanism that exists at the ICJ, a decision apparently unreasonably taken by the Council could be reversed on appeal.[57]

Clearly, any decision taken by the Council following a demand under Article 84 of the *Chicago Convention* would most likely be based largely on political grounds. We can certainly question whether such a method of adjudicating disputes is fit for our purpose in the present context. In fact, the first president of the ICAO Council, Dr. Edward Warner, was already of the opinion in 1945 that "no international agency composed of representatives

Annexes to the said Convention and to recommend them to the Council. See Weber, *supra* Note 25 at 38.

49 Milde, *supra* Note 3 at 199.
50 Ibid.
51 Council Minutes 29 July 1971 (C-Min. 74/6).
52 Milde, *supra* Note 3 at 199; Dempsey, *supra* Note 3 at 734.
53 *Chicago Convention*, Art. 50 (c).
54 Dempsey, *supra* Note 3 at 734.
55 Bae, *supra* Note 16 at 71.
56 Ibid.
57 Ibid.

of States could be expected to bring judicial detachment to the consideration of particular cases in which large national interests were involved."[58]

10.7 THE CONSIDERATION OF ENVIRONMENTAL PROTECTION AND SUSTAINABLE DEVELOPMENT BY THE ICAO COUNCIL

Under Article 2.2 of the Kyoto Protocol,[59] States shall pursue limitation of greenhouse gases emission (GHG) by working through the ICAO. Nevertheless, the ICAO does not consider that the said provision grants a mandate to the Organization to act specifically on that matter.[60] In fact, as correctly pointed out by Professor Dempsey, a literal reading of the Kyoto Protocol suggests that only certain States are obliged to address the issue of GHG emissions from international aviation.[61] In fact, the ICAO is not bound under the *Chicago Convention* or the Kyoto Protocol to develop a policy with respect to GHG emissions, but is also not precluded from doing so.[62] The ICAO is viewed as a forum where States can discuss any such issues.[63] Without any desire of its Member States, the ICAO does not have a specific obligation to consider such a matter. Nevertheless, the signature of the Kyoto Protocol seems to have been the starting point for the ICAO Assembly to take actions in order to deal with the issue of aviation and climate change.[64] A review of ICAO Assembly Resolutions since 1998 certainly demonstrates the political will of the EU and of certain Member States to tackle that subject.[65] However, the adoption of an international scheme to limit GHG emissions from aircraft in international flight remained a matter of great controversy until the decisions of the ICAO at its 39th Assembly in October 2017.

58 E. Warner, "The Chicago air conference accomplishments and unfinished business," *Foreign Affairs*, **23** (1945), 406 at 415.

59 *Protocol to the United Nations Framework Convention on Climate Change* (signed December 11, 1997, entered into force February 16, 2005), UN Doc FCCC/CP/1997/7/Add.1.

60 A. Piera, *Greenhouse Gas Emissions from International Aviation* (The Hague: Eleven International Publishing, 2015), 44.

61 Dempsey, *supra* Note 3 at 450.

62 Such opinion has been argued *inter alia* by the former Director of the ICAO Legal Bureau, Mr. Denys Wibaux. "The text under consideration, if combined with the Chicago Convention, could be interpreted to indicate that there was no legal obligation for ICAO to develop a policy or rules in respect of aviation GHG emissions, nor was there obviously any legal obstacle, either in the UNFCCC, the Kyoto Protocol or the Chicago Convention, to ICAO developing policies or rules aimed at reducing aviation GHG emissions." See C-MIN 181/21 at 256, para 22.

63 Piera, *supra* Note 60 at 44.

64 Ibid.

65 Ibid. at 44–45, n 17.

The agreement reached at the Conference of the Parties in Paris in December 2015 (COP21) did not make any reference to civil aviation or the ICAO. In fact, the preliminary paragraph on aviation was surprisingly removed completely from the final agreement.[66] However, the momentum created at Paris continued to put pressure on States at the ICAO to address aviation emissions through the implementation of a distinct MBM scheme.[67] This was finally achieved at the 39th Assembly of the ICAO with the adoption of Resolution A39–3 in October 2017, prior to the adoption of Resolution A39–3 calling for the design and adoption by the ICAO Council of global Market-Based Measures (MBM) to reduce GHG emissions from aircraft. This Resolution was the culmination of many years of difficult negotiations in the ICAO and reflected the sense of urgency felt by many states attending the ICAO Assembly as a result of commitments made at the Paris Climate Change Summit earlier in 2015.[68] Resolution A39–3 calls for the adoption by the ICAO Council of a scheme of MBM, taking the form of a Carbon Offsetting and Reduction Scheme for International Aviation (CORSIA) to be ready for the next Assembly in 2019. Prior to that, the only scheme in existence was that of the EU-ETS, adopted unilaterally, which entered into force in 2012.[69] In the face of considerable opposition, the EU-ETS was withdrawn by the EU and is unlikely ever to be reintroduced, unless the ICAO scheme fails to be adopted. However, the EU-ETS remains the most concrete model currently in existence.

Since the *Chicago Convention* was adopted in 1944, at a time when environmental protection was not an issue for the international community, it did not include any provision with respect to environmental protection or sustainable development.[70] Therefore, any dispute with respect to the implementation of the EU-ETS or Resolution A39–3 could certainly raise questions

[66] See UNFCCC, "Proposal by the President, Paris Agreement" (December 12, 2015), https://unfccc.int/resource/docs/2015/cop21/eng/l09r01.pdf last accessed October 18, 2017.

[67] Green Air Online, "COP21 President says growing emissions from aviation and shipping sectors must be tackled this year" (January 22, 2016), greenaironline.com/news.php?viewStory=2188 last accessed October 18, 2017.

[68] See UNFCC, "Climate change conference – November 2015," https://unfccc.int/process/conferences/pastconferences/marrakech-climate-change-conference-november-2016/events-and-programme/climate-change-studio last accessed October 24, 2017.

[69] European Commission, Directive 2008/101/EC of the European Parliament and of the Council of 19 November 2008 amending Directive 2003/87/EC so as to include aviation activities in the scheme for greenhouse gas emission allowance trading within the Community, OJ 2008 No. L8/3.

[70] See B. F. Havel and G. S. Sanchez, *The Principles and Practice of International Aviation Law* (New York: Cambridge University Press, 2014), 228.

regarding *inter alia* the jurisdiction and suitability of the Council to handle such matters under Article 84 of the said Convention. Nonetheless, since the Council has broad jurisdiction with respect to the "interpretation and application" of the *Chicago Convention* there appear to be few limits on the exercise of its jurisdiction.[71] Thus, it would be highly unlikely that the Council would refuse to take into consideration the principles of environment and sustainable development while examining a potential application with respect to the unilateral implementation of the EU-ETS or if it were called upon to rule on a challenge to the application of Resolution 39.3. In fact, environmental protection is one of the five strategic objectives of the Organization, and to refuse such consideration would be against certain ICAO Assembly Resolutions adopted within the past few decades.[72] Also, as a great number of States elected on the Council are also Parties to the Kyoto Protocol and all supported the Paris Summit Declaration on Climate Change, it would be incongruous for States to adopt a position in one *forum* and do the opposite in another. However, the weight to be accorded to the principle of sustainable development in a particular case can only be a matter of conjecture.[73]

10.8 EXAMPLES OF LEGAL PROCEEDINGS WHICH COULD BE INITIATED AGAINST THE EU

In the event that a dispute occurs in the coming years in the field of sustainable development and environmental protection, arising either out of the reimposition of the EU-ETS or disputes concerning the application of the MBM scheme adopted by the Council pursuant to Resolution A39–3 and applied by states, it is most likely that certain States would challenge these measures before the Council and possible in other fora. For example, prior to the 38th session of the Assembly, several States expressed their objections to the EU Directive on

71 Bae, *supra* Note 16 at 79.

72 See ICAO Assembly Resolutions, A32–8; A33–7; A35–5; A36–22; A37–19 and A38–18. See also Piera, *supra* Note 60 at 44–45, note 17. Moreover, taking urgent actions to combat climate change and its impact is one of the UN Sustainable Development Goals. To this end, as a UN agency, the ICAO is already involved in a number of activities in order to contribute to tackling the established targets. See ICAO, "ICAO and the United Nations sustainable development goals," https://www.icao.int/about-icao/aviation-development/Pages/SDG.aspx accessed October 18, 2017.

73 See Chapter 11, which examines the principle of sustainable development in WTO law and in public international law.

ETS through various statements, actions, or even lawsuits.[74] One of the most important of these is the Joint Declaration of the Moscow Meeting on Inclusion of Civil Aviation in the EU-ETS, adopted in Moscow in February 2012.[75] This declaration gives an idea of the range of actions that could possibly be taken by States wishing to avoid the EU measures.[76] This declaration was affirmed prior to the 38th session of the ICAO Assembly. Since the 39th ICAO Assembly adopted Resolution A39–3 on the establishment of global market-based measures and charged the Council to implement such a scheme by 2019, the 2012 declaration is now obsolete. However, one can note that a range of measures were threatened to stop the EU from moving forward with its EU-ETS. The first measure was to file an application to the ICAO Council under Article 84 of the *Chicago Convention*.[77] Had that actually occurred, the Council would have faced a range of procedural and substantive arguments, which are discussed in the next section. Should disputes ever arise out of the MBM scheme that is currently under consideration before the Council and is to be implemented by 2019 similar questions may well arise.

74 For a list of the principal reactions to the EU-ETS see P. M. de Leon, "Enforcement of the EU ETS: The EU's convulsive efforts to export its environmental values," *Air & Space L*, 37 (2012), 286 at 292ff; Piera, *supra* Note 60 at 135 ff.

75 Green Air, "Joint declaration of the Moscow meeting on inclusion of civil aviation in the EU-ETS" (February 22, 2012), www.greenaironline.com/photos/Moscow_Declaration.pdf last accessed October 18, 2017. [*Moscow Declaration*]. The Moscow Declaration has been supported by Armenia, Argentina, Republic of Belarus, Brazil, Cameroon, Chile, China, Cuba, Guatemala, India, Japan, Republic of Korea, Mexico, Nigeria, Paraguay, Russian Federation, Saudi Arabia, Seychelles, Singapore, South Africa, Thailand, Uganda, and the United States.

76 Ibid. at Attachment A.

77 (1) Filing an application under Art. 84 of the *Chicago Convention* for resolution of the dispute according to the ICAO Rules for the Settlement of Differences (Doc 7782/2); (2) using existing or new State legislation, regulations, or other legal mechanism to prohibit airlines/aircraft operators of that State from participating in the EU-ETS; (3) holding meetings with the EU carriers and/or aviation-related enterprises in their respective States and apprising them about the concerns arising out of the EU-ETS and the possibility of reciprocal measures that could be adopted by the State, which may adversely affect those airlines and/or entities; (4) mandating EU carriers to submit flight details and other data; (5) assessing whether the EU-ETS is consistent with the WTO Agreements and taking appropriate action; (6) reviewing Bilateral Air Services Agreements, including Open Skies with individual EU Member States, and reconsidering the implementation or negotiation of the "Horizontal Agreement" with the EU; (7) suspending current and future discussions and/or negotiations to enhance operating rights for EU airlines/aircraft operators; (8) imposing additional levies/charges on EU carriers/aircraft operators as a form of countermeasure; and (9) any other actions/measures.

10.9 THE AMBIGUOUS STATUS OF THE EU AT THE ICAO

Currently, the EU has only an *ad hoc* observer status at the ICAO. In law, the EU cannot accede to the Organization due to the provisions of the *Chicago Convention* with respect to membership,[78] which only allow sovereign States to become members.[79] To complicate matters, a recent judgment of the European Court of Justice (ECJ) affirmed that the EU is not bound by the *Chicago Convention* since it is not a party.[80] A potential application under article 84 of the *Chicago Convention* opposing an EU measure would have to be taken against all EU Member States in the ICAO as was done in 2000 for the "hushkit case."[81] Therefore, even if the status of the EU remains an exception at the ICAO, it seems that EU Member States would have to answer for their actions pursuant to EU decisions.

10.10 MEANS OF RESOLVING A POTENTIAL DISPUTE WITH RESPECT TO THE EU-ETS BEFORE THE COUNCIL

If a dispute arises involving the EU-ETS scheme or measures taken pursuant to Resolution A39–3, it is most likely that the Council would handle the matter in a manner similar to the Hushkit case.[82] The Council would certainly first seek mediation and conciliation rather than adjudication,[83] and would encourage negotiations at different stages of the proceedings.[84] It is also foreseeable that the

[78] See A. de Mestral and M. Vaugeois, "La reconnaissance de l'Union européenne à l'Organisation de l'aviation civile internationale: une perspective canadienne," Policy Brief Series, Canada-Europe Transatlantic Dialogue, Carleton University, Ottawa, May 2015, http://labs.carleton.ca/canadaeurope/wp-content/uploads/sites/9/Vaugeois-policy-paper-20152.pdf last accessed October 17, 2017.

[79] *Chicago Convention*, Art. 92.

[80] *Air Transport Association of America (ATA) and US airlines* v. *UK Secretary of State for Energy and Climate Change* (December 21, 2011), CJEU Case 366/10. See B. F. Havel and J. Q. Mulligan, "The triumph of politics: Reflections on the judgment of the Court of Justice of the European Union validating the inclusion of non-EU airlines in the emissions trading scheme," *Air & Space L*, 37 (2012), 3; P. M. de Leon, "Enforcement of the EU ETS: The EU's convulsive efforts to export its environmental values," *Air & Space L*, 37 (2012) 287.

[81] P. Manzini and A. Masutti, "The application of the EU ETS system to the aviation sector: From legal disputes to international retaliations," *Air & Space L*, 37 (2012) 313, note 13.

[82] Bae, *supra* Note 16 at 78.

[83] D. Maniatis, "Conflict in the skies: The settlement of international aviation disputes," *Ann Air & Sp L*, 20 (1995), 167 at 192–93.

[84] *Rules*, Art. 14 (1).

President of the Council might at some point during the potential proceeding be designated as a Conciliator among the parties.[85]

If the EU were to proceed again with unilateral enforcement of its ETS, or a dispute arose out of the implementation of Resolution A39–3, the ensuing dispute would have worldwide implications. Consequently, it is questionable how any State Member of Council would be able to act impartially in such case. EU states on Council would have to recuse themselves as being directly involved in the dispute, as would any state taking measures pursuant to Resolution A39–3. EU States might possibly be tempted to submit a counter claim intended to deprive non-EU States not party to the dispute of their voting rights, due to their indirect implication in the dispute.[86] If such claim succeeded, it would affect the quorum needed to allow the Council to take a decision.[87] It would also be argued that other States members of Council would be at the same time judge and indirectly party to the dispute. Moreover, certain States could be viewed in the judicial process as already biased due *inter alia* to their signature in 2012 of the Moscow Declaration. One could even argue that all non-EU States flying to and from the EU were equally situated, and therefore "Parties" to the dispute. Unfortunately, no provisions exist in the *Chicago Convention* with respect to the appearance of impartiality of States while performing their duties under Article 84.[88] Therefore, as pointed out by Dr. Jon Bae, a preliminary objection of the EU member states with respect to the lack of impartiality of the Council might well not be successful.[89]

With the adoption of Resolution A39–3 a more likely scenario for a possible dispute between ICAO member states might involve differences of opinion as to its application to developing states who consider that they should be exempt, or attempts by major aviation states to impose the scheme on recalcitrant states. In such circumstances the states imposing the scheme might well invoke both the fact of the Resolution and the need to ensure its broadest application in order to protect the atmosphere from further degradation. In such cases the Council will be faced with claims justifying the Resolution and unilateral measures to enforce it based on the need to protect the global environment and sustainable development.

85 Maniatis, *supra* Note 83 at 191.
86 Bae, *supra* Note 16 at 79.
87 Art. 52 of the *Chicago Convention* stipulates that "[d]ecisions by the Council shall require approval by a majority of its members." See Bae, *supra* note 16 at 79.
88 Bae, *supra* Note 16 at 78.
89 Ibid.

10.11 CONCLUSION

Despite all the obstacles, it appears that the dispute settlement mechanism set out at Article 84 of the *Chicago Convention* could still certainly be invoked in a potential dispute in the field of sustainable development and environmental protection. As demonstrated, it seems that a dispute involving a large number of States would be somewhat different from previous cases, which were regional and bilateral in nature. Nevertheless, this dispute settlement mechanism remains relevant and appropriate for a highly political dispute such as the one involving the EU-ETS, where conciliation and mediation will be prioritized. The procedural hurdles are considerable. Equally uncertain is the willingness of members of the ICAO Council to base their decision on principles of sustainable development. The *Chicago Convention* does not require this result but equally it need not frustrate the recourse to evolving standards of environmental protection.

11

International Civil Aviation and Sustainable Development

The Application of WTO Law

Emilie Conway and Armand de Mestral*

This chapter seeks to determine whether the Emissions Trading System of the European Union (EU-ETS) might be challenged or justified under the law of the World Trade Organization (WTO). In principle, much of the law of international air transport governed by the Chicago Convention is not covered by WTO law, but, arguably, certain important aspects may be covered. This chapter considers whether the principles of sustainable development might be used as justification of the EU-ETS should it be challenged under the WTO Dispute Settlement Understanding. It is argued that the principles of sustainable development would be invoked in WTO dispute settlement involving the EU-ETS.

11.1 INTRODUCTION

This chapter considers whether the law of the World Trade Organization (WTO) might arguably apply to the exercise of rights and duties under a greenhouse gas emissions scheme covering emissions from civil aircraft on international flights, adopted unilaterally by a state or group of states, or adopted pursuant to the recent decisions of the Assembly of the International Civil Aviation Organization (ICAO) in October 2016. Among these decisions is Resolution A39–3, which calls for the design and adoption by the ICAO Council of Global Market-Based Measures (MBM) taking the form of a Carbon Offsetting and Reduction Scheme for International Aviation (CORSIA).[1] This Resolution was the culmination of many years of difficult

* The views represented in this chapter are strictly personal and not to be attributed to any other entity directly or indirectly associated with the authors.

[1] ICAO, "Consolidated statement of continuing ICAO policies and practices related to environmental protection – Global Market-Based Measure (MBM) scheme," Res A39–3 (October 6, 2016)

negotiations in the ICAO and reflected the sense of urgency felt by many states attending the ICAO 39th Assembly as a result of commitments made at the Paris Climate Change Summit earlier in 2016. Prior to the adoption of Resolution A39–3, the only scheme in existence was that of the European Union (EU), adopted as part of its ongoing efforts to curb climate change through reduction of carbon emissions. The EU scheme adopted pursuant to directive 2008/101/EC[2] (the Aviation Directive) extended the comprehensive EU Emission Trading System (ETS)[3] to include the aviation industry. Accordingly, effective as of January 1, 2012, all airline companies – EU and non-EU airlines, without distinction – were to be subject to a greenhouse gas emission allowance trading scheme, a "cap and trade" system, providing for the acquisition and surrender of allowances for emissions generated by flights coming in and out of European airports.

While the rationale behind the ETS scheme appears to have won broad support, as reflected by the international consensus on climate change issues, evidenced by the recent Paris Agreement on climate change,[4] its unilateral extension to aviation services elicited strong reactions, both in the International Civil Aviation Organization and other international fora.[5] Pending negotiations for a global scheme applicable to all states to be adopted by the ICAO, the EU agreed to suspend some of its requirements and limit its

[2] European Commission, Directive 2008/101/EC of the European Parliament and of the Council of 19 November 2008 amending Directive 2003/87/EC so as to include aviation activities in the scheme for greenhouse gas emission allowance trading within the Community, OJ 2008 No. L8/3 [Directive 2008/101/EC].

[3] European Commission, Directive 2003/87/EC of the European Parliament and of the Council of 13 October 2003 establishing a scheme for greenhouse gas emission allowance trading within the Community and amending Council Directive 96/61/EC, OJ 2003 No. L 275/32.

[4] The Paris Agreement was signed on December 12, 2015 and entered into force on November 4, 2016.

[5] For example, a consortium of US-based airline companies challenged the measures undertaken by the United Kingdom to implement Directive 2008/101/EC before the High Court of Justice of England and Wales, which then referred the case for a preliminary ruling by the Court of Justice of the European Union (CJEU). The CJEU's ruling, which was delivered in 2011, upheld the validity of the ETS: [ATAA]. Case c-366/10, *Air Transport Association of America* v. *Secretary of State for Energy and Climate Change*. [2012] OJ C49/7; [2012] 2 CMLR 4. [ATAA]; On the political front, a group of twenty-three opposing countries adopted the *Joint Declaration of the Moscow Meeting on Inclusion of International Civil Aviation in the EU-ETS* in February 2012, which was intended "as a clear manifestation of their unanimous position that the EU and its Member States must cease application of the Directive 2008/101/EC to airlines/ aircraft operators registered in third States," www.ruaviation.com/docs/1/2012/2/22/50/ [Moscow Joint Declaration]. Finally, some States have forbidden their national airlines from complying with the scheme.

geographical scope to flights within the European Economic Area.[6] The Aviation Directive is unlikely to be reinstated in its original form unless the ICAO scheme fails to be implemented.[7] However, the EU scheme remains the most concrete model currently in existence, and offers a good testing ground for compatibility with WTO rules.

For the moment, the adoption of ICAO Assembly Resolution A39–3 reduces the likelihood of any formal dispute between states concerning an MBM scheme for the immediate future, at least until the ICAO scheme is proposed and adopted by 2019. Thus, a WTO dispute is only a theoretical possibility at this point. Nevertheless, invocation of WTO law in the context of an MBM scheme would likely have far-reaching implications for the trade/environment linkage. This is because the MBM touches upon some of the most contentious aspects in WTO jurisprudence, namely the interface between multilateral environmental agreements (MEAs) and trade rules, process and production methods, and extraterritorial application of environmental measures. For this reason, while the immediate likelihood of a dispute has been postponed, the questions posed are of great interest to environmental, trade, and air lawyers.

Drawing on the environmental justification given for the EU scheme and now for ICAO Resolution A39–3, this chapter examines whether, in the event of a WTO dispute, the principle of sustainable development might successfully be invoked to justify either the EU Directive as originally drafted or ICAO Resolution A39–3 under WTO law.

Section 11.2 examines how the EU scheme could be subject to WTO rules, and more particularly with provisions of the *General Agreement on Tariffs and*

6 In the face of strong opposition, the EU decided to stop the clock until work in the ICAO resumed. See European Commission, Decision No. 377/2013/EU of the European Parliament and of the Council of April 24, 2013 derogating temporarily from Directive 2003/87/EC establishing a scheme for greenhouse gas emission allowance trading within the Community, OJ 2013, No. L 113/1; Regulation (EU) No 421/2014 of the European Parliament and of the Council of 16 April 2014 amending Directive 2003/87/EC establishing a scheme for greenhouse gas emission allowance trading within the Community, in view of the implementation by 2020 of an international agreement applying a single global market-based measure to international aviation emissions Text with EEA relevance, OJ 2014 No. L 129, April 30, 2014.

7 The European Commission has recently proposed to maintain the reduced geographical scope of the EU-ETS beyond 2016: European Commission, "Proposal for a regulation of the European parliament and of the council amending Directive 2003/87/EC to continue current limitations of scope for aviation activities and to prepare to implement a global market-based measure from 2021" (February 3, 2017) COM(2017) 54 final, eur-lex.europa.eu/legal-content/EN/TXT/PDF/?uri=CELEX:52017PC0054&from=EN last accessed October 21, 2017.

Trade (GATT).[8] It also considers whether ICAO Resolution A39–3 is compatible with WTO law and whether unilateral attempts to apply the ICAO MBM scheme to recalcitrant states might come into conflict with WTO law. Section 11.3 then analyses whether the principle of sustainable development may provide an effective defense against allegations of violation of WTO law.

11.2 THE EU EMISSIONS TRADING SYSTEM AND WTO LAW

In order to set solid groundwork for discussion, a few words are first warranted about the background and functioning of the EU's Aviation Directive (11.2.1) to understand how it might eventually be challenged by a WTO Member before a dispute panel (11.2.2).

11.2.1 *Extending the European Trading System to Aviation*

The EU-ETS came about in the context of the desire of the EU authorities to give effect to the international community's commitment to limit climate change, as set out under the United Nations Framework Convention on Climate Change (UNFCCC) and the Kyoto Protocol.[9] The Kyoto Protocol, which entered into force in 2005, imposes upon State parties listed in its Annex 1 the obligation to reduce their greenhouse gas emissions according to given targets.[10] Although such targets do not apply to international aviation, section 2(2) of the Protocol requires "[t]he Parties included in Annex I [to] pursue limitation or reduction of emissions of greenhouse gases not controlled by the Montreal Protocol from aviation … working through the International Civil Aviation Organization."[11] It had proved difficult to reach a consensus on the appropriate approach to alleviate climate impacts of international aviation under the auspices of the ICAO before 2016. The limited scope of proposed measures in the ICAO negotiations in the early years of the new century

8 *General Agreement on Tariffs and Trade, Annex 1A of the Marrakesh Agreement establishing the World Trade Organization* (adopted April 15, 1994, entered into force January 1, 1995) 1869 UNTS 426 () [GATT]. In this chapter, we have purposely left aside the question relating to the Aviation Directive's compatibility with the General Agreement on Trade in Services.

9 *United Nations Framework Convention on Climate Change*, (adopted June 12, 1992, entered into force March 21, 1994), 1771 UNTS 107, (1992) 31ILM 849 [UNFCCC]; *Kyoto Protocol to the United Nations Framework Convention on Climate Change*, (adopted December 11, 1997, entered into force February 16, 2005), FCCC/CP/1997/L.7/Add. 1, 37 ILM 22 [Kyoto Protocol].

10 Kyoto Protocol, ibid., Art. 3.

11 Ibid., Art. 2(2).

prompted the EU to develop its own strategy by expanding its Emission Trading System to cover international air transport through directive 2008/101/EC.[12]

In a nutshell, directive 2008/101/EC establishes a global ceiling for greenhouse gas emissions by fixing a limited quantity of allowances issued to aircraft operators each year. Emission quantities are to be adjusted annually according to a sliding scale.[13] Under the scheme, aircraft operators are required to monitor their yearly emissions – calculated in terms of tons of CO_2 – and surrender an equivalent number of emission allowances.[14] Such obligations are imposed upon all aircraft operators for "flights which depart from or arrive in an aerodrome situated in the territory of a Member State," whether they be passenger or cargo flights, intra-EU flights or flights between EU and non-EU airports.[15] Part of the controversy surrounding the Aviation Directive stemmed from the fact that it was designed to apply not only to flights within the EU, but also to the portion of international flights between the EU and a non-EU destination.[16] Sanctions for noncompliance range from monetary penalties – 100 euros per ton of carbon dioxide emitted in excess of allowances surrendered – to outright operating bans.[17]

[12] In the ICAO context, see ICAO, "Consolidated statement of continuing ICAO policies and practices related to environmental protection," Res A36–22 (September 28, 2007), at para 1(b)(1), www.icao.int/env/A36 last accessed October 19, 2017 (discouraging unilateral action); ICAO, "Consolidated statement of continuing ICAO policies and practices related to environmental protection," Assembly Res A37–19 (October 8, 2010), at para 6(c), https://www.icao.int/environmental-protection/37thAssembly/A37_Res19_en.pdf last accessed October 19, 2017 (showing a degree of openness by recognizing that some States may choose to take more ambitious actions but reminding the need to engage in consultations and negotiations before implementing unilateral measures). Many States lodged reservations to the 2010 Resolution: See ICAO, https://www.icao.int/Meetings/AMC/Assembly37/Documents/ProvisionalEdition/a37_res_prov_en.pdf last accessed October 19, 2017 (on the one hand, the EU member States and states members of the European Civil Aviation Conference issued a reservation stating that the *Chicago Convention* does not require States to obtain prior consent from other States before applying market-based measures to their national airline operators; on the other hand, another group of States added a reservation stressing that unilateral measures are prohibited).

[13] Directive 2008/101/EC, *supra* Note 5, Art. 3(c) (1)(2) (initially at 97 percent of a benchmark based on the industry's average carbon emissions over the years 2004–2006 and at a 95 percent rate starting in 2013 and onward.)

[14] Ibid., Art 3(g), 14(3).

[15] Ibid. Annex 1 (definition of "Aviation"). Annex 1 also contains a list of excluded aviation activities for example, military flights and humanitarian flights, *inter alia*.

[16] L. Bartels, "The WTO legality of the application of the EU's trading system to aviation," *EJIL*, **23** (2012), 429 at 430 [Bartels, "ETS"].

[17] Directive 2008/101/EC, *supra* Note 5, Art 16(3)(5).

Application of the ETS would likely have economic repercussions on WTO Members, to varying degrees.[18] In this regard, it can be said that the obligation to purchase emissions allowances, or the imposition of fines or plain denial of entry into the EU for refusal to respect the Directive might constitute violations of the EU's WTO obligations. For example, the Directive could fall under the application of GATT disciplines on trade in goods, insofar as it imposes restrictions – albeit indirectly – on goods being transported on international flights to and from Europe. The assumption here is that the aviation directive's compliance costs – i.e. the purchase of emission allowances – would be passed on to the importers of the goods, thus translating to increased air transportation costs, and ultimately, higher product prices.[19] If the Directive ever came under the purview of WTO law, the next question becomes whether it is likely to contravene trade rules.

11.2.2 *Application of WTO Law to the Aviation Directive*

The legal nature of the Aviation Directive has so far inspired many legal analyses by scholars.[20] Rather than repeating the exercise of qualifying the ETS under WTO, we choose to focus on the most pertinent aspects for our purposes.

Commentators attempting to characterize the ETS under WTO law have usually first started by determining whether it constitutes a fiscal measure within the meaning of GATT article III:2 – which prohibits subjecting imported products to "internal taxes and other internal charges of any kind

[18] There are various estimates as to the costs of the Directive, depending on the actors involved and the projection of the carbon market. For an overview see Bartels, "ETS," *supra* Note 20 at 432 (from his compilation, the costs assessment range between €360 and €3–4 billion. The author, however, emphasizes the fact that these costs do not necessarily translate into losses for the aviation industry).

[19] Ibid.; J. Meltzer, "Climate change and trade – The EU aviation directive and the WTO," *JIEL*, 15 (2012) 111 at 120; S. Hiesinger and P. C. Mavroidis, "Planes, trains and automobiles: The EU legislation on climate change and the question of consistency with WTO law," in C. Bakker and F. Francioni, (eds.), *The EU: The US and Global Climate Governance* (Aldershot: Ashgate, 2014), 127 at 130.

[20] See for example Meltzer, ibid.; Bartels, "ETS," *supra* Note 20; L. Bartels, *The Inclusion of Aviation in the EU ETS: WTO Law Considerations* (Geneva: International Centre for Trade and Sustainable Development, Trade and Sustainable Energy Series, issue paper no. 6, 2012); Hiesinger and Mavroidis, *supra* Note 23; W. H. Maruyama, "Climate change and the WTO: Cap and trade versus carbon tax," *J World Trade*, 45 (2011), 679; E. Vranes, "Climate change and the WTO: EU emission trading and the WTO disciplines on trade in goods, services and investment protection," *J World Trade*, 43 (2009), 707.

in excess of those applied, directly or indirectly, to like domestic products."[21] This question has attracted divergent answers. Joshua Meltzer, for example, suggests that the ETS may be tantamount to an indirect tax imposed upon aircraft operators, if it is "understood as a requirement to pay 100 Euros per ton of CO_2 unless airlines had purchased sufficient allowances to cover their CO_2 emissions."[22] He further adds that this obligation generates fiscal revenues for EU Member States, for them to use as they see fit, which tends to bring the Aviation Directive closer to taxes.[23] Lorand Bartels, for his part, argues that the ETS does not equate to a fiscal measure. He insists on the proprietary aspect of the scheme, which in his view sets it apart from regular fiscal measures, in that airline companies obtain a "tradable property right" in exchange of purchasing emission allowances.[24] Another reason is that, "the 'price' paid for an allowance is not fixed by the state in advance, but depends on free market forces" according to supply and demand.[25]

Conversely, if the ETS is held not to be a fiscal measure under GATT article III:2, it might be characterized as an "internal measure" under GATT article III:4. This article forbids WTO Members from according foreign products less favorable treatment to that accorded to "like" domestic products with regard to "laws, regulations and requirements affecting their internal sale, offering for sale, purchase, transportation, distribution or use."[26] Much has been said about what constitutes a "like product" in WTO jurisprudence.[27] In *Japan-Taxes on Alcoholic Beverages*, the Appellate Body identified four relevant factors to ascertain whether products will be deemed to be like: physical

[21] GATT, *supra* Note 12 Art. III:2. The second sentence of article III:2 refers to the first paragraph of the same article, which states that internal taxes and other internal charges "should not be applied to imported or domestic products so as to afford protection to domestic production." The second sentence of Art. III:2, read together with Ad Note III, requires a complainant to demonstrate that the imported and domestic products are directly competitive or substitutable and are not similarly taxed.

[22] Meltzer, *supra* Note 23.

[23] Ibid.

[24] Bartels, "ETS," *supra* Note 20 at 439.

[25] Ibid. (noting that this was the conclusion reached by both Advocate General Kokott and the Court in its ruling – albeit in the context of the EU–US Open Skies Agreement and the *Chicago Convention*). Contra Meltzer, *supra* Note 23 at 130 (in the author's opinion, the CJEU's finding that the ETS is not a charge or a tax has "limited relevance for the meaning of tax or charge in GATT Art. III.2." This is because the scope of GATT Article III.2 is much broader than the equivalent provisions in the EU–US Open Skies Agreement and the *Chicago Convention*).

[26] GATT, *supra* Note 12, art. III:4.

[27] See generally W. M. Choi, *"Like Products" in International Trade Law: Towards a Consistent GATT/WTO Jurisprudence* (Oxford: Oxford University Press, 2003).

characteristics, end-uses, tariff classification, and consumer's tastes.[28] If we consider the Aviation Directive, it would seem impossible to determine, simply by looking at a product, whether it was imported via air transport. Then there is the question of whether the ETS affords less favorable treatment to imported products than to "like" domestic products.[29] Meltzer argues it does, given the "additional costs to be borne by imported products" associated with airfreight.[30]

Beyond the national treatment provisions described previously, the ETS could also be found to violate the most favored nation obligation (MFN) laid down in GATT article I:1, which provides that "any advantage, favor, privilege or immunity granted by any contracting party to any product originating in or destined for any other country shall be accorded immediately and unconditionally to the like product originating in … the territories of all other contracting parties."[31] In this case, the likeness requirement would not involve

[28] *Japan – Taxes on Alcoholic Beverages* (1996), WTO Doc WT/DS 8, 10, 11/AB/R (Appellate Body Report) at 21 [Japan – Alcoholic Beverages II (Appellate Body Report)].

[29] A measure may be found inconsistent with Art. III:4 of the GATT if: (i) the imported and domestic products are "like products"; (ii) the measure at issue is a "law, regulation, or requirement affecting the internal sale, offering for sale, purchase, transportation, distribution, or use" of the products at issue; and (iii) the treatment accorded to imported products is "less favourable" than that accorded to like domestic products, WTO, *United States – measures concerning the importation, marketing and sale of Tuna and Tuna products – recourse to Art. 21.5 of the DSU by Mexico – panel report*, WT/DS381/RW, para. 7.470 (referring to Appellate Body Reports, EC – Seal Products, para. 5.99). The latter condition implies that "there must be in every case a genuine relationship between the measure at issue and its adverse impact on competitive opportunities for imported versus like domestic products to support a finding that imported products are treated less favorably" within the meaning of GATT Art. III:4. See: WTO, *Thailand – Customs and fiscal measures on cigarettes from the Philippines – Report of the appellate body* (July 15, 2011), WT/DS371/AB/R, DSR IV, 2203, para. 134; WTO, *United States – measures concerning the importation, marketing and sale of Tuna and Tuna Products – recourse to Art. 21.5 of the DSU by Mexico – panel report*, para. 7.477.

[30] Meltzer, *supra* Note 23; Bartels, "ETS," *supra* Note 20 at 444 (the author finds that there is no violation considering that section III:4 only applies to intra-EU flights: "[t]he result is that the EU's scheme does not appear to violate Art. III:4 GATT to the extent that it applies to foreign non-imported products carried on intra-EU flights").

[31] GATT, *supra* note 12, Art. I:1 In order to establish inconsistency with Art. I:1, it must be demonstrated that: (i) that the measure at issue falls within the scope of application of Art. I:1; (ii) that the imported products at issue are "like" products within the meaning of Art. I:1; (iii) that the measure at issue confers an "advantage, favor, privilege, or immunity" on a product originating in the territory of any country; and (iv) that the advantage so accorded is not extended "immediately" and "unconditionally" to "like" products originating in the territory of all Members: WTO, *United States – measures concerning the importation, mrketing and sale of Tuna and Tuna products – Recourse to Art. 21.5 of the DSU by Mexico* (December 3, 2011), Add.1 and Corr.1, as modified by Appellate Body Report WT/DS381/AB/RW, para. 7.405 (referring to Appellate Body Reports, EC – Seal Products, para. 5.86). As for GATT Art. III:4,

a comparison between "like" domestic and imported products, but rather between "like" products originating from those countries that control CO_2 emissions and those that do not.

The four criteria put forward in *Japan – Taxes on Alcoholic Beverages* give some indications for the purposes of determining whether goods from different countries might be considered to be like under Article I:1.[32] Once again, it would seem difficult to distinguish between products imported from a country that holds a good carbon report card according to ETS standards and one that does not. Although the third criterion, consumers' perspectives, could in theory include sustainability considerations, it is far from obvious whether it would be sufficient to render two products unlike within the meaning of the MFN provisions in the current state of WTO jurisprudence. In any event, the international aspect of the EU aviation scheme – i.e. regulation of emissions for flights outside the EU – is likely to breach the MFN clause inasmuch as it accords an advantage to like products from different WTO members in the form of additional "costs on products from certain origins according to the distance they travel by air to the EU."[33]

The Aviation Directive could also prove problematic in light of article XI:1 GATT, which proscribes quantitative restrictions, that is "prohibitions or restrictions other than duties, taxes or other charges, whether made effective through quotas, import or export licenses or other measures" on the importation, exportation, or sale for export of any product destined for another Member.[34] Bartels points out that the term "other measure" has received a broad interpretation by WTO panels and is thus considered to cover "any form of limitation imposed on, or in relation to importation."[35] With regard to the Aviation Directive, the limitation will likely take the form of increased

this provision has been interpreted as aiming to protect "expectations of equal competitive opportunities for like imported products from all Members," rather than the "the actual trade effects of a measure"; WTO, *European Communities – measures prohibiting the importation and marketing of seal products – Report of the appellate body* (2014) WT/DS400, 401/AB/R at para. 5.87 citing Panel Reports, *US – COOL*, para. 7.571 (referring to Panel Report, *Colombia – Ports of Entry*, para. 7.236, in turn referring to Panel Report, *Argentina – Hides and Leather*, para. 11.20, in turn referring to Appellate Body Reports, *Japan – Alcoholic Beverages II*, p. 16, DSR 1996: I, p. 109; and *Korea – Alcoholic Beverages*, paras. 119, 120, and 127).

32 Meltzer, *supra* Note 23 at 138.

33 Bartels, "ETS," *supra* Note 20 at 445.

34 GATT, *supra* Note 12, art XI:1.

35 Bartels, "ETS," *supra* Note 20 at 440, citing *Colombia – Ports of Entry* (2009), WTO Doc WT/DS366/R at para. 7.227 and Appellate Body Report, *China – Raw Materials*, WT/DS394/AB/R at para. 320. See also more recently: Panel Reports, *Argentina – Measures Affecting the Importation of Goods*, WT/DS438/R and Add.1 / WT/DS444/R and Add.1 / WT/DS445/R and Add.1, adopted January 26, 2015, as modified (WT/DS438/R) and upheld (WT/DS444/R / WT/

transportation costs for airlines that elect to comply with the scheme, and penalties for those who decline, and therefore be covered by GATT Article XI:1.[36]

It follows from the foregoing that, in the event of a dispute, the Aviation Directive might be found to breach a number of GATT provisions, namely articles III:2 and III:4 (national treatment), article I:1 (most favored nation obligation), and XI:1 (quantitative restrictions).[37] Those potential breaches may, however, be justified under the GATT article XX exceptions regime, which permits an otherwise GATT-inconsistent measure to be maintained for enumerated policy reasons, in certain limited circumstances. Two paragraphs are of direct assistance in this case: article XX(g), which allows WTO members to adopt measures "in relation to the conservation of exhaustible natural resources," provided that such measures are "made effective in conjunction with restrictions on domestic production or consumption,;" and article XX(b), which permits WTO members to take measures necessary for the protection of human, animal, or plant life or health.[38] Article XX consists of a two-tier analysis whereby a Member defending a measure must prove that: (1) the measure at issue falls under one of the exceptions listed in article XX; (2) and it also satisfies the requirements of the GATT article XX chapeau.[39]

Commentators tend to agree that the Aviation Directive would likely survive the first step of the analysis, which requires examining whether the measure at hand displays a sufficient degree of connection with the policy objective it seeks to achieve.[40] In the context of article XX(g), the measure must be "relating to" the conservation of exhaustible natural resources, meaning that the means must be reasonably related to the ends, and must also be "made effective in conjunction with restrictions on domestic production and consumption."[41] The Aviation Directive's stated objective is to mitigate climate change through reduction of aviation emissions.[42] One can easily draw a parallel with *US – Gasoline*, where the Appellate Body found that clean air

DS445/R) by Appellate Body Reports WT/DS438/AB/R / WT/DS444/AB/R / WT/DS445/AB/R, paras. 6.245–6.248.

36 Ibid.

37 While the EU-ETS may also be contrary to Article V relating to freedom of transit, we chose to focus on the main GATT disciplines.

38 GATT, *supra* Note 12, Art. XX.

39 WTO, *United States – Standards for reformulated and conventional gasoline – Report of the appellate body* (1996), WT/DS2/AB/R at 22 [*US – Gasoline* (Appellate Body Report)].

40 Bartels, "ETS," *supra* Note 20 at 450–51; Meltzer, *supra* Note 23 at 140–43.

41 GATT, *supra* Note 12, art XX(g).

42 The need for the Aviation Directive was presented by the EU as follows: European Commission, "Communication from the commission to the council, the European

was an exhaustible natural resource,[43] which led commentators to conclude that the atmosphere could arguably qualify as an exhaustible natural resource.[44] Moreover, the ETS might indirectly contribute to protect living and nonliving natural exhaustible resources that are vulnerable to climate change impacts.[45] In terms of connection between ends and means, the Aviation Directive is designed to capture the largest volume of CO_2 emissions by targeting both EU and non-EU airlines.[46] It has also been adopted in concert with domestic restrictions on production and consumption, as it applies to both EU and non-EU airlines and serves to complement the ETS, which has already instituted such restrictions on EU domestic activities.[47]

The necessity test contained in paragraph XX(b) dictates that a measure must be necessary to the protection of human, animal, or plant life or health, which means that it must be "apt to produce a material contribution to the achievement of [this] objective."[48] For some commentators, the Aviation Directive may end up having very little impact on the patterns of carbon emission in the aviation industry, with compliance costs being passed on to consumers.[49] It is, however, plausible that the Aviation Directive could be considered to make a material contribution if we adopt a long-term view, as suggested by *Brazil – Measures Affecting Imports of Retreaded Tires*, in which the Appellate Body acknowledged that: "[t]he results obtained from certain actions – for instance, measures adopted in order to attenuate global warming

parliament, the European economic and social committee and the committee of regions, reducing the climate change impact of aviation" (September 27, 2005) COM (2005) 459 final at 2. ("Although aviation's share of overall greenhouse gas emissions is still modest (about 3%), the rapid growth undermines progress made in other sectors. If the growth continues as up to now, emissions from international flights from EU airports will by 2012 have increased by 150 % since 1990. This growth in the EU's international aviation emissions would offset more than a quarter of the reductions required by the Community's target under the Kyoto Protocol. In the longer run, aviation emissions will become a major contributor if current trends continue").

43 Bartels, "ETS," *supra* Note 20 at 449; *US – Gasoline* (Appellate Body Report), *supra* Note 50 at 14–15.

44 Bartels, ibid. at 449–50.

45 Ibid. at 450.

46 Meltzer, *supra* Note 23 at 141.

47 Ibid. at 142; Bartels, "ETS," *supra* Note 20 at 450.

48 WTO, *Brazil – measures affecting imports of retreaded tires – Report of the appellate body* (2007) WT/DS332/AB/R, para. 150 [*Brazil – Retreaded Tires* (Appellate Body Report)]. See also WTO, *Korea – Measures affecting imports of fresh, chilled and frozen beef – Report of the appellate body* (2000) WT/DS161,169/AB/R at paras 161, 164, and 166.

49 Meltzer, *supra* Note 23 at 143; Bartels, "ETS," *supra* Note 20 at 450–51.

and climate change ... can only be evaluated with the benefit of time."[50] In order for a measure to be necessary, there must be no reasonable alternative measures that are less trade restrictive.[51] Although it seems difficult to assess at this point whether alternative measures are available, there is also reason to believe that the Aviation Directive will meet these criteria. For Bartels, "[a]t most, it is possible to say that excluding international flights, or non-EU airlines, would not meet the EU's objectives, as too few emissions would be captured."[52]

Once it is demonstrated that the measure falls within the ambit of listed exceptions, it must still meet the requirements of the GATT article XX introductory clause, which stipulates, *inter alia*, that measures should not be applied in a manner constituting "a means of arbitrary or unjustifiable discrimination between countries where the same conditions prevail."[53] For Bartels, the Aviation Directive might create discrimination in two instances: (1) between products from WTO members situated at varying distance from the EU; (2) between products imported from countries equidistant from the EU, if it is easier to transport the products from one country on an indirect flight to the EU.[54] In the second scenario, goods flown on an indirect flight would probably be subject to lower compliance costs, as only the last portion of the flight would be accounted for in the calculation of emissions. While discrimination may be rationally justified in the first case – because it is logical, from the perspective of reducing carbon emissions, that the volume of emissions, and therefore the compliance costs, be correlated to distance flown – the second case is less defensible.[55] In this regard, Meltzer observes

50 *Brazil – Retreaded Tires* (Appellate Body Report), *supra* Note 59 at 151. While in subsequent cases, the Appellate Body focused its analysis on the actual (rather than possible) contribution of a measure, it seems to have left some room for the "apt to make a contribution" test, especially with regard to situations where it faces the "challenge of assessing the contribution of a measure that formed part of a broader policy scheme, and that was not yet having, or likely itself to produce, an immediately discernible impact on its objective," in which may be appropriate to "project what contribution will be brought about by the measure": WTO, *European Communities — Measures prohibiting the importation and marketing of seal products*, paras. 5.213, 5.224. See on this point: Ming Du, "The necessity test in world trade law: What now?" *Chinese Journal of International Law*, 15 (2016), 817 at 829–30.

51 WTO, *European Communities – measures affecting asbestos and asbestos-containing products – Report of the appellate body* (2001), WT/DS 1 35/AB/R, para 172. [EC – *Asbestos* (Appellate Body Report)].

52 Bartels, "ETS," *supra* Note 20 at 451.

53 GATT, *supra* Note 12, art XX (the measure must neither be a "disguised restriction on international trade").

54 Bartels, "ETS," *supra* Note 20 at 458.

55 Ibid.

that distinguishing between direct and indirect flights may in fact yield counterproductive effects, as it provides an incentive for airline companies to transit through other countries, which may result in a higher overall volume of emissions.[56] These elements suggest that the Aviation Directive may not sustain careful examination under the GATT article XX chapeau.

Finally, it should be borne in mind that the Aviation Directive was designed to apply, in its original form, not only to aircraft flying over European airspace but also to flights between EU and non-EU airports, over the airspace of third countries and the high seas. This is the controversial "last leg" of the flight, which has given rise to allegations of extraterritoriality and breach of other countries' sovereignty.[57]

The Aviation Directive may very well be deemed extraterritorial and hence in violation of WTO law if we look back at the GATT decision in *Tuna – Dolphin*, wherein the panel took the view that trade-restrictive measures should be limited to the territory of the Member undertaking them.[58] Some consider that this interpretation still holds true today; despite growing acceptance of certain extraterritorial measures over the years, it has been left seemingly unfettered by WTO panels.[59] For example, in the *US – Shrimp*, often considered as implicitly authorizing extraterritorial measures, the Appellate Body refused to address whether "there is an implied jurisdictional limitation in Article XX(g)."[60]

For Bartels, the extraterritorial dimension of the Aviation Directive does not necessarily represent an insuperable hurdle, as it would probably meet the "nexus" requirement and thus be justified under GATT article XX.[61] In the *US - Shrimp* decision, the Appellate Body found that sea turtles migrating to US waters had sufficient jurisdictional nexus with the US territory.[62] As Bartels

56 Meltzer, *supra* Note 23 at 145.

57 Ibid. at 151–53.

58 *United States – Restrictions on Importations of Tuna (Complaint by Mexico)* (1991) GATT Doc DS21/R, paras 5.25–5.29.

59 E. Ruozzi, "The EU directive on renewable sources and WTO: Towards a solution of the PPMs and extraterritoriality measures?" European and Comparative Law Issues, Working Paper series, Instituto Universitario di Studi Europei (2012), at 7.

60 WTO, *United States – import prohibition of certain shrimp and shrimp products – Report of appellate body* (1998), WT/DS58/AB/R, para 133.WTO, *European Communities – measures prohibiting the importation and marketing of seal products – Report of the appellate body* (2014), WT/DS400, 401/AB/R at para. 5.173, where the Appellate Body similarly declined to address the issue, stating that while it recognized "the systemic importance of the question of whether there is an implied jurisdictional limitation in Article XX(a), and, if so, the nature or extent of that limitation, [it had] decided in this case not to examine this question further."

61 Bartels, "ETS," *supra* Note 20 at 450.

62 *US–Shrimp* (Appellate Body Report), *supra* Note 73 at para 133.

rightly points out "[t]he 'atmosphere' that the EU seeks to protect has, if anything, an even closer 'jurisdictional nexus' to the EU."[63]

11.3 RESOLUTION A39–3 AND WTO LAW

As the Aviation Directive fades from prominence and ICAO Resolution A39–3 becomes the primary focus of concern, it is necessary to subject the Resolution to the same analysis with respect to WTO law. A further and possibly more pressing question is to determine whether unilateral or collective measures taken by ICAO Member States to impose a multilaterally agreed ICAO scheme on recalcitrant states, after its adoption in 2019, would violate WTO law. At this point much is hypothetical, but the most likely scenario might involve the United States, the EU, and other states supporting early implementation of the scheme to be adopted by the ICAO Council pursuant to Resolution A39–3 taking unilateral measures to force recalcitrant states to obey the scheme. The Resolution does indicate which states will be subject to the scheme and the air traffic routes on which it should be applied, but the Resolution is not mandatory. It excepts certain states on a *de minimis* basis and calls for respect of the principle of differential application to developing states; therefore, some states, such as India, which have objected to the EU-ETS may also decide not to adopt the scheme for its own aircraft or obey the scheme on routes where it is applied by others. This could well lead certain major international air traffic destinations such as the United States and the EU to impose the scheme on all aircraft regardless of registry. There is precedent for this in the efforts made by the United States and the EU to ban from their airspace aircrafts registered in certain states or flying with certain companies not deemed to have sufficiently high safety standards.[64]

The questions posed here are very much hypothetical, but some points can certainly be raised. In the first case, many of the issues raised with respect to the EU-ETS – with the possible exception of extraterritoriality – remain relevant. The issue of unilateral decisions to exclude aircraft of certain states but not others would also pose serious legal questions, as they have in the past

63 Bartels, "ETS," *supra* Note 20 at 450.

64 See for example, in the context of the EU, the "Community list of air carriers which are subject to an operating ban within the Community," established pursuant to Regulation (EC) No 2111/2005 of the European Parliament and of the Council of December 14, 2005 on the establishment of a Community list of air carriers subject to an operating ban within the Community and on informing air transport passengers of the identity of the operating air carrier, and repealing Article 9 of Directive 2004/36/EC.

with respect to the threatened exclusion by the EU of aircraft whose engines were not modified to reduce their noise levels.[65] Nondiscrimination is a central aspect of WTO law and refusal to admit aircraft that were not participating in the ICAO scheme might well be met with objections similar to those raised in the past.

One of the most interesting legal arguments that might be posed by any attempt to exclude aircraft that were not complying with the ICAO scheme would be the argument that the scheme was a multilateral agreement designed to protect the environment and hence justified under that heading. Various justifications can be advanced based on this argument, as they have been successfully made before the WTO in the past.[66] Finally, the argument that the ICAO scheme might be justified on the basis of the need to adopt policies of sustainable development is dealt with Section 11.4, with respect to the EU-ETS but also ICAO Resolution A39–3.

11.4 JUSTIFYING THE ETS AND RESOLUTION A39–3 UNDER WTO LAW

The possibility of raising sustainable development as a defense in a WTO dispute involving the Aviation Directive or ICAO Resolution A39–3 (11.4.2) is largely contingent upon its status and relationship to trade law, which first need to be explored (11.4.1).

11.4.1 *Sustainable Development and Trade Law: An Overview*

In this first subsection, we look briefly at the status of sustainable development under international law (11.4.1.1) before we analyze its degree of acceptance in WTO practice (11.4.1.2).

65 The so-called Hushkits controversy, which resulted in the EU deciding not to implement measures that it had adopted in order to reduce aircraft noise levels. See European Commission, Regulation (EC) No 925/1999 of 29 April 1999 on the registration and operation within the Community of certain types of civil subsonic jet aeroplanes which have been modified and recertificated as meeting the standards of volume I, Part II, Chapter 3 of Annex 16 to the Convention on International Civil Aviation, third edition, OJ (1993) No. L 115, 04/05/1999.

66 See for example WTO, *United States – Import prohibition of certain shrimp and shrimp products, recourse to Article 21.5 by Malaysia – Panel report* (2001), WT/DS58/RW at para 5.54 [*US – Shrimp, Recourse to Article* 21.5 (Panel Report)], discussed in more detail in the next section.

11.4.1.1 Status of Sustainable Development under International Law

Since the 1987 *Brundtland Report*, which marked its emergence in the lexicon of international environmental law, the concept of sustainable development has suffered from a lack of certainty, which still represents one of the main obstacles in its applicability.[67] Despite reaching global acceptance and being endorsed in a growing number of national,[68] regional,[69] and international[70] legal instruments, from the perspective of WTO diplomats and those involved in WTO dispute settlement, controversy remains on practical and conceptual levels with regard to the concept's scope, implications, and definition.[71]

67 "Our Common Future." Report of the World Commission on Environment, UNWCED, 42d Sess., Annex, Provisional Agenda Item 83(e), UN Doc. A/42/427 (1987). Other documents prior to 1987 have paved to way to the Brundtland Report: *Stockholm Declaration on the Human Environment of the United Nations Conference on the Human Environment* (June 16, 1972), UN Doc A/Conf 48/14/Rev.l, 11 ILM 1416; *Convention on international trade in endangered species of wild fauna and flora* (signed March 3, 1973, entered into force July 1, 1975)993 UNTS 243, 12 ILM 1085; UNGA, "World charter for nature," GA Res 37/7 (October 28, 1982) UN Doc A/Res/37/7.

68 OECD, "Good practices in the national sustainable development strategies of OECD Countries" (2006), www.oecd.org/greengrowth/36655769.pdf last accessed October 17, 2017..

69 M. C. C. Segger, "Sustainable development in regional trade agreements," in L. Bartels and F. Ortino, eds., *Regional Trade Agreements and the WTO Legal System* (Oxford: Oxford University Press, 2006) 331. See for example recently, in the European context: H. G. Ruse-Khan, "A real partnership for development? Sustainable development as treaty objective in European economic partnership agreements and beyond," JIEL (2010), 1; L. Kramer, "Sustainable development in EC law," in H. C. Bugge and C. Voigt, eds., *Sustainable Development in International and National Law: What Did the Brundtland Report Do to Legal Thinking and Where Can We Go from Here?* (Groningen: Europa Law Publishing, 2008), 377.

70 *Rio Declaration on Environment and Development*, UN Conference on Environment and Development, UN Doc. A/CONE151/Rev. 1 (1992), 31 ILM 874 (1992); *UNECD Agenda 21: Programme of Action for Sustainable Development* (New York: UN Department of Public Information, 1992); *United Nations Convention on Biodiversity*, June 5, 1992, 1760 UNTS 79, 143; 31 ILM 818 (1992); *United Nations Convention to Combat Desertification in those Countries Experiencing Serious Drought and/or Desertification, Particularly in Africa*, 15 October 1994, 33 ILM 1328; *Cartagena Protocol on Biosafety to the Convention on Biological Diversity*, January 29, 2000, 39 ILM 1027 (entered into force November 11, 2003). For a history of codification of sustainable development in international law treaties, see: Segger, "Sustainable development in international law," in Bugge and Voigt, ibid. at 87.

71 For an overview, see *inter alia* C. Voigt, *Sustainable Development as a Principle in International Law: Resolving Conflicts between WTO Law and Climate Measures* (The Hague: Martinus Nijhoff Publishers, 2009) [Voigt, *Resolving Conflicts*]; N. Schrijver, *The Evolution of Sustainable Development in International Law: Inception, Meaning and Status* (The Hague: Martinus Nijhoff Publishers, 2008); S. A. Atapattu, *Emerging Principles of International Environmental Law* (Ardsley: Transnational Publishers, 2006) at 182–94; V. Barral., "Sustainable development in international law: Nature and operation of an evolutive legal norm," *EJIL*, **23** (2012), 377.

Pursuant to the often-cited definition put forward in the *Brundtland Report*, sustainable development is understood as "development that meets the needs of the present without compromising the ability of future generations to meet their own needs." States thus undertake a "collective responsibility to advance and strengthen the interdependent and mutually reinforcing pillars of sustainable development – economic development, social development and environmental protection – at the local, national, regional and global levels."[72] More than twenty-five years after it was first drafted, the wording of sustainable development continues to raise many questions. What are its operational content and meaning? How are its three pillars to be implemented? And mostly, what does a commitment to sustainable development entail in practice?[73]

Equally uncertain, from the WTO perspective, is the concept's normative status under international law. Despite abundant scholarly work on this subject, the debates surrounding the legal significance of sustainable development have not yet been put to rest. As Christina Voigt remarks, a wide spectrum of views on the appropriate degree of normativity that should be assigned to sustainable development exists.[74] While some scholars deny sustainable development any legal value – characterizing it, for example, as an idealistic aspiration,[75] soft law, a meta-principle,[76] or a source of conceptual guidance,[77] – some have gone as far as to contend that it is an emerging principle or custom of international environmental law.[78] Others argue that it should rather be construed as a principle of interpretation, or an interstitial norm, which serves to reconcile conflicting social, economic, and

[72] *Johannesburg Declaration on Sustainable Development* (September 4, 2000), UN Doc A/Conf. 199/20 at 5.

[73] For attempts at fleshing out the content of sustainable development, see: International Law Association, *New Delhi Declaration on Principles of International Law Related to Sustainable Development* (New Delhi: ILA, 2002), http://cisdl.org/tribunals/pdf/NewDelhiDeclaration.pdf last accessed October 18, 2017.

[74] Voigt, *Resolving Conflicts*, *supra* Note 84 at 161–62.

[75] Ibid.

[76] V. Lowe, "Sustainable development and unsustainable arguments," in A. Boyle and D. Freestone (eds.), *International law and sustainable development: Past achievements and future challenges* (Oxford: Oxford University Press, 1999), 30.

[77] E. B. Lydgate, "Biofuels, sustainability and trade-related regulatory chill," *JIEL*, 15 (2012), 158.

[78] Ibid.; M. C. C. Segger and A. Khalfan, *Sustainable Development Law: Principles, Practices and Prospects* (Oxford: Oxford University Press, 2005), 45. Some authors dot not see sustainable development evolving into a legal norm, be it customary or not: Lowe, *supra* Note 89 at 23–24 (arguing "the concept of sustainable development is inherently incapable of having the status … of a rule of law addressed to States and purporting to constrain their conduct"); A. Boyle and D. Freestone, *International Law and Sustainable Development: Past Achievements and Future Challenges* (Oxford: Oxford University Press, 1999), 16–18.

environmental norms.[79] Finally, others have opted for a middle ground solution, which conceptualizes sustainable development both as a substantive area of law sitting at the intersection of international economic law, international environmental law, and international social law, and an independent legal principle of reconciliation powerful enough to modify other obligations, whether customary or treaty-based.[80]

Within this context of conflicting views, the International Law Association Committee on International Law on Sustainable Development observed, in its 2012 report, that "there has in fact been little movement in the development of the legal foundations of sustainable development," qualifying the discussions on the legal status of sustainable development as "sterile."[81] This latent ambiguity has earned sustainable development a timid, yet promising reception in WTO law. Arguably, the legal weight of the sustainable development principle with respect to the protection of air quality has been strengthened by the success of the Paris Agreement on Climate Change.

11.4.1.2 Sustainable Development and Substantive WTO Law

At the outset, it should be remembered that WTO law itself is not exempt from sustainability considerations. On the contrary, the Preamble of the 1994 *Marrakesh Agreement* relevantly states that trade liberalization

> should be conducted with a view to raising standards of living, ensuring full employment and a large and steadily growing volume of real income and effective demand, and expanding the production of trade in goods and services, while allowing for the optimal use of the world's resources in accordance with the objective of sustainable development, seeking both to protect and preserve the environment and to enhance the means for doing so in a manner consistent with their respective needs and concerns at different levels of economic development.[82]

This has been since reiterated in the 2001 Doha Declaration and numerous other WTO documents.[83] Despite its nonbinding nature, WTO dispute

[79] Lowe, *supra* Note 89 at 19.

[80] Segger and Khalfan, *supra* Note 91 at 49.

[81] International Law Association, "International law on sustainable development" (Sofia Conference, 2012) 2002 Report, 6, www.ila-hq.org. last accessed October 19, 2017.

[82] *Marrakesh Agreement Establishing the World Trade Organization* (adopted April 15, 1994 entered into force January 1, 1995) 1867 UNTS 154, 33 ILM 1197.

[83] WTO, "Doha Ministerial Declaration" (November 14, 2001), WT/MIN(01)/DEC/1,7; *Marrakesh Trade and Environment Decision*, April 15, 1994, 33 ILM 1267, at 1267 (1994) ("there should not be, nor need be, any policy contradiction between upholding and safeguarding an

settlement system bodies have utilized the Preamble language on a few occasions since 1994. For example, in the important *US – Shrimp* case, the Appellate Body used sustainable development, as cited in the *Marrakesh Agreement* Preamble, to support an evolutionary interpretation of the term "exhaustible natural resources" (article XX(g)) in order to include not only inert natural resources but also living creatures, in this case sea turtles:

> The words of Article XX(g), "exhaustible natural resources," were actually crafted more than 50 years ago. They must be read by a treaty interpreter in the light of contemporary concerns of the community of nations about the protection and conservation of the environment.
>
> ...
>
> From the perspective embodied in the preamble of the WTO Agreement, we note that the generic term "natural resources" in Article XX(g) is not "static" in its content or reference but is rather "by definition, evolutionary." It is, therefore, pertinent to note that modern international conventions and declarations make frequent references to natural resources as embracing both living and non-living resources. [footnotes omitted][84]

More recently, in *Brazil – Retreated Tires*, the Panel, in analyzing article XX (b) relating to the preservation of animal and plant life and health, reiterated the Appellate Body's observation in *US-Shrimp* to the effect "that the preamble of the Marrakesh Agreement establishing the WTO showed that the signatories to that Agreement were, in 1994, fully aware of the importance and legitimacy of environmental protection as a goal of national and international policy."[85]

These developments have led authors to conclude that significant progress has been made in terms of acknowledgment of sustainable development before the WTO dispute settlement bodies. For example, Christina Voigt commends "the systematic inclusion of the concept within WTO DSB jurisprudence, which indicates a significant change, not only for the dispute settlement system, but for the WTO in general. The reference to sustainable development and the inclusion of concerns entailed by other multilateral agreements, illustrate the extent to which the judicial function (at least within

open, non-discriminatory and equitable multilateral trading system on the one hand, and acting for the protection of the environment, and the promotion of sustainable development on the other"); WTO Secretariat, "Sustainable Development," www.wto.org, last accessed October 18, 2017.

84 *US – Shrimp* (Appellate Body Report), *supra* Note 73 at paras 129–30.

85 *Brazil – Measures affecting imports of retreaded tyres* (2007), WTO Doc WT/DS332/R (Panel Report), at para 7.112.

the WTO context) has departed from formal positivism."[86] For his part, Markus W. Gehring underscores the fact that "the objective of sustainable development has become an integral part of the world trading system," as "[l]egal arguments encompassing an integrated developmental and environmental approach have been made by the parties and accepted by the relevant dispute settlement organs."[87]

However, as important as it may be, this recognition should not obscure the fact that WTO dispute settlement bodies, like most international bodies, have generally been reluctant to give sustainable development full legal effect, partly due to the concept's perceived indeterminacy.[88] For instance, in the famous *US – Shrimp* and *US – Shrimp, Recourse to Article 21.5* cases, the WTO Panel referred to sustainable development as an "objective"[89] or a "concept,"[90] rather than a legally binding principle. Indeed, the use of sustainable development before WTO dispute settlement bodies has so far been limited to that of an interpretative tool. Accordingly, in *US – Shrimp*, the Appellate Body declared that the objective of sustainable development must "add colour, texture and shading to our interpretation of the agreements annexed to the WTO Agreement."[91] In a follow-up to the same dispute, the Panel held that the notion of sustainable development should inform its interpretation of GATT's article XX introductory clause, as it reflects the "object and purpose" of the WTO Agreement.[92]

Notwithstanding the fact that many WTO decisions have highlighted the importance and relevance of sustainable development, none have so far dismissed a claim on sustainability grounds.[93] This suggests that the status of sustainable development in the WTO remains somewhat contradictory: "despite its conceptual centrality and wide acceptance in principle, it is very controversial when applied through trade-restrictive regulation."[94] The

86 Voigt, *Resolving Conflicts*, *supra* Note 84 at 142–43.
87 M. Gehring, "Sustainable development in world trade law – A short history," in Bugge and Voigt, *supra* Note 82, 271 at 290.
88 See M. C. C. Segger, "The role of international forums in the advancement of sustainable development," *Sustainable Dev L & Pol'y*, 10(2009–2010) 18.
89 *United States – Import Prohibition of Certain Shrimp and Shrimp Products, Recourse to Article 21.5 by Malaysia* (2001), WTO Doc. WT/DS58/RW at para 5.54 (Panel Report) [*US – Shrimp, Recourse to Article 21.5* (Panel Report)].
90 Ibid. at footnote 202; see also *US – Shrimp* (Appellate Body Report), *supra* Note 98 at footnote 107.
91 *US – Shrimp* (Appellate Body Report), ibid. at 153.
92 *US – Shrimp, Recourse to Article 21.5* (Panel Report), *supra* Note 89 at para 5.54.
93 M. E, Rancourt, "Promoting sustainable biofuels under the WTO legal regime," *McGill Int'l J Sust Dev L & Pol'y*, 5 (2009), 73 at 82.
94 Lydgate, *supra* Note 90 at 170.

concept's breadth and vagueness also pose very concrete challenges in the WTO context. As Emily Barrett Lydgate points out, it might be quite difficult to justify comprehensive and far-reaching regulations such as the ETS, "solely based on its contribution to the abstract concept of sustainability."[95] In and of itself, sustainable development appears to provide insufficient grounds to implement trade-restrictive measures because it is difficult to discern what it prescribes, allows, or prohibits and whether, in short, it contains any executable normative obligation. Lydgate adds that sustainability is a "process-oriented concept," which seeks to promote sustainable processes and production methods that are not always visible in the physical characteristics of the end product (non–product-related process and production methods (PPM)).[96] It is sufficient to note that the WTO Members and WTO dispute settlement bodies have historically been hostile to the establishment of regulatory distinctions based on nonproduct-related PPMs.[97] But perhaps more fundamentally, the applicability of sustainable development is further complicated by the interaction between WTO law and public international law (PIL) in general.

11.4.2 *Sustainable Development as a Justification for Nonconforming ETS or ICAO Measures*

As we shall see, the role of public international law in WTO dispute settlement (11.4.2.1) greatly shapes and constrains the ways in which sustainable development may be raised to defend the Aviation Directive or an eventual ICAO MBM scheme (11.4.2.2).

11.4.2.1 The Role of Public International Law in WTO Dispute Settlement

It is now trite to say that WTO law "should not be read in clinical isolation from public international law."[98] But working out the exact terms and

95 Ibid.

96 Ibid. at 171.

97 On the PPM debate see in general S. Charnovitz, "The Law of environmental PPMs in the WTO: Debunking the myth of illegality," *Yale J Int'l L*, 27 (2002) 59; R. Read, "Like products, health and environmental exceptions: The interpretation of PPMs in recent WTO trade dispute cases," *Estey Centre J Int'l L & T Pol'y*, 5 (2004) 123; S. E. Gaines, "Process and production methods: How to produce sound policy for environmental PPM-based trade measures?" *Columb J Envtl L*, 27 (2002) 383; R. Howse and D. Reagan, "The product/process distinction – An illusory basis for disciplining unilateralism in trade policy," *EJIL*, 11 (2000) 24.

98 *US – Gasoline* (Appellate Body Report), *supra* Note 54 at 17. On the issue as to whether WTO law is a self-contained regime: J. H. Jackson, "Fragmentation or unification among international institutions: The world trade organization," *NYU J Int'l L & Pol*, 31(1999) 823;

conditions that should govern the WTO/PIL relationship is no easy feat. While it is beyond the scope of this contribution to reconstruct the debates on this matter, it is worth recalling the main doctrinal trends involved. In an effort to elucidate the role of non-WTO norms in dispute settlement, scholars have traditionally drawn a distinction between treaty interpretation and treaty application.[99] Simply put, this means that we can either resort to non-WTO rules to *interpret* WTO rights and obligations, or use them as *applicable law*.

The WTO *Dispute Settlement Understanding* (*DSU*) does not contain a provision explicitly stating the applicable law before WTO dispute panels.[100] Articles 3.2, 7.1 and 11 *DSU* are, however, used to provide some guidance in this area. Let us start with section 7.1 *DSU*, which defines the mandate of the dispute settlement bodies in the following terms:

> To examine, *in the light of the relevant provisions in (name of the covered agreement(s) cited by the parties to the dispute)*, the matter referred to the DSB by (name of party) in document … and to make such findings as will assist the DSB in making the recommendations or in giving the rulings provided for in that/those agreement(s). [emphasis added]

Some commentators have suggested that this provision limits both the WTO's substantive jurisdiction and applicable law to the covered agreements, thus excluding the application of non-WTO rules.[101] They have drawn the same inference from article 11 *DSU*, which describes the panel functions as "[making] an objective assessment of the matter before it, including an objective assessment of the facts of the case and the applicability of and conformity with the relevant covered agreements" [emphasis added]. Other scholars vigorously oppose the proposition that the applicable law should be

D. M. McRae, "The WTO in international law: Tradition continued or new frontier?" *JIEL*, **3** (2000) 27; B. Simma and D. Pulkowski, "Of planets and the universe: Self-contained regimes in international law," *EJIL*, **17** (2006), 483.

99 G. Marceau, "A call for coherence in international law: Praises for the prohibition against 'clinical isolation' in WTO dispute settlement," *J World Trade*, **33** (1999) 87 at 113 [Marceau, "Praises for the Prohibition"]; Chang-fa Lo, "The i between treaty interpretation and treaty application and the possibility to account for non-WTO treaties during WTO treaty interpretation," *Ind Int'l & Comp L Rev*, **22** (2012), 1.Contra: A. D. Mitchell and D. Heaton, "The inherent jurisdiction of WTO tribunals: The select application of public international law required by the judicial function," *Mich J Int'l L*, **31** (2010) 559 (arguing that the distinction between treaty application and treaty interpretation is in practice very thin).

100 *Understanding on Rules and Procedures Governing the Settlement of Disputes, Annex 2 of the Marrakesh Agreement establishing the World Trade Organization* (adopted April 15, 1994, entered into force January 1, 1995), 1869 UNTS 401 [*DSU*].

101 G. Marceau, "WTO dispute settlement and human rights," *EJIL*, **13** (2002), 753 at 767; J. I. P. Trachtman, "The domain of WTO dispute resolution," *Harv Int'l LJ*, 40 (1999) 333 at 342.

delimited by the covered agreement.[102] In his seminal 2001 article,[103] Joost Pauwelyn argues that the multiple references to covered agreements in the *DSU* do not serve to circumscribe applicable law, but rather strictly concern the WTO's jurisdiction.[104] Therefore, they do not bar the application of *other* rules of public international law in deciding on WTO claims.[105]

Article 3:2 *DSU* is also regularly cited for the purposes of determining applicable law. This provision describes the role of the dispute settlement system as "preserv[ing] the rights and obligations of Members under the covered agreements, and … clarify[ing] the existing provisions of those agreements in accordance with customary rules of interpretation of public international law." Two conclusions have been drawn from this article. First, WTO panels may apply international customary law in the context of dispute settlements.[106] Second, this reference to customary law does not necessarily preclude the application of other PIL norms.[107] Commentators rely upon the case *Korea – Measures Affecting Government Procurement*, in which the Panel declared that there is "no basis here for an *a contrario* implication that rules of international law other than rules of interpretation do not apply."[108]

[102] D. Palmeter and P. C. Mavroidis, "The WTO legal system: Sources of law," *Am J Int'l L*, **92** (1998) 398 at 399. See also L. Bartels, "Applicable law in WTO dispute settlement proceedings," *J World Trade*, **35** (2001), 499 at 505 [Bartels, "Applicable law"] ("Nowhere do these paragraphs say that the law applicable in Panel proceedings is limited to that contained in the covered agreements. According to Article 7.1, Panels are to examine the matter referred to the DSB by the complainant *in the light of* the relevant provisions in the relevant covered agreement. The phrase 'in the light of' does not limit the sources of law that might be relevant in examining the 'matter'."); E. Vranes, "Jurisdiction and applicable law in WTO proceedings," *German Y B Int'l L*, 48(2005), 265.

[103] J. Pauwelyn, "The role of public international law in the WTO: How far can we go?" *Am J Int'l L*, **95** (2001), 535 [Pauwelyn, "How far can we go?"]; from the same author. J. Pauwelyn, "Bridging fragmentation and unity: International law as a universe of inter-connected islands," *Mich J Int'l L*, **25** (2003–2004) 903 [Pauwelyn, "Bridging Fragmentation"].

[104] Pauwelyn, "How far can we go?" ibid. at 560 (in his opinion, "the fact that the substantive jurisdiction of WTO panels is limited to claims under WTO covered agreements does not mean that the applicable law available to a WTO panel is necessarily limited to WTO covered agreements").

[105] Ibid. at 561.

[106] *Korea – Measures Affecting Government Procurement* (2000), WTO Doc WT/DS163/R at para 7.96 (Panel Report) [*Korea – Procurement*] ("Customary international law applies generally to the economic relations between the WTO Members. Such international law applies to the extent that the WTO treaty agreements do not 'contract out' from it. To put it another way, to the extent there is no conflict or inconsistency, or an expression in a covered WTO agreement that implies differently, we are of the view that the customary rules of international law apply to the WTO treaties and to the process of treaty formation under the WTO").

[107] Bartels, "Applicable law," *supra* Note 116 at 506.

[108] *Ibid*; *Korea – Procurement, supra* Note 120 at footnote 753.

There is, however, one important caveat to this, which also derives from article 3.2: "in their findings and recommendations, the panel and Appellate Body cannot add to or diminish the rights and obligations provided in the covered agreements."[109] According to Pauwelyn, it follows that a WTO member could in practice invoke rules of international law as a defense, subject to the condition that the opposing party is also legally bound by the same rules. This is because, in accordance with article 3.2 *DSU*, "[t]he complaining party cannot see its WTO rights diminished on the basis of a rule of international law by which it is not bound."[110] As attractive as it may be on paper, the approach delineated here does not yet seem to constitute *lex lata*. In fact, dispute settlement bodies have generally declined to rule on a dispute based on treaties not explicitly included in the covered agreements.[111]

Public international law may also assist dispute settlement bodies in the interpretation of WTO disciplines. Over the years, the Appellate Body interpreted 3.2 *DSU* as incorporating article 31 of the *Vienna Convention on the Law of Treaties*, which calls for a treaty to be interpreted in light of its context, object, and purpose.[112] Together with the treaty "context," interpreters should take into account, *inter alia*, "any relevant rules of international law applicable in the relations *between the parties*." [emphasis added][113] There have been some disagreements about the proper scope of this provision: Must "outside WTO rules" bind all WTO Members[114] in order to be used as interpretative tools, just the parties to the dispute, or only one party?[115] The case law on this

[109] *DSU*, *supra* Note 114, art 19.2

[110] Pauwelyn, "How far can we go?" *supra* Note 117 at 566.

[111] Bartels, "Applicable law," *supra* Note 116 at 509 (noting, after reviewing the practice of dispute bodies that there "then, is an inconsistency in the treatment of 'outside' law considered prima facie to be applicable, but which, if applied, would conflict with the covered agreements. In some cases, the rules of the Vienna Convention on the Law of Treaties are used to exclude this law, while in others it is claimed that the law does not apply because it is not contained in a covered agreement. And in other cases again, the covered agreements are simply assumed to 'override' the other law").

[112] *Vienna Convention on the Law of Treaties* (adopted May 23, 1969,entered into force January 27, 1980) 1155 UNTS 331 [*Vienna Convention*]; *US – Gasoline* (Appellate Body Report), *supra* Note 54 at 17; *Japan – Alcoholic Beverages II* (Appellate Body Report), *supra* Note 34 at 10; *European Communities – Customs Classification of Certain Computer Equipment* (1998), WTO Doc. WT/DS62, 67, 68/AB/R at para 86 (Appellate Body Report); *US – Shrimp* (Appellate Body Report), supra Note 98 at para 114 and note 82.

[113] *Vienna Convention*, *supra* Note 126 Art. 31(1)(c).

[114] Pauwelyn, "Bridging fragmentation," *supra* Note 117 at 910 (affirming that the relevant rules that may assist a panel in the process of treaty interpretation should be limited to "non-WTO rules reflecting the common intentions of all WTO Members").

[115] Marceau, "Praises for the prohibition," *supra* Note 113 at 124.

issue is ambiguous. For instance, in *US – Shrimp*, the Appellate Body did not hesitate to resort to multilateral environmental agreements – notably the *United Nations Convention on International Trade in Endangered Species of Wild Fauna and Flora*, the *Convention on the Conservation of Migratory Species of Wild Animals*, and the *Convention on Biological Diversity* – to impart meaning to the term "exhaustible natural resources" (GATT article XX (g)), even though these agreements were not binding upon all parties to the dispute.[116] In *European Communities – Measures Affecting the Approval and Marketing of Biotech Products*, the Panel nevertheless rejected the argument of the EU to the effect that the *Convention on Biological Diversity* and the *Cartagena Protocol on Biosafety* – by which the United States was not bound– should be used to interpret the parties' obligations.[117] Aside from being "a relevant rule applicable between the parties," sustainable development may also be contemplated as the "object and purpose" of a treaty, which is probably the most appropriate solution in the present case.

11.4.2.2 Sustainable Development as Defense: Between Interpretation and Application

If we now turn to sustainable development, the foregoing developments direct us to two possible points of entry into WTO law. First, following Pauwelyn's prospective approach, one could consider sustainable development to be applicable law within the meaning of section 3.2 of the *Dispute Settlement Understanding*.[118] Defining the legal nature of sustainable development here becomes crucially important. If we qualify sustainable development as a customary norm, it may well become applicable law in a dispute involving the Aviation Directive. In light of this, it is, however, safe to say that sustainable development is not "ripe" for such a qualification yet. Furthermore, a WTO panel might be reluctant to characterize sustainable development as a new source of customary law. It should indeed be borne in mind that in the *European Communities – Measures Concerning Meat and Meat Products* case, the Appellate Body displayed extreme caution in refusing to decide

[116] *US – Shrimp* (Appellate Body Report), *supra* Note 98 at footnote 111.

[117] *European Communities – Measures affecting the approval and marketing of biotech products* (2006) WTO Doc WT/DS291, 92, 93/R at paras 7.74–7.75 [*EC – Approval and Marketing of Biotech Products*].

[118] *DSU*, *supra* Note 114, Art. 3.2.

whether the precautionary principle had reached the status of customary international law.[119]

Alternatively, if we conceive sustainable development as an obligation imposed by an MEA, and thus embodied in a legal instrument, it may be invoked as a defense, with the important limitation that such legal instrument must bind both parties to the dispute.[120] This poses a few challenges in the context of the Aviation Directive. First, it is questionable whether the Aviation Directive can be considered as a measure implementing an MEA. Although the *UNFCCC* and the *Kyoto Protocol* both make multiple references to sustainable development,[121] it is open to argument, given this concept's breath and complexity, that it did not specifically require the EU to adopt the Aviation Directive. Marie-Ève Rancourt notes that "State Parties under the UNFCCC and the Kyoto Protocol have absolute discretion as to how they fulfil their obligations."[122] Consequently, these conventions cannot be invoked to justify the modalities and necessity of a disputed measure.[123] The language of article 2(2) of the *Kyoto Protocol* – which invites States to work toward aviation emissions reduction within the ICAO framework – appears to be of little assistance in this case. Its vagueness was underscored in the CJEU's *ATAA* ruling in the following terms:

> Article 2(2) of the Kyoto Protocol, mentioned by the referring court, provides that the parties thereto are to pursue limitation or reduction of emissions of certain greenhouse gases from aviation bunker fuels, working through the ICAO. Thus, that provision, as regards its content, cannot in any event be considered to be unconditional and sufficiently precise so as to confer on individuals the right to rely on it in legal proceedings in order to contest the validity of Directive 2008/101.[124]

[119] WTO, *European Communities – measures concerning meat and meat products (Hormones)* (1998), WT/DS26/AB/R at para 123 (concluding that it was "unnecessary, and probably imprudent, for [it] in this appeal to take a position on this important, but abstract, question").

[120] Pauwelyn, "How far can we go?" *supra* Note 117 at 566.

[121] For example, the objective of the UNFCCC, as laid out in its section 2 is to stabilize greenhouse gas concentrations "within a time-frame sufficient to allow ecosystems to adapt naturally to climate change, to ensure that food production is not threatened, and to enable economic development to proceed in a sustainable manner." Perhaps more evidently, section 3 (4) of the Convention states that State parties have a right to and a duty to promote sustainable development. In a similar fashion, the Kyoto Protocol identifies the promotion of sustainable development as one of the key obligations incumbent upon State parties.

[122] Rancourt, *supra* Note 107 at 81.

[123] Ibid.

[124] *ATAA*, *supra* Note 8, at para 73.

Moreover, relying upon article 2(2) may be a slippery slope, as it paradoxically highlights the Aviation Directive's alleged unilateral and extraterritorial nature.

Second, it remains uncertain, if the Aviation Directive or the ICAO scheme were to be challenged before the WTO, whether all the parties to the dispute would be bound by the *Kyoto Protocol.* The European Union being a party to the *Kyoto Protocol,* this treaty's provisions "form an integral part of [its] legal order."[125] Conversely, the United States, which may be a potential party to a WTO dispute, has signed but not ratified the *Protocol.* It should be noted that both the EU and the United States are parties to the *UNFCCC* and *the Paris Agreement.* However, contrary to the *Kyoto Protocol,* which provides for binding and mandatory emissions reduction commitments, the UNFCCC is more aspirational in nature, as it solely enjoins States to limit their emissions, without obliging them to do so.[126] These difficulties, coupled with the WTO's unfavorable jurisprudence, render the direct application of sustainable development highly implausible.

More realistically, sustainable development may be used as a means to interpret the WTO-covered agreements in a manner that is more compatible with the Aviation Directive. As a preliminary matter, we must rule out the application of sustainable development as "relevant rules of international law applicable in the relations between the parties," pursuant to article 31(1)(c) of the *Vienna Convention.* Recent WTO case law indeed suggests that all parties to the dispute must be bound by "outside" WTO rules used in interpreting WTO obligations.[127] As previously discussed, this requirement may not be met in a dispute involving the Aviation Directive. Contrary to section 31(1)(c) of the *Vienna Convention,* relying upon sustainable development as the "object and purpose" of WTO Agreements does not require all parties to have ratified MEAs under which trade-restrictive measures are adopted. The "object and purpose" of WTO-covered agreements applies in virtually all disputes, since all WTO Members share a common commitment to sustainable development through the Marrakesh Agreement Preamble.[128]

There are several advantages to using sustainable development as an interpretation aid. First, it bypasses the problems of indeterminacy: in this context, sustainable development "does not purport to bind states in the form of a

[125] Ibid. at para 54.

[126] The ICAO 2004 and 2007 resolutions, by which the Members reiterated their desire to address the aviation sector's impact on global warming, may at best be characterized as soft-law.

[127] *EC – Approval and Marketing of Biotech Products, supra* Note 131 at paras 7.74–7.75.

[128] M. A. E. de Carranza, "MEAs with trade measures and the WTO: Aiming towards sustainable development?" *Buff Envtl LJ,* **15** (2007–2008) 43 at 87–88.

specific obligation entailing an executable substantive order, [nor] does [it] need to prescribe any specific integrated outcome"; "[h]ere, regardless of the identified ambiguity, the concept can still perform a general steering role towards integrative decision-making processes."[129] Second, it may help instill greater flexibility in trade rules, by supporting a broad and teleological interpretation of WTO provisions.[130] How may sustainable development add "color, texture and shading" in the case at hand?

One example is the open-ended "likeness requirement" at the heart of WTO nondiscrimination provisions (articles I:1, III:2, III:4 GATT) – which the Aviation Directive is, considering the foregoing, likely to breach. Conceivably, the likeness test could take a different turn if interpreted in light of sustainable development. As Rancourt notes, it could, for instance, integrate new social and environmental considerations, and in particular non–product-related process and production methods, insofar as they have an impact on consumers' tastes and preferences.[131] In *EC – Asbestos*, the Appellate Body found that the health risks associated with a product were relevant to a likeness assessment, in that they influence consumer's behavior.[132] By extension, could the depletion of exhaustible resources and health risks associated with aviation emissions become pertinent to determine whether products flown on ETS-compliant airlines are "like" other products imported without regard to carbon emissions? It might seem far-fetched, but the logic is the same: If production methods indeed have an impact on consumers' decisions, then the products may not necessarily be "like" and differential treatment may be justifiable.[133] Proving the existence of widespread consumer concerns over climate change issues would, of course, require strong evidence, but it is not unfeasible.

In addition, sustainable development could help ease the conditions of the GATT exceptions regime to ensure that nonprotectionist or nondiscriminatory measures furthering MEA objectives are not unduly dismantled. This would sometimes mean giving the Defendant Member the benefit of the doubt, and may eventually lead, as Marceau suggests, to a presumption that MEA-motivated trade restrictions meet the requirement of GATT article XX in certain circumstances.[134] In the case of the Directive, two examples easily

[129] Ruse-Khan, *supra* Note 82 at 35.
[130] Carranza, *supra* Note 142 at 89.
[131] Rancourt, *supra* Note 107 at 93–94.
[132] *EC – Asbestos* (Appellate Body Report), *supra* Note 62 at para 121; Rancourt, ibid.
[133] Rancourt, ibid. at 94.
[134] Carranza, *supra* Note 142 at 88–89; Marceau, "Praises for the prohibition," *supra* Note 113 at 131.

come to mind: The first relates to the "necessity test" contained in article XX (b), and the second to the requirements of the article XX chapeau.

First, sustainable development could help support the view that the Aviation Directive's contribution to the objective of combating climate change should be analyzed in a long-term perspective, in line with the Appellate Body's findings in *Brazil – Retreated Tires*. Not only is the Aviation Directive in itself insufficient to prevent climate change, but its effects are unlikely to be obvious in the near future. However, this should not preclude a WTO body from finding that the measure was necessary. Likewise, sustainable development could encourage WTO panels to adopt a more holistic view of the contribution of the measure to the objective it seeks to achieve. In the case of the Aviation Directive, for example, one should not only examine its results in terms of reduction of carbon emissions, but also the positive impact it may have in inciting other countries to adopt similar measures and changing behavior in the aviation sector.[135] Second, concerning the controversial "last leg" of the flights that the Aviation Directive intends to regulate, sustainable development could help offer a justification for the fact that it is being applied in a "discriminatory and arbitrary manner." On a practical level, one possible explanation why the Directive only applies to the last portion of international flights is that, as Bartels points out, the "EU cannot obtain data relevant to flights without a terminal point in the EU."[136] This is largely due to administrative constraints, which could eventually amount to a valid justification in a sustainable development perspective. As Bartels notes, there is, in fact, some "room for justifying discrimination under the Chapeau on the basis of genuine administrative constraints."[137] In *Brazil – Retreated Tires*, the Appellate Body acknowledged the fact that climate change measures might not immediately bring visible results. We see no reason why it should not also acknowledge the difficulties inherent with designing a scheme that is both balanced and effective in preventing climate change. As for the risk of increasing aviation emissions due to the incentive to transit, an approach inspired by sustainable development may help look beyond individual cases where the Directive may have such negative effects, and instead consider general changes in emissions patterns and behavior modification in the aviation sector.

135 Ibid.
136 Bartels, "ETS," *supra* Note 20 at 459.
137 Ibid. at 456.

PART IV

Future Directions

12

Getting to Global Cooperation

The ICAO and Climate Change

Alejandro Piera

International aviation is growing at a rate of roughly 5 percent per year. Its greenhouse gas (GHG) emissions are forecast to increase by 3–4 percent per year. At present, international aviation's contribution to global GHG emissions is approximately 2 percent. However, these emissions are expected to increase considerably under a business-as-usual scenario.

Although the International Civil Aviation Organization (ICAO) has discussed environmental protection in connection with aviation since the 1970s, climate change issues are relatively new. Ever since the Kyoto Protocol entrusted the ICAO with handling GHG emissions from international aviation, the Organization has been at the center of the storm. This chapter seeks to explore the ICAO's involvement in climate change issues, and its merits and shortcomings, as well as identifying better ways for the organization to handle GHG emissions from international aviation, in particular bearing in mind the recent agreement to develop a global market-based measure (MBM) scheme. Understanding the constraints under which the ICAO operates is central to determining its limitations and establishing realistic corrective actions to facilitate not only its adoption and implementation but, more importantly, participation in the ICAO's global MBM.

To this end, the chapter discusses two main topics. First, it analyzes the suitability of the ICAO's institutional setting to handle climate change issues. Secondly, the chapter studies the ICAO's specific involvement in climate change issues. Although the ICAO has in the past taken many initiatives to tackle climate change, the chapter focuses on five key aspects: (1) the CO_2 standard; (2) State action plans; (3) the aspirational goals; (4) the framework for MBMs; and, (5) the global scheme. These topics adequately illustrate the challenges faced and the political implications involved. Finally, the chapter provides some concluding observations with some suggested realistic corrective actions that the ICAO may take to better handle the issue of GHG emissions from international aviation.

12.1 INTRODUCTION

The success of international aviation has not been without cost. As the sector continues to achieve unyielding growth rates, concerns over its environmental impact have risen in tandem. Although the ICAO has discussed environmental protection in connection with aviation since the 1970s, climate change issues are relatively new. Ever since the Kyoto Protocol entrusted the International Civil Aviation Organization (ICAO) with handling GHG emissions from international aviation, the organization has been at the center of the storm. This chapter seeks to explore the ICAO's involvement in climate change issues, and its merits and shortcomings, as well as identifying better ways for the organization to handle GHG emissions from international aviation, in particular bearing in mind the recent decision to implement a global market-based measure (MBM) in the form of a carbon offsetting and reduction scheme for international aviation (CORSIA). Understanding the constraints under which the ICAO operates is central to determining its limitations and establishing realistic corrective actions to facilitate not only its implementation but, more importantly, participation and its enforcement.

To this end, the chapter discusses two main topics. First, it analyzes the suitability of the ICAO's institutional setting to handle climate change issues. It digs into the organization's aims and objectives as set out in the Chicago Convention and its strategic objectives. It examines whether the lack of a specific reference to "environmental protection" in the organization's constitutional framework presents a problem. In addition, this chapter looks into the ICAO's governing structure and considers whether it facilitates or inhibits participation by member States. Given aviation's global nature, broad participation and member State engagement are desired attributes of any measures intended to address climate change issues. Also, this chapter explores the nature of the organization's constituency, the influence of industry stakeholders in the formulation of environmental policy, and the lack of presence of representatives of international civil society. It pays close attention to the work of the ICAO's Committee on Environmental Protection (CAEP), the merits and shortcomings thereof, and perceived structural deficiencies. CAEP has been at the forefront of the development of environmental regulations applicable to international aviation and will continue to play a leading role in addressing GHG emissions given that it handles most of the technical work.

Second, through an examination of all relevant Assembly resolutions and discussions within the Council, the chapter studies the ICAO's specific involvement in climate change issues. Although the ICAO has in the past taken many initiatives to tackle climate change, the chapter focuses on five key aspects: (1) the CO_2 standard; (2) State action plans; (3) the aspirational goals; (4) the framework for MBMs; and, (5) the global scheme. These topics adequately illustrate the challenges faced and the political implications involved. Similarly, they highlight unresolved issues and various opportunities for improvement that lie ahead. These will be enormously valuable in designing and bringing CORSIA into operation. Finally, the chapter provides some concluding observations with some suggested realistic corrective actions that the ICAO may take to better handle the issue of GHG emissions from international aviation.

12.2 THE ICAO'S INSTITUTIONAL SETTING

Adopted on December 7, 1944 and having entered into force on April 4, 1947, the Chicago Convention serves as the constitutional framework for international air transport.[1] In addition to setting out basic rules to promote the safe and orderly development aviation,[2] the Chicago Convention established the ICAO.[3] To date, 191 States are party to the Chicago Convention and therefore members of the ICAO.[4] Through the adoption of its standards and recommended practices (SARPs), this specialized UN agency has been instrumental in laying down the foundational grounds that have allowed international civil aviation to evolve from perilous beginnings to the safest mode of transportation.[5]

[1] See Convention on the International Civil Aviation (adopted December 7, 1944, entered into force April 4, 1947)15 UNTS. 295, 61 Stat 1180, ICAO Doc. 7300/06 [Chicago Convention]. See generally P. S. Dempsey, *Public International Air Law* (Montreal: Institute and Center for Research in Air & Space Law, 2008) [Dempsey, *Public International Air Law*].

[2] Among others, these rules address issues such as the principle of exclusive sovereignty over a State's airspace, exclusion of military aircraft, prohibition on the use of weapons against civil aviation, right of nonscheduled flights, cabotage, requirement of prior approval of the State concerned for pilotless aircraft, provisions on prohibited areas, customs and immigration, measure to prevent spread of communicable diseases, airport and air navigation charges, nationality of the aircraft, search and rescue, fuel tax exemptions, and adoption of standards and recommended practices. See Ibid., *Chicago Convention*, Arts. 1–42.

[3] Ibid., Art. 43.

[4] See *Chicago Convention, supra* Note 1.

[5] See *Chicago Convention, supra* Note 1, Arts. 37, 38.

12.2.1 *Objectives*

The Chicago Convention sets out the ICAO's main objectives.[6] These may be summarized as follows: (i) develop principles to foster progress of international air transport; (ii) ensure safe and orderly growth; (iii) encourage infrastructure expansion; (iv) avoid discrimination; and, (v) play a vigilant role to ensure that the rights of all member States are respected.[7] These objectives were established in the early days of aviation when the organization's institutional framework served to encourage the growth of the sector and to ensure its stability in the post-World War II era. In anticipation of aviation's potential benefits of enhancing connectivity and encouraging economic prosperity, the drafters of the Chicago Convention wanted to guarantee that international air transport would develop in a "safe, regular, efficient, and economical" manner to "meet the needs of the people of the world."[8] Never in their wildest dreams could they have envisioned that the tiny air transport sector would have reached its current dimensions. It is not surprising that the word "environment" is not even mentioned once throughout the Chicago Convention; the text pays much more attention to "growth" and "development," which, at the time, were main concerns of the drafters. As China has noted, "the development of international air transport is [ICAO's] priority."[9]

This historical context explains why the ICAO's institutional framework heavily favors the expansion of air transport.[10] Some commentators therefore see the organization's objectives as "seemingly weighted against the needs of the climate system."[11] Similarly, others claim that the ICAO's own legal framework and its institutional setting are not necessarily conducive to addressing environmental issues such as climate change.[12]

6 Ibid., Art. 44.
7 Ibid.
8 Ibid., Art. 44 (d).
9 See ICAO, A37/WP-181 at 2.4.
10 See Transport and Environment, "Global deal or no deal? Your free guide to ICAO's triennial assembly," www.transportenvironment.org/sites/te/files/publications/2013%2009%20Your%20Guide%20to%20ICAO_final.pdf last accessed October 18, 2017. [Transport & Environment, Global Deal or no Deal] (suggesting that being "aware of the sector's environmental impacts" since the 1970s, the ICAO has demonstrated "no willingness to constrain growth").
11 See A. Macintosh, "Overcoming the barriers to international aviation greenhouse gases emissions abatement," *Air & Sp. L.*, **33** (2008) at 411. [Macintosh].
12 See K. Kulovesi, "Addressing sectoral emissions outside the United Nations Framework Convention on Climate Change: What roles for multilateralism, minilateralism and unilateralism," *RECIEL*, **21** (2012) 193 at 198 [Kulovesi, Addressing Sectoral Emissions].

The ICAO's structural characteristics and its natural tendency to promote the growth and development of the air transport sector pose major challenges when the organization considers policies oriented at curbing aviation's environmental externalities. Environmental policy at the ICAO must be limited to measures that reduce aircraft engine emissions without constraining the growth of air transport in any way. Above all, these are the organization's core aims and objectives.

The ICAO's constitutional framework places severe limitations on what the organization can actually accomplish in the environmental field. There might be times when specific measures ought to be put in place in certain regions or locations seeking precisely to restrict growth in order for international civil aviation to develop in a sustainable manner. Yet these measures would directly conflict with the aims and objectives of the ICAO as set out in the Chicago Convention. It is on the basis of this contradiction that the ICAO's constituents will most likely argue against or simply reject any such growth-limiting proposals. By way of illustration, some States have argued that emissions-related charges are incompatible with the aims of the Chicago Convention since they place incremental burdens on the orderly development of air transport.[13]

Within the ICAO, there is also a strong perception that the organization's core business is to deal with issues of air navigation, safety, and security.[14] For instance, while pointing out that the ICAO has devoted too much attention to climate change issues, one State "expressed doubt that [climate change] carried the same weight as safety and security and other tasks."[15]

In an effort to remedy the absence of a clear environmental objective in the Chicago Convention, the ICAO has, through various proposals developed by the Secretary General with input from the Council, adopted a number of different strategic objectives addressing environmental issues. For instance, for the first time ever, the ICAO conducted a reassessment of its main objectives in 1997.[16] Following this exercise, the Council approved an action plan with strategic objectives addressing issues such as SARPs, strengthening the legal framework, air navigation, and technical cooperation.[17] Although the growing

[13] See ICAO, CSG-LAEC/1 at 3–1.

[14] See L. A. Dupuis, Discours d'adieu du Représentant permanent du Canada au Conseil de l'OACI, Doyen des Membres du Conseil (June 29, 2011) (on file with the author) (noting that safety and air navigation are the ICAO's priorities).

[15] See ICAO, C-MIN 199/13 at 15.

[16] ICAO, "Guiding international civil aviation into the 21st century," www.icao.int/Documents/strategic-objectives/sap1997_en.pdf, last accessed October 19, 2017.

[17] Ibid.

concern over aviation's environmental impact was noted in the action plan, the ICAO did not establish a specific objective for environmental protection.[18] In addition to laying down the organization's vision and mission, the ICAO developed a new set of strategic objectives in 2005.[19] At this time, "[m]inimizing the adverse effect of global civil aviation on the environment" became one of the aims of the organization.[20] For the 2010–2013 triennium, the ICAO adopted three strategic objectives, one of which dealt with "environmental protection and sustainable development of air transport."[21] Here, the objective was to "[f]oster [a] harmonized and economically viable development of international civil aviation, [while] not unduly [harming] the environment." Finally, in 2013, the 38th Assembly endorsed a proposal of the Council to adopt new strategic objectives for the 2013–2016 triennium. While addressing key areas of concern to the ICAO such as safety, security, and air navigation, this latest iteration of the objective de-links air transport from environmental protection.[22] In other words, the objective seeks to "[m]inimize the adverse environmental effect of civil aviation activities," while "[fostering] ICAO's leadership in all aviation-related environmental activities."[23]

The fact that environmental protection now forms part of the ICAO's strategic objectives is very indicative of the relevance that this issue bears for the organization's activities. There is no doubt that presently, the ICAO is much more engaged with environmental issues than it previously was, and it has allocated significantly more financial resources to the issue.[24] However,

18 Ibid.

19 ICAO, "Strategic objectives of ICAO for 2005–2010," www.icao.int/Documents/strategic-objectives/strategic_objectives_2005_2010_en.pdf, last accessed October 19, 2017.

20 Ibid.

21 ICAO, "Strategic objectives 2011–2012–2013," www.icao.int/Documents/strategic-objectives/strategic_objectives_2011_2013_en.pdf, last accessed October 19, 2017.

22 See ICAO, "Budget of the organization 2014–2015–2016," Doc. 10030, at 24 [ICAO, Budget 2014–2016].

23 ICAO, "Strategic objectives 2013–2016," www.icao.int/about-icao/Pages/Strategic-Objectives.aspx last accessed October 20, 2017. See also ICAO, "Strategic objectives," www.icao.int/about-icao/Council/Pages/Strategic-Objectives.aspx last accessed October 20, 2017.

24 While the ICAO's budget for the triennium 2008–2010 only provided for CA$ 5.1 million for the strategic objective of environmental protection, this jumped to CA$ 8.5 million for the following triennium (2011–2013); See ICAO, "Budget for the organization 2008–2009–2010," Doc. 9895, at 11; ICAO, "Budget for the organization 2011–2013–2013," Doc. 9955 at 12; For the triennium 2014–2016, the 38th Assembly approved a budget of roughly CA$ 14 million for environmental protection activities; See ICAO, "Budget for the organization 2014–2015–2016," Doc. 10030, at 10. While environmental protection still represents less than 2 percent of the ICAO's overall budget, safety accounts for roughly 10 percent and air navigation for 9.5 percent; Ibid. Of all the strategic objectives established for the 2014–2016 triennium, environmental protection showed the largest increase compared to the previous triennium. Ibid.

these strategic objectives by themselves do not amount to an amendment or a rewriting of the organization's aims as set out in the Chicago Convention. In practice, the fact that the Chicago Convention does not spell out "environment" as one of the ICAO's main objectives does pose a problem. Arguably, in cases of conflict, the development of air transport would trump environmental protection. For instance, one State has said that "ICAO should put the development of international air transport as its first priority bearing in mind the mandate of Article 44 on the aims and objectives of ICAO in the Chicago Convention."[25] In spite of the foregoing, it seems very unlikely that, at least in the near future, the Chicago Convention will be amended to correct these deficiencies.

12.2.2 *Governing Structure*

The ICAO consists primarily of an Assembly, a Council, a Secretariat, and other technical bodies that report to the Council such as the Air Navigation Commission (ANC).[26] For the purpose of this thesis, consideration will be given to the Assembly and the Council.

As the supreme body of the organization, the Assembly is responsible for (i) electing States to the Council; (ii) approving the budget; (iii) considering proposals to amend the Chicago Convention; (iv) delegating prerogatives to the Council; and, (v) considering reports from the Council.[27] Initially, the Chicago Convention stipulated annual Assembly meetings.[28] However, on June 14, 1956 the Assembly adopted a Protocol to amend the Chicago Convention and changed the annual frequency of its meetings to no less than once every three years – in practice this has meant a meeting every three years.[29]

This amendment marks one of the most unnoticed but profound structural changes that the ICAO has ever undertaken. Less frequent sessions have diminished the Assembly's role[30] while "strengthening the position and

[25] See ICAO, A37-WP/181 EX/32.
[26] See Chicago Convention, *supra* note 1 Arts. 48, 50, 56, 58 & 59.
[27] Ibid., Art. 49.
[28] Ibid., Art. 48.
[29] See ICAO, "Protocol relating to the amendments of Articles 48 (a), 49 (e) and 61 of the Convention on International Civil Aviation," DOC 7300, Amendments 12/12/56, https://www.icao.int/publications/Documents/7300_1ed_amend_dec56.pdf last accessed October 20, 2017.
[30] See M. Milde, "Chicago convention – 50 years later: Are major amendments necessary or 'desirable'?" *Ann. Air & Sp. L.* 19 (1994), 401 at 429.

influence of [the Council]."[31] As one commentator notes, with this change, "the powers of the Assembly have eroded."[32] The change has progressively dissuaded active participation of member States other than those fortunate enough to have Council representation. Although member States do attend the ICAO's triennial Assembly sessions, they do so in a rather passive manner. The tremendous backlog of massive working papers makes it impossible for delegates to really grasp what the Assembly is supposed to consider in a short two-week session. In addition, the more infrequent these sessions have become, the farther member States have moved from the day-to-day activities of the organization. Commentators also point out that this structural change in the ICAO has led to the "majority of States simply [not contributing] to the advancement of the international aviation."[33] In 2013, the 38th Assembly considered a proposal to hold its meetings once every two years. The Council reported that such a proposal would represent an additional cost of US$ 2.4 million over a period of six years. To no one's surprise, the Assembly quickly discarded the proposal.[34] What the Council did not present to the Assembly was a cost-benefit analysis on changing the nature of the Council from a permanent to an ad hoc political body.

Initially, the Council, the organization's permanent political body, consisted of twenty-one States.[35] At present, however, the Council has thirty-six States.[36] As one environmental nongovernmental organization puts it, the Council "has been carefully nurtured over the years to call all the shots."[37] The Council is headed by a President who is also a permanent employee of the organization.

The Council's functions may roughly be summarized as follows: (i) execution of the mandates given by the Assembly; (ii) management of the organization's finances; (iii) appointment of the Secretary General; (iv) adoption of standards and recommended practices (SARPs); and, (v) reporting of infractions to the Chicago Convention.[38] The fact that extremely important

[31] See P. A. A. Fossungu, "A critique of the powers and duties of the assembly of the international civil aviation organization," unpublished LLM thesis, McGill University (1996), 21.

[32] See M. Milde, *International Air Law and ICAO*, 2nd edn. (The Hague: Eleven International Publishing, 2012), 130 [Milde, *International Air Law and ICAO*].

[33] See P. A. A. Fossungu, "999 University, please help the third world (Africa) help itself: A critique of council elections," *J. Air L. & Com.*, 64 (1999) 339.

[34] See ICAO, A38-WP/18 EX 13.

[35] Membership to the Council increased from twenty-one States to thirty, to thirty-three, and finally to thirty-six States.

[36] See *Chicago Convention*, *supra* Note 1, Art. 50.

[37] See Transport & Environment, Global Deal or no Deal, *supra* Note 10.

[38] See *Chicago Convention*, *supra* Note 1, Art. 54.

functions such as the adoption of SARPs (the ICAO's uncontested core activity) and the appointment of the Secretary General are vested in the Council is very indicative of its influential role. As Milde points out, it is the Council that is without a doubt "the real focus of the ICAO decision-making" process.[39] It is with reason then that some have ventured to call it a genuine "executive committee."[40]

The foregoing may explain why States continue to suggest that Council membership should be increased. In 2007, at the 36th Assembly, fifteen Arab States presented a proposal to increase Council membership from thirty-six to thirty-nine States.[41] These States argued that the "increasing importance of civil aviation in the Arab region, particularly in the Gulf area, [justified] a higher weight of participation in supervisory bodies in the field of international civil aviation."[42] They also contended that "many regions of the world are over-represented compared to the 22 Arab States, such as the Northern European States as well as Central and Latin America."[43] Three years later, in 2010, at the 37th Assembly, Saudi Arabia tabled a similar proposal.[44] At the time, the Assembly referred the matter to the Council for consideration. Although noting "the need and growing desire by many States to be represented on the Council," the Council observed that "increasing membership may not be the most appropriate means to address this matter."[45] The Council therefore did not endorse an increase of its membership to thirty-nine.[46] In 2013, the 38th Assembly followed the Council's recommendation and the proposal was abandoned.

In 2016, the political landscape shifted. Turkey placed enormous pressure on European States to be included as part of Europe's quota in the Council. As a result of this, other European States saw Turkey's position as a threat that may jeopardize their longstanding presence in the Council. The Asian States also expressed their views that, for a long time, they have been under-represented. Other Gulf countries also signaled their intention to take part in the Council. Because of this, the Council tabled a concrete proposal to the

39 See Milde, International Law and ICAO, *supra* Note 32 at 130.

40 See I. H. Ph. Diederiks-Verschoor, *An Introduction to Air Law*, 8th edn., (The Netherlands: Kluwer Law International, 2006) at 45.

41 See ICAO, A36-WP/258 EX 86.

42 Ibid. at 3.

43 Ibid.

44 See ICAO, "Assembly 37th Session – Working Papers by numbers," https://www.icao.int/Meetings/AMC/Assembly37/Pages/Working%20Papers%20by%20Numbers.aspx last accessed October 20, 2017.

45 See ICAO, A38-WP/17 EX 12.

46 Ibid.

Assembly to increase its membership from thirty-six to forty States.[47] The proponents of the Council membership increase argue that since 1990 – the last time the membership was increased to thirty-nine States – twenty-nine new States have joined the ICAO.[48]

The proposals to increase the Council membership echo a growing feeling within member States that in order to participate in the organization's activities one must be a member of the Council. If not, their contributions to the organization become much less significant. Some States with significant aviation activity are currently not members of the Council. These include, among others, Indonesia, Thailand, Qatar, Turkey, Ireland, Luxembourg, Ethiopia, Taiwan, Finland, Philippines, Israel, and Colombia.[49]

The existing structure poses significant barriers to participation and engagement from member States, *a sine qua non* for addressing aviation and climate change issues. The more disengaged and the less informed the majority of member States are on this issue, the stronger their inclination to reject collaborative action and block global proposals. Participation is a key element in the development of a global MBM scheme to address GHG emissions from international aviation.

12.2.3 *Constituency*

Most attendees to ICAO events are delegates from civil aviation authorities and ministries of transport of member States. In fact, it is rare to find someone with a background other than aviation at an Assembly. Council composition is not much different. Permanent Representatives to the Council are either civil servants from civil aviation authorities or career diplomats attached to their ministries of foreign affairs. Likewise, with very few exceptions, most staff members of the ICAO Secretariat possess a technical aviation background. It is unlikely that a predominantly aviation-oriented constituency will weigh in heavily on environmental considerations. In this context, it should not be a surprise that the ICAO constituency has the tendency to examine climate change issues from an aviation perspective and not vice versa.

47 See ICAO, A39-WP18 EX 6.

48 Ibid., Appendix A at A-3.

49 According to ICAO statistics, these countries rank in the top thirty-six in terms of international aviation activity, albeit not Council members. See ICAO, "Civil aviation: 2012 international RTK by State of Air Operator Certificate (AOC)," www.icao.int/Meetings/a38/Documents/International%20Scheduled%20RTK%20(Annual%20Report).PDF last accessed October 20, 2017.

12.2.4 *The ICAO's Committee on Aviation Environmental Protection (CAEP)*

On December 5, 1983, the Council merged the Committee on Aircraft Noise (CAN) and the Committee on Aircraft Engine Emissions (CAEE) and thereby established the Committee on International Aviation Environmental Protection (CAEP), a body of interdisciplinary experts, to formulate recommendations on issues involving technical, economic, social, and policy aspects of aviation and the environment.[50] CAEP is first and foremost a committee of the Council. The Council approves its meetings, directives, terms of reference, agenda, and work program. The CAEP work program is carried out over a cycle of three years, during which various steering and working groups meet regularly. At the end of the cycle a two-week meeting is convened in Montreal to prepare a final report with proposed recommendations for consideration and approval by the Council.

CAEP has been instrumental in the ICAO's work on environmental issues. Its initial focus was geared toward standard setting on aircraft engine emissions, air quality, technical aspects, cost effectiveness, and vapor displacement from fuel tanks.[51] Later, just before its second meeting, the ICAO Council refined CAEP's terms of reference to specifically tackle issues relating to the control of aircraft noise and gaseous emissions from aircraft engines.[52] It was only after the conclusion of the 1992 United Nations Conference on Environment and Development that the 31st Assembly decided to entrust CAEP with a very broad mandate to expand its work plan to include climate change issues associated with aviation and to work closely with other organizations such as the UNFCCC and the IPCC.[53]

CAEP recommendations are adopted following a six-fold test that includes technical feasibility, environmental effectiveness, economic reasonableness, the interdependencies of measures, developments in other fields, and national and international programs.[54] Under technical feasibility, CAEP seeks to

50 See ICAO, C-WP/13520 at 1.1 and 1.2.

51 See ICAO, CAEP/1-WP/97 at 4–1.

52 See ICAO, CAEP/2-WP/1.

53 At present, experts from the following States are members of CAEP: Argentina, Australia, Brazil, Canada, China, Egypt, France, Germany, India, Italia, Japan, Netherlands, Poland, Russian Federation, Singapore, Spain, Sweden, Switzerland, South Africa, Tunisia, Ukraine, United Kingdom, and the United States. The following States serve as observers: Greece, Indonesia, New Zealand, Norway, Turkey, and United Arab Emirates.

See ICAO, "CAEP – Members and observers," www.icao.int/environmental-protection/Pages/CAEP.aspx, last accessed October 19, 2017.

54 ICAO, "CAEP terms of reference," www.icao.int/environmental-protection/Documents/CAEP/Images/CAEPToR.jpg last accessed October 19, 2017;. See also ICAO, "Environmental

ensure that a recommended environmental regulation is viable from a technical perspective in order not to jeopardize aviation safety. This part of the test has been criticized as favoring technical conservatism where market forces – often summarized as the views of the industry – and not ICAO regulations determine what is technically feasible.[55] Under environmental effectiveness, CAEP seeks to ensure that the proposal will in fact produce concrete environmental benefits. In considering the economic reasonableness of recommendations, CAEP looks into the most cost-effective ways to carry them out. There have been concerns that economic reasonableness considerations now include complex cost-benefit analyses that do not factor in the cost of internalizing externalities that aviation creates for the environment. In other words, the test does not consider the application of the polluter pays principle through the imposition of an environmental externality on airlines and consumers to be economically reasonable.[56] In connection with interdependencies of measures, CAEP assesses the link between the different components of environmental protection to avoid situations in which, for instance, a CO_2 reduction measure may generate an increase in NO_x emissions.[57] Yet perhaps the most serious criticism that CAEP's six-pronged test has received relates to the fact that it fails to recognize the cost to society of aviation's unsustainable development.[58] CAEP's test also looks into what other sectors are doing to address GHG emissions, as well as examining programs being implemented at national or international levels.

Another criticism that CAEP has attracted relates to its imbalanced membership. At CAEP/1, the original roster included experts from thirteen ICAO member States, of which seven were European States.[59] Later, at CAEP/3 membership was increased to fifteen States with two new European additions.[60] At CAEP/5, held in 2001, nearly eighteen years after its formation,

protection," www.icao.int/environmental-protection/Pages/Caep.aspx, last accessed October 19, 2017.

55 See E. Duthie, "ICAO regulation: Meeting environmental need?" *Air & Sp. Europe*, 3 (2001), 27. [Duthie].

56 Ibid. at 28.

57 For instance, See D. S. Lee and R. Sausen, "New directions: Assessing the real impact of CO2 emissions trading by the aviation industry," *Atmos. Environ.*, 34 (2000), 5337 at 5338. Note that any initiative to reduce aviation's CO_2 emissions must also factor in the effect that such measure may have on radiative forcing, for it may produce an increase of the latter.

58 Ibid.

59 CAEP's original members were Australia, Brazil, Canada, Denmark, France, Germany, Italy, Japan, Netherlands, Sweden, USSR, United Kingdom, and United States. AAC, IATA, and ICCAIA joined as observers. See ICAO CAEP/1-WP/97.

60 Although Denmark dropped out of CAEP at its third meeting, Poland, Spain, and Switzerland joined. The Council also decided to add Norway as an observer State. This produced a net get

membership was expanded to eighteen ICAO member States in order to include experts from Singapore, Egypt, and South Africa.[61] For the first time, regional diversity became a relevant factor in determining CAEP's membership. An expert from China, the fastest growing domestic aviation market in the world, was only admitted in 2007 during the CAEP/7 cycle. Later, experts from Nigeria and Ukraine became members in 2009.[62] At present, CAEP is composed of experts from twenty-four ICAO member States with an additional five experts having observer status.[63] European countries account for roughly 41 percent of CAEP's membership including observer States, whereas developing countries only account for 34.4 percent.[64] While six industry trade associations provide experts to CAEP as observers, only one environmental NGO is allowed to participate.[65]

CAEP's notorious imbalance in favor of a heavily represented European constituency may be attributed to the fact that at the time of its origin the predominant issue in its work program referred to aircraft noise – a subject about which the European countries were profoundly concerned. Progressive European liberalization policies prompted rapid expansion of air transport, causing severe issues of airport congestion. Countless local areas neighboring airport premises were affected, provoking frequent public outcry. At the time, aircraft noise became the major aviation environmental issue in Europe. It was therefore the European push that forced the Council to include noise-related topics in CAEP's agenda. However, in regions where aircraft noise was not the subject of much attention, the environmental issues surrounding aviation seemed mostly remote. Countries from these regions did not see an acute need to participate in CAEP and neither did the ICAO encourage them to join. In the ICAO's defense, it is also true that these countries did almost nothing to engage in CAEP's discussions. It is not surprising that, during the early days of CAEP, Brazil – an aircraft manufacturing country – was the only developing country to take part in its proceedings. Japan was the only representative from Asia, and there were no members from Africa. This historical

gain for Europe of two additional member States and one observer State. At the time, no other country from any other of the ICAO's geographical regions became a CAEP member. See ICAO, CAEP/3.

61 See ICAO, CAEP/5-WP/86.

62 See ICAO, CAEP/8-WP/80 at 1.

63 See ICAO, "CAEP members and observers," www.icao.int/ENVIRONMENTAL-PROTECTION/Pages/CAEP.aspx last accessed October 19, 2017.

64 Ibid. On the other hand, experts from developed States account for 65.5 percent of CAEP's membership.

65 Ibid.

imbalance also helps to explain why today aviation's environmental problems, including climate change, are to some extent perceived as a European phenomenon only, to which developing States try somewhat to distance themselves to the greatest extent possible.

CAEP will continue to play a leading role in the formulation of ICAO standards and guidance material, as well as in providing policy advice on delicate issues. CAEP's work will be instrumental in CORSIA's design and implementation. In fact, in October 2016, the 39th Assembly tasked CAEP to develop sustainability criteria for offsets or carbon credits eligible for CORSIA.[66] The 39th Assembly also entrusted CAEP with the mandate to work on monitoring, reporting, and verification (MRV) standards, and the establishment of registries.[67] Because of the significant role CAEP is likely to have in the development of these standards, as well as other tasks that the Council may assign later, the imbalance in CAEP's membership and the participation of its experts should be revisited.

12.2.5 *Industry Participation*

Nobody can question the value of industry involvement in an international organization's rule-making process.[68] At the ICAO, industry stakeholders play a significant role. Yet, outsiders have already pointed out that the organization echoes the interests of industry stakeholders such as air carriers far too strongly.[69] Some years ago, this was subject to noteworthy scrutiny, particularly in the case of the ICAO's Legal Committee. In June 2009, the Working Group on Governance and Policy (WGOG) recommended an amendment to the committee's rules of procedure with regard to the participation of (industry) observers.[70] The WGOG report argued that, in pursuit of consistency with the procedures of other United Nations specialized agencies, a clear

66 ICAO, "Consolidated statement of continuing ICAO policies and practices related to environmental protection – Global Market-based Measure (MBM) scheme," Res A39–3 (October 6, 2016); See also ICAO, C-DEC 200/4; ICAO, MIN-200/4; ICAO, "Committee on Aviation Environmental Protection – CAEP – Informal Briefing to the Council" (January 31, 2014) (on file with the author).

67 Ibid.

68 See P. Canan and N. Reichman, "Lessons learned," in D. Kaniaru (ed.), *The Montreal Protocol: Celebrating 20 Years of Environmental Progress* (London: Cameron May Ltd, 2007) at 114 (highlighting that strong industry involvement was important for the successful adoption of the Montreal Protocol on Ozone Depleting Substance).

69 See R. Janda, "Passing the torch: Why ICAO should leave economic regulation of international air transport to the WTO," *Ann. Air & Sp.*, **21**(1995), 409 at 413.

70 See ICAO, C-WP/13399.

differentiation was needed between member States and observers, since "[observers] have neither the same responsibilities nor the same duties [as member States]."[71] Although the Legal Committee did not agree with WGOG's recommendation to change its rules of procedure to restrict participation of industry stakeholders, the proposal serves to illustrate the discontent of some States.[72]

Industry observers bring invaluable technical expertise and advice to the ICAO. Their participation helps to ensure that rules are drafted in a manner that recognizes the practicalities of the market and the realities of a sector that is technical by definition. International rulemaking should not adopt the form of a unilateral set of commands that fail to take into account the views of those who are the subject of intended regulations. As Fuller notes, this should be an interactive process where all parties involved actively participate as opposed to "only a unidirectional exercise of authority."[73] It is precisely this interaction between lawgivers – ICAO – as the regulating agency – and law subjects – industry stakeholders as their ultimate recipients – that "gives meaning to this law [-making]" process.[74]

Having said this, it is also uncontested that this interaction cannot be to the detriment of the participation of member States, the ICAO being first and foremost an organization of sovereign States. Industry's overwhelming involvement in CAEP, for instance, exemplifies what ought not to be the standard. Should this trend continue, it will only perpetuate a practice that thus far has only disengaged State participation.

Although unsuccessful on this occasion, the WGOG proposal also illustrates the growing discontent among some States with role of industry stakeholders at the ICAO. Arguably, there is a perception that industry has become either too powerful or too successful in its lobbying tactics, making it intricate for some States to dissect what their legitimate concerns are from those that are purely self-interested dogmatic statements with no sound foundation. Complex issues such as aviation and climate change may only accentuate this imbalance where the asymmetry of information gives a significant advantage to industry. Perhaps there is the need to mark the boundaries within which industry stakeholders may participate at the ICAO, but restricting industry participation will not – by itself – resolve the dilemma, for it will only help to isolate a leading actor whose unquestionable contribution is

71 Ibid.
72 See ICAO, Legal Committee 34th Session, Doc 9926-LC/194 (September 9–17, 2009) at 3.1.
73 L. L. Fuller, *The Morality of Law* (New Haven, CT: Yale University Press, 1964) [Fuller] at 223.
74 Ibid. at 195.

desperately required. Without industry input, the ICAO will quickly lose touch with the practical needs and realities of the market on a number of regulatory issues including climate change.

12.2.6 NGO *Participation*

It is interesting to compare the role of industry stakeholders with that of organizations representing civil society at large. Arguably, industry enjoys greater access to the ICAO process than environmental NGOs. It is not unusual that industry is invited to participate in the ICAO's discussion, whereas NGOs are not. For instance, when the 38th Assembly agreed to develop a global MBM for international aviation, it tasked the Council to "finalize work on the technical aspects . . . of the possible options for a global MBM scheme . . . taking into account . . . the proposal of the aviation industry."[75] There is no reference to proposals from those sectors representing civil society.

NGOs bring a completely different perspective on climate change issues that may be worth considering. Perhaps this surreptitious bias has been due to the fact that, historically, the ties between the ICAO and some industry trade organizations have been very strong. For instance, one of IATA's own objectives is precisely to "cooperate with [ICAO]."[76] The fact that IATA is headquartered in Montreal is because of the ICAO. The Airport Council International (ACI) – the international trade association of the world's airports – has also relocated its headquarters to Montreal. The industry–ICAO symbiosis may also be explained from the perspective that as a specialized institution, the ICAO deals with technical issues on which input from industry stakeholders is usually extremely important.

Yet, this should not be translated into a perpetual advantage. Climate change is a complex issue characterized by different interests. It should be in the best interest of the whole process that all parties, including those representing civil society at large, are given a fair opportunity to participate. Restricting access to these organizations or not providing them with a level playing field may reflect an unintentional bias that may be detrimental to the rule-making process.

[75] See ICAO, "Consolidated statement of continuing ICAO policies and practices related to environmental protection – Climate change," A38–18, preamble, para. 19 (a) [ICAO, A38–18].

[76] See IATA, "Articles of Association," Art. 4 (3), www.iata.org/about/Documents/articles-of-association.pdf last accessed October 19, 2017.

12.3 THE ICAO AND CLIMATE CHANGE

The ICAO has an impressive track record when it comes to the production of guidance materials directly or indirectly relating to aviation and climate change issues.[77] Yet, the main criticism against the work of the organization is that GHG emissions from international aviation continue to grow in spite of all its efforts. To date, there is no system in place to reduce or limit these emissions. In addition to describing the evolving challenges that the ICAO has faced, this section focuses on key elements that are expected to play a significant role in the organization's future work on GHG emissions.

12.3.1 *Historical Background*

In 1998, less than a year after the adoption of the Kyoto Protocol, the 32nd Assembly tasked the Council with exploring "policy options to limit or reduce greenhouse gas emissions from civil aviation, taking into account the IPCC special report and the requirements of the Kyoto Protocol."[78] CAEP then established a working group to look into policy options such as charges, fuel taxes, offsetting schemes, and emissions trading.[79] Three years later, the 33rd Assembly noted CAEP's recommendation that an "open emissions-trading system"[80] was a "cost effective measure to limit or reduce" GHG emissions

77 See ICAO Doc. 9949, *Scoping study of issues related to 'linking' open emissions trading systems involving international aviation*, 1st edn. (2011); ICAO, Doc. 9931 AN/476, *Continuous descent operations (CDO) Manual*, 1st edn. (2010); ICAO, Doc. 9574 AN/934, *Manual on a 300 m (1000 ft) vertical separation minimum between Fl 290 and FL 410 inclusive*, 3rd edn. (2012); ICAO Doc. 9885, *Guidance on the use of emissions trading for aviation*, 1st edn. (2008); ICAO Doc. 9977 AN/489, *Manual on civil aviation jet fuel supply*, 1st edn. (2012); ICAO Doc. 9988, *Guidance on the development of States' action plans on CO_2 emissions reductions activities*, 1st edn. (2013); ICAO, Doc. 9501 AN/929, "Environmental technical manual," 1st edn., Doc. 9501 AN/929 (2010); ICAO Doc. 10018, *Report of the assessment of Market-based Measures*, 1st edn. (2013) [ICAO, Global MBM Assessment]; ICAO, Doc. 9997 AN/498, *Performance-based navigation (PBN) operational approval manual*, 1st edn. (2013); ICAO, Doc. 9993 AN/495, *Continuous climb operations (CCO) manual*, 1st edn. (2013); ICAO Doc. 9992 AN/494, *Manual on the use of performance-based navigation (PBN) in airspace design*, 1st edn. (2013); ICAO Circular 134-AN/94, *Control of aircraft engine emission*,1st edn. (1977); ICAO, Circular 334-AN/184, *Guidelines for the implementation of lateral separation minima*,; ICAO Circular 303 AN/176, *Operational opportunities to minimize fuel use and reduce emissions* (2003).

78 See ICAO, "Consolidated statement of continuing ICAO policies and practices related to environmental protection," app. F, para. 4 [ICAO, A32–8].

79 See ICAO, "MBM activities chronology," [unpublished] (on file with the author) [ICAO, MBM Chronology].

80 ICAO defines an open emissions trading as the "system where allowances can be traded in and outside the given scheme or sector." ICAO, Doc. 9885, "Guidance on the use of emissions

from international civil aviation.[81] Due to the lack of political will, the Assembly did not adopt such a system. Instead, the Assembly encouraged States to address the aviation sector's carbon footprint through the adoption of voluntary measures.[82] It also tasked the Council to "develop guidance for States on the application of [MBMs]."[83] For the next three years, CAEP conducted a number of studies on several subjects, including the impact of environmental levies on developing countries, emissions trading, and the possibility of implementing voluntary agreements.[84] In 2004, the 35th Assembly, "[endorsed] the further development of an open emissions trading system."[85] It also tasked the Council to continue carrying out feasibility studies.[86] At that time, the fact that the Assembly was unable to implement concrete measures to address the sector's GHG emissions but rather continue in a "studying mode" *sine die* was perceived as a *de facto* rejection of emissions trading.[87] CAEP nevertheless developed guidance on emissions trading. The ICAO also formed a group of legal experts to examine the legality of emission-related levies and GHG charges.[88]

The next session of the Assembly took place in September 2007,[89] more than two years after of the European Union announced its intention to rope foreign aircraft operators into its emissions trading scheme (EU-ETS). This announcement ignited fierce international opposition never seen in the context of international civil aviation. To no one's surprise, the deliberations that took place at the 36th Assembly were clearly aimed at sending a strong message to Europe that the international community will not tolerate the inclusion of foreign aircraft operators in such a unilateral regime. In fact, the Assembly stated categorically that a State should not include foreign aircraft

trading for aviation," at xiv. In other words, the aviation sector would be permitted to purchase allowances from other industry sectors; Ibid.

81 See ICAO, "Consolidated statement of Continuing ICAO policies and practices related to environmental protection," Res A33–7, app. I, Preamble. [ICAO, A33–7]

82 Ibid., Appendix I, para. 2 (1).

83 Ibid., Appendix I, para. 1.

84 See ICAO, MBM Chronology, *supra* Note 80.

85 See ICAO, "Consolidated statement of continuing ICAO policies and practices related to environmental protection," Res A35–5, app. I, para. 4 (c) (1) [ICAO, A35–5].

86 Ibid., app. I, para. 4 (c) (2).

87 See Transport & Environment, "Global deal or no deal," *supra* Note 10 (suggesting that the 35th Assembly turned down emissions trading as a policy option).

88 See ICAO, MBM Chronology, *supra* Note 80. See also ICAO, "Guidance on the use of emissions trading for aviation," 1st edn. (2008); ICAO, "Council special group on legal aspects of emissions charges" (Montreal, September 6–9, 2005) [ICAO, CSG-LAEC/1].

89 See ICAO, "Assembly 36th Session," www.icao.int/Meetings/AMC/36th/Pages/default.aspx last accessed October 21, 2017.

operators into its emissions trading scheme unless it has previously sought and obtained consent from the home State(s) of the foreign aircraft operators.[90] It is an understatement to say that the issue of mutual consent dominated the Assembly's discussions on climate change. Moreover, in light of the significant disagreements and the failure to adopt a system to regulate GHG emissions, the Assembly tasked the Council with establishing a High-Level Group on International Aviation and Climate Change (GIACC) to provide policy recommendations on what the Assembly described as "an aggressive Program of Action."[91]

After numerous meetings, GIACC provided three key recommendations, namely, the need to develop: (i) a CO_2 aircraft emission standard; (ii) a framework for MBMs; and, (iii) State action plans.[92] In October 2009, the ICAO convened a High-Level meeting on International Aviation and Climate Change (HLM-ENV/09).[93] Building upon GIACC's work, HLM-ENV/09 adopted a nonbinding declaration suggesting that as part of the ICAO's action plan on climate change, States should embrace an aspirational, nonattributable goal "to achieve a global annual average fuel efficiency improvement of 2 per cent over the medium term until 2020."[94] HLM-ENV/09 also recommended that a framework for MBMs should be adopted and that States should develop action plans.[95] The following year, in 2010, signifying progress in three specific areas, the 37th Assembly instructed the Council to: (i) develop a CO_2 standard for aircraft emissions;[96] (ii) develop a framework for MBMs;[97] and (iii) explore the feasibility of a global scheme for MBMs.[98] At the time, the possibility of developing a global scheme seemed extremely remote. Three years later, however, the 38th Assembly finally agreed to develop a global MBM scheme for international aviation.[99]

90 See ICAO, "Consolidated statement of continuing ICAO policies and practices related to environmental protection," app. L, para. 1 (b) (1) [ICAO, A36–22].
91 Ibid., app. K, para. ph 2 (a).
92 See ICAO, "Group on international aviation and climate change (GIACC) Report" (June 1, 2009) at 5–6.
93 See ICAO, "Report of the high-level meeting on international aviation and climate change," Doc. 9929 (Montreal October 7–9, 2009) [HLM-ENV/09 Report].
94 Ibid. at 20, para. 2.
95 Ibid. at 20, paras. 5 and 7.
96 See ICAO, "Consolidated statement of continuing ICAO policies and practices related to environmental protection – Climate change," Res A37–19, para. 24 (e) [ICAO, A37–19].
97 Ibid., para. 13.
98 Ibid., para. 18.
99 Ibid., para. 18.

12.3.2 *The Long Road to the CO_2 Standard*

The process leading to the development of the CO_2 standard for aviation emissions has involved some highly controversial environmental policy debates at the ICAO. The case is illustrative of the challenges that an international organization such as the ICAO faces when industry is not necessarily on board or convinced that regulation is warranted. As will be seen in this chapter, it is also symptomatic of the limitations embedded in the regulation.

In simple words, a CO_2 standard refers to the minimum certification requirements applicable to aircraft engine emissions. Based on type certification, these standards apply solely to aircraft engines.[100] To date, some countries have established minimum fuel consumption standards for road vehicles. However, there are no fuel efficiency standards in existence in any country for purposes of aircraft certification. As a result of successful industry lobbying efforts, market forces – nonregulatory intervention – helped determine fuel efficiency and CO_2 emissions.[101] For a long time, aviation industry advocates, with consistent support from free market champions, have strongly opposed emissions standards on the grounds that market forces have already ensured aircraft fuel efficiency. Aircraft and engine manufacturers have sufficient incentives to produce the most fuel-efficient aircraft. This is precisely what their customers (mostly commercial airlines) demand. With ever-increasing fuel prices and with fuel being the major element in the cost structure of most airlines, reducing fuel consumption is not just an environmental crusade for airlines but also a significant part of their everyday survival mode. Should inefficiencies arise, free market advocates argue that the market's invisible hand will correct them. They point to the US capacity cutbacks that were experienced in 2008 as a result of the fuel spike, which translated into lower fuel consumption levels than those of the year 2000.[102] Free market advocates claim that since CO_2 emissions are directly proportional to the amount of fuel consumed, there is no need to develop such a standard.[103]

[100] See Duthie, *supra* Note 56 at 27.

[101] See B. Metz et al., *Climate Change 2007: Mitigation. Contribution of Working Group III to the Fourth Assessment Report* (Cambridge: Cambridge University Press, 2007) [IPCC/4] at 353.

[102] See M. Locke, "Aviation & the environment: Issues for considering global aviation emissions" ICAO Workshop on Aviation Carbon Markets (June 19, 2008), at 5, https://www.icao.int/Meetings/EnvironmentalWorkshops/Documents/WACM-2008/5_Locke.pdf last accessed October 21, 2017.

[103] See ICAO, CAEP/5-WP/86 at 1–2.

Adhering strictly to this rationale, CAEP/5 completely ruled out the possibility of developing a CO_2 standard in 2001.[104] While this line of reasoning may be true, it also fails to recognize that even if market forces may drive fuel efficiency standards to some extent, this only applies to the acquisition of new equipment. Market forces bear almost no impact at all on the retirement or upgrading of existing, aged fleet – a severe problem in certain regions.[105]

The ICAO's longstanding reluctance to adopt a CO_2 standard gradually came to an end when the GIACC recommended the development of the standard in its final report. However, the recommendation was limited in scope in that it was applicable exclusively to new aircraft types.[106] On June 30, 2009, the Council accepted the GIACC's recommendation and directed the Secretariat to work through CAEP on establishing such a standard.[107] Later, in October 2009, the ICAO's HLM-ENV recommended that the organization should "seek to develop a global CO_2 standard for new aircraft types,"[108] thereby implicitly reaffirming the Council's earlier decision. At this stage, pressure was mounting. Aircraft manufacturers could no longer resist, and it was evident that the standard would have to be developed. A year later, as mentioned in the previous section, the 37th Assembly formally instructed the Council to develop the CO_2 standard.

According to CAEP's reports, the ICAO is pursuing three major objectives in establishing a CO_2 standard. First, the standard seeks to provide additional incentives to improve aircraft fuel efficiency performance.[109] Second, the standard will measure such performance across different aircraft types.[110] And finally, the ICAO intends to minimize counterproductive incentives and adverse interdependency effects.[111] In early 2013, CAEP finally agreed on a common metric for the standard.[112] On March 6, 2017, the Council adopted the new emissions CO_2 standard, which will apply to aircraft type

[104] Ibid.
[105] See Duthie, *supra* Note 56 at 27.
[106] See ICAO, C-WP/13385.
[107] See ICAO, C-DEC 187/14.
[108] See HLM-ENV/09 Report, *supra* Note 94 at 21.
[109] See ICAO, CAEP/8, at 2–18.
[110] Ibid.
[111] Ibid.
[112] See ICAO, "ICAO environmental protection committee delivers progress on aircraft CO_2 and noise standards," www.icao.int/Newsroom/Pages/ICAO-environmental-protection-committee-delivers-progress-on-new-aircraft-CO2-and-noise-standards.aspx last accessed October 21, 2017.

designs from 2020, and to aircraft type designs already in-production as of 2023.[113] The new CO_2 standard imposes a significant restriction.[114] By 2028, in-production aircraft will not be permitted to operate, unless their designs are modified in accordance with the new requirements set forth by the CO_2 standard.[115]

Critics would highlight a number of shortcomings in the CO_2 standard. It will have almost no effect on aircraft in service or those that are already on the production line. In practical terms, from an environmental perspective, the effect of the CO_2 standard will be limited. In fact, the CO_2 standard is nothing more than what industry is already doing or willing to concede. In this respect and as will be discussed later, the case of the CO_2 standard is very similar to that of the global scheme for MBMs.

Yet, one must also bear in mind the enormous opposition that this issue has attracted. For almost ten years, industry and some States were reluctant to even entertain the idea of a CO_2 standard – let alone its metric or scope of applicability. The fact that the ICAO has now adopted such a standard should be seen as a major accomplishment. Should there be the necessary political will, the ICAO and its member States could expand the scope of the CO_2 standard to aircraft in service.

12.3.3 *State Action Plans*

In 2009, GIACC suggested that the ICAO "should encourage States to develop action plans."[116] In an apparent follow up effort on this suggestion in 2010, the 37th Assembly "[encouraged] States to submit their action plans [by June 2012] outlining their respective policies and actions, and annual reporting on international aviation CO_2 emissions to ICAO."[117] As a tool for the achievement of the ICAO's aspirational goals, action plans essentially seek to induce States to monitor their aviation emissions and, as well, to identify measures to address their carbon footprint.[118] To this end, the Assembly suggested that States should establish a baseline or counterfactual basis to

[113] See ICAO, "ICAO council adopts new CO_2 standard for aircraft," www.icao.int/Newsroom/Pages/ICAO-Council-adopts-new-CO2-emissions-standard-for-aircraft.aspx last accessed October 21, 2017.

[114] Ibid.

[115] Ibid.

[116] See GIACC Report, *supra* Note 93 at 4.

[117] ICAO, A37–19, *supra* Note 97, para. 9.

[118] ICAO, "Climate change: Action plans," www.icao.int/environmental-protection/Pages/action-plan.aspx last accessed October 21, 2017.

assess their progress.[119] In 2013, at the 38th Assembly, the ICAO reported that sixty-one States had submitted action plans.[120] Later, in 2016, the 39th Assembly reported that "94 member States that represent more than 88 per cent of the global international air traffic voluntarily prepared and submitted actions plans to ICAO."[121] As of the date of this writing, many States had made their action plans public.[122]

Although it is not yet possible to determine actual GHG emission reductions as a result of the actions plans, this has arguably proved to be one of the ICAO's major achievements in addressing climate change issues. It is true that the development of these action plans is still undergoing a trial-and-error phase, but it has been a gigantic step toward instilling among member States the culture of addressing GHG emissions from international aviation. Even if one remains skeptical about the content of these actions (e.g. accuracy of data, over-emphasis on technological and operational measures, or in some cases, lack of evidence that concrete measures have been put in place to limit or reduce GHG emissions), the sole fact that States discuss measures and options to address climate change issues at large is a major accomplishment. Here, one must bear in mind that the predominant transport-oriented culture within the vast majority of ICAO member States is not necessarily conducive to tackling climate change issues.

Presumably, State action plans have been an invaluable tool to engage a broader audience. The fact that the ICAO Secretariat has attempted to link technical assistance for some States to the preparation of these action plans is a step in the right direction. Obviously, here the availability of additional funds and resources will be of paramount importance. For the future, the ICAO should consider whether the submission of these action plans should be made mandatory, possibly through the adoption of a special ICAO standard. The action plans could also form part of the ICAO audit process. At present, the ICAO only audits States on the basis of their level of compliance with aviation safety and security standards.[123]

119 See ICAO, "Guidance material for the development of states' action plans," www.icao.int/environmental-protection/Documents/GuidanceMaterial_DevelopmentActionPlans.pdf last accessed October 21, 2017.

120 See ICAO, A38-WP/30.

121 See ICAO, "Consolidated statement of continuing ICAO policies and practices related to environmental protection – Climate change," Res A39–2.

122 ICAO, "Action Plans," www.icao.int/environmental-protection/Pages/action-plan.aspx last accessed October 21, 2017.

123 At present, the ICAO safety audits only include airworthiness protocols related noise certification standards of Annex 16 (Environmental Protection). See generally, ICAO, *Universal safety oversight audit program continuous monitoring manual*, Doc. 9735 AN/960, 3rd

12.3.4 *Aspirational Goals*

In 2010, moving beyond HL-ENV/09, the 37th Assembly adopted three aspirational goals. First, the sector should strive to achieve "a global annual average fuel efficiency improvement of 2 per cent."[124] Second, this goal should also be maintained from 2020 to 2050.[125] And finally, from 2020 onward, the Assembly also decided to cap the growth of aviation emissions at 2020 levels.[126] This is what industry refers to as carbon neutral growth (CNG).[127] In working toward CNG, the Assembly called upon States to take into account a number of factors, such as "the special circumstances and respective capabilities [SCRC] of developing countries, the maturity of aviation markets, [and the fact] that some States may take more ambitious actions prior to 2020, which may offset an increase in emissions from the growth of air transport in developing states."[128]

Although no State objected to the fuel efficiency goals, fifty-one States filed reservations against the CNG goal. For forty-four European States and the United States, such a goal was not stringent enough.[129] Instead of CNG, European States had proposed a 10 percent reduction in emissions by 2020 but with a 2005 baseline – a significantly more aggressive goal.[130] The United States, along with Canada and Mexico, in turn, had proposed CNG from 2020 onward with a 2005 baseline.[131] On the other hand, six States claimed that it was unfair for developing countries to commit to such goals.[132] According to them, only developed States should take the lead and implement CNG.[133] Given the divergence in views and how far apart the positions were, it is in fact remarkable that the Assembly was able to adopt such goals – albeit subject to numerous reservations. It was interesting though that the "middle

edn. (ICAO, 2011); ICAO, *Safety management manual (SMM)*, 3rd edn. (ICAO, 2013); ICAO, *Universal security audit program*, 2nd edn. (ICAO, 2010).

124 See ICAO, Res A37–19, *supra* Note 97, para. 4.

125 Ibid.

126 Ibid., para. 6.

127 See ICAO, A37-WP/217 EX/39.

128 See ICAO, A37–19, *supra* Note 97, paras 6 (a), (c), and (d).

129 See ICAO, "Reservations to A37–19," www.icao.int/Meetings/AMC/Assembly37/Documents/ReservationsResolutions/10_reservations_en.pdf last accessed October 21, 2017. [ICAO, Reservations to A37–19].

130 See ICAO, A37-WP/108 EX/26.

131 See ICAO, A37-WP/186 EX/35.

132 See ICAO, Reservations to A37–19, *supra* Note 133.

133 See ICAO, A37-WP/181 EX/32.

ground" lay exactly at the same place where industry struck. To a large extent, these goals are strongly industry-oriented.[134]

These goals are nonbinding, neither are they assigned or "attributed" to States or aircraft operators. All States are encouraged to collectively strive to achieve them. This was done to delink the ICAO's goals from the notion of binding emissions reduction commitments applicable under the UNFCCC/ Kyoto regime. For some developing States, the fact that these goals were "global" and did not set different obligations for developed and developing countries made them unacceptable. This explains why a number of developing countries filed reservations. For other developed States, the suggestion by the Assembly that some States may take action to offset the growth of emissions in developing countries was perceived as a camouflaged incarnation of the CBDR principle at the ICAO. The United States, Canada, and Australia expressed strong reservations on this issue.[135] It would seem that, for both developing and developed States, these discussions at the ICAO bear implications for the broader climate change negotiations at the UNFCCC.[136]

The ICAO's goals have been the subject of severe criticism.[137] Some commentators doubt that they will in fact lead to meaningful emission reductions.[138] The ICAO itself admits that fuel efficiency improvement by itself will be insufficient.[139] In spite of this, one must also recognize that the goals have been instrumental in setting a reference point, which also serves as a basis for the ICAO's work on climate change. This is important in determining whether the implementation of technical and operational measures will be sufficient, or whether MBMs ought to be developed. Even if these goals prove later to be insufficient, it would be almost impossible to make any progress without them. One could argue that, in light of the current growth trends of the air transport sector, the ICAO should consider more aggressive goals. To date, however, it is not clear that there is sufficient political will to do

[134] See ICAO, A37-WP/217 EX/39.

[135] See ICAO, Reservations to A37–19, *supra* Note 133.

[136] See ICAO, C-MIN 197/6 at 8 (Statement of India) (suggesting that climate change issues involving international aviation cannot be disassociated from UNFCCC developments).

[137] See C. Lyle, "Mitigating international air transport emissions through a global measure: Time for some lateral thinking" (2014), www.greenaironline.com/news.php?viewStory=1820last accessed October 21, 2017. (describing the ICAO's global aspirational goals as "tenuous") [Lyle, Mitigating International Air Transport Emissions through a Global Measure].

[138] See Green Air "Climate researchers find even Carbon-neutral growth from 2020 will not be enough to stave off climate impacts," www.greenaironline.com/news.php?viewStory=1761 last accessed October 21, 2017.

[139] See ICAO, Res A37–19, *supra* Note 95, preamble.

so. In this context, it is very likely that these goals will remain untouched and that they will continue to be nonbinding.

12.4 A FRAMEWORK FOR MBMS

Ever since Europe announced its intention to include foreign aircraft operators in its ETS, one of the industry's greatest concerns has been the potential emergence of a patchwork of multiple regimes attempting to address the sector's GHG emissions.[140] In the words of Giovanni Bisignani, IATA's former Director General, "a global industry [requires] a global solution."[141] The industry's preference for a coordinated approach was self-evident. At this juncture, however, the possibility of adopting a single global scheme seemed a far-fetched proposition.[142] Cognizant of the industry's concerns, both GIACC and HLM-ENV/09 recommended that a framework for MBMs should be pursued.[143] The framework was perceived as a tool to induce coordination among different regimes, avoid market distortions, and shield the industry from additional financial burdens and redundant compliance.[144] At this stage, there was not much information as to what the framework should be, neither was there any indication as to whether it should be adopted through a binding or nonbinding instrument.

In 2010, the 37th Assembly tasked the Council "to develop a framework for [MBMs]."[145] Unlike many other provisions of the 2010 ICAO climate change resolution, this task did not receive a single reservation.[146] Arguably, States saw in the framework a tool to avoid uncoordinated approaches and, for some, an instrument to send a strong political message to Europe in connection with its decision to include foreign aircraft operators in its ETS.[147]

After the Assembly session, much of the work on the framework remained dormant for more than a year following the Council's declaration of a one-year cooling-off period.[148] The ICAO resumed discussions on the framework

140 See G. Bisignani, *Words of Change* (Geneva: IATA Corporate Communications, 2011) at 52 [Bisignani, *Words of Change*].

141 Ibid.

142 In fact, "GIACC acknowledged that the implementation of a unique global sectoral system would face major challenges, particularly in the short and medium-term." GIACC Report, *supra* Note 91 at 16.

143 See GIAAC Report, *supra* Note 93 at 5–6; HLM-ENV/09 Report, *supra* Note 94 at 20, para. 5.

144 Ibid., GIAAC Report at 16.

145 See ICAO, A37–19, *supra* Note 97, para. 13.

146 See ICAO, Reservations to A37–19, *supra* Note 133.

147 See ICAO, HGCC/2-WP/9.

148 See ICAO, C-DEC 192/6 at 2.

in 2012. At this time, all non-EU States joined in the effort to stop the application of the EU-ETS. In this context, it seemed reasonable to push for the development of the framework. At the invitation of the United States, a group of States opposing the EU-ETS met in Washington DC on July 31 and August 1, 2012 to discuss international aviation emissions.[149] These States concluded that the ICAO's work on the framework should be prioritized.[150] Other political factors also explain the preference for a framework as opposed to a global scheme. For instance, the US presidential elections were scheduled for November 2012. Seeking re-election, and given tremendous difficulties encountered with the US Congress on other domestic issues, the Obama administration was very concerned about any potential spill-over effects that could be triggered if it expressed support for the concept of a global scheme.

The framework must be clearly distinguished from CORSIA.[151] In essence, it is only a set of common, nonbinding principles[152] aimed at guiding those States or group of States that voluntarily decide to implement an MBM to the extent that such a measure is applicable to foreign aircraft operators.[153] The framework does not seek to impose on States the obligation to adopt MBMs. There have been different views of what the purpose of the framework should be. For instance, the United States suggested that the framework should be a "safety zone" that seeks to provide guidance to those States or group of States wishing to implement MBMs.[154] As another State brilliantly noted, the "safety zone" approach seeks to act as a "dispute settlement mechanism to resolve controversies amongst States. It seeks to set out the conditions of [the framework's] applicability and scope. Rather than enabling action to reduce GHG emissions from international aviation, this view is much more concerned with restricting the reach and the implementation of existing MBMs."[155] For others, the framework's main purpose is to "drive commonality and harmonization in order to avoid duplicative measures [and constitute] the building

[149] See Meeting on International Aviation Emissions, Chair's Summary, July 31–August 1, 2012, Washington D.C. (on file with the author) [Washington Meeting].

[150] Ibid. at 2.

[151] See ICAO, C-WP/13861 at 3–4.

[152] Although States did discuss different instruments (e.g. convention, Assembly resolutions, standard), they have always assumed that the framework will be adopted through an Assembly resolution. See ICAO, HGCC/2-WP/6.

[153] See ICAO, C-WP/13861 at 3–4. See also ICAO, HGCC/3-WP/4 at 3 (noting that the framework should be a set of guiding principles that seek to guide States in the implementation of domestic and regional MBMs, when these measures are applied to foreign aircraft operators).

[154] See ICAO, HGCC/2-WP 9.

[155] ICAO, HGCC/3-WP/4 at 3.

blocks for a future global scheme."[156] The Secretariat also suggested that the framework should "contribute to the achievement of [ICAO's global aspirational goals]."[157]

Although the Secretariat highlighted other areas where policy guidance was warranted,[158] States focused their discussions on the most controversial issue associated with the framework: the so-called geographical scope. In other words, States focused on whether a State implementing an MBM could include foreign aircraft operators, and if so, under what conditions and to what extent.[159] Depending on the approach adopted, the geographical scope of an MBM may provide the basis for allegations of extraterritorial application to be made. Moreover, emissions were computed for the whole duration of the flight. It suffices to note here that the central argument against the EU-ETS was precisely that the extraterritorial elements present in the scheme were impermissible.[160]

The ICAO Secretariat identified three different approaches to the geographical scope. First, an MBM could be applied only to flights departing from airports situated in the implementing States.[161] The scheme would cover emissions for the whole duration of the departing flight.[162] A second alternative would capture all emissions produced by aircraft registered in the implementing State.[163] Finally, a third approach would be to allow the implementing State to cover all flights, both incoming and outgoing, of both national and foreign aircraft operators, but only for the portion of emissions generated within its national airspace.[164]

At the time when States were discussing potential options for the geographical scope for the framework, Europe had already announced the temporary suspension of its ETS. As a result, Europe was aware that it needed to make some concessions and show some flexibility. This explains why Europe

156 ICAO, HGCC/3-WP/4 at 2.

157 ICAO, HGCC/2-WP/4, app. A.

158 These included issues such as whether the framework should incorporate provisions to accommodate the special needs of developing countries, whether the participants to an MBM scheme should be aircraft operators or the States themselves. See ICAO, HGCC/1-WP/5.

159 As the State of registry, there is no question that the implementing State may apply an MBM to aircraft operators registered in such a State.

160 Here it is worth bearing in mind that the 36th Assembly had said that an emissions trading scheme should only cover foreign aircraft operators to the extent that their respective home States consented to. See ICAO, A36–22, *supra* Note 91, app. L.

161 See ICAO, HGCC/1-WP/3 at 2. See also ICAO, HGCC/2-WP/4 at 2.

162 See ICAO, HGCC/1-WP/3 at 2.

163 Ibid.

164 Ibid.

supported the option of departing flights.[165] Most other States, however, supported the notion of national airspace.[166] Although this option would seem to be better aligned with principles such as the exclusive sovereignty over a State's territory, it is less attractive from an environmental perspective since it leaves out emissions produced over the high seas.[167] Some States suggested that as long as the implementing State is in conformity with the framework, such a State would not require the consent of other States to include foreign aircraft operators.[168] Other States, such as India, strongly advocated the need for mutual consent in all cases.[169]

During discussions held prior to the 38th Assembly, States were not able to reach consensus on the geographical scope of the framework. It was evident, however, that a majority of States favored the national airspace approach.[170] In fact, the text of the resolution that had been prepared for the 38th Assembly incorporated the notion of national airspace.[171] Industry, however, lobbied extensively against this provision, alleging that it could be interpreted as a license or encouragement for States to implement their own schemes.[172] This was perceived as a real threat to the future of the global scheme.[173] In other words, this recognizes that States may adopt measures outside the auspices of the ICAO.

The incorporation of the national airspace approach as part of the Assembly resolution was also perceived as legitimizing a scaled-down version of the EU-ETS. Consequently, with strong industry intervention, the 38th Assembly opted to remain silent on the issue of the geographical scope.[174] In fact, the Assembly resolution does not even mention the word framework.[175] However, according to the resolution, if a State wishes to implement a "new" or "existing" MBM, the State should "engage in constructive bilateral and/or

[165] See ICAO, HGCC/3-WP/7.
[166] See for instance, ICAO, HGCC/2-WP 9.
[167] See ICAO, HGCC/3-WP/4 at 4.
[168] See ICAO, HGCC/1-WP/2 at 1–2.
[169] See ICAO, HGCC/3-WP/5 at A-4.
[170] See V. Volcovici, "Shuttle diplomacy under way on global aviation emissions deal," *Reuters* (July 22, 2013), uk.reuters.com/article/2013/07/22/us-eu-aviation-emissions-idUKBRE96L0ZJ 20130722 last accessed October 21, 2017.
[171] See ICAO, A38-WP/34 EX/29.
[172] See Green Air, "Aviation industry calls for global agreement and climate change leadership by governments ahead of ICAO assembly," www.greenaironline.com/news.php?viewStory=1745, last accessed October 21, 2017
[173] Ibid.
[174] See ICAO, A38–18, *supra* Note 76.
[175] Ibid.

multilateral consultations and negotiations with other States to reach an agreement."[176]

For some States, the requirement of an agreement equates to mutual consent in practice. In other words, the implementing State cannot include foreign aircraft operators, unless the affected States provide their consent. This would even be applicable to emissions generated over the implementing State's national airspace. For other States, on the other hand, this requirement only serves as a suggestion that they should use their best efforts to consult the other States concerned and attempt to reach an agreement. However, failure to reach an agreement does not stop the implementation of the scheme. In any case, this provision does not override the principle of exclusive sovereignty over a State's territory. In other words, consent is not required to include in a State's MBM scheme emissions produced over the implementing State's national airspace by foreign aircraft operators.

The development of the framework has been a fascinating story in many ways. First, it was conceived as a tool to correct the potential threat of uncoordinated approaches. Yet it also became its own worst foe as it was essentially abandoned in order not to encourage the surge of other schemes outside of the realm of the ICAO. Second, for better or worse, the framework serves to demonstrate the enormous influence that the EU-ETS has had on climate change discussions at the ICAO.[177] From its initial conception to its actual abandonment by the 38th Assembly, the framework became more than a technical issue – a political battle that was seen by non-EU States as an appropriate avenue to demonize the EU-ETS. For European States, however, this provided a means to legitimize the EU-ETS. Third, the framework is a classic example of a situation in which States get entangled into a political discussion with little or no legal or policy justification. From the get-go, it was self-evident that a nonbinding framework will have no persuasive effect on the intended target. In other words, it is unrealistic to expect that European States would comply with the letter of a framework that would seem to contradict the very notion of the principle of exclusive sovereignty (e.g. the requirement to obtain the consent of other States over emissions produced within the airspace of the implementing State).

[176] See ICAO, A38–18, *supra* Note 76 para. 16 (a).

[177] See contra ICAO, C-MIN 196/7 at 9 (Statement of Cuba) (stating that ICAO was working under the mandate given by the Assembly and not as a result of the external pressure exerted by the EU-ETS).

12.5 A GLOBAL SCHEME FOR MBMS: THE ROAD TO CORSIA

Pursuant to the task of exploring the feasibility of a global MBM scheme assigned to the Council at the 37th Assembly, the President of the Council formed an Ad Hoc Working Group on MBMs (AHWG) on January 20, 2012 during the 195th Session of the Air Transport Committee.[178] The purpose of the AHWG was to identify potential measures for a global MBM scheme for international aviation with the assistance of a group of experts.[179] After extensive work, the experts assisting the AHWG along with the Secretariat identified the following four potential measures for a global scheme: (i) offsetting; (ii) offsetting with a revenue generation mechanism; (iii) emissions trading (cap & trade); and, (iv) emissions trading (baseline & credit).[180]

Offsetting envisages a scheme where either States or aircraft operators (participants) are required to purchase emissions reduction units (ERUs) from other sectors.[181] The scheme's design involves the establishment of a set of criteria to determine which units will be eligible, as well as setting out a baseline.[182] Taking the ICAO's CNG aspirational goal as an example, offsetting will mean that, in order to compensate for the growth in their emissions, participants will, as of 2021, be required to purchase Emission Credit Units (ECUs) taking into account their 2020 emissions levels (baseline).[183] This was the least complicated alternative, and so it was not surprising that the airline industry would express its preference for this option.[184]

The second option, offsetting with a revenue generation mechanism, follows exactly the same principles, the only difference being that it includes a revenue generating mechanism, either through the imposition of a transaction fee or through the establishment of a price for emissions.[185] The rationale for adding the revenue generation mechanism lies in the fact that such funds may be used for broader purposes such as climate change mitigation and adaptation in developing countries.[186] This closely resembles other proposals aimed at establishing a rebate mechanism or a re-channeling of funds to

[178] See ICAO, C-WP/13894, app. C; See also ICAO, C-WP/13799 at 2.
[179] See ICAO, HGCC/3-WP/4 at 2.
[180] See ICAO, C-WP/13861 at 2.
[181] Ibid., app. A-1.
[182] Ibid.
[183] Ibid.
[184] See ICAO, A38-WP/68 EX/33 at 3 (noting that "a simple carbon offsetting scheme would be the quickest to implement, the easiest to administer and the most cost-efficient").
[185] Ibid. at A-7.
[186] Ibid.

address equity issues. This, however, creates a fairly complex scheme as decisions will have to be made on matters such as the quantum of such levy; how and who will collect them; the purposes to which the revenues will be applied; and the beneficiaries thereof. Given the well-known industry rejection of fees and taxes as well as the position of some aviation-oriented States, it is unlikely that this option will ever see the light of day.[187]

The third option envisages an emissions trading scheme.[188] Here, the system would cap the sector's overall international emissions.[189] It would then allocate allowances to the participants.[190] In essence, the allowance is a license to emit a specified quantity of CO_2.[191] The system would also establish compliance periods and would require participants to monitor their emissions.[192] If their emissions should exceed their allowances over a given compliance period, participants must purchase either ECUs or additional allowances.[193] The main difference between this option and offsetting is that under this option, allowances become a negotiable property right.[194] The presence of allowances, however, adds a layer of significant complexity to the scheme.

The fourth option also involves emissions trading but based on a baseline and credit system. Here, instead of allowances, the scheme establishes a baseline.[195] Should a participant emit more than the established baseline, such participant will be required to purchase ECUs.[196] If, on the other hand, at the end of the compliance period a participant's emissions are below the established baseline, the participant may either earn credits or bank them for future use.[197] In establishing the baseline, an efficiency metric may be taken into account.[198] Because of aviation's projected growth trends, it is expected that participants will have to purchase ECUs.[199] Therefore, this option does in

187 See ICAO, MIN 196/7 at 8 (Statement of the UAE) (recommending abandoning consideration of offsetting with a revenue generation mechanism).
188 See ICAO, C-WP/13861 at 2.
189 Ibid., app. A-8.
190 Ibid.
191 Ibid.
192 Ibid.
193 Ibid.
194 Ibid.
195 Ibid., app. B.
196 Ibid.
197 Ibid.
198 Ibid.
199 Ibid.

fact closely resemble the offsetting scheme. In light of this, the Council ultimately decided to discard this option.[200]

All of these options will require the adoption of monitoring, reporting, and verification systems (MRVs); the establishment of a compliance period and enforcement mechanisms; a determination as to who the participants will be (in other words, whether States or aircraft operators will bear compliance obligations); an assessment of the legal vehicles needed; and a means for distributing baselines and allocating allowances.[201]

The work of the experts assisting the AHWG sufficiently demonstrated that all of the options are "technically feasible and have the capacity to contribute to achieving [ICAO's aspirational goals]."[202] The studies have also revealed that the financial impact on the industry is expected – at least for the time being – to be minimal.[203] On the basis of these findings, the 38th Assembly, working under intense pressure to demonstrate leadership and deliver results,[204] finally "[agreed] to develop a global MBM scheme for international aviation."[205] This decision attracted strong endorsement from the industry and no reservations were filed against it.[206] To develop such a scheme, the Assembly instructed the Council to consider a number of factors, including proposals made by the industry;[207] the special circumstances of States;[208] the need to explore a route-base and incremental approaches;[209] and the recognition of fast-growing carriers as well as those who have taken early action (e.g. early movers who have invested heavily in technology).[210] The Assembly also instructed the Council to present a concrete proposal to the 39th session scheduled for 2016.[211] In October 2016, the 39th Assembly finally adopted CORSIA – a global MBM scheme that will be implemented as of January 2020.

200 See ICAO, C-DEC 196/7 at 2.

201 See ICAO, C-WP/13861, app. A1–9 and B.

202 See ICAO, C-WP/139894; ICAO, C-DEC 197/6.

203 For instance, the ICAO estimates that the cost of MBM could represent 0.8–1 percent of the industry's revenues. See ICAO, "Assessment of the impact of Market-Based Measures (MBMs)" (Council Informal Briefing, June 11, 2013) (on file with the author) at 11.

204 See ICAO, A38–18, *supra* Note 76, para. 19.

205 See ICAO, A38-WP/68 EX/33.

206 See ICAO, "Summary listing of reservations to resolution A38–18," www.icao.int/Meetings/a38/Documents/Resolutions/summary_en.pdf last accessed October 21, 2017. [ICAO, Reservations to A38–18].

207 Ibid., para. 19 (a).

208 Ibid., para. 20.

209 Ibid., para. 21.

210 Ibid., para. 22.

211 Ibid., para. 19 (d).

12.6 CONCLUSION

Environmental protection was not part of the ICAO's original objectives as set out in its constitutional framework. Yet, through the adoption of various strategic objectives, the Secretary General and Council have attempted to gradually incorporate environmental concerns as one of the organization's priorities. It is true, however, that the absence of a specific reference to the environment in the Chicago Convention is problematic, particularly when environment-related initiatives would seem to be in conflict with the convention's overarching goals, such as fostering the development of the sector (i.e. growth). The ICAO's governing structure seems to have strengthened the role of the Council. This poses some challenges when the need to engage a broader audience beyond those States that form part of the Council arises – the non-Council member States have much less connection with the organization. Yet, in spite of all these structural deficiencies, the ICAO continues to be the best forum to handle this issue.

In theory, all of these deficiencies could be addressed through the introduction of substantial amendments to the international legal regime. This, however, is extremely unlikely to occur. The Council has already considered a proposal recommending amendments to the Chicago Convention, and the predominant view was that the septuagenarian instrument still provides an appropriate framework to address current and emerging challenges. For a number of reasons that extend beyond the realm of aviation and climate change issues, this view is not expected to change in the near future.

In this context then, the ICAO should explore other alternatives to further engage its membership. Perhaps, this could be done through empowering its seven regional offices. These should be in much closer contact with its member States. For instance, in an effort to address CAEP's imbalanced membership during the 38th Assembly, Argentina recommended that the regional offices should be much more involved in disseminating the committee's work within their respective regions.[212] Although unnoticed by the vast majority of States attending the Assembly, the Argentinean proposal was targeted at one of the ICAO's most acute deficiencies: the disconnection between the organization and those member States that are neither members of the Council nor participants in the technical work of the organization. This is not a problem unique to the ICAO. However, a proper resolution of this

[212] See ICAO, A38-WP/318 EX/110.

deficiency will go a long way to facilitate the design and implementation of the global MBM scheme for international aviation in the ultimate analysis.

Ever since the Kyoto Protocol enjoined States to address the aviation sector's carbon footprint through the ICAO, the organization has been extremely active in exploring alternatives, conducting studies, and presenting concrete proposals. The fact that GHG emissions continue to be unregulated is certainly not the ICAO's fault, but it rather reflects the unwillingness of its member States to undertake any serious commitments. Obviously, there are a number of exogenous and endogenous factors that explain the lack of political will on the part of member States.

In spite of the enormous difficulties faced, what is clear is that the ICAO has made concrete progress. The CO_2 standard is on track for adoption. This will not be a major technological breakthrough, but it is a significant step forward. Arguably, the State action plans are also a success story. They are in the process of changing the attitude of member States toward climate change issues. As a result of the State action plans, a large number of States are beginning to address issues involving aviation's climate change impact for the first time ever. In the near future, it will be desirable for the State action plans to become mandatory and also included in the ICAO audits.

The decision by the 39th Assembly to adopt CORSIA has strengthened the ICAO's leadership. Arguably, there is consensus that this is the best way forward to address GHG emissions from international aviation. However, forming consensus on the actual elements of the scheme will not be an easy task. Although the work of the group of experts has already provided a solid starting point for the development of the global scheme, a number of unresolved issues still remain. Tackling these issues will not only require technical and policy considerations, but above all, political decisions.

13

Seeking Global Environmental Harmony in Aviation

Peter Paul Fitzgerald

Over the last twenty years the number of flights has mushroomed, increasing GHG emissions from airlines and causing crowded skies and congested airports. Competitor jets follow each other across the sky and where an airline might have served a route with two planes in 1992, today it uses three. Both of these practices are routed in theories that argue that business travelers will prefer the airline with more frequent flights.

Proposed aircraft like the 300-seat Large Aircraft for Short Range (LASR) with the potential to dramatically reduce greenhouse emissions cannot emerge in the current climate. This chapter is motivated by regulatory decisions that have supported Metal Neutral Joint Ventures in North America and Europe and by capacity sharing arrangements between competitors on domestic routes in the United States and Mexico in the 1970s and 1980s. Just as such arrangements were used to provide greater consumer choice, it will be proposed that such arrangements could be used in current circumstances to reduce both the GHG impact of a flight and the amount of congestion in our skies.

This chapter proposes legal structures that would facilitate the sharing by two or more airlines of the same large aircraft. It ensures that any inter-carrier arrangement would promote competition between them and further proposes that environmental benefits, in particular a reduction in GHG emissions, be considered as part of any analysis to grant antitrust immunity to a joint venture or merger.

13.1 INTRODUCTION

Around the world, three interlocking themes are discussed at aviation conferences: growing airport congestion and the related demands on air traffic management (ATM) systems; the role of commercial aviation in contributing to greenhouse gas (GHG) emissions; and the increasing cost of jet fuel and its impact on airline balance sheets. Increasingly, engineers are promoting new aircraft designs that would fly more people at one time and be up to 70 percent more efficient than current aircraft.[1] It is hoped that the ICAO's adoption of the Carbon Offsetting and Reduction Scheme for International Aviation (CORSIA)[2] to implement market-based measures in order to reduce aircraft emissions will foster the emergence of such new technology.

However, current market conditions and competition laws promote high frequency with small aircraft and, therefore, on many long-established routes over the past twenty years, airlines have down-gauged their aircraft by roughly 30 percent so that three flights in 2012 carried roughly the same number of passengers as two flights did in 1992. Competition is such that it is not uncommon to see competitor's jets follow each other across the skies.[3] Such a reality suggests that if the practice could be reversed, so that two aircraft in 2017 would replace three aircraft in 2012, GHG targets would be more attainable and there would be a corresponding decline in the demand for Air Traffic Service (ATC) and airport infrastructure. Such a practice would be known as up-gauging and, in order to reach its full potential, changes to competition policy will be required.

Such practice would further sustainable development in aviation in that it would immediately reduce the impact both in terms of GHGs and ATM of commercial aviation, and it would also reduce the consumption of nonrenewable hydrocarbons on a per-seat basis. Moreover, if up-gauging could be adopted on a widespread basis, this might boost the business case for aircraft such as the Large Aircraft for Short Ranges (LASR), identified later in this chapter. Airbus predicts that air traffic in terms of passenger-kilometers will grow by an average of 4.6 percent annually from 2015 to 2034.[4] At the same time, it is obvious that there is a need to reduce not just the number of GHGs emitted per passenger/kilometer, but the total number of GHGs emitted by

1 See E. de la Rosa Blanco and E. M. Greitzer, "Subsonic civil aircraft for 2035," *MIT AeroAstro* (2009–2010), web.mit.edu/aeroastro/news/magazine/aeroastro7/n-3.html last accessed October 18, 2017.

2 ICAO, "Consolidated statement of continuing ICAO policies and practices related to environmental protection – Global-Market-Based Measures (MBM) Scheme," Res A39–3 (October 6, 2016).

3 This practice has been observed on domestic routes within Australia, Canada, and in the United States.

4 See Airbus, "Global market forecast; flying by numbers 2015–2034," https://espas.secure.europarl.europa.eu/orbis/sites/default/files/generated/document/en/Global_Market_Forecast_2015_Book.pdf Last accessed October 18, 2017.

the airline industry worldwide. Sustainability for the airline industry will require new technologies and new approaches; this chapter promotes the latter to stimulate the former.

The idea of up-gauging as a way of reducing both GHGs and ATM impact is not new. As early as February 2011, Lufthansa was planning to replace its two wide-body Frankfurt–New York JFK flights with a single Airbus A-380 flight and, in May 2012, Delta called on its commuter partners to replace inefficient 50-seat regional jets with more modern and more capacious 76-seat versions. The trend accelerated in 2016 with mainline carriers beginning to use their own aircraft on routes previously served by commuter partners.[5] Clearly up-gauging can, in certain cases, be implemented by a single carrier. Nonetheless, if competition policies were amended, one could imagine significant up-gauging on routes operated pursuant to a code-share or metal neutral joint venture.[6]

The challenge is to provide for the GHGs and airport infrastructure benefits that up-gauging might allow, while avoiding the competitive distortions often associated with code-shares and alliances. This chapter will propose a creative approach: that, in limited and defined circumstances, competitive rivals and even rival alliances be encouraged to share the use of an efficient capacious aircraft that is larger than either would have flown on its own account. There are precedents and structures that confirm that such an approach could be implemented without competitive distortions and with the positive externalities described in this section.

Up-gauging would not be incompatible with the *Chicago Convention*,[7] but it might require the re-negotiation of some of the Bilateral Air Service Agreements (BASAs) concluded pursuant to it. This is because commercial air traffic rights are not regulated by the International Civil Aviation Organization (ICAO) but through the clauses of the BASAs concluded between ICAO member States. For example, Canada's 1989 BASA with Thailand[8] has clauses limiting capacity for single carrier operation but offers

5 See K. C. "Regional airlines, more communities threatened as partners shift flying to mainline," *Forbes* (January 27, 2016), www.forbes.com/sites/kathryncreedy/2016/01/27/regional-airlines-more-communities-threatened-as-partners-shift-flying-to-mainline/#5c383ee35228 last accessed October 18, 2017.

6 "Metal neutral joint venture" is discussed in this chapter.

7 *Convention on International Civil Aviation* (adopted December 7, 1944, entered into force April 4, 1947), 15 UNTS 295, 61 Stat 1180 [*Chicago Convention*].

8 *Agreement between the Government of Canada and the Government of the Kingdom of Thailand on Air Services* (signed May 24, 1989, entered into force June 30, 1989) Can TS 1989 No 16.

greater flexibility with respect to codeshare arrangements. If up-gauging were to be deployed on a widespread basis on intercontinental routes, this might require the renegotiation of certain BASAs.

13.2 AIR TRAFFIC INCREASES AND THE S-CURVE

In Canada, the United States, and, to a lesser extent, the European Union (EU),[9] airlines are offering more flights with smaller aircraft. This is partly due to the S-Curve Theory, which posits that airlines that achieve a frequency-share advantage attain disproportionately high market shares[10] and, consequently, revenues, since business travelers value schedule flexibility.

Thus airlines have reacted by offering greater frequencies and have managed to maintain load factors by reducing aircraft size in a practice known as down-gauging. Initial research[11] indicates that, from 1992 to 2010, over five routes flown between extremely busy airports, namely New York JFK–Los Angeles, Newark–Chicago ORD, Detroit DTW–Chicago ORD, London LHR–Paris CDG, and Toronto–Vancouver, the average number of seats per flight has declined by 36 percent, 27 percent, 53 percent, 33 percent, and 25 percent, respectively.

These dramatic reductions in seats/flight can be explained in part by the fact that many of the aircraft used in the late 1980s and early 1990s were overly capacious,[12] and that major airlines have since contracted flights to regional airlines operating much smaller aircraft.[13] Nonetheless, given that US carriers flew 26 percent more revenue passengers in July 2012 than in July 1996,[14] and

[9] The EU's explosive traffic growth and rising emissions due to aviation are at least partly due to regional subsidy policies. See generally, P. P. Fitzgerald, "Europe's emissions trading system: Questioning its raison d'être," *Issues Aviation L & Pol'y*, 10 (2011) 189–229..

[10] See W. E. Fruhan, *The Fight for Competitive Advantage: A Study of the United States Domestic Trunk Air Carriers* (Boston, MA: Harvard Graduate School of Business Administration, 1972) 126–30.

[11] This involved contrasting flights and average seat offerings on two intervals in the summer of 1992 and 2010. Information was retrieved from the Official Airline Guides, *OAG Desktop Flight Guide: North American Edition* (August 1992) vol.18, no.21,the Official Airline Guides, OAG *Desktop Flight Guide: Worldwide Edition* (August 1992) vol.17, no. 16. as well as from airline timetables in August 2010.

[12] See S. Morrison and C. Winston, *The Evolution of the Airline Industry* (Washington, DC: Brookings Institution Press, 1995) 91.

[13] See A. Mozdzanowska, R. John Hansman, and J. Histon, "Emergence of regional jets and the implications on air traffic management," MIT International Center for Air Transportation, 2003, http://dspace.mit.edu/handle/1721.1/35881 accessed October 18, 2017.

[14] See Research and innovative technology administration bureau of transportation statistics information at http://apps.bts.gov/xml/air_traffic/src/datadisp.xml.last accessed October 18, 2017.

that many of the regional carriers operate high frequency flights over big city–big city routes that were previously flown by larger aircraft, the influence of the S-Curve cannot be denied. More often than not, these practices result in the same number of passengers being carried by more flights, with a corresponding increase in take-offs and landings, slot and gate requirements, and GHG emissions per passenger.

13.3 UP-GAUGING

While North American and European carriers are offering fewer seats per departure, Japanese carriers are forced to recognize the value of an airport and the impact of imported jet fuel. Japan's busiest route is between two heavily strained airports Tokyo (Haneda) and Osaka (Itami). Over that route between 1992 and 2010, growing demand (107 percent) prompted Japanese carriers to increase frequency by 81 percent and average seat count by 14 percent by up-gauging aircraft size.[15] In Japan, the idea of increasing the number of seats per flight is compatible with environmental goals and increasing the efficient use of high demand airport infrastructure assets such as slots and gates.

13.3.1 *Up-Gauging and S-Curve*

Inherently, it would seem that up-gauging is counterintuitive; if higher frequencies imply disproportionately higher revenue, any reduction in frequency would tend to dilute revenue. Yet in February 2011, Lufthansa replaced two of its Frankfurt–New York JFK flights with a single Airbus A380,[16] resulting in a reduction of the daily seat capacity by seventeen seats or 1.97 percent and a reduction in the number of flights by 33 percent.[17] Here, the A380's attraction

[15] In August 1992, Japanese carriers offered 16 daily Tokyo–Osaka flights, with an average capacity of 406 seats. By 2010, demand had nearly doubled and carriers offered 29 daily flights with an average of 464 seats per flight. See Official Airline Guides, OAG *Desktop Flight Guide*, worldwide edn. (OAG, August 1992) at 945; Oneworld, *Oneworld Timetable* (May 14, 2010–June 11, 2010); Star Alliance, *Star Alliance Timetable* (May 1, 2010– July 18, 2010) at 353.

[16] Travelio, "Lufthansa flying to New York with the A380" (December 14, 2010) https://www.travelio.net/lufthansa-flying-to-new-york-with-the-a380.html, last accessed October 16, 2017. Lufthansa's A380 has 526 seats.

[17] The other flight is a Boeing 747–400 with 322 seats. See Star Alliance, *Star Alliance Timetable* (May 1, 2011–July 17, 2011) 164.

to business passengers[18] may offset potential S-Curve impacts but Metal Neutrality also played an important role.

13.3.2 *Metal Neutrality Is Compatible with Up-Gauging*

On July 23, 2008, Air Canada, Continental, Lufthansa, and United filed an application before the US Department of Transportation (DOT) asking for, *inter alia,* blessing for a highly confidential proposed four-way joint venture called Atlantic Plus-Plus (A++).[19] The DOT stated:

> A++ aims to foster "metal neutrality" – a commercial environment in which joint venture partners share common economic incentives to promote the success of the alliance over their individual corporate interests. By pooling resources to improve the overall service offering, and by sharing gains and losses, the partners are able to harmonize the global network and become *indifferent as to which of them collects the revenue and operates the aircraft on a given itinerary*. They are then able to focus on gaining the customer's business by providing the best available fare and routing between two cities.[20]

Indeed, the fact that Lufthansa had received antitrust immunity to cooperate with United and Air Canada in the A++ metal neutral joint venture in 2009[21] means that, even after the up-gauging, Lufthansa is part of a group that offers five flights a day between Frankfurt and New York.[22] The only other airlines offering nonstop service are Delta[23] and Singapore Airlines.[24]

Here, cognizant of the low probability of revenue dilution as a result of frequency reduction, the A++ partners made a business-based decision that reduced the number of flights operated, and consequently the demands on the ATM system, airport infrastructure, and GHGs emitted.

18 See Lufthansa, "The A380: Be part of it," http://a380.lufthansa.com/TAKEPART/#/DE/EN/HOME last accessed October 19, 2017.

19 See US DOT, "Joint Application of Air Canada, Austrian, bmi, LOT, Lufthansa, SAS, Swiss, TAP, and United to Amend Order 2007–2-16 under 49 U.S.C. §§ 41308 and 41309 so as to Approve and Confer Antitrust Immunity," Docket OST-2008–0234 (July 23, 2008).

20 US DOT, Show Cause Order 2009–4-5, Docket OST-2008–0234 (April 7, 2009) [emphasis added].

21 US DOT, Order No 2009–7-10 (July 10, 2009).

22 Lufthansa's A-380 flight number is LH 400; United lists the flight as UA 8841. Lufthansa and United also operate from Frankfurt to Newark. See United Airlines, "United System Timetable" (June 30, 2012–July 28, 2012) 171.

23 Delta offers a single daily flight. See Delta, "Timetable for August 2012."

24 Star Alliance, "Star Alliance Timetable" (July 21, 2012–August 2, 2012) 155.

13.3.3 *Up-Gauging Makes Business Sense*

Two factors initially made up-gauging more attractive to airlines; fuel prices that rose dramatically between 1998 and 2005,[25] and government strategies to reduce airport congestion.[26] Thus, in May 2012, Delta announced a major up-gauging initiative. It would acquire 88 100-seat Boeing B717s and require its commuter partners to dispose of 281 50-seat regional jets, cap the 70-seat regional jet fleet at 102, and increase by 70 the size of the 76-seat two-class regional jet fleet to 325.[27] The plan might set an up-gauging "precedent that could spell a sea-change in the structure of the U.S. air transport business."[28]

Although there are obviously cases where airlines will up-gauge of their own volition, the S-curve and other factors discourage it and, therefore, progress in this area may be slower than would be ideal.

13.4 THE LIMITS OF UP-GAUGING

While it is obvious that more capacious aircraft will be heavier than their less capacious competitors, in some cases they will even be heavier on a per seat basis. A European study noted that capacious aircraft are designed for long-haul routes and this limits the potential GHG gain from their use:

> To make a better use of available runway capacity and to reduce the environmental impact from aircraft operation, especially at large airports, a large (wide body) aircraft designed for short haul operation would be required.[29]

[25] A 2005 report from the U.S. Government Accountability Office observed that the cost of aviation fuel had increased between 1998 and 2005 by 280 percent. See US GAO, *Report* GAO-05–945 *Commercial Airline Bankruptcy and Pensions* (Washington, DC: GAO 2005) 6.

[26] In January 2008 the FAA proposed a two-part landing fee to help relieve congestion at major airports. See US DOT, Office of the Secretary FAA, *Policy Regarding Airport Rates and Charges*, 73 FR 3310 (January 17, 2008). See also See *Air Transport Association of America, Inc. v. DOT, et al.* (D.C. Cir. 2010) Case: 08–1293.

[27] Delta Air Lines, "Delta to take delivery of Boeing 717 aircraft upon ratification of pilot tentative agreement" (Press release, May 22, 2012), http://news.delta.com/index.php?s=43&item=1624 last accessed October 19, 2017.

[28] G. Polet, "Delta deal seals fate of hundreds of 50-seat jets," *AIN Air Transport Perspective* (July 2, 2012), www.ainonline.com/aviation-news/2012-07-02/delta-deal-seals-fate-hundreds-50-seat-jets last accessed October 21, 2017.

[29] M. Givoni and P. Rietveld, "Comparing the environmental impact from using large and small passenger aircraft on short haul routes," Working paper No. 1033 (Transport Studies Unit Oxford University Centre for the Environment, 2008) at 18, www.tsu.ox.ac.uk/pubs/1033-givoni-rietveld.pdf last accessed October 21, 2017.

Another study argues that, using present technology, it is possible to specifically design a Large Aircraft for Short Ranges (LASR)[30] with a capacity of 300 passengers but weighing 26 percent less and being 22 percent more fuel efficient than similar sized long-range aircraft.[31] However, the design and creation of a LASR is unlikely in the near future as airlines seem to prefer offering small aircraft and high frequency service on routes between congested airports.[32] Although Boeing foresees "a modest increase in the average size of airplanes in operation,"[33] unless a business case can be made for the creation of the LASR, the plane will never leave the drawing board.

13.5 A LEGAL CHANGE IN FAVOR OF UP-GAUGING

Indeed, up-gauging only makes commercial sense if the larger aircraft can maintain a profitable load factor and if the above-average yields associated with the S-Curve can be preserved.

13.5.1 *Code-Share Agreements*

The legal underpinning of the A++ joint venture is the code-share, where one carrier operates the flight and a second markets the seats and the flight carries the two digit IATA flight code of each.[34] The joint venture goes well beyond this, but the basic code-share agreement may be enough to facilitate significant up-gauging and the consequent reduction in GHGs. Although code-share agreements are most frequently present between allied carriers, an alliance is by no means a condition precedent to such an accord. Moreover, the quest to reduce GHG emissions through up-gauging may warrant the

30 See M. Mane, N. Davendraingam, and W. Crossley, Exploration of designing short-range high-capacity aircraft (12th AIAA Aviation Technology, Integration, and Operations (ATIO) Conference and 14th AIAA/ISSMO Multidisciplinary Analysis and Optimization Conference, September, 2012).

31 G. K. W. Kenway, et al., "Reducing aviation's environmental impact through large aircraft for short ranges"(48th AIAA Aerospace Sciences Meeting Including the New Horizons Forum and Aerospace Exposition, Orlando, Florida, 2010), http://oddjob.utias.utoronto.ca/dwz/Miscellaneous/LASROrlando2010.pdf, last accessed October 21, 2017.

32 Givoni and Rietveld, "Comparing the environmental impact from using large and small passenger aircraft on short haul routes," 18 .

33 Boeing, "Current Market Outlook 2012–2031," www.boeing.com/commercial/cmo/pdf/Boeing_Current_Market_Outlook_2012.pdf last accessed October 21, 2017.

34 See generally, *The Commissioner of Competition* v. *Air Canada, United Continental Holdings Inc., United Airlines Inc., and Continental Airlines Inc*, CT-2011–004, Affidavit of Hugh Dunleavy, August 24, 2011, at 9. See further, C. Hadrovic, "Airline globalization: A Canadian perspective," *Transp. L.J.*, 19 (1990–1991) 193. [Hadrovic].

conclusion of code-share agreements between competitors and, although such an idea may appear unorthodox, it is not without precedent and is worthy of further exploration.

13.5.1.1 Block Space Agreements

Code-share arrangements often include a Block Space contract, where the marketing carrier buys, and resells as its own, a percentage of seats on the operating carrier's aircraft. Here, the two carriers compete with each other with respect to the sale of the seats within their allotment and, thus, the seats of the marketing carrier are essentially a "virtual flight"[35] within the aircraft of the operating carrier. One observer described the operation of the two blocks of seats sold by competing airlines but carried in the same fuselage as "[t]wo planes flying wing to wing."[36]

HARD BLOCK CODE-SHARE In a Hard Block code-share, the marketing carrier purchases a defined number of seats from the operating carrier at an agreed price and forfeits the money if the seats are unsold.[37] This means that both the airlines assume the cost if they do not sell their full complement of hard block allocated seats.[38] In this arrangement, the marketing carrier is competing with the operating carrier with respect to the sale of seats on the same flight.[39] Here, the two carriers will "independently sell and market their fares on the code-share service. Each carrier will set its own prices; determine its own fare classes and rules; operate its own independent yield management systems and; sell its products through its respective independent sales networks."[40]

13.5.2 *Domestic Code-Share*

The type of domestic code-share envisaged to reduce GHGs is not the subcontracting of an airline's routes to a commuter carrier, but rather a

35 Ibid., 11.
36 John P. McCaffrey, former Vice President of Pan Am, in conversation with the author.
37 S. D. Gleave, *Competition Impact of Airline Code-Share Agreements, Final Report* (Brussels; European Commission Directorate General for Competition, 2007) 11 and 84.
38 Independent Consumer and Competition Commissioner, *Code Share Arrangement between Airlines of Papua New Guinea Limited (Airlines PNG) and Pacific Blue Airlines (Aust) PTY Limited and Virgin Blue Airlines PTY Limited* (Canberra; ICCC, September 2008) 4.
39 Ibid., 20.
40 Ibid., 25.

limited scope code-share between two competitors of roughly equal commercial standing and reputation.

13.5.2.1 The US Examples

United and Northwest have long competed on United States–Japan routes.[41] However, prior to its 2008 merger with Delta Airlines, Northwest offered no service between Arizona and California, and was unable to match United's service from Phoenix to Tokyo via either San Francisco or Los Angeles. As a result, Northwest concluded a code-share agreement with US Air with respect to certain flights between Arizona and California, and also between San Francisco and Los Angeles. This enabled the carrier to compete with United in the Arizona–Asia and Arizona–Australia markets.[42]

The situation was one of the few, if not the only, examples of a major US airline code-sharing on a competitor's jet flights within the contiguous forty-eight states.[43] Indeed, the agreement was extraordinary. On the selected routes, there was unique cooperation; elsewhere was business as usual. Thus, while Northwest was putting its code on a number of US Air flights,[44] the two were clearly competing with each other across the rest of the country. Each had a full coast-to-coast route network and international services to Canada and Europe. Each was a member of different international alliances; US Air was then a British Airways partner and Northwest was in league with KLM. Finally, on the routes where the two would offer competing nonstop services, there was no hint of any collaboration between them.[45] Northwest also

[41] Each served Tokyo from Honolulu, Los Angeles, San Francisco, Seattle and 3 other U.S. cities. See Northwest, "Airlines System Timetable" (June 8, 2006–August 21, 2006). See United, "Worldwide Timetable" (July 2006).

[42] This agreement was in effect from roughly 1994 to the January 7, 1999 Northwest-Continental code-sharing agreement which covered approximately 850 domestic and international flights to 95 destinations (as a result of Northwest's January 27, 1998 acquisition of voting control of Continental Airlines). The agreement was reprised in 2008 after Continental began its merger talks with United. Source; author's personal files.

[43] There are several examples of two major carriers blocking space on the same "commuter" carrier. Horizon Air (a "commuter" under the Alaska Airlines umbrella) allowed Northwest to block-space and code-share on some of its turboprop services to Vancouver and Victoria from Seattle. Thus two competitors, Alaska Airlines and Northwest, both listed the same Horizon flight as their own. This was not extraordinary; the "commuter" and the "major" were rarely, if ever, in direct competition.

[44] Northwest code-shared on three US Air flights from Los Angeles to San Francisco, six from San Francisco to Los Angeles and one round-trip flight between Los Angeles and Las Vegas.

[45] The two competed on three routes, Baltimore–Detroit, Detroit–Pittsburgh and Minneapolis–Pittsburgh. Of the five flights they each offered between Detroit and Pittsburgh, two departed

concluded a similar agreement[46] with America West[47] to facilitate the former's services to Australasia from Arizona and Nevada.[48]

13.5.2.2 Mexican Examples

If the US experience shows that it is possible for two domestic carriers to code-share on selected routes while competing vigorously on others, all in the best interests of consumers, the Mexican experience takes this theory a step further. Both major airlines of the country, namely Aeromexico and Mexicana (now defunct),[49] were owned by the same government-run holding company: the Corporación Internacional de Aviación, S.A. de C.V. (Cintra). Aeromexico was a Skyteam member and Mexicana was in the Star Alliance. They competed aggressively against each other, often siphoning passengers to the connecting flights of foreign partners rather than to their domestic rival.[50]

However, an intriguing situation existed on the Acapulco–Mexico route, where Aeromexico and Mexicana code-shared seven evenly-spaced daily flights.[51] The code-share was justified on the basis that a quick connection to Acapulco was needed from virtually every flight that arrived in Mexico City. In every other sense they competed. Thus, Aeromexico listed Mexicana's 12 PM. departure as the connection for the former's Mexico–Paris service, while Mexicana urged Francophiles on the same 12 PM. departure to remain onboard until the final stop in Chicago where they could connect to a Paris-bound flight on United Airlines. The two competed head-to-head on routes to Los Angeles, New York, and Miami, and, thus, the Acapulco–Mexico arrangement could be described as a "limited cooperation where necessary but not necessarily cooperation." However, this unique code-share enhanced competition, giving passengers a choice of carriers and itineraries and, ultimately, prices.

within twenty minutes of a competing flight offered by the other. This was also the case with one of the three flights that each offered between Minneapolis and Pittsburgh.

46 The date of this agreement is hard to confirm as both carriers have since merged with others. Northwest provided some financial assistance to America West in August 1991. See "America West Holdings," The agreement was in place in 1999. Source: author's files.

47 America West bought US Air in 2005.

48 Without the agreement, Northwest would have had to route the traffic via Minneapolis.

49 Mexicana ceased operations on August 28, 2010.

50 All the data in this section is based on Aeromexico and Mexicana timetables for 1998 and 1999.

51 Ibid.

13.5.3 *Code-Share Lessons Learned*

These three code-share examples – Northwest–US Air, Northwest–America West, and Aeromexico–Mexicana – confirm that rival airlines may enter into limited-scope code-share agreements to further their objectives. Northwest's code-share agreements gave it the ability to effectively compete against United Airlines for Australasia traffic from Arizona and Nevada. The Aeromexico–Mexicana agreement resulted in shuttle service between Acapulco and Mexico City, and increased competition on routes between Acapulco and Europe.

In each case, the code-share agreement facilitated increased competition over an intercontinental route, such as Phoenix–Tokyo or Acapulco–Frankfurt, and did so without being any more comprehensive than absolutely necessary. These code-share examples illustrate code-share arrangements between otherwise unaffiliated equal carriers. Each of the five airlines chosen for these examples – Aeromexico, America West, Mexicana, Northwest, and US Air – was, at the time of the agreement, a fully independent network carrier with a nationwide route system and international services.

These examples stand as precedent for an unusual proposition, the creation of limited-scope code-share agreements between two strong competitors with respect to joint service over a domestic route. If such agreements can be justified on the basis of increased connectivity, it should also be possible to justify and encourage such agreements on the basis of reducing GHGs.

13.6 ANTITRUST IMMUNITY PRINCIPLES

Every major jurisdiction has anti-combines and anti-monopoly legislation. Article 101(1) of the *Treaty on the Functioning of the European Union* (TFEU),[52] section 90.1(1) of Canada's *Competition Act*,[53] and America's *Sherman Act*[54] all prohibit anti-competitive activities. However, some of the debate surrounding the passage of the 1890 predecessor to the current US Antitrust law considered whether a monopoly whose efficiencies decreased consumer prices might be acceptable in certain situations.[55]

[52] Consolidated Version (2010) The Treaty on the Functioning of the European Union, OJ 2010, C 83/47 at 89.

[53] *Competition Act*, RS 1985, c. 34, s. 901(1).

[54] *Sherman Act*, 26 Stat 209 (1890). See also 15 USC § 1.

[55] See C. Grandy, "Original intent and the Sherman antitrust at: A re-examination of the consumer-welfare hypothesis," *J Econ Hist*, 53 (1993), 359 at 365. See the amendment to the Bill proposed by Senator Aldrich.

Thus, Article 101(3) of the TFEU, section 90.1(4) of Canada's *Competition Act*, and 49 USC § 41308(b) permit anti-competitive activities, where they:

- "improve the production or distribution of goods or to promoting technical or economic progress, while allowing consumers a fair share of the resulting benefit";[56]
- are "likely to bring about gains in efficiency";[57]
- are deemed to be in the public interest[58] (a term which embraces a "likelihood that consumers would benefit"),[59] or give "new service options and fare benefits for consumers";[60] or
- are "likely to generate substantial public benefits to the traveling and shipping public."[61]

European concerns can be met if the merged entity or joint venture will "provide air passengers with a greater choice of destinations and services without having to pay a higher price on those routes where their presence is the strongest,"[62] and sometimes for Canadian authorities the threshold is met if there is a "minimum disruption to service, no loss of jobs, no bankruptcy and not a nickel in subsidy."[63]

It is proposed that environmental benefits, in particular a reduction in GHG emissions, be considered as part of any analysis to grant antitrust immunity to a joint venture or merger. For example, as part of the ongoing EU investigation of the A++ joint venture,[64] EU authorities should consider Lufthansa's aircraft up-gauging on the Frankfurt–New York JFK route, and

[56] *Consolidated Version (2010) The Treaty on the Functioning of the European Union*, OJ 2010, C 83/ 47. See also *Council Regulation (EC) No 1/2003 of 16 December 2002 on the implementation of the rules on competition laid down in Articles 81 and 82 of the Treaty*, OJ 2003 (L. 1/ 1 (EC).

[57] *Competition Act* (RS 1985, c. 34, s. 90 1(4).

[58] For exemption from the antitrust laws, see 49 U.S.C. § 41308.

[59] US DOT, Order No. 2008–5-32 (May 22, 2008), at 3.

[60] US DOT, Order No. 2009–7-10 (July 10, 2009), at 1.

[61] US DOT, Order No. 2010–7-8 (July 20, 2010) at 1. Identical language is used in DOT Order 2010–11-10 (November 10, 2010), at 1.

[62] European Commission, "Commission clears merger between Air France and KLM subject to conditions" (Press Release IP/04/194, February 11, 2004) 4.

[63] The Hon. David Collenette, then Canada's Minister of Transport, on March 31, 2000 addressing legislation (Bill C-26 an *Act to amend the Canada Transportation Act*) to allow Air Canada to acquire financially troubled Canadian Airlines. See Parliament of Canada, *House of Commons Debates*, vol. 136, No. 76, 5512.

[64] See European Commission, "Communication of the Commission published pursuant to Article 27(4) of Council Regulation (EC) No 1/2003 in Case COMP/39.595 – Continental/ United/Lufthansa/Air Canada," OJ 2012 C. 396/21, eur-lex.europa.eu/legal-content/EN/TXT/?uri=CELEX%3A52012XC1221(02) last accessed October 21, 2017.

require as a condition of approval that the A++ joint venture partners up-gauge future operations on routes from Frankfurt to Chicago, San Francisco, Toronto, and Washington. This is because, if EU authorities approve the joint venture, the A++ partners will be alone in offering nonstop flights over these routes and, therefore, S-Curve considerations do not apply. The same philosophy should apply to EU consideration of Skyteam or Oneworld proposals, and result in similar up-gauging where approval would make the carriers dominant on the route in question.

It is argued that public benefit tests should be read to include "reduced GHG emissions associated with the operation of the joint venture as contrasted with those of the individual airlines involved." At present, there are no examples of two or more airlines seeking to justify an endeavor on environmental grounds. Nonetheless, given the increased global preoccupation with the airline industry's connection to climate change and the need for achieving sustainable development in aviation, regulators in Canada, the United States, and the EU should consider including "environmental" or "ecological" in the grounds for ATI relief on routes, especially where there is a substantial likelihood of up-gauging.

13.6.1 Antitrust Immunity Leads to Up-Gauging

In past airline mergers, on routes where two former rivals competed with each other using smaller aircraft, up-gauging was often a result. The 1988 acquisition of Wardair by Canadian Airlines saw changes to routes from Toronto to Edmonton, Calgary, and Vancouver; in the first case frequency was cut by 42 percent while seat count was reduced by only 14 percent.[65] In 2008, after the Delta–Northwest merger,[66] in three instances on the Minneapolis–Atlanta route, a Delta 65-seat CR7 regional jet and a Northwest 122-seat DC9 were replaced with a single Delta 186-seat 757.[67] Comparable up-gauging occurred on the routes from Detroit to Atlanta and from Minneapolis to Salt Lake City. Similar up-gauging is believed to have occurred on routes between United and Continental hubs, such as Denver–Newark, Houston–Chicago, Houston–Denver, and Houston–San Francisco. Nonetheless, the difficulty of accessing data makes confirmation difficult.

[65] See Canadian Airlines Timetable (October 1988), Wardair Canada Schedule (January 1989), Canadian Airlines Timetable (October 1989)

[66] The merger was completed on October 29, 2008.

[67] See "Executive Travel SkyGuide" (June 2008) 271–272; d Delta, "Worldwide Timetable" (July 2012), 246.

Without antitrust immunity, airlines cannot coordinate schedules and certainly cannot agree to share one large aircraft rather than each flying its own smaller aircraft. Yet it is precisely this kind of thinking that is a precondition to the development of LASRs, as in almost every other case, one airline cannot obtain enough customers for a short-range flight without sacrificing the frequency that is the essence of S-Curve revenues. Thus, in the absence of some sort of antitrust immunity, rival airlines are very unlikely to ever give serious consideration to the idea of sharing the capacity of a large aircraft rather than flying two competing small aircraft.

13.7 IMPLEMENTING UP-GAUGING

Initially, the two airlines would have to negotiate a "Hard Block" Space Agreement between an operating carrier and a marketing carrier such that the economic risk of the flight was equally shared between the rival carriers, and that each would assume full responsibility for marketing and selling its respective share of the aircraft's capacity.

If, for example, such an arrangement were to occur between Delta and United on the route between Chicago and Detroit, Delta might offer Chicago passengers connections to its Europe-bound flights at Detroit, whereas United would offer Detroit passengers connections to its Asia-bound fights at Chicago. By doing so, each airline would be using the flight to carry passengers from a "spoke city" through its hub to another destination.

Here, the rivals would compete not only with respect to the passengers traveling between the two cities but also for international and transcontinental traffic at their respective hub cities. Through sharing the operation of a large aircraft, GHGs could be reduced as would demands on ATM and airport infrastructure. However, as the example illustrates, it is possible to design such a code-share in order to minimize any potential competitive distortions. Nonetheless, in cases where the up-gauging would potentially require a LASR, conditions must be created to favor the design and manufacture of such an aircraft.

13.8 CONCLUSION

The fact that airlines, such as Delta and Lufthansa, have concluded that up-gauging makes commercial sense should encourage other airlines to embrace it. However, in a world focused on S-Curve concerns, and painfully aware of the power of over-capacity to depress yields, airlines may be less than fully enthusiastic about adopting this strategy. If regulators in different jurisdictions can be encouraged to create situations where rivals can safely discuss how to best share the capacity of an up-gauged aircraft, which in turn promotes two public goods, efficient transportation and a clean environment, the world will be better off. If airlines and States are committed to meeting the increasingly ambitious emissions targets of CORSIA,[68] up-gauging must be considered.

Implementation of such a strategy will not be easy. Relatively few airlines have extensive experience participating in a code-share arrangement that does not involve either a subordinate partner airline or an alliance partner. Nonetheless, there are reasons to believe that such an approach has merit; carefully structured code-share agreements between rivals have promoted intercontinental travel in Mexico, Canada, and the United States. If such arrangements can be concluded in the furtherance of international relations, how much greater will their potential be when applied to address climate change concerns?

Aircraft such as the LASR have enormous potential to reduce congestion, GHGs, and fuel consumption. Nevertheless, their existence depends to a large extent on re-examining existing approaches to competition on high-density routes. Quite simply, the S-Curve world of competing small jets following each other across the sky is incompatible with their design.

Some airlines have already embraced up-gauging and others have used innovative code-share arrangements with competitors to offer increased access to customers. The use of Hard Block Code-Share agreements between competitors on short-haul high-density routes will help create the business case for the LASR. But regulatory encouragement from authorities in Canada, the United States, and Europe will be necessary to spur such agreements.

There has been much discussion on aviation and the environment, and much examination of incremental changes of technology, engine design, or fuel types. The LASR requires a rethink of existing competitive practices on short-haul routes, both from the perspective of the airline executive and of the regulator. When airlines propose alliances or metal neutral joint ventures, if regulators see the potential of rivals to share a more capacious aircraft, they should find ways to enable such practices and thereby incite the type of rethink that will enable real reductions in GHGs from aviation.

[68] See *CORSIA*, *supra* Note 2.

14

Inspirations from Sustainable Maritime Development

Jeffrey J. Smith

This chapter addresses the historical, international, and legal roots of environmental protection in the global shipping industry. The discussion begins with a review of the initial efforts among states to regulate the industry and the creation of the International Maritime Organization. The original maritime environmental treaties of the 1960s are considered and the early success of a 1970s era global treaty is then assessed. The particular challenge of regulating greenhouse gas emissions under the UNFCCC-Kyoto Protocol-Paris Agreement regime is reviewed. Concluding lessons about sustainability are offered.

14.1 INTRODUCTION

The growth of maritime transportation has continued relentlessly in the twenty-first century. One need only visit the great port cities of the world – Hamburg, Hong Kong, Rotterdam, and Singapore – to confirm that humanity trades significantly by sea. Maritime transport, after the advent of safer navigation practices, improved technology, and ever-decreasing operating costs, has never been more efficient or widely available to states and those who would trade by sea. The revolution in shipbuilding and maritime commerce that began with the invention of steam propulsion technology two centuries ago is sure to continue.[1]

As with all transportation, whatever the specific human use and setting – national and international – maritime shipping has costs or externalities that

1 Maritime trade accounts for the vast majority of the volume and weight of goods moved in global commerce but not always its value, for which aviation has a significant share. See United Nations Conference on Trade and Development, *Review of Maritime Transport 2016: The Long-Term Growth Prospects for Seaborne Trade and Maritime Businesses* (Geneva: UNCTAD, 2016). The report notes that in 2015 global seaborne trade for the first time since UNCTAD was created in 1964 exceeded an estimated 10 billion tonnes.

extend beyond its industry. One that has been grappled with extensively is the environmental impact from the construction, operation, and dismantling of ships. The approach, led by regulators including national governments and the International Maritime Organization (IMO) from the 1950s to the present, has been incremental and remedial, in response to the high-profile problems of each era. After oil pollution concerns in the 1960s came the regulation of operator competence to avoid catastrophic ship losses, followed by improved design of ships with particular risks (including roll on-roll off vehicle ferries and bulk carriers) and, more recently, air emission controls in populated coastal areas. These advances, increasingly negotiated and implemented by states through the IMO, have not occurred in isolation from each other. They have been realized as part of the IMO's great project to regulate for the safety of life at sea. And environmental protection in the maritime industry has advanced under the aegis of significant state commitment and implementation of measures in the 1982 United Nations Convention on the Law of the Sea.[2]

This chapter surveys the landscape of environmental protection and sustainable development in the international maritime industry. The review is necessarily historic, because the remedial dimensions of early responses to environmental impacts and creating sustainable shipping are useful to gauge the future development of regulation and the limits of legal responses. Treaty-making by states in the IMO and in bilateral, regional, and global settings is then considered. This activity, until recently at least, has been successful, ensuring the safer operation of cleaner ships. The topics of oil pollution, adverse air emissions, and dismantling of ships – each regulated by treaties of global application – are reviewed. The challenge of reducing greenhouse gas (GHG) emissions is particularly addressed, including for cross-regime lessons in aviation. Thematic observations are also offered in a bid to assess the maritime industry's progress toward sustainable development.[3]

2 *United Nations Convention on the Law of the Sea* (adopted December 10, 1982 entered into force November 16, 1994) 1833 UNTS 397 [*UNCLOS*]. As of January 2017, 192 states have signed UNCLOS with 168 of them ratifying the Convention (including the Cook Islands, the European Union, Palestine, and Niue). Fifteen states and UN observer entities have not signed UNCLOS, among them Israel, Peru, Syria, Turkey, the United States, and Venezuela.

3 Sustainable development is a modern term, given importance as the principal definition of the conduct of economic progress with regard to environmental protection. It entered the policymaking canon of states and international organizations such as the IMO and the ICAO after the report of the UN General Assembly-created World Commission on Environment and Development, *Our Common Future* (Oxford: Oxford University Press, 1987), known as the Brundtland Report, for which, see also, UN doc. A/42/427, "Sustainable development is development that meets the needs of the present without compromising the ability of future generations to meet their own needs. It contains within it two key concepts: the concept of

14.2 THE HISTORICAL ROOTS OF SUSTAINABLE DEVELOPMENT IN THE MARITIME INDUSTRY

The world's maritime states have long regulated the environmental impacts of shipping. Their concern was mostly local: what ships might discharge in port, wastes that would foul inshore areas, and ballast materials discarded into shallow waters.[4] Until the nineteenth century states took little interest in maritime jurisdiction beyond their immediate coastal areas, and none in respect of environmental matters. The progressive growth in coastal areas claimed by states during this era, at first in Scandinavia, followed by continental Europe and the United Kingdom, was attributable to technology, primarily the advent of the marine steam engine, but also iron-hulled ships, improvements in navigation methods, and communication by undersea telegraph cable.[5] The growth of seaborne trade would mean attendant losses of ships and lives at sea after 1850 (an era that saw increased trade and the arrival of iron-hulled ships), which led to the first efforts to regulate safety at sea, for example the standards for basic vessel construction and stability pursued by Samuel Plimsoll, the reform-minded British Member of Parliament.[6]

'needs', in particular the essential needs of the world's poor, to which overriding priority should be given; and the idea of limitations imposed by the state of technology and social organization on the environment's ability to meet present and future needs ... In essence, sustainable development is a process of change in which the exploitation of resources, the direction of investments, the orientation of technological development; and institutional change are all in harmony and enhance both current and future potential to meet human needs and aspirations." Ibid., Chapter II, paras. 1 and 15. The Agenda 21 priorities resulting from the 1992 UN Conference on Environment and Development and those in the "The Future We Want" declaration of the 2012 Río + 20 conference have consistently applied the concept. The maritime industry can be conceived as having an *internal sustainability*, that is, constancy of its economic activity with environmental impact, and *external sustainability*, its contribution or place generally within sustainable development.

4 See e.g. the United Kingdom, *Thames Conservancy Act*, 1932, 22 & 23 Geo. 5, c. xxxvii. s. 121 prohibits "any substance which has been used as ballast" from being deposited in the Thames River. The statute originates from the 1535 *Thames Conservancy Ships' Ballast, etc., Act*, 28 Hen. VIII, c. 18.

5 In some respects, these developments resulted in and were further driven by decisions of European states at the Conference of Berlin in 1884–85 to divided colonial areas among themselves, notably in Africa. Efficient maritime transport had brought the last economically attractive areas within efficient reach of colonial powers.

6 The concern of the era was to preserve lives at sea. See N. Jones, *The Plimsoll Sensation: The Great Campaign to Save Lives at Sea* (London: Little, Brown, 2006).

It was the large loss of life in the 1912 sinking of the RMS *Titanic* that prompted the initial work for collective regulation of maritime safety among states. The first Safety of Life at Sea (SOLAS) treaty resulted, although it never became formally effective because of the First World War.[7] The widespread adoption of oil fuel for ships in preference to coal over the following decades created the industry's original large-scale pollution problem: What to do with waste oils that were uneconomical to retain and could not be processed aboard? The response was the 1954 International Convention for the Prevention of Pollution of the Sea by Oil.[8] The Convention regulated operating waste and tank washing discharges from all ships but not the accidental loss of oil from tankers. The middle part of the twentieth century was a period of technical change; commercial vessels becoming larger in all categories (e.g. bulk carriers, tankers, and passenger vessels), constructed and registered in more countries, and the change in ship propulsion from the large, inefficient triple expansion engine to the steam turbine and internal combustion diesel.[9]

The 1950s also marked the start of the codification of international maritime law, a project conceived during the League of Nations era. This would have a significant influence on common understandings of states' environmental obligations for shipping in later decades. In 1956 the International Law Commission had recommended such a step, thereby setting the stage for a conference in Geneva two years later.[10] The continuing creation of new states, the growth in commercial fisheries extending across vast distances, and the start of an era of expansive claims by states to offshore areas yielded a consensus that such matters were properly to be regulated by treaty. The 1958 conference yielded four instruments that were the foundation of UNCLOS in 1982: (i) the Convention on the Territorial Sea and Contiguous Zone; (ii) the

7 *Convention for the Safety of Life at Sea* (adopted January 20, 1914) (London: HMSO, 1914). The twelve states participating committed to adoption of prescribed measures in their national legislation and to a follow-up conference by 1920. Subsequent conferences, which resulted in modest technical and operating prescriptions for commercial vessels, were held in 1929 and 1948.

8 *International Convention for the Prevention of Pollution of the Sea by Oil* (adopted May 12, 1954, entered into force July 26, 1958), 327 UNTS 3. By 1954, the customary international law obligation for states to prevent transboundary pollution and to warn others had been established, confirmed by the *Trail Smelter (Canada* v. *USA)* (1941) 3 RIAA 1905 and *Corfu Channel (United Kingdom* v. *Albania)* (Merits) [1949] ICJ Rep 4 decisions.

9 After the Second World War there was a revolution in efficient propulsion for ships and aircraft, without which the growth in both industries would not have been possible. See V. Smil, "The two prime movers of globalization: History and impact of diesel engines and gas turbines," *Journal of Global History*, 2 (2007), 373–394.

10 See ILC, "Report of the international law commission on the work of its eighth session" (April 23–July 3, 1956) UN Doc CAN.4/104) in UNGA (1956) UNYB vol. 2, at 253.

Convention on the High Seas; (iii) the Convention on Fishing and Conservation of Living Resources of the High Seas; and (iv) the Convention on the Continental Shelf.[11] That principles long accepted by states could be reduced to treaty provisions fostered confidence in the maintaining of a balance between traditional rights and access to maritime resources within acceptable restrictions.

14.3 CENTRE STAGE: THE ROLE OF THE INTERNATIONAL MARITIME ORGANIZATION

It was the creation of the IMO that led to regulation of environmental protection and the promotion of sustainable development in the maritime industry. First styled as the Intergovernmental Consultative Maritime Organization (IMCO) under a 1948 UN-sponsored treaty for shipping states, the IMO did not begin operation until a decade later.[12] It had a coordinating mandate "to provide machinery for co-operation among Governments in the field of governmental regulation and practices relating to technical matters of all kinds affecting shipping engaged in international trade, and to encourage the general adoption of the highest practicable standards in matters concerning maritime safety and efficiency of navigation."[13] Governance was to be through a biennial conference of parties with a delegation of administration to an elected Council.[14] The interests of leading shipping states, those with large fleets generally in Global North states, along with flag of convenience states

[11] Respectively: (i) (adopted April 29, 1958, entered into force September 10, 1964) 516 UNTS 205; (ii) (adopted April 29, 1958, entered into force September 30, 1962) 450 UNTS 11; (iii) (adopted April 29, 1958, entered into force March 20, 1966) 559 UNTS 285; and (iv) (adopted April 29, 1958, entered into force June 10, 1964) 499 UNTS 311.

[12] *Convention on the Intergovernmental Maritime Consultative Organization* (adopted March 6, 1948, March 17, 1962) 298 UNTS 3; [IMO Treaty]. The IMO Treaty required ratification by twenty-one states, at least seven with commercial fleets exceeding one million tonnes. As of January 2017, 172 states were IMO members, Belarus joining that year. Three other entities have Associate status: the Faroe Islands, Hong Kong, and Macao. Numerous states have declared when acceding to the Treaty that the IMO should not exceed its mandate into areas of economic regulation.

[13] IMO Treaty, Art. I(a),The IMCO had an important secondary trade role, namely to liberalize commercial shipping between states in order to eliminate discrimination in the use of nationally registered fleets.

[14] IMO Treaty, Arts. 13–38. A fourteen-member standing Marine Safety Committee – with at least eight members from the largest ship-owning states – was created to pursue improvements to "aids to navigation, construction and equipment of vessels, manning from a safety standpoint, rules for the prevention of collisions, handling of dangerous cargoes, maritime safety procedures and requirements . . . marine casualty investigation, salvage and rescue, and any other matters directly affecting maritime safety."

offering a practically reduced regulatory and taxation burden to shipowners such as Liberia and Panama, have tended to dominate IMO regulation-making, both for safety of life at sea and environmental matters.

Although the IMO had no express regulation-making role, the new organization arranged the 1960 SOLAS II conference with a goal of creating a comprehensive instrument for common vessel construction and marine safety standards.[15] Building on the event, and with a Secretariat able to obtain technical advice and coordinate proposed regulation-making, the IMO planned an ambitious agenda in pursuit of maritime safety. Some measures were anodyne, to make standard requirements not yet adopted universally among states such as the 1966 *Load Lines Convention*, while others were in response to technical advances in shipping such as nuclear-powered vessels and prominent marine casualties.[16]

Several events put environmental protection in the maritime industry firmly on the agenda of states and the IMO. One was the loss of the oil tanker m.v. *Torrey Canyon* off southwest England in March 1967.[17] A second was the decision of the UN General Assembly the following year to begin preparatory work for the UN Conference on the Human Environment that would take place in Stockholm in 1972.[18] The third was the UN General Assembly's

[15] *International Convention for the Safety of Life at Sea* (adopted June 17, 1960 entered into force May 26, 1965) 536 UNTS 27. Significant amendments were proposed from 1966 through 1973 but did not come into force because of a formula requiring acceptance by two-thirds of member states.

[16] *International Convention on Load Lines* (adopted April 5, 1966, entered into force July 21, 1968) 640 UNTS 9159. The convention marked the start of the IMO's approach to providing for specific technical and operating matters by individual treaty instead of amendments to the 1960 and 1974 SOLAS treaties. Ships are required to carry current load line (loading capacity) certificates that can be reviewed by a port state to better ensure the safety of such activity. The measure is an early example of the more comprehensive regime of port state control inspections for the safety of shipping that began in the 1980s following UNCLOS.

The sinking of the SS *Yarmouth Castle* in 1965 between Miami and Nassau was a typical casualty of the time, one resulting in regulatory changes. See US Coast Guard, *Marine Board of Investigation: SS Yarmouth Castle*" (Washington, DC: Department of the Treasury, 1966).

[17] The *Torrey Canyon* incident resulted in the first multilateral oil spill response treaty, the *International Convention Relating to Intervention on the High Seas in Cases of Oil Pollution Casualties* (adopted November 29, 1969, entered into force May 6, 1975), 970 UNTS 212 complemented by the 1969 *International Convention on Civil Liability for Oil Pollution Damage* (adopted November 29, 1969, entered into force June 19, 1975) 973 UNTS 3, 9 ILM 45 and the 1971 *International Convention on the Establishment of an International Fund for Compensation for Oil Pollution Damage* (adopted December 18, 1971, entered into force October 16, 1978), 1110 UNTS 57.

[18] UNGA, "Problems of the Human Environment," Resolution 2398 (XXIII) (December 3, 1968). The Preamble called "for intensified action at the national, regional and international level in order to limit and, where possible, eliminate the impairment of the human environment [and]

recognition that a comprehensive law of the sea regime would be useful and that negotiations for it should be pursued.[19] Humanity's sense of the limits of the environment was evolving.[20] The call by civil societies in many states that their governments should act was being heard.

A 1973 treaty to regulate the "harmful discharge" of substances from ships into the marine environment, the *International Convention for the Prevention of Pollution from Ships*, marked the IMO's turn to environmental protection.[21] At first, MARPOL regulated only the prevention of oil pollution from ships, replacing the 1954 convention. It would next be amended in 1978 to include pollution from noxious substances. To these Annexes I and II of the treaty were later added measures to control pollution from packaged substances (Annex III, in force in 1991), sewage from ships (Annex IV, in force 2003), garbage discharge (Annex V, in force 1998), and air pollution (Annex VI, in force 2005). Such entry-into-force dates can be misleading because new technical regulations are now adopted regularly across the annexes, as they are for ship design and construction under SOLAS. MARPOL's arrival saw the 1974 creation of the IMO's Marine Environment Protection Committee and the later agreement of member states that stringent standards for pollution control could be adopted in geographically designated "special areas" (for Annex I, II, IV, and V substances) and "emission control areas" to regulate sulphur oxide (SO_x) and nitrogen oxide (NO_x) emissions in coastal areas under Annex VI.[22]

to protect and preserve the natural surroundings in the interest of man." See "Declaration of the United Nations Conference on the Human Environment" (June 16, 1972), UN doc A/Conf.48/14/Rev. 1(1973).

19 UNGA, "Convening of a conference on the law of the sea" Resolution 2750 (XXV) (C) (December 17, 1970).

20 Another factor was the continuing expansion in maritime zones by coastal states including fishery areas to 200 nautical miles offshore. A typical case of the conflict between states was *Fisheries Jurisdiction (United Kingdom of Great Britain and Northern Ireland* v. *Iceland)*, Merits, ICJ Reports 1974, 3.

21 *International Convention for the Prevention of Pollution from Ships* (adopted November 2, 1973, entered into force October 2, 1983) 1340 UNTS 184 amended by its 1978 Protocol (MARPOL).
The IMO had also seen negotiations for the *Convention on the Prevention of Marine Pollution by Dumping of Wastes and Other Matter* (adopted December 29, 1972, entered into force August 30, 1975) 1046 UNTS 120 [*London Dumping Convention*]. This was a treaty to regulate marine disposal of wastes from land, such as dredging materials from coastal areas and derelict ships, a matter arguably outside the IMO's burgeoning environmental mandate.

22 For a list of such areas, see IMO, www.imo.org, last accessed October 20, 2017. Emission control areas are negotiated between coastal states concerned before being adopted by the IMO through the MEPC. See the US Environmental Protection Agency explanation of that created for Canada, France, and the United States in North America in 2012, US EPA, "Designation of north American emission control area to reduce emission from ships," www.epa.gov/

MARPOL lacked provisions for monitoring and enforcement between member states, the preferred approach being for states to individually enact legislation adopting the treaty's detailed regulations. As such, the IMO environmental regime came to have four layers: (i) the 1948 IMO Treaty; (ii) the wide-ranging Safety of Life at Sea Convention (SOLAS) framework; (iii) MARPOL itself; and (iv) regulations in declared resolutions of the IMO's Marine Environment Protection Committee (MEPC).[23] However, the entry into force of MARPOL Annex I in 1983, together with the concept of regional seas environmental agreements created under a just-concluded UNCLOS, as well as port state control agreements by which like-minded states in various regions would inspect and require the fixing of sub-standard shipping, fostered meaningful compliance by the industry.[24] These elements of enforceability are integrally part of the marine environmental protection regime for shipping that prevails today.

From a rule-making perspective, the IMO was successful in a relatively short period of time because of several features of its governance framework. The first is that of the sustained existence and credible program of the Organization over an inception period of several decades; a focal point for states to arrive at common, detailed technical standards to regulate the industry. The second was the creation of a secretariat led by the authority figure of the IMO Secretary-General that ensured administrative continuity of complex matters. In an era that now takes as common the significant role of standing secretariats for treaty bodies, this innovative step should not go unrecognized.[25] A third factor has certainly been the reduction of negotiated

regulations-emissions-vehicles-and-engines/designation-north-american-emission-control-area-marine last accessed October 20, 2017.

23 Treaty-making for safer shipping has been extensive through the IMO, from the 1977 *Torremolinos International Convention for the Safety of Fishing Vessels* to the *International code of safety for ships operating in polar waters* (the *Polar Code*) expected to enter into force in 2017.

24 Regional seas marine environmental protection areas now exist in numerous areas, including the North Sea, the Baltic, the Mediterranean, the Arabian/Persian Gulf, and off west Africa. See United Nations Environment Programme: https://www.unenvironment.org/explore-topics/oceans-seas/what-we-do/working-regional-seas/why-does-working-regional-seas-matter last accessed October 20, 2017.

UNCLOS Art. 219 requires a port state to assess a ship that may be unseaworthy and "thereby threatens damage to the marine environment," and permits such a ship to be detained and repaired. Port state control agreements (memoranda of understanding) for the exchange of information about sub-standard ships now exist in most shipping areas of the world and between all significant commercial ports. For Europe see Europe, "the 1982 Paris MoU," www.parismou.org last accessed October 20, 2017.

25 Credible secretariats confer actual and perceived competence. Within the IMO, the presence of the MEPC as a standing entity accepted as the place to pursue negotiated technical rules exemplifies this. See G. Ulfstein, "Reflections on institutional design – especially treaty

agreements to stand-alone treaties. It is true that the core of marine safety governance can be captured in detailed rules efficiently prescribed in treaty-regulation form, in distinction to more ethereal operating principles, human factors governance, and economic standards. Common agreement on prescriptive rules for such things as load line standards and tonnage rules can be readily achieved. But the SOLAS system with its many detailed instruments, including MARPOL, an impressive codification, could not have held without a high degree of confidence among states.[26] A fourth element of such consensual rule-making success has been the entry-into-force and amending formulae in the suite of IMO treaties. They have ensured a negotiated result can be brought to fruition by a tacit acceptance process, a problem that persists in multilateral environmental treaties of general application.[27]

All environmental treaty-making has limits. The global distribution and ownership of commercial ships reflects this acutely. State administrations may not have sufficient capacity to prescribe and implement MARPOL and related rules. Addressing sub-standard ships – the category of which disproportionately account for maritime accidents and environmental problems – is a constant demand on governmental resources. The IMO has recognized this, and that is why environmental standards are increasingly accompanied by soft standards or guidelines developed by the Organization. Some examples include: (i) the *Polar Code* in its post-2002 inception phase as "guidelines" of recommend practice for ships operating in ice-covered waters; (ii) "goal based construction" standards for the improved design and building of ships to ensure their in-service reliability and therefore the avoidance of accidents; and (iii) addressing the environmental impact of ships in their routine operation by creation of recommended practices to detail construction materials and for end-of-life dismantling.[28]

bodies," in J. Klabbers and A. Wallendahl (eds.), *Research Handbook on the Law of International Organizations* (Cheltenham: Edward Elgar, 2011), 431–447.

26 Marine classification societies such as Det Norske Veritas-Germanischer Lloyd, Bureau Veritas, Lloyd's Register, and the American Bureau of Shipping have been influential in improving shipping standards and performance. The International Association of Classification Societies has a pronounced role in the MEPC's work as an observer member.

27 Amendments to SOLAS and MARPOL have a long inception period through recognition of a needed rule change, to negotiation, and then implementation. The *Polar Code* is an example. First proposed as nonbinding guidelines in 2002, it was adopted by the IMO states in 2014 for application in 2017 to newly constructed ships and in 2018 to all others trading in polar waters.

28 In 2009, the IMO Assembly adopted the *Hong Kong International Convention for the Safe and Environmentally Sound Recycling of Ships* (adopted May 15, 2009, not in force) IMO doc. SR/CONF/45. Art. 17 is worth noting. It prescribes the requirement for entry-into-force, to occur twenty-four months after: (i) ratification by fifteen states; (ii) ratification by states that have registered between them at least 40 percent of the tonnage of global commercial shipping; and

14.4 SUSTAINABILITY AND ITS CHALLENGE FOR THE IMO: CLIMATE CHANGE REGULATION

The regulation of greenhouse gas emissions from commercial shipping has presented the IMO with its most complex environmental problem to date. More than a decade after the Kyoto Protocol came into force and in the wake of the 2015 Paris Agreement, a long-term solution – by treaty, guidelines, or consensus of IMO member states – has yet to be achieved. This is not surprising in view of the similar experience of civil aviation and industries within states, and recent economic problems faced by much of the global shipping industry. The 1992 UN Framework Convention on Climate Change contained no provision for the control of GHGs from shipping or the maritime industry.[29] It would fall to the Convention's 1998 Kyoto Protocol to confer the needed regulation to the IMO. This was not a delegation as such, but the agreement of contracting states that the issue would be addressed through the IMO.[30] MARPOL would be the focal point for the needed regulation because it had a relatively mature regime for air emissions standards and widespread acceptance among shipping states. However, because the regulation of GHGs has a substantial economic aspect, there would be limits in a traditional, formal approach to controlling a "pollutant" not attributable from case to case to a single point source and for which there was no ready technical solution.

MARPOL was revised in the 1990s to provide for air emissions from ships so as to protect coastal air quality and, thereby, human health. This created a basis for GHG control measures under Annex VI of the treaty in 2005.[31] The initial requirement was to reduce NO_X and SO_X emissions that result from

(iii) the first fifteen (or any greater number needed) ratifying states having achieved a maximum annual ship recycling (i.e. dismantling) volume of not less than 3 percent of the combined tonnage of such states during the past ten years.

29 *United Nations Framework Convention on Climate Change* (adopted June 4, 1992, entered into force March 21, 1994) 1771 UNTS 107 [UNFCCC].

30 *Kyoto Protocol to the United Nations Framework Convention on Climate Change* (adopted March 16, 1998, entered into force February 16, 2005) 2303 UNTS 148. [*Kyoto Protocol*]. Art. 2 (2) provides that: "The Parties included in Annex I shall pursue limitation or reduction of emissions of greenhouse gases not controlled by the Montreal Protocol from aviation and marine bunker fuels, working through the International Civil Aviation Organization and the International Maritime Organization, respectively." The 1987 Montreal Protocol is for the control and elimination of ozone-depleting substances. The IMO had started to regulate such substances, mainly refrigerants and solvents, under air emission standards in MARPOL Annex VI.

31 IMO, "IMO policies and practices related to the reduction of greenhouse gas emissions from ships," Res A. 963(23) (March 4, 2004), www.imo.org last accessed October 20, 2017.

combustion of fuel, with the needed measures detailed in Regulations 13 and 14 of Annex VI.[32] The IMO's approach to more fuel-efficient engines emerged from the need to reduce NO_X concentrations in engine exhaust and is to be achieved in three stages through 2016.[33] The 2008 introduction of Regulation 18 for fuel quality demanded the gradual elimination of sulphur from marine fuels, first to concentrations of no more than 4.5 percent by 2012, 3.5 percent in the eight years following, and 0.5 percent after 2020.[34] These initiatives were helped by an increase in the cost of marine fuels after the 1990s, which gave impetus to the better design of engine efficiency and operational measures. Regulation here has two challenges, namely, the inherent limits in the efficient conversion of fuel energy to motive power in diesel engines, and the capital cost for construction of ships with efficient engines. The UN Conference on Trade and Development (UNCTAD) expressed the desired rule-making approach for the IMO to pursue in these terms:

> The aim is the adoption in 2009 of a binding, coherent and comprehensive IMO regulatory framework on GHG emissions from ships. IMO's Marine Environment Protection Committee (MEPC) agreed that, among other things, the framework should be: (a) effective, binding all flag States; (b) cost effective; (c) practical; (d) transparent; (e) fraud-free; and (f) easy to administer. It should have limited competitive distortion, support technical innovation, promote sustainable development and not penalize trade.[35]

The same year, the IMO MEPC established a GHG Working Group that would conceive the Energy Efficiency Design Index (EEDI) for mandatory application to newbuilds, and the Ship Energy Efficiency Management Plan

[32] See by comparison the directives of the European Environmental Agency and the European Commission, respectively at: www.eea.europa.eu/themes/air and ec.europa.eu/environment/air/quality/standards.htm.

[33] Tier I applies to ships constructed after January 1, 2000, for example regulating NO_X emissions at 9.8 grams per kilowatt hour (g/kwh) when engine speed exceeds 2000 RPM, and then 7.7 g/kwh after January 1, 2011. (Comparable stepped reductions apply for engine speeds below 2000 RPM and below 130 RPM). Tier III requirements, to come into effect on January 1, 2016, see the same requirement then at 2.0 g/kwh. Tier III standards apply in designated coastal areas only, such as the Baltic Sea and North Sea Emissions Control Areas. Nitrous oxide is a GHG and is designated as such in the Kyoto Protocol.

[34] Nothing in Regulations 13, 14, and 18 of Annex VI is intended to reduce GHG emissions as such. January 1, 2020 was affirmed by the MEPC in October 2016 as being the implementation date for a "global sulphur cap of 0.50%." See IMO Meeting Summary, "Marine Environment Protection Committee (MEPC), 70th session, 24–26 October 2016," www.imo.org last accessed October 22, 2017.

[35] UNCTAD, "Summary of Proceedings: Multi-Year Expert Meeting on Transport and Trade Facilitation: Maritime Transport and the Climate Change Challenge, 16–18 February 2009, Geneva," UNCTAD/DTL/TLB/2009/1 (December 1, 2009) at 10.

(SEEMP) for all vessels.[36] These measures, added to Annex VI as Regulations 19–23, were adopted in July 2011 and became effective in 2013.[37] The EEDI at Regulation 21 is the most tangible of GHG reduction measures. Over a ten-year period, it is intended to result in up to 30 percent improved energy efficiency in several categories of ships propelled by diesel engines, although not "non-conventional propulsion" systems such as diesel-electric and gas turbine plants. In general, three phase-in periods provide for efficiency improvements of 10 percent (2015–2019), 20 percent (2020–2024), and 30 percent (after January 1, 2025) for vessels constructed in each period. Vessels are required to maintain an International Energy Efficiency Certificate that details routine surveys and maintenance of efficiency, and subjects ships to being checked under the port state control regime.[38]

Regulations 22 for SEEMP and 23 for technology transfer and cooperation round out the present Annex VI GHG framework. The SEEMP is a soft measure intended to "establish a mechanism for a company and/or a ship to improve the energy efficiency of a ship's operation."[39] It seeks improvements to "a ship's efficiency through four steps: *planning, implementation, monitoring*, and *self-evaluation and improvement*."[40] As with aircraft, ship speed is the primary determinant of fuel consumption and, therefore, efficiency on a unit basis of tonnage moved over distance, and, hence, tangible measures are geared to better voyage planning with more direct passages at lower average speeds. High fuel costs, set to increase with the elimination of heavy fuel oils in order to meet Regulations 14 and 18 sulphur reduction targets, have practically compelled shipping operators to consider such approaches, although informally.[41] The IMO's latest regulatory measure in this area is the requirement for states to ensure vessels registered to them monitor and

36 The EEDI and SEEMP were developed in 2010 and 2012 inter-sessions of the Working Group on Energy Efficiency Measures for Ships. States and technical organizations such as the International Association of Classification Societies (IACS) made proposals including for the establishment of baseline standards across various ship types.

37 See IMO, Res MEPC.203(62), 62th Sess, Annex 19 (2011) 1.

38 Such ships are not required to be built to the Regulation 21 EEDI standard, but must demonstrate "attained" EEDI: Regulation 20. At present, ships entirely operating in national waters and those in government service are exempted from the EEDI scheme. The Guidelines for calculation of EEDI for new ships continue to be amended with the benefit of experience. See e.g. IMO, Resolution MEPC.263(68) (adopted on May 15, 2015).

39 "2012 guidelines for the development of a ship energy efficiency management plan," Resolution MEPC.213(63) (2012) 1 at para 3.2 (SEEMP).

40 SEEMP at para 3.6.

41 See e.g. G. Lloyd, "In focus: Ship efficiency and emission reduction" (January 2013), www.dnv.com last accessed October 22, 2017.

report ship-by-ship fuel consumption under a "statement of compliance" scheme, with data annually submitted by the state to the IMO for analysis.[42]

Two economic factors will affect the success of this scheme, namely, variations in the market price of ship fuels, and operating costs of existing ships and the capital cost to replace them. When it comes to cost, although shipyard capacity remains high (including in those states – China, Japan, and South Korea – which build the majority of the global fleet captured by the Regulation 21 EEDI standard) and capital continues to be inexpensive, there continues to be from about 2014 an oversupply of ships, which suggests new-builds (which have increased every year since 2000) must decline.[43] With the collapse in the market price of petroleum in late 2014, ship operating costs have eased compared to those of a decade earlier, recalling that for most ship types, such as bulk carriers, container ships, and tankers, fuel is routinely half or more of such cost.

MARPOL has arguably reached its limits as a regulatory instrument to govern GHG reductions in the global shipping sector. The rules in Annex VI to ensure air emission quality – to reduce pollution that impairs human health – have worked through a combination of factors, including strong consensus for their creation, long introductory periods, the salutary effect of high fuel prices in recent years, a continuing trend of new shipbuilding, adoption and local enforcement of air quality standards by states, the supporting role played by marine classification societies, and the international nature of enforcement for shipping by a port state control inspection regime encompassing many areas of the world. IMO member states accept objective technical design and performance standards for shipping. But they have yet to allow additional cost and taxation-like burdens on national shipping industries, however fair or redistributionist that may be. This can be seen in the

[42] "Under the new requirements, ships of 5,000 gross tons and above will have to collect consumption data for each type of fuel oil they use, as well as other, specified data including proxies for transport work. These ships account for approximately 85% of CO2 emissions from international shipping. The data collected will provide a firm basis on which future decisions on additional measures, over and above those already adopted by the IMO, can be made." IMO, "New requirements for international shipping as UN body continues to address greenhouse gas emissions" (Press briefing, October 28, 2016), www.imo.org last accessed October 20, 2017. [IMO Press briefing] Regulation 22A "Collection and reporting of ship fuel oil consumption data" is to come into force on March 1, 2018.

[43] See the reports of the OECD Workshop on Shipbuilding and the Offshore Industry held on November 24, 2014. OECD, "Workshop on Shipbuilding and the Offshore Industry," www.oecd.org, last accessed October 20, 2017; and see UNCTAD, *Review of Maritime Transport 2016*.

response to the Paris Agreement.[44] No new technical measures for efficiency or to control output resulted, the MEPC deciding in October 2016 that a "roadmap" is to be developed from 2017 through 2023 toward a comprehensive strategy for the reduction of GHG emissions from ships.[45] And there has been no sustained suggestion of economic or market measures to reduce and re-allocate the use of petroleum fuels in the industry. Meaningful regulation of GHG reduction, modestly underway after a decade of experience with NO_X and SO_X emissions and the recent adoption of the EEDI requirement for new ships, has not yet arrived for the global maritime industry.

Sustainable development in the global shipping industry has made impressive strides during the past half century. This success has turned on the increasing acceptance and development of the rule of law in the international order, together with a coherent regime in the SOLAS and MARPOL treaty family now universally accepted by shipping states. Where there has been a high-profile pollution incident or a demonstrable human health concern such as coastal air quality in air emissions from ships, a remedial response has routinely yielded durable regulations by the IMO. An additional factor toward a sustainable regime has been the legitimacy of an IMO not competed with by other agencies and to which states increasingly resort for negotiated, uniform standards across the industry. Another has been monitoring and enforcement of basic pollution control standards in most global shipping under the UNCLOS-inspired port state control system. The greatest challenge for environmental protection in a still growing global shipping industry has arrived in the form of climate change. The IMO regime is increasingly revealed as lagging that of the post-Paris consensus of states, with a reckoning of the shipping industry's complete and seemingly permanent dependence on petroleum fuels now only faintly perceptible.[46] The transition to reduced GHG emissions will demand technical innovation, a consensus among states and interested actors, a measure of economic sacrifice by industry operators, and therefore the use of international law as never before.

44 *Paris Agreement* (December 12, 2015) UN doc. FCCC/CP/2015/L.9/Rev.1 (Annex) (in force November 4, 2016). *Paris Agreement under the United Nations Framework Convention on Climate Change* (adopted December 12, 2015, entered into force November 4, 2016), UN Doc. FCCC/CP/2015/L.9/Rev.1, Annex. The Agreement contains no provisions or direction for GHG reduction measures in the IMO, leaving the Kyoto Protocol Article 2 delegation of governance the formal measures for states and the IMO to address GHG regulation in the shipping industry.

45 IMO Press briefing *supra* Note 42.

46 The nature of ship propulsion is that petroleum – diesel/gas oil, medium fuel oil, heavy fuel oil, LPG, and LNG, together with ethanol – will long be needed as fuel for present-technology prime movers. The result is that, in a future era of declining petroleum use, the global shipping industry (and naval fleets) will generate increasing portions of globally emitted GHGs.

15

Corporate Social Responsibility in the Aviation Industry

Peter Paul Fitzgerald and René David-Cooper

Corporate Social Responsibility (CSR) is rooted in the idea that corporations must focus on issues beyond the balance sheet. For instance, CSR has had an impact in reducing child labor in developing countries, making extractive industries more responsible to local communities, and reducing the environmental impact of hotels. It is also applicable to the airline industry where it has promoted various types of positive behavior. In a world increasingly concerned with climate change and that sees as problematic the airline industry release of greenhouse gas (GHG) emissions at high altitude, regulators are about to set emissions reduction targets for the airline industry. Given that fuel is the single greatest cost for airlines, and that any reduction in fuel consumed involves a consequential reduction in GHGs emitted, the airline industry is generally eager to reduce GHG emissions. However, several emerging CSR best practices in civil aviation have incentivized the industry to become more environmentally friendly in recent years. In this context, this chapter argues that CSR should encourage airlines to go beyond mere self-interest or regulatory compliance in leading the way to meeting increasingly ambitious GHG reduction targets.

15.1 INTRODUCTION

Corporate Social Responsibility (CSR) is the idea that corporations are responsible to parties beyond merely their shareholders and that management, in addition to focusing on their balance sheets and income statements, should also turn their attention to corporations' greater impact on the society in which they exist. Corporations in all types of industries have embraced CSR as a way of proving themselves to be good corporate citizens. In each case the CSR challenges are slightly different; with a manufacturer, it might involve respect of collective bargaining or a prohibition on the use of child labor, a multinational mining company might have to train local employees and adopt safer work practices. However, airlines are unique in that as corporations they face many of the reputational challenges of their homologues, but as operators of jet aircraft they are also held to a unique responsibility with respect to reducing GHG emissions from their industry, especially at high altitude.

Given the nature of the industry, one must also wonder if we can realistically expect airlines operating in a competitive market with vulnerable financial health and annual net profit margins hovering around 1 percent[1] to adequately balance profitability with environmental objectives, as the financial health of airlines cannot *always* be divorced from their ability to comply with their legal and corporate obligations.[2] We cannot ignore that in times of financial distress, which seemingly reoccur every decade, airlines have demonstrated behaviors of self-destructive practices to remain profitable.[3] Anemic profitability has even driven airlines to curtail costs, including safety-related expenses, to remain afloat.[4] If unhealthy economics can threaten flight safety,[5] the same could certainly happen with CSR and environmental matters.

Thus, this chapter investigates a simple question; does corporate social responsibility induce airline management to go further than they would otherwise in reducing GHG emissions? The question must be situated in context; most often there is a direct correlation between a reduction of GHG emissions and a reduction of fuel consumption. If the reduction of fuel consumption results from lighter aircraft, from more fuel efficient engines, or from better air navigation practices, such benefits flow to the environment but they also flow to the airline's bottom line. However, environmental measures require, especially in aviation, a considerable upfront cost to be implemented, with no prospect of a short-term return. The expected savings for the environment are neither proven nor guaranteed, *yet*. It is therefore important to identify situations where the GHG reduction is not solely due to the quest for lower fuel costs, but rather out of recognition that

1 P. S. Dempsey, "The financial performance of the airline industry post-deregulation," *Hous L Rev*, 45 (2008), 421 at 424–427; "Why airlines make such meagre profits," *The Economist* (February 23, 2014), www.economist.com/blogs/economist-explains/2014/02/economist-explains-5 last accessed October 21, 2017.

2 P. S. Dempsey and A. R. Goetz, *Airline Deregulation and Laissez-Faire Mythology* (Westport, CT: Quorum Books, 1992) at 304.

3 P. S. Dempsey and L. E. Gesell, *Airline Management Strategies for the 21st Century*, 3rd edn. (Chandler, AZ: Coast Aire Publication, 2012) at 193–97.

4 P. S. Dempsey, "Transportation deregulation – On a collision course?" *Transp Law J*, 13 (1984), 329 at 352.

5 P. S. Dempsey, "The rise and fall of the civil aeronautics board-opening wide the floodgates of entry," *Transp L J*, 11 (1980), 91 at 167.

airlines are corporate citizens with a responsibility to the planet in whose skies they operate.

15.2 AN EXPLANATION OF CORPORATE SOCIAL RESPONSIBILITY AND HOW IT EVOLVED

The concept of CSR has been in existence for nearly seventy years; as early as 1946 Fortune Magazine surveyed business people with respect to their social responsibilities.[6] By 1953, it was characterized in terms of business leaders being "responsible for the consequences of their actions in a sphere somewhat wider than that covered by their profit-and-loss statements."[7]

While some may consider a corporation's support of the Arts or of charitable organizations to be an example of CSR, such actions may be more connected to tax incentives or public relations than to a genuine sense of CSR. Increasingly, especially in States where society holds corporations to certain standards, it is important to draw a distinction between the rhetorical and the substantial aspects of CSR.[8] At a minimum, CSR involves two elements:

> First, [corporations] must not knowingly do anything that could harm their stakeholders – notably, their investors, employees, customers, suppliers, or the local community within which they operate. Second, if corporations do cause harm to their stakeholders, they must then rectify it whenever the harm is discovered and brought to their attention.[9]

Moreover, to the extent that the rectification of harm is required by legal or social norms, failure to do so would constitute socially irresponsible behavior. This is because compliance with legal and social norms is a minimum behavioral standard and CSR must exist above this standard.[10]

Additionality is a concept initially linked with the international climate change legal regime and has specifically been mentioned in the *Kyoto Protocol* (Kyoto).[11] Additionality refers to an effort that is supplemental to or

[6] See A. B. Carroll, "Corporate social responsibility: Evolution of a definitional construct," *Business & Society*, 38 (1999), 268–95, 269.

[7] Ibid., 270, quoting Howard R. Bowen, *Social Responsibilities of the Businessman* (1953) at 44.

[8] See J. L. Campbell, "Why would corporations behave in socially responsible ways? An institutional theory of corporate social responsibility," *Academy of Management Review*, 32 (2007), 946–67,

[9] Ibid., 951.

[10] Ibid., 951.

[11] *Kyoto Protocol to the United Nations Framework Convention on Climate Change* (adopted December 11, 1997, entered into force February 16, 2005),2303 UNTS 148, s. 1.3. [*Kyoto Protocol*].

beyond what would have been achieved in a business-as-usual (BAU) scenario.[12] Thus, to the extent that legal compliance could be considered to be a BAU scenario, any CSR must have the properties of additionality in order to be substantial.

John L. Campbell argues that a corporation's CSR will be likely to be substantial rather than merely rhetorical when most of the factors listed here are present:

(1) the corporation is profitable and operating in a healthy economic environment;[13]
(2) there is healthy competition between corporations and a level playing field;[14]
(3) there are well-enforced regulations to ensure such behavior;[15]
(4) well-organized self-regulation in place and perceived threat of government regulation if self-regulation fails;[16]
(5) there is pressure from private independent organizations, including NGOs, who monitor compliance and lobby to enforce it;[17]
(6) compliance is institutionalized in business publications and business school curricula;[18]
(7) where corporation belongs to a trade or employer association that promotes socially responsible behavior; and/or[19]
(8) where corporations are engaged in institutional dialogue with unions, employees, community groups, investors, and other stakeholders.[20]

Consumers are becoming increasingly aware of social issues, and just as consumers have boycotted certain companies in the past, there is a growing segment of the population that factors CSR into making purchasing decisions.[21] At the same time, CSR is now being seen as a tool to achieve various

[12] See, C. C. Gomez Wichtendahl, "Biodiversity offsets in a public lands context: A romantic concept or a practical tool to balance economic development and biodiversity conservation goals?" unpublished Doctoral thesis, University of Ottawa (2017), See also *Kyoto Protocol*, s.2.3.3 Additionality.

[13] Campbell, "Why would corporations behave in socially responsible ways?" *supra* Note 8 at 952.

[14] Ibid. at 953.

[15] Ibid. at 955.

[16] Ibid. at 956.

[17] Ibid. at 958.

[18] Ibid. at 959.

[19] Ibid. at 960.

[20] Ibid. at 962.

[21] See L. A. Mohn, D. J. Webb, and K. E. Harris, "Do consumers expect companies to be socially responsible? The impact of corporate social responsibility on buying behaviour," *The Journal of Consumer Affairs*, 35 (2001), 45–72.

outcomes such as reducing poverty,[22] eliminating forced child labor,[23] or fighting bribery and corruption.[24]

There is debate as to what types of social change public corporations should support[25] and whether the return on investment is negative or positive.[26] Indeed, the impact of CSR is, to a certain extent, based on current consumer perceptions of the corporation and its activities.

> Consider McDonald's and Subway restaurants. Although they are both in the same industry and so face similar competitive conditions, were each to contribute $1 million to efforts to curb obesity, it is unlikely they would experience identical financial returns. In fact, their returns could differ radically, with one achieving a positive return and the other experiencing losses.[27]

Thus, CSR probably works best when the goals are aligned with those of the company, and where CSR simply pushes the company slightly further than would have been achieved by market principles alone. Thus, the Body Shop used an externally verified process for "understanding, measuring, reporting on and improving the organisation's social, environmental and animal testing performance."[28] Such practice is consistent with the Body Shop's image, but using an externally verified process would not typically be required by market forces acting alone. Similarly, Hilton has a comprehensive CSR that details its commitment to "equal opportunity and diversity, human rights, health and safety, and environment and sustainability."[29] Its CSR is consistent with the corporation's image and some of its environmental practices such as encouraging guests staying multiple nights to consider reusing towels and linens to save water, energy, and ultimately money.[30]

[22] See R. Jenkins, "Globalization, corporate social responsibility and poverty," *International Affairs*, 81 (2005), 525–40.
[23] Ibid. at 528.
[24] Ibid. at 539.
[25] See M. L. Barnett, "Stakeholder influence capacity and the variability of financial returns to corporate social responsibility," *Academy of Management Review*, **32** (2007), 794–816.
[26] Ibid.
[27] Ibid. at 795.
[28] See P. S. Brønn and A. B. Vrioni, "Corporate social responsibility and cause-related marketing: An overview," *International Journal of Advertising*, **20** (2001), 207–22, 211.
[29] See J. L. Holcomb, R. S. Upchurch, and F. Okumus, "Corporate social responsibility: What are top hotel companies reporting?" *International Journal of Contemporary Hospitality Management*, **19** (2007), 461–75, 465.
[30] Ibid. at 464.

15.3 CSR CAN REDUCE ENVIRONMENTAL IMPACT OF HUMAN ACTIVITIES

Due to the nature of resource extraction, and the fact that it is often conducted by multinational corporations at locations outside the European Union or North America, CSR often serves in the place of regulation with respect to the disclosure of the social, economic, and environmental impact. In an effort to be seen as partners with the people, huge corporations such as Anglo American, and Rio Tinto support the Extractive Industries Transparency Initiative, a campaign that helps citizens of resource-rich development countries to hold their governments accountable for the revenues from those resources.[31] The campaign has the added benefit of making community members aware of the magnitude of resource revenues. Mining giants like these and BHP Billiton have found that open disclosure of information and an engagement in sustainable development help to earn the necessary social license.[32]

> These companies have been publishing combined health, safety, environment and community reports for some time, and have developed combined social and environmental policies and codes of business conduct that are aligned with the principles of sustainable development.
>
> [T]hey have a wide financial and geographic impact, which both increases their potential for social and environmental impacts and provides them with the financial resources to perform well in the disclosure of such issues.[33]

In particular, for companies engaged in resource extraction, CSR helps to balance the imperative to protect the environment with the need to make a profit.[34] An argument can be made that without CSR, there would be more environmental damage as a result of extractive industries.

[31] See H. J. and N. Yakovleva, "Corporate social responsibility in the mining industry: exploring trends in social and environmental disclosure," *Journal of Cleaner Production*, 14 (2006), 271–84, 276.

[32] See T. M. Devinney, "Corporate social responsibility in the mining industry: Exploring trends in social and environmental disclosure," *Academy of Management Perspectives*, 14 (2000), 44–56, 45. Devinney suggests that while CSR may enable these corporations to operate in foreign jurisdictions, it does not guarantee lack of protests at home.

[33] Jenkins, *supra* Note 31 at 281.

[34] Ibid. at 272.

15.4 STIMULATING CSR AND FOSTERING BUSINESS SUSTAINABILITY IN THE AIR PASSENGER MARKET

15.4.1 *Current Industry Challenges*

Airlines must embrace CSR to a greater degree than companies in other industries. However, corporate decisions by air carriers are shaped by economic, political, and operational impediments, all of which may positively or adversely impact our common well-being,[35] including the environment. At first glance, it may seem improbable that, in an aviation market that has been largely deregulated, airlines will openly embrace CSR into their business models with the prospect of fostering further growth and expansion. In environmental matters, CSR is certainly not *always* viewed as a profitable business strategy *per se*.

Given that airlines operate in a capital-intensive industry and have often struggled to amass the necessary capital to upgrade their fleets in compliance with emerging safety norms,[36] why would not the same occur for environmental goals and treaties? If faced with a CSR to "go green," an airline must either absorb the consequential costs of environmental measures or pass them on to the consumer; two scenarios which are undesirable from a business standpoint.[37]

As has been the case with air safety,[38] we can expect that the economic strains created by intensive airline competition can also have a deleterious effect on a carrier's ability to meet CSR environmental goals, unless the industry is presented with compelling reasons to seek an alternate approach. The true question is: How can air carriers around the world be incentivized to

35 R. D. Cooper, "The transition to safety management systems (SMS) in aviation: Is Canada deregulating flight safety?" *J Air Law Commer*, 81 (2016), 33 at 34.

36 P. S. Dempsey, "The financial performance of the airline industry post-deregulation," *Houst Law Rev*, 45 (2008), 421 at 445; P. S. Dempsey, "Airlines in turbulence: Strategies for survival," *Transp Law J* 23 (1995), 15 at 23; Dempsey and Goetz, *Airline Deregulation and Laissez-Faire Mythology*, at 225 ("[D]eregulation has brought about cutthroat pricing, a miserable level of industry profitability, insufficient capital to reequip aging fleets, and a deterioration of service. Since deregulation began, the airline industry has suffered the worst economic losses in its history.")

37 M. Friedman, "The social responsibility of business is to increase its profits," *The New York Times Magazine* (September 13, 1970) "In each of these cases, the corporate executive would be spending someone else's money for a general social interest. Insofar as his actions in accord with his 'social responsibility' reduce returns to stockholders, he is spending their money. Insofar as his actions raise the price to customers, he is spending the customers' money. Insofar as his actions lower the wages of some employees, he is spending their money."

38 P. S. Dempsey, "The rise and fall of the civil aeronautics board–opening wide the floodgates of entry," *Transp Law J*, 11 (1980) at 167; Dempsey and Goetz, *supra* Note 2 at 304.

embrace CSR in a liberalized market where airlines constantly struggle to balance profitability with a set of already stringent regulations?[39]

While CSR is desirable in principle, it can be a tough sell in the aviation industry where there is a genuine fear among its stakeholders that passengers will be reluctant to personally stomach the cost of impending environmental measures, namely carbon credits and aircraft fleet modernization. Nonetheless, there are important incentives for airlines to justify CSR on their balance sheets.[40]

15.4.2 *Legal Incentives*

The social norms of today embodied in CSR are a presage of tomorrow's laws, as CSR practices may eventually convert into industry norms over time and, in some cases, subsequently become the law. *Vice versa*, a practice that is viewed by the existing laws of today as "legal" may not be lawful a decade later as the airline industry's landscape evolves over the years with newer technology and altered social norms.

CSR therefore increases an airline's ability to adjust progressively, rather than abruptly, to environmental concerns, particularly when onerous regulatory changes come into effect. Conversely, the absence of CSR in an airline's business model will often catch up to it when a social norm formally becomes a binding industry requirement, given that social responsibilities often translate into legal obligations as an industry evolves over time. Given that civil aviation is well acquainted with alterations to its regulatory landscape, good CSR mitigates the risk of airlines becoming noncompliant overnight when a new era of regulations is introduced.

[39] P. S. Dempsey and L. E. Gesell, *Air Transportation: Foundations for the 21st century* (Chandler, AZ: Coast Aire Publication, 1997) at 42.

[40] The Center for International Environmental Law, "(Mis)calculated risk and climate change - are rating agencies repeating credit crisis mistakes?" (2015), www.ciel.org/wp-content/uploads/2015/10/ciel-rpt-credits-10.15-webv2smaller.pdf last accessed October 20, 2017. In the contrary, the proactive implementation of CSR can increase an airline's financial health on paper. For instance, the Center for International Environmental Law (CEIL) suggests that industries and individual companies that comply with environmental norms should benefit in the future from higher credit ratings as they experience an "easier transition to a less carbon-intensive economy and avoid the potential for massive downgrades and consequential shocks to capital markets." The CIEL concludes that current finance models relying on BAU scenarios do not, however, address the probability of climate impacts, including the potential financial risks of experiencing a severe economic crisis once environmental concerns compel industries around the world to suddenly change their business models. Hence, a BAU approach to the environment distorts the actual financial health of a company, and hides the wealth of those with good CSR. When financial institutions and investors start considering this factor in their analyses, the credit ratings of companies will start depending partly on their compliance with environmental norms, thus resulting in a financially enviable position for airlines wishing to foster further growth.

When one reflects on the history of air transportation, CSR has existed in civil aviation since its inception at the dawn of the twentieth century, at least implicitly or instinctively. Safety being the "social norm" at the time, CSR aimed to ensure, in some respects, that air carriers were operating safely by transporting passengers to their destination *alive and uninjured*. In the primitive stages of civil aviation, safety was the additionality of CSR, as there were no regulatory requirements governing air safety, nor were there any express legal requirements to operate an aircraft in a manner to prevent bodily harm or death.[41] But the industry nonetheless adopted corporate practices[42] to ensure that passengers were safely transported to their destination, given that safety was a "public good."[43] It was, in a very elementary manner, good CSR to protect the safety and security of passengers, but also to maintain business and avoid producing large holes in major cities with collateral effects on society.[44]

Of course, protecting and ensuring air safety in civil aviation quickly became the overarching legal priority throughout the world as it turned into the ICAO's primary focus and gained an *erga omnes* character,[45] even though it was merely a desirable goal at the time aviation was first used as a mode of transportation over a century ago. If one looks at the current regulatory requirements in international air transportation, many take their origins from earlier CSR principles, which eventually made their way into the written provisions of international treaties and domestic laws.[46] If we follow the

41 For instance, no laws existed a century ago to prevent pilots from flying poorly maintained aircraft or into dangerous weather conditions. Put bluntly, CSR in the industry at the time was taking the necessary measures to prevent too many casualties and injuries; this was the additionality of CSR in air transportation.

42 Even today, there are many examples of airlines exceeding safety requirements. See P. P. Fitzgerald, "Questioning the regulation of aviation safety," *Ann Air & Space Law*, 37(2012), 44–45.

43 T. Ahmad, "Achieving global safety in civil aviation: A critical analysis of contemporary safety oversight mechanisms," *Ann Air & Space Law*, 37 (2012), 81 at 84–85.

44 Dempsey and Andrew, *supra* Note 2 at 304–6 "No one can quarrel with the basic economic principle that if an airline kills off its passengers, it won't have any." Consumers, for obvious reasons, will not support or fly with airlines that frequently generate accidents and fatalities.

45 J. Huang, "Aviation safety, ICAO and obligations *erga omnes*," *Chin J Int Law*, 8 (2009) 63; J. Huang, *Aviation Safety through the Rule of Law: ICAO's Mechanisms and Practices* (The Netherlands: Kluwer Law International, 2009), c 5; M. Ratajcyk, "Regulatory framework for a 'performance-based' approach to air safety management in the European Union," *Air and Space Law*, 36 (2011), 401 at 402; this CSR precept lies at the core of the fundamental principles of civil aviation that eventually led the ICAO to regulate safety under a formal legal framework now endorsed by 191 Member States.

46 In practice, numerous other examples exist in the aviation industry. When pilot fatigue was first regulated with the implementation of flight and duty time limitations, airlines with sound employment policies and balanced work schedules reflecting a consideration for the human

evolution of CSR in relation to emerging concerns in aviation, the environmental goals of today could very well translate into the binding legal norms of tomorrow,[47] hence the legal incentive of embracing CSR proactively.

It is therefore a flawed approach to resist the adoption of CSR as part of one's business model on the premise that the increased costs associated with noncompulsory measures, such as implementing and exceeding environmental goals, are unjustified from a business perspective. On the contrary, good CSR often places an airline ahead of the queue when industry changes are just around the corner. CSR enables airlines to be cognizant of subtle industry changes and current trends before their cumulative influence triggers larger regulatory changes where some air carriers are simply too far behind others to catch up and sustain their presence in the market.

The most compelling example of CSR in aviation lies in the field of aircraft noise pollution. When operating out of an airport, being a good corporate citizen entails that airlines owe respect and tranquility to their host city, namely the individuals living near the airport it flies into. This was, for the longest time, a "gentleman's agreement" between the airline industry and society, where efforts were made by air carriers to mitigate noise pollution and safeguard the enjoyment of people above whom airliners were being flown. Again, there were no laws prohibiting aircraft noise at the dawn of aviation, albeit there has always been a persistent tension between individual land occupiers and the entities operating aircraft above them.[48]

nature of each employee saw very few changes to their operations due to good CSR. On the other hand, airlines with draconian and intensive aircrew schedules either scrambled to comply operationally and financially with the new regulations or entered a dark age of noncompliance, threatening in both scenarios their survival as a business. While it increased their operational costs at first, even though there were no rules to enforce pilot fatigue previously, airlines with good CSR, which had already provided their employees with fair working conditions, benefited from their CSR in the long run once those norms became the law.

47 By analogy, the same could be said about CSR in relation to our environment today; there are no express domestic laws or ICAO SARPs at the time of this writing preventing air carriers from polluting the atmosphere.

48 See *United States* v. *Causby*, 328 US 256, 261 (1946); *Lord Bernstein of Leigh* v. *Skyviews & General Ltd.* [1977] 2 All ER 902 at 907; *R.* v. *Air Canada*, 1978 CanLII 2210 (MB CA), 86 D.L.R. (3d) 631. (In *Causby*, the respondent owned a chicken farm located less than half a mile from an active United States military airport, where airplanes would fly as low as twenty-five meters above his farm, which terrified his animals so much that they stopped laying eggs, while others would fatally run into the sides of the chicken coop. Nowadays, safety regulations govern the minimum altitudes above which aircraft can overfly built-up areas, with even more stringent regulations in the case of agricultural farms housing animals).

With the introduction of larger jetliners in the second half of the twentieth century,[49] airlines and airports with good CSR quickly became cognizant of this predicament and adopted voluntary and proactive measures to reduce aircraft noise with alternate air routes and flight times, while aircraft manufacturers saw a business opportunity to develop new technology addressing this social concern.[50] At the time, this was the "social norm" in aviation. Noise reduction eventually became an industry practice and when Annex 16 to the *Chicago Convention*[51] was adopted in 1971,[52] it became a legal requirement to comply with noise restriction standards and recommended practices (SARPs),[53] while more stringent national laws in some States restricted or banned noisy aircraft from flying into their domestic airspace.[54] As a result, airlines with sound CSR in the area of noise pollution emerged with aircraft already compliant with the new regulations, while others struggled or vanished.[55] History could very well repeat itself for air carriers who fail to embrace CSR in environmental matters.

While airlines must avoid falling into the trap of embracing CSR solely as a means to further increase their profitability,[56] one must retain from this point that

49 P. S. Dempsey, *Public International Air Law* (Montreal: McGill University Institute and Center for Research in Air and Space Law, 2008) at 415. The ICAO has regulated aircraft noise since 1968. While there are no international standards prohibiting the use of noisier aircraft, several countries have now banned aircraft producing too much noise from flying into their airspace.

50 Ibid.

51 ICAO, "International standards and recommended practices: Annex 16 to the *Chicago Convention*: Aircraft engine emissions," vol. 2 (2008).

52 Dempsey, *Public International Air Law, supra* Note 49 at 415–44.

53 Ibid. at 417–18.

54 Ibid. at 421.

55 Ibid. at 415. While some airlines with good CSR had already protectively and voluntarily invested in reducing aircraft noise with newer aircraft fleets or modified engines, complacent carriers lagging behind modern engine noise technology were faced with a Hobson's Choice of either making considerable investments to modernize their aircraft fleets and maintain their market position under the new regulations, or abdicate and terminate their operations in that market with deleterious consequences for their finances. In any case, airlines with proactive and innovative CSR in the field of noise pollution ensured their sustainability in the airline market, whereas the ones who did not eventually disappeared.

56 Friedman, *supra* Note 37 "Of course, in practice the doctrine of social responsibility is frequently a cloak for actions that are justified on other grounds rather than a reason for those actions . . . [T]here is a strong temptation to rationalize these actions as an exercise of 'social responsibility.' In the present climate of opinion, with its wide spread aversion to 'capitalism,' 'profits,' the 'soulless corporation' and so on, this is one way for a corporation to generate goodwill as a by-product of expenditures that are entirely justified in its own self-interest. It would be inconsistent of me to call on corporate executives to refrain from this hypocritical window-dressing because it harms the foundations of a free society. That would be to call on them to exercise a 'social responsibility'! If our institutions, and the attitudes of the public make it in their self-interest to cloak their actions in this way, I cannot summon much indignation to denounce them. At the same time, I can express admiration for those individual proprietors or

innovative CSR will often provide insurance for legal compliance and long-term market sustainability. The liberalization of the airline market has indeed taught us that disobedience with emerging industry standards, such as safety regulations, will often doom the viability of a noncompliant airline.[57] Like any regulation in civil aviation, environmental standards must be viewed as the operational floor – not the ceiling.[58] Airlines who embrace CSR for environmental matters will often lie beyond that floor and remain unaffected when the regulatory bar is raised, given that the new rules were, up to that time, already exceeded by the airline.

Conversely, if an airline ignores CSR and operates strictly within the existing legal boundaries with a view that regulations are the ceiling – not the floor – it will painfully struggle to keep operating every time the regulatory floor is elevated and squeezes the airline against the operational roof outside which it refuses to operate. It will do so until the airline suffocates and takes its last breath within the confines of its obsolete business model.[59] Unless an airline adheres to CSR, the reality of law and business, when these two factors intertwine in civil aviation, is that Adam Smith's invisible hand will inevitably vindicate the environmental impact of a disobedient and polluting airline by strangling the economic life out of it.[60]

As environment goals evolve into a universal and nonreciprocal responsibility in the aviation industry, airlines struggling to comply with emerging environmental concerns will become vulnerable when CSR practices evolve into binding legal obligations. Embracing CSR therefore ensures the sustainable compliance of airlines with evolving legal norms and, consequently, protects their ability to continue operating.

15.4.3 *Social Incentives*

At the very core of environmental law lies first and foremost a *social* value. Under CSR, the industry's cognizance and adherence to contemporary social

owners of closely held corporations or stockholders of more broadly held corporations who disdain such tactics as approaching fraud."

57 Dempsey and Goetz, *supra* Note 2 at 306.

58 Ibid. at 303.

59 For instance, air carriers operating piston-engine aircraft utilizing a polluting leaded-aviation gasoline ("Avgas" or "100LL") will likely struggle to survive whenever this fuel is either banned or restricted due to carbon emissions restrictions, or when the availability of this fuel becomes scarce, as the only feasible solution will be to retire their fleet or upgrade it at considerable expense.

60 See Dempsey and Goetz, *supra* Note 2 at 298–308.

values have a crucial impact on how passengers will perceive each individual airline and potentially influence their decisions when they decide whether to fly with a particular carrier. CSR will necessarily follow our society's contemporary values as airlines attempt to seduce the passenger market by branding and marketing an image that reflects social norms. Bad CSR opposed to current social values may, on the other hand, have a significant business impact.

An example of poor CSR is found in Air Canada's alleged price-gouging incidents during the Fort McMurray wildfire evacuation in 2016, when most of the city was burning to the ground.[61] This was a profit-oriented choice that defied, in times of emergency, many elementary humanitarian considerations and consequently triggered a massive public backlash with financial ramifications, as competitors took a contrary approach and were praised for offering discounted travel prices for evacuees.[62] The reality of CSR is that, in the context of marketing strategies, it projects a "human" image for the airline, which appeals to the average consumer.[63] In the Fort McMurray evacuation, there were no legal prohibitions or obligations to lower or increase the airfare

[61] K. Coorsh, "Air Canada addresses accusations of price-gouging during Fort McMurray evacuation," *CTV News* (May 6, 2016), www.ctvnews.ca/business/air-canada-addresses-accusations-of-price-gouging-during-fort-mcmurray-evacuation-1.2891081 last accessed October 22, 2017. For instance, in a matter of twenty-four hours during the beginning of the evacuation, an Air Canada flight from Edmonton to Fort McMurray jumped from C$585 to C $4059.

[62] E. Atkins, "Rail, flight companies offer deals to Fort McMurray wildfire evacuees," *Globe Mail* (May 9, 2016), www.theglobeandmail.com/report-on-business/transportation-companies-offer-deals-to-fort-mcmurray-wildfire-evacuees/article29945420 last accessed October 22, 2017.

[63] C. Zdanowicz and E. Grinberg, "Passenger dragged off overbooked United flight," *CNN* (April 11, 2017), http://edition.cnn.com/2017/04/10/travel/passenger-removed-united-flight-trnd/index.html?iid=EL last accessed October 22, 2017; J. Bachman, "Will outrage towards united impact ticket sales?" *Bloomberg* (April 11, 2017), www.bloomberg.com/news/videos/2017-04-11/will-social-media-outrage-for-united-impact-sales-video last accessed October 22, 2017; D. Rushe and D. Smith, "United airlines CEO offers softer apology after stock nosedives," *The Guardian* (April 12, 2017), www.theguardian.com/us-news/2017/apr/11/united-airlines-shares-plummet-passenger-removal-controversy last accessed October 22, 2017. One can only think about how the inhumane treatment of a passenger forcibly dragged off a United Airlines aircraft, which contravenes many basic social norms and principles of human dignity, can have a damaging effect on the image of an airline, its finances, and even its stock value. While the legality of this business-oriented measure is questionable, it certainly did not showcase the airline's respect for social norms and proper CSR in the twenty-first century. In addition to injuring its reputation, this incident was followed within twenty-four hours by a 2.8 percent drop in United Airlines' stock value and a loss of $600 million dollars on the value of its holding company. Hence, CSR certainly has a financial aspect that cannot be ignored.

for various flight routes. But ultimately, CSR efforts, for example by WestJet, who added flight frequencies at reduced costs, donated money, and flew in relief supplies,[64] paid off as it gained the admiration of the public and likely the loyalty of many passengers.[65]

If we revert to the environmental context, the hard truth these days is that "greener" transportation is "sexier" from a consumer's perspective. From a competitive standpoint, airlines have an incentive to be "greener" than their competitors to satisfy the consumer's appeal for environmentally friendly practices.[66] For instance, Bombardier's C-Series jetliner became in 2016 the first aircraft to ever receive an environmental designation – the Environmental Product Declaration (EPD),[67] which independently assesses the environmental

64 G. Sartsky, "Update on WestJet efforts to support Fort McMurray evacuation," *WestJet* (May 4, 2016), https://blog.westjet.com/update-westjet-efforts-fort-mcmurray-evacuation/ last accessed October 22, 2017.; R. Drinkwater, "Fort McMurray hospital staff move patients to safety, some flown on WestJet planes to Edmonton," *CTV News* (May 4, 2016), www.ctvnews.ca/canada/fort-mcmurray-hospital-staff-move-patients-to-safety-some-flown-on-westjet-planes-to-edmonton-1.2888383 last accessed October 20, 2017.

65 Perhaps as a consequence of this, WestJet now flies Suncor employees. See A. Stephenson, "Suncor eliminates in-house aviation department, WestJet picks up contract," *Calgary Herald* (September 21, 2016), http://calgaryherald.com/business/local-business/suncor-eliminates-in-house-aviation-department-westjet-picks-up-contract last accessed October 22, 2017.

66 L Bershidsky, "Diesel scandal hurt the environment more than VW," *Bloomberg* (December 16, 2016), www.bloomberg.com/view/articles/2016-12-15/the-diesel-scandal-hurt-the-environment-more-than-vw last accessed October 22, 2017; P. Campbell, "Diesel faces global crash as electric cars shine," *Finance Times* (December 11, 2016),www.ft.com/content/b7d0c024-be1e-11e6-8b45-b8b81dd5d080 last accessed October 22, 2017; R. Hotten, "Volkswagen: The scandal explained," *BBC News* (December 10, 2016), www.bbc.com/news/business-34324772, last accessed October 22, 2017. One can only think, for example, of the Volkswagen Emissions Scandal where Volkswagen falsely advertised, as part of a large marketing campaign, engine emissions results lower than other competitors, which certainly made their product more appealing, although it was later found that the test results were fixed. This not only tarnished Volkswagen's corporate image and temporarily drowned its sales, but also triggered the probable disappearance in the next ten years of diesel engines in the automobile sector, as electric and hybrid cars have become more appealing as a result of the scandal according to industry experts. In the long run, the same could very well happen in aviation. Perhaps an airline or a manufacturer will be accused of operating or manufacturing a polluting aircraft model previously promoted as being "greener" than it really is.

67 Bombardier, "Bombardier CS100 aircraft receives the first environmental product declaration in the industry," *Bombardier* (September 26, 2016), http://news.commercialaircraft.bombardier.com/bombardier-cs100-aircraft-receives-the-first-environmental-product-declaration-in-the-industry/ last accessed October 22, 2017.

"Bombardier is delighted to announce the Environmental Product Declaration for the CS100 aircraft during ICAO's World Aviation Forum," said Fred Cromer, President, Bombardier Commercial Aircraft. "ICAO is widely recognized as the leading organization pursuing unified and coordinated measures to reduce civil aviation's impact on the environment, and Bombardier is proud to be the first in the aerospace industry to release an

impact of aircraft.[68] In addition, the EPD's independent analysis provided confirmation of the aircraft's ability to meet environmental goals, thus making the C-Series more appealing to airlines wishing to satisfy their environmental agenda in light of the ICAO's proposed emissions caps in civil aviation.[69] Again, this illustrates how a product going beyond the BAU scenarios will usually appeal more to the individual consumer as social values evolve. Of course, this will also give Bombardier a competitive advantage over major competitors who have yet to obtain their EPD designation at the time of this writing, such as Airbus, Boeing, or Embraer, whenever regulatory changes are imposed worldwide on the design of commercial aircraft.

If airlines ignore social norms in their business models and corporate decisions, they will inevitably suffer the economic consequences of their corporate social irresponsibility, namely the loss of consumer appeal, reduced sales, and injury to their market share. As environmental practices become the norm in civil aviation, oversight of environmental practices will become more and more frequent with individual countries and international organizations assessing the environmental compliance of airlines worldwide. Investigative reports on the environmental footprint of an airline will be published and are likely to generate adverse political, economic, punitive, and reputational effects upon individual airlines if they fail to endorse CSR with compliant

EPD®. Sustainability is a key factor guiding our thoughts and business processes, and the C Series family of aircraft is testament to our commitment to a greener future for aviation. We thank our suppliers whose ongoing contributions are immensely valuable."

"The publication of the EPD® is another C Series aircraft program milestone that reflects Bombardier's focus on industry-leading product innovation, commitment to environmentally sustainable business practices, and determination to exceed customers' expectations," said François Caza, Vice President, Product Development and Chief Engineer and Head of Bombardier's Design Approval Organization. "Led by our Eco-Design team, our product innovation life-cycle process – from the design and manufacture of the aircraft to its end-of-life – was applied throughout the development of the C Series family of aircraft to minimize the airliners' impact on the environment."

68 EPD International Secretariat, "What is an EPD?" www.environdec.com/en/What-is-an-EPD last accessed October 22, 2017. "An EPD® (Environmental Product Declaration) is an independently verified and registered document that communicates transparent and comparable information about the life-cycle environmental impact of products. Having an EPD® for a product does not imply that the declared product is environmentally superior to alternatives – it is simply a transparent declaration of the life-cycle environmental impact."

69 ICAO, "New aerospace environmental product declaration announced at ICAO world aviation," www.icao.int/Newsroom/Pages/highlight-New-Aerospace-Environmental-Product-Declaration-Announced.aspx last accessed October 22, 2017; K. Owram, "Bombardier's C – Series receives environmental designation as emissions talks get underway," *Financial Post* (September 26, 2016), http://business.financialpost.com/news/transportation/bombardiers-cseries-receives-environmental-designation-as-emissions-talks-get-underway last accessed October 22, 2017.

environmental measures.[70] Such findings, when made in a field like that of air transport where customer confidence often depends on intangibles, could irreparably injure the image of individual airlines and have an immediate effect on goodwill given that aviation is a highly competitive industry where a modest decline in the number of passengers can be financially catastrophic.[71]

Historically, passengers' loyalty toward a carrier has indeed been fickle and in circumstances, where its public image is damaged, some airlines have been unable to recover from the travelling public's negative perception.[72] For example, the "name and shame" effect of blacklisting unsafe airlines has pressured countries to comply with international standards[73] and has proven to be effective, as it can generate severe economic consequences.[74] Under CSR, it is not unlikely that individual states or international organizations will eventually produce "Green Lists" of compliant airlines, or even blacklists citing polluting airlines or ICAO Member States that disobey environmental norms. The identification and stigmatization of a particular carrier who fails to meet environmental norms may affect its ticket sales and its reputation, thus persuading it to take corrective actions and embrace CSR with added environmental measures.

The public availability of these lists could therefore influence consumer behavior,[75] even more so if the newspaper, television, or online media outlets were to broadcast an airline's poor environmental report card.[76] Given how

70 P. S. Dempsey, "Independence of aviation safety investigation authorities: Keeping the foxes from the henhouse," *Journal of Air Law and Commerce*, 75 (2010), 223. See, by analogy, how safety investigation reports have generated similar impacts on the reputation and branding of individual airlines.

71 Dempsey, *supra* Note 2.

72 F. M. Isaac, "Is it safe up there?" *Transp Law J*, 25 (1997), 183 at 185. For instance, ValuJet never recovered from the public's negative perception following the crash of ValuJet Flight 592. Similarly, the Lockerbie disaster induced passengers to fly on airlines other than Pan Am at a time when it urgently needed to fill its planes; an impact that hastened the carrier's bankruptcy. See R. Sanders, *The Executive Decision Making Process: Identifying Problems and Assessing Outcomes* (Westport, CT: Greenwood, 1999) at 148.

73 Ahmad, *supra* Note 43 at 108; Dempsey, *supra* Note 49 at 93.

74 P. S. Dempsey and L. E. Gesell, *Public Policy and the Regulation of Commercial Aviation* (Chandler, AZ: Coast Aire Publication, 2013) at 284; Dempsey, *supra* Note 49 at 79. "When economically powerful States, such as the United States or the European Union, blacklist a nation's carriers, the economic impact can be severe."

75 Ahmad, *supra* Note 43 at 108–9.

76 See for instance how public disclosure can affect the business reputation of an airline: R. D. Cooper, "Implementing safety management systems (SMS) in Canada: Is flight safety on a collision course with the forced disclosure of SMS data?" *Issues in Aviation Law and Policy*, 15 (2015) at 106.

the media's powerful influence can construct entirely new public opinions,[77] consumer knowledge that an airline may not endorse CSR in the field of aviation might very well influence in the future how passengers select carriers and present an opportunity for carriers having already implemented innovative environmental measures to challenge the market share of a disobedient competitor.[78]

15.4.4 *Political Incentives*

Airlines are not like any other business. They have strong historic ties to government in the form of previous government ownership,[79] government subsidies,[80] "equivalent-to-financial support" through the granting by a State of lucrative international route operating rights,[81] the subsidization of a route,[82]

77 J. Habermas, "Political communication in media society: Does democracy still enjoy an epistemic dimension? The impact of normative theory on empirical research," *Commun Theory*, 16 (2006), 411 at 419.

78 See P. S. Dempsey, Predation, competition and antitrust law: Turbulence in the airline industry, *Journal of Air Law and Commerce*, 67 (2002), 685, 707–15; Dempsey and Goetz, *supra* Note 2 at 306 "No one can quarrel with the basic economic principle that if an airline kills off its passengers, it won't have any." Consumers, for obvious reasons, will not support, or fly with, airlines that frequently generate accidents and fatalities. By analogy, consumers can also be expected to dislike an airline that is reported by the media and State actors as "killing the environment."

79 See M. Staniland, *Government Birds: Air Transport and the State in Western Europe* (Lanham, MD: Rowman & Littlefield Publishers, 2003).

80 In the EU, the subsidization of airlines in certain countries was so problematic that EU authorities had to intervene. In 1998, the EU demanded that Greece cease subsidies to Olympic Airlines. See K. Button and R. Stough, *Air Transport Networks: Theory and Policy Implications* (Cheltenham: Edward Elgar Publishing, 2000) at 164. Greece was still trying to justify these subsidies in 2005. See Case C – 415/03, *Commission* v. *Greece* [2005] ECR I-3894. In the United States operators of wide-body aircraft may receive government support if they make these aircraft available to the U.S. Air Force on request. See Civil Reserve Air Fleet (CRAF) program, 10 USC § 9512 (2011); 49 CFR Part 93 (2011). See also Department of Defense Authorization Act, 1982, Pub L No 97–86, s. 9513, 95 Stat 1099 at 1128 (codified at 10 USC § 9513).

81 For an overview of how Trans World Airlines (TWA) got its international routes, see A. Sampson, *Empires of the Sky: The Politics, Contests and Cartels of World Airlines* (London: Hodder & Stoughton, 1984) at 77–82.

82 49 USC s. 41742 (2012) is the U.S. Essential Air Service (EAS) program and pays a subsidy to residents of communities beyond a defined distance from a medium or major airport. Airlines bid for the route and the winning carrier must offer a minimum number of daily flights over a designated route. Thus, this subsidy does not distort competition.

government support for airports,[83] or even support by regional airports of low-cost airlines.[84]

The ties between government and airlines are both deep and all-encompassing;[85] even in the United States, where no airline has ever been state-owned, governments have used airlines to foster diplomatic ties,[86] to provide cargo lift to the military in times of national emergency,[87] to facilitate espionage activities,[88] and to support military operations.[89]

> American-Flag air transport abroad is part of our nation's air power. World leadership for peace demands continued leadership by our Flag on the airways of the world. By making the finest air service available to more and

83 This is particularly evident from recent government decisions to turn former military airfields into civilian airports. In the United States, the former Plattsburgh Air Force Base, south of Montreal, has become Plattsburgh International Airport as a result of the Military Airports Program and is now trying to lure Montreal passengers. See "Plattsburgh becomes newest member of military airport program," *Airports*, 19 (July 2002) (July 23, 2002) 3; "Plattsburgh campaign uses new terminal to lure Montreal pax," *Airports*, 25:20 (May 22, 2007) 1; In Europe, Frankfurt Hahn and Paris Beauvais are former air force bases. See Frankfurt Hahn Airport, "Wizz Air flies 3 routes to Frankfurt-Hahn" (Press Release, April 13, 2005), www.hahn-airport.de/default.aspx?menu=press_archive&cc=en&dataid=508458 last accessed October 22, 2017; Discover France, "Practical information on Beauvais-Tillé Airport," air-travel.discoverfrance.net/bva_info.shtml last accessed October 19, 2017.

84 See European Commission Decision 2004/393/EC of 12 February 2004 concerning advantages granted by the Walloon Region and Brussels South Charleroi Airport to the airline Ryanair in connection with its establishment at Charleroi, OJ 2004, No. L 137/1; See also V. J. G. Power, "Ryanair v. European Commission: The European court of first instance's judgment on alleged state aid at Charleroi airport," *Issues in Aviation Law and Policy*, 8 (2008–2009), 183. (Para. 357 of the Court decision shows how the subsidy was saved in part due to its ability to created jobs in an economically depressed region.)

85 See P. P. Fitzgerald, *A Level Playing Field for "Open Skies": The Need for Consistent and Harmonized Regulation of Aviation* (The Hague: Eleven International Publishing, 2016) at 13–24.

86 Pan Am's "joint-venture" agreement with Aeroflot facilitated New York–Moscow flights in 1988. See "Company News: Pan Am, Aeroflot Plan Joint Venture," *The New York Times* (October 3, 1987), https://www.nytimes.com/1987/10/03/business/company-news-pan-am-aeroflot-plan-joint-venture.html last accessed October 22, 2017.

87 Under America's Civil Reserve Air Fleet, US airlines offer their aircraft in times of national emergency through agreements with the Department of Defense and are given preference in carrying commercial peacetime cargo and passenger traffic for the Department. See online: US Department of Transportation, www.dot.gov/mission/administrations/intelligence-security-emergency-response/civil-reserve-airfleet-allocations last accessed October 22, 2017.

88 For the activities of Pan Am, Braniff, and Continental see Sampson, *supra* Note 81 at 84–85.

89 Pan Am played a crucial role in the Berlin airlift of 1948–49 and operated "rest and relaxation" flights for US soldiers in Vietnam in the early 1960s. See C. M. Hartt et al., "Guiding the space age from the ground up: Pan Am, cold war and guided missiles," *Management and Organizational History*, 4 (2009), 229–45.

> more people, the men and women of Pan American, at home and abroad, are keeping the American Flag in first place on the air routes of the world.[90]

While government ties to the airline industry are diminishing, as recently as 2007 the President of Venezuela ordered state-owned Conviasa[91] to link his country with Iran.[92] Even in 2017, government-owned major international airlines included Aeroflot,[93] Air India,[94] Air China,[95] Air New Zealand,[96] China Airlines,[97] Emirates,[98] Etihad,[99] Finnair,[100] LOT Polish Airlines,[101] Malaysian Airlines,[102] Pakistan International Airlines,[103] Qatar

[90] Ibid., 32 quoting Pan American Airways, "1948 Annual Report," at 17.

[91] President Hugo Chavez established Conviasa by a Presidential Decree, published in the Official Gazette on March 31, 2004, as Presidential Decree No. 37.910.

[92] See S. Romero, "Venezuela and Iran strengthen ties with Caracas-to-Tehran flight," *The New York Times* (March 3, 2007), www.nytimes.com/2007/03/03/world/americas/03caracas.html?_r=0 last accessed October 22, 2017.

[93] See Aeroflot, "Company Profile," www.aeroflot.com/ru-en/about/company_profile last accessed October 22, 2017.

[94] See A. Majumder, "Air India opposes changes to ownership norms," *Business Standard* (March 17, 2017), www.business-standard.com/article/companies/air-india-opposes-changes-to-ownership-norms-117031601147_1.html last accessed October 22, 2017.

[95] Air China is 80 percent owned by the China State-Owned Assets Supervision and Admn. Commission. See 4-traders, "Air China LTD. (601111)," www.4-traders.com/air-china-ltd-6499026/company/ last accessed October 20, 2017.

[96] Air New Zealand is 52 percent government owned. See Air New Zealand Investors Centre, "Frequently asked questions," www.airnewzealand.co.nz/investor-centre-frequently-asked-questions last accessed October 19, 2017.

[97] China Airlines is roughly 50 percent government owned. See "Losses from CAL strike hit NT $500m: chairman," *Taipe Times* (June 28, 2016) www.taipeitimes.com/News/taiwan/archives/2016/06/28/2003649658 last accessed October 20, 2017.

[98] Emirates is wholly owned by the Government of Dubai. See The Emirates Group, "Emirates," www.theemiratesgroup.com/english/our-brands/air-transportation/emirates-airline.aspx last accessed October 20, 2017.

[99] Etihad is wholly owned by the Government of Abu Dhabi. See Etihad, "Etihad airways: Our story," www.etihad.com/en-us/about-us/keep-the-skies-open/our-story/ last accessed October 20, 2017.

[100] Finnair is 55 percent owned by the Government of Finland. See Finnair, "Shareholders," https://investors.finnair.com/en/shareholders last accessed October 19, 2017.

[101] In 2014 the Polish government owned 99.7 percent of LOT and was planning to buy out minority shareholders. See K. Wajszczuk, "Treasury to up LOT ownership to 100%," *Warsaw Business Journal* (December 2, 2014), http://wbj.pl/treasury-to-up-lot-ownership-to-100/ last accessed October 19, 2017. The government has not sold its shares since.

[102] Malaysian Airlines is wholly owned by Khazanah Nasional Bhd, the Malaysian government's sovereign wealth fund. See Malaysia Airlines, "Malaysia Airlines Group," www.malaysiaairlines.com/my/en/corporate-info/malaysia_aviation_group.html last accessed October 20, 2017.

[103] See A. Yusuf and A. Shahbazi "The big debate: To sell or not to sell PIA?" *Dawn* (February 2, 2016), www.dawn.com/news/1234527 last accessed October 20, 2017.

Airways,[104] Scandinavian Airlines,[105] Singapore Airlines,[106] and Thai Airways.[107] These are simply the largest international carriers on a long list of government-owned airlines in all regions of the world,[108] and their status confirms that the longstanding bond between government and airlines is far from over.

Indeed, in February of 2017, Qatar Airways seeking to claim the record of the world's longest flight, inaugurated nonstop service between Doha and Auckland, 334 km further and 75 minutes longer than Emirates' Dubai–Auckland flight.[109] Whereas Emirates had been serving New Zealand via Australia since 2003[110] and only began its nonstop service to Auckland in 2016,[111] Qatar Airways, which had never served New Zealand, announced the nonstop service in 2017 with a press release heralding the launch of "the world's longest flight."[112] Whether a nongovernment-backed carrier would have found a commercial basis to launch such a service is not clear, but the new route confirms the value of governmental ties to the airline industry.

[104] See A. Dron, "Qatar Airways becomes state-owned," *Air Transport World* (May 23, 2014), http://atwonline.com/finance-data/qatar-airways-becomes-state-owned last accessed October 20, 2017.

[105] Scandinavian Airlines is 50 percent owned by the governments of Denmark (14.3 percent), Norway (14.3 percent), and Sweden (21.4 percent). See Scandinavian Airlines, "SAS – Four airlines in three countries," www.flysas.com/upload/International/SKI/Media-center/Mediakit/Oct08/Scandinavian%20Airlines.pdf last accessed October 20, 2017.

[106] Singapore Airlines is 55 percent owned by Temasek Holdings, a state-owned holding company. See Singapore Airlines, "Stocks and Shareholding Information," www.singaporeair.com/en_UK/us/about-us/information-for-investors/shareholding-info/ last accessed October 20, 2017.

[107] Thai Airways is 53.16 percent owned by the Thai Ministry of Finance. See Thai Airways "Annual Report 2015," http://thai.listedcompany.com/misc/ar/20160325-thai-ar2015-en.pdf last accessed October 20, 2017, at 14.

[108] There are well over 150 government-owned airlines worldwide. See ICAO, "List of Government-owned and privatized airlines (unofficial preliminary compilation)" (July 4, 2008), www.icao.int/sustainability/Documents/PrivatizedAirlines.pdf last accessed October 20, 2017.

[109] See C. Adams, "Qatar airways coming to NZ – Confirmed ," *New Zealand Herald* (March 10, 2016), www.nzherald.co.nz/business/news/article.cfm?c_id=3&objectid=11603279&ref=NZH_FBpage last accessed October 20, 2017. Service started February 6, 2017. The longer flying time is due to Qatar Airways use of the Boeing 777–200 LR, which has a slightly lower cruising speed than the Airbus A-380 used by Emirates on its Dubai–Auckland flight.

[110] Emirates serves Auckland from Dubai via Brisbane, Melbourne, or Sydney. It inaugurated service to Auckland via Singapore and Brisbane in 2003. See AAP, "Emirates touches down in Brisbane," *Sydney Morning Herald* (October 27, 2003), www.smh.com.au/articles/2003/10/27/1067213200929.html last accessed October 20, 2017.

[111] See Emirates, "Emirates and New Zealand; Creating connectivity and driving economic growth," https://cdn.ek.aero/downloads/ek/pdfs/fact_sheets/NZ_fact_sheet.pdf, last accessed October 20, 2017.

[112] See Qatar Airways, "A historic moment for Qatar Airways as it launches the world's longest flight on new Auckland service," www.qatarairways.com, last accessed October 20, 2017.

The enduring government–airline relationship is based on a simple fact; whether from a perspective of providing national infrastructure or facilitating connectivity to far-flung regional or isolated destinations, airlines have a "public good" component to them, especially in the context of affordable flights aimed at the general public. Indeed, it is this status as a public good that allows the airline industry to attract financial support, whether direct or indirect.[113]

Even in countries where a former state-owned airline has been privatized, and where no route-specific subsidies or support are available, indirect support is often provided. Thus, the granting of international routes has an economic value,[114] as does granting relief from pension funding obligations[115] or requiring government employees to travel with national carriers.[116]

Each of these policies drives home a simple reality; no matter how market-focused an airline might become it can never fully escape its characterization as a public good and the consequential inextricable ties with government. So deep are the ties that even today, a person born on an Air Canada jet flying between Buenos Aires and Santiago as part of a South America–Canada service, will have Canadian citizenship.[117]

It follows therefore that airlines are not purely commercial enterprises in the same way as an investment fund or a printing company. They have a unique relationship with government and therefore must embrace government-backed initiatives such as CSR. The fact that the vast majority of today's government-owned airlines have comprehensive CSR initiatives confirms that CSR is a natural fit with the international airline industry.

This also explains why politics can strongly influence the adoption of CSR in international aviation. As social norms evolve, individuals across the globe will

[113] R. R. Nelson, *Technology, Institutions, and Economic Growth* (Cambridge, MA: Harvard University Press, 2005) at 216. See also N. K. Taneja, *Simpli-Flying: Optimizing the Airline Business Model* (Aldershot: Ashgate Publishing, 2004) at 59.

[114] Thus, Air Canada was able to use some of its Pacific routes, slots, and leaseholds as collateral for financing. See Air Canada "Annual Report 2016" (2016), 97. www.aircanada.com last accessed October 20, 2017,

[115] Thus regulations are routinely passed so that Air Canada is relieved from its obligation to fund the deficit of its defined benefit pension plans in accordance with the minimum standards for funding under the *Pension Benefits Standards Act*, 1985. See *Air Canada Pension Plan Funding Regulations*, 2014, SOR/2013–244.

[116] 49 U.S.C. 40118 – Government-financed air transportation, also known as the "Fly America Act," requires travelers to use US carriers for all air travel funded by the US government.

[117] Article 17 of the *Chicago Convention* recognizes the nationality of aircraft, and some States, including Canada, use that status to determine the nationality of babies born aboard aircraft. See *Convention on International Civil Aviation* (adopted December 7, 1944, entered into force March 5, 1947), 15 UNTS 295, 61 Stat 1180 Art. 17. [*Chicago Convention*]; *Citizenship Act*, RSC 1985, c. C-29, s. 2(2)(a).

become more and more cognizant of emerging environmental issues affecting society, a process that naturally politicizes contemporary social issues and brings them to the forefront of domestic politics and foreign affairs.[118] The same phenomenon is now taking place in the realm of environmental law, with several countries spearheading changes in civil aviation with regards to environmental matters. The impact of these forecasted changes is certainly a political incentive for airlines to adopt CSR and introduce environmental goals into their business strategies.

In February 2017, the European Commission presented a proposal to include international civil aviation in its EU Emissions Trading System (EU-ETS).[119] In 2016, Canada reiterated its international environmental commitments by announcing its intention to adhere to a carbon pricing plan in various industries by 2018, with Air Canada already paving the way in civil aviation.[120] It made this claim on the basis that it was responsible for maintaining its *political* promises, both with Canadians and the international community at large.[121] On the international stage, sixty-seven States, representing more than 87.5 percent of international aviation activity,[122] have, at the time of this writing, adhered to the ICAO's *Carbon Offsetting and Reduction*

118 Dempsey, *supra* Note 49 at 422. For instance, it is public pressure coupled with technological advancements that drove ICAO Member States to address aircraft noise issues. Nowadays, CSR drives airports and air carriers to adopt a balanced approach, where aircraft noise is reduced not only by regulations, but under an approach favoring land use planning, operational procedures, and operational restrictions.

119 European Commission, "Proposal for a Regulation of the European Parliament and of the Council amending Directive 2003/87/EC to continue current limitations of scope for aviation activities and to prepare to implement a global market-based measure from 2021" (February 3, 2017), COM(2017) 54 final, eur-lex.europa.eu/legal-content/EN/TXT/PDF/?uri=CELEX:52017PC0054&from=EN last accessed October 21, 2017.

120 "Prime Minister Trudeau delivers a speech on pricing carbon pollution" (October 3, 2016), pm.gc.ca/eng/news/2016/10/03/prime-minister-trudeau-delivers-speech-pricing-carbon-pollution last accessed October 20, 2017.

121 Ibid. "First, that when we see a problem, we don't walk away from it, or deny that it exists. Instead, we lean in. We work hard – and we work together – to solve the problems that come our way. And second, when we say we're going to do something, we follow through. We live up to our commitments. The world expects that of us. So do the markets. And so do our fellow Canadians. It is in that very Canadian spirit of solving problems and keeping promises that I address the House today, and share the government's plan for pricing carbon pollution. After decades of inaction, after years of missed opportunities, we will finally take real and concrete measures to build a clean economy, create more opportunities for Canadians, and make our world better for our children and grandchildren. Mr. Speaker, we will not walk away from science, and we will not deny the unavoidable. With the plan put forward by the government, all Canadian jurisdictions will have put a price on carbon pollution by 2018."

122 ICAO, "Carbon offsetting and reduction Scheme for international aviation (CORSIA)," www.icao.int/environmental-protection/Pages/market-based-measures.aspx last accessed October 20, 2017.

Scheme for International Aviation (CORSIA)[123] to address annual increases in emissions from the aviation industry above the 2020 levels.[124]

On a larger scale, public awareness raised by the adoption of the *United Nations Framework Convention on Climate Change*,[125] the *Kyoto Protocol*, the *Paris* Agreement,[126] and the United Nations' *Sustainable Development Goals* (SDGs)[127] has enshrined CSR into the governance of most industries, including civil aviation.

The cumulative impact of these environmental commitments signifies that environmental norms, which were mere social objectives a generation ago, are now firmly anchored in the political realm. The political threat of impending environmental regulations certainly incentivizes airlines to embrace CSR as a proactive strategy to align themselves now, rather than later, with current and anticipated political decisions reflecting existing international commitments, including those found in various treaties. They also benefit from CSR as governments and international organizations model and align their political approach around the industry's best practices in environmental matters. Hence, CSR permits the industry to actively participate in the changes of tomorrow by shaping its own best practices, rather than having airlines put in the effort of working around the regulator's imposed rules.

Furthermore, political power is a powerful incentive for adopting CSR in environmental matters, as the political pressure induced by their citizens may very well compel States to take action against one or more carriers with poor environmental practices. A foreign air operator viewed as a high contributor to environmental pollution may not gain favorable political treatment from a foreign State, for example, when it wishes to negotiate bilateral agreements or when landing slots are allocated. International politics could therefore have a considerable weight in an airline's ability to enter or continue operating in a foreign market in the future.

Conversely, a domestic airline that disregards or fails to meet its country's environmental goals and commitments will attract little sympathy from its government, for instance, during regulatory reviews, operator certificate approvals, or

[123] At its 39th General Assembly, the ICAO adopted CORSIA, which is scheduled to come into effect in 2021 under a pilot phase.

[124] ICAO, "What is CORSIA and how does it work?" https://www.icao.int/environmental-protection/Pages/A39_CORSIA_FAQ2.aspx accessed October 20, 2017.

[125] *United Nations Framework Convention on Climate Change* (adopted June 12, 1992, entered into force March 21, 1994), 1771 UNTS 107 (1992) 31ILM 849 [UNFCCC].

[126] *Paris Agreement under the United Nations Framework Convention on Climate Change* (adopted December 12, 2015, entered into force November 4, 2016), UN Doc. FCCC/CP/2015/L.9/Rev.1, CN92.2016.TREATIES-XXVII.7.d of 17.

[127] UNGA, "Transforming our world: The 2030 agenda for sustainable development" (September 25, 2015), A/Res/70/1.

even when seeking financial assistance from the State. If an airline ignores CSR and continues flying polluting aircraft, nothing prevents a State regulator from adopting specific rules to prohibit nonenvironmentally friendly air carriers, although the same approach for a foreign operator may be legally troublesome.[128]

Hence, there is a strong benefit for political actors to foster relationships with carriers with a good environmental CSR, and turn away those who do not. Good CSR in the environmental field brings, both domestically and internationally, a unique standing in the political arena, which can either benefit an airline's growth and viability or contribute to its downfall when political pressure compels decision makers to terminate or suspend their operator's certificate.

As mentioned earlier, the failure to embrace CSR also exposes airlines to the risk of waking up one day and realizing, upon a regulatory change such as the adoption of a new Annex to the *Chicago Convention*[129] addressing environmental measures, that they are no longer compliant with international civil aviation standards in the field of environment. In practice, political pressures may then permit an ICAO Member State to, at its entire discretion, prohibit the entry of a foreign carrier into its country's airspace on the basis that it, or its State of registry, has breached its international environmental commitments as an ICAO Member State.[130]

There may also be a time when States will negotiate or terminate bilateral agreements on the basis of CSR principles reflected in international environmental instruments. It is even more likely that some States will refuse to enter or renew bilateral agreements with another country on the political grounds that its air carriers do not comply with environmental practices found in international treaties, including those that are isolated from the ICAO's

[128] Dempsey, *supra* Note 49 at 424.

[129] See *Chicago Convention*, *supra* Note 117.

[130] P. S. Dempsey, "Compliance and enforcement in international law: Achieving global uniformity in aviation safety," *N C J Int Law and Com. Reg.*, 30 (2004) 1 at 132–33; M. Milde, *International Air Law and ICAO: Essential Air and Space Law* (The Hague: Eleven International Publishing, 2008) at 161–64; P. S. Dempsey, *Law and Foreign Policy in International Aviation* (Ardsley, NY: Transnational Publishers Inc., 1987) at 312. Under articles 37 and 38 of the *Chicago Convention*, there exists a fundamental principle of legal uniformity, which encourages all ICAO Member states to adhere to a common set of rules of the air by complying with the ICAO's SARPs enshrined in its nineteen annexes. Under Article 12, countries have an affirmative obligation to maintain their compliance with ICAO SARPs (e.g. upcoming environmental norms), or else they risk political consequences, such as restrictions or prohibitions from flying into certain countries. Indeed, Article 33 of the Convention affirms that the failure of a State to comply with ICAO SARPs allows another country to refuse the entry of airlines registered in the delinquent country and even terminate any existing bilateral transport agreements between both States. Hence, the effectivity of environmental measures is greatly insured through these political incentives and hence, by the inclusion of environmental norms into international treaties (e.g. into an annex of the *Chicago Convention*).

jurisdiction. Countries may even one day incorporate into bilateral agreements reciprocal obligations to satisfy specific environmental goals. Political forces can therefore act as powerful leverage when ensuring the effectivity of international environmental commitments.

In sum, CSR and its underlying environmental objectives are not devoid of any significance as they enter the realm of international treaties more and more. With impending regulatory changes announced by the ICAO and several of its Member States, CSR and its environmental goals may soon become powerful political bargaining chips for airlines seeking to enter new passenger markets, but also to keep their existing presence in other regions intact. Consequently, CSR will likely shape more and more the political relationships between States, but also between States and individual airlines.

15.5 CSR IN THE AIRLINE INDUSTRY

China Airlines won an award in 2005 for its CSR policy but this included employee relations, welfare of employees, and participating in social or community voluntary activities.[131] Similarly, the very comprehensive CSR policy of Scandinavian Airlines (SAS) includes both environmental responsibility and social responsibility, both of which resonate strongly in the airline's home base.

SAS sees social responsibility in terms of working conditions, equality, and diversity for its employees; however, the airline's recent decision to move airline reservation positions to India has resulted in it placing a greater emphasis on its environmental record.[132]

> In addition to saving money, [through environmental actions] management at SAS believe that it can boost earnings by gaining and maintaining corporate customers who are demanding environmental responsibility of their suppliers because of requirements for certifications such as ISO 14000.[133]

SAS is based in a region of the world where conservation of the environment is seen as more important than economic growth.[134] In this context, its environmental policies have various important benefits:

[131] See W. H. Tsai and J. L. Hsu, "Corporate social responsibility programs choice and costs assessment in the airline industry – A hybrid model," *Journal of Air Transport Management*, 14 (2008) 188–96.

[132] See J. K. Lynes and M. Andrachuk, "Motivations for corporate social and environmental responsibility: A case study of Scandinavian Airlines," *Journal of International Management*, 14 (2008), 377–90, 384.

[133] Ibid. at 383.

[134] Ibid. at 382.

- Direct and often immediate cost savings through eco-efficiencies (i.e. the "low-hanging fruit");
- Investment in green technology that will result in long-term savings;
- Operational changes aimed at minimizing environmental taxes and charges;
- Boosted earnings by maintaining ethical credibility and avoiding costs incurred by having a bad environmental image or reputation;
- First-mover advantages of being one of the environmental leaders in the industry;
- Improved productivity of employees through sense of pride; and
- Better investor relations could be a future selling point for the airline (to both attract corporate clients and increase shareholder value).[135]

The airlines' former CEO, Jan Stenberg, was so dedicated to environmental issues that in 1995 he actually overrode the SAS executive management group and approved, "the purchase of a new fleet of aircraft with engines that produced significantly less NOx emissions, but which also added approximately US $40 million to the total cost of the fleet."[136]

In North America, Air Canada won an award in 2017 for its 2015 Corporate Sustainability Report.[137] Among the highlights of the 2015 report[138] were a 3 percent reduction in injuries, successful completion of the IATA Operational Safety Audit, a $312 million contribution to its pension plan, fuel efficiency savings of 11,000 tonnes and a consequent reduction of 35,000 tonnes of GHG emissions, and a 10 percent increase in funding of the Air Canada foundation.[139]

Moreover, in 2015 the International Council on Clean Transportation ranked Air Canada as number 4 among the top 20 most fuel-efficient carriers on a transatlantic route.[140] When one considers that Air France, British Airways, and Lufthansa all operate the A380 on transatlantic routes, the importance of Air Canada's ranking becomes more evident.

[135] Ibid. at 383.

[136] Ibid. at 386.

[137] See "Air Canada receives award for best corporate sustainability report – Transportation from the finance and sustainability initiative," *CNW* (January 26, 2017), www.newswire.ca/news-releases/air-canada-receives-award-for-best-corporate-sustainability-report—transportation-from-the-finance-and-sustainability-initiative-611907515.html last accessed October 20, 2017. [AC_CNW].

[138] Air Canada, "Citizens of the world, corporate sustainability report 2015," www.aircanada.com/content/dam/aircanada/portal/documents/PDF/agents/en/documents/csr_2015_report_en.pdf, last accessed October 20, 2017 [AC_CSR_2015].

[139] See AC_CNW, *supra* Note 137.

[140] See AC_CSR_2015, *supra* Note 138 at 26.

Air Canada's report confirmed its 2009 adoption of the industry's four pillar approach based on seeking improvements in technology (new aircraft and biofuel initiatives), operations (reducing flying weight and operating more direct routes), air traffic management (continuous descent paths), and industry-wide market-based measures.[141] The report also set ambitious targets for 2016, such as launching Canada's Biojet Supply Chain Initiative (CBSCI) with partners, advancing bio jet supply logistics in Canada, and completing analysis on the Air Canada Environmental Management System to align it with the recently updated ISO 14001 standard.[142]

Obviously, if Air Canada burns less fuel, not only does it reduce GHG emissions, it also reduces fuel costs, therefore the airline has a direct interest in fuel efficiency. However, depending on oil prices, biofuel can be significantly more expensive than jetfuel[143] and thus Air Canada's support for CBSCI must be seen from a CSR perspective and be seen as consistent with Air Canada's desire to be seen as a good corporate citizen in a country that is increasingly concerned about climate change.

> While much of what we do to reduce the environmental footprint of our operations is about "leaving less," we also need to do more – more with our partners, and more in our communities and with employees and customers – to ensure the future sustainability of the world we live in.
>
> At Air Canada, doing more is about commitment and leadership. It's about reaching beyond the status quo to embrace partnerships and opportunities to work together towards common goals. And, it's about connecting people with the world we live in to ensure that it's there for future generations.[144]

15.6 THE GROWING IMPORTANCE OF INTERNATIONAL AVIATION IN THE EFFORTS TO COMBAT CLIMATE CHANGE

Increasingly, researchers are confirming a greater-than-anticipated impact of aviation emissions on climate change. It is not just the emissions of GHGs by the airline industry; jet aircraft emit substances other than CO_2 and the impact of all of these emissions at typical cruising altitude is up to ten times as great as

[141] Ibid. at 26–30.

[142] Ibid. at 6.

[143] See K. Atsonios, et al., "Alternative thermochemical routes for aviation biofuels via alcohols synthesis: Process modeling, techno-economic assessment and comparison," *Applied Energy*, 138 (2015), 346–66.

[144] Air Canada, "Leaveless," www.aircanada.com/ca/en/aco/home/about/corporate-responsibility/environment/leaveless.html#!/do-more/more-commitment.

it would be at sea level.[145] This reality had made the airline industry the target of regulations in the European Union[146] in 2008 and the ICAO's CORSIA in 2016.[147]

An earlier section of this chapter illustrated how substantive CSR is often a proactive reaction of perceived threat of government regulation if self-regulation fails.[148] The airline industry understands three things:

(1) The public is concerned about the link between GHGs and Climate Change.
(2) Airline activity is harmful to the environment.
(3) The best way to avoid binding harsh regulation is to be seen to be environmentally friendly.

Thus, an increasing number of airlines are implementing and reporting CSR initiatives;[149] more airlines are recognizing the "the need for environmental reporting and have demonstrated various degrees of effort"[150] both with respect to CSR reporting and to being seen to be engaged in the fight against climate change. A study of fourteen airlines[151] revealed "Reduction of CO2emissions was reported and measured by all 14 airlines. It was the only goal to be implemented and measured by all the airlines studied."[152] This confirms that insofar as airlines are concerned, the central focus of any CSR initiative is to convince the public that airlines are part of the solution rather than part of the problem in the battle against climate change.

15.7 APPLICATION OF CSR TO REDUCING AVIATION GHGS – THE ELEMENT OF ADDITIONALITY

An essential element of any application of CSR to the airline industry must be additionality, the idea that one goes further than required by regulations or

[145] See A. C. Smith and D. de Grosbois, "The adoption of corporate social responsibility practices in the airline industry," *Journal of Sustainable Tourism*, 19 (2011), 59–77 at 61.

[146] See EC, *Directive 2008/101/EC of the European Parliament and of the Council of 19 November 2008 amending Directive 2003/87/EC so as to include aviation activities in the scheme for greenhouse gas emission allowance trading within the Community* [2009] OJ, L 8/3.

[147] ICAO Assembly Res A39–3, 39th Sess, online: ICAO www.icao.int/environmental-protection/Documents/Resolution_A39_3.PDF.

[148] Campbell, *supra* Note 8 at 956.

[149] Smith and de Grosbois, *supra* Note 145 at 62.

[150] Ibid. at 63.

[151] The airlines were All Nippon Airways, Air France KLM, Asiana, British Airways, Cathay Pacific, China Southern, Finnair, Iberia, Japan Airlines, Korean Air, Lufthansa-Swiss, Qantas, SAS, and Singapore Airlines.

[152] Allen Cowper-Smith, *supra* Note 145 at 66.

competitive norms. Given that fuel is one of the principle expenses of commercial aviation and its combustion is the primary source of aviation-related GHG emissions, airlines have a double incentive to seek fuel efficiency. Winglets, more fuel-efficient engines, lighter aircraft, electronic flight bags, better fuel management, and direct flight routes are all tools in the fight against climate change,[153] but in reducing an airline's fuel bill, they increase the bottom line.

However, to the extent that the above factors are part of a Business as Usual (BAU) or new BAU scenario, they must be considered to be part of the new normal. Here, in order to be substantial, a CSR initiative must be additional, in that it must push the company to go beyond what it would have done in the absence of CSR.

For example, to the extent that biofuel is more expensive than jetfuel,[154] Air Canada's support of Canada's Biojet Supply Chain Initiative,[155] as part of its CSR,[156] would be considered as additional, as the difference between the price/liter of jetfuel and the price/litre of biofuel is something Air Canada might not have considered in the absence of its CSR. To the extent that its CSR exceeds Air Canada's BAU scenario, its CSR has elements of additionality and can be considered to be substantial. In this respect, Air Canada sets a standard for other airlines to match.

[153] For instance, modern Performance Based Navigation (PBN) has allowed air traffic control in the United States to closely schedule commercial aircraft with more precise and efficient flight paths around airports. PBN is defined by the ICAO as "[a]rea navigation based on performance requirements for aircraft operating along an ATS route, on an instrument approach procedure or in a designated airspace [where] airborne performance requirements are expressed in navigation specifications in terms of accuracy, integrity, continuity and functionality needed for the proposed operation in the context of a particular airspace concept." It encompasses both Area Navigation (RNAV) and Required Navigation Performance (RNP). For the major airports in California (KSFO, KLAX and KSAN), Texas (KIAH and KDFW), Charlotte (KCLT), and the Washington DC area (KDCA, KIAD, and KBWI), PBN technology has allowed airlines to make a cumulative annual reduction in CO_2 emissions ranging approximately between 219,000 and 519,000 metric tons and annual fuel savings ranging between 61 million and 145 million US Dollars. ICAO, *Performance-Based Navigation (PBN) Manual – Doc9613 AN/937*, 3rd edn. (Montreal: ICAO, 2008); FAA, "Performance based navigation: Untangling the airspace" (June 2014), www.faa.gov/nextgen/library/media/getSmart_PBN.pdf; FAA, "The PBN toolbox: Building the performance based national airspace system" (October 16, 2012), www.icao.int/Meetings/PBN-Symposium/Presentations/Session%202/2%20Lynn%20Ray%20-%20FAA/ICAO%20Presentation%20Lynn%20Ray%20Final%201.pdf last accessed October 22, 2017.

[154] See Konstantinos Atsonios, *supra* Note 143.

[155] BiofuelNet, "Canada's Biojet supply chain initiative: Enabling 2020 carbon neutral growth," Waterfall Group, http://www.biofuelnet.ca/nce/wp-content/uploads/2015/11/Aviation-TF-KT-Fund-application-v1.pdf last accessed 18, October 2017.

[156] See *supra* Note 138 at 6.

Emirates' 2008 launch of its Dubai–San Francisco route employed similar types of thinking. Rather than simply fly between the two cities, the airline entered into negotiations with Canada, Dubai, Iceland, Russia, and the United States to create a much more direct route than usual.[157] The use of polar flights was not new, but sitting down with various governments to seek permission for an even more direct flying route is new. To the extent that the initiative was motivated by CSR, this would be another example of CSR driving GHG emissions. Here the additionality is not measured in financial terms, but in the spending of diplomatic and political capital.

15.8 EXAMPLES OF HOW AIRLINE CSR BEST PRACTICES HAVE REDUCED GHG EMISSIONS

A University of Warwick study in 2016 found that Finnair had the smallest carbon footprint of any large airline in 2014.[158] The study's author, Federik Dahlmann, stated:

> Finnair performs best due to the age and type of its planes, the routes it flies and the overall number of connections it offers. Plus it is probably among the most advanced when it comes to accounting for and managing its emissions over time.[159]

In 2015, Finnair brought its materiality analysis for corporate responsibility into accord with the GRI G4 reporting[160] guidelines.[161] The materiality analysis helps to identify the key economic, environmental, and social impacts in Finnair's value chain as well as impacts on business and stakeholder decision making. The previous year, IATA recognized Finnair as European leader in environmental management systems.[162] In 2015 the airline confirmed its goal of reducing CO_2 emissions by 20 percent per one hundred tonne kilometers

157 See J. Sharkey, "Polar route saves fuel, but did Santa clear it?" *The New York Times* (December 3, 2008), www.nytimes.com/2008/12/23/business/23road.html last accessed October 22, 2017.

158 WBC, "Finnair found to be cleanest airline in new study" (April 26, 2016), www.wbs.ac.uk/news/finnair-found-to-be-cleanest-airline-in-new-study1/ last accessed October 22, 2017.

159 Ibid. at 63.

160 These will be replaced by the GRI sustainability reporting standards on July 1, 2018. See Global Reporting, "G4 sustainability reporting guidelines," www.globalreporting.org/information/g4/Pages/default.aspx last accessed October 22, 2017.

161 Finnair, "GRI DATA 2015," www.finnair.com/go/2016-12-15/documents/PDFs/Finnair_GRI_data_2015.pdf last accessed October 22, 2017.

162 Ibid. at 22. Finnair became the first European airline to receive IATA Environmental Assessment (IEnvA) Stage 2 certification for its environmental management systems.

flown by 2017, using 2009 as the baseline.[163] It was also evaluating the prospect of opening a biofuel hub at its main base in Helsinki.[164]

Another example of an airline using CSR to reduce GHG emissions is KLM. The airline is aggressively exploring the use of biofuels, noting that if biofuels were broadly used, CO_2 emissions could be cut by 80 percent.[165] In 2016, the airline announced that all Los Angeles–Amsterdam flights would be operated with biofuels for a period of three years.[166] Also, in 2016 the airline launched a series of Oslo–Amsterdam biofuel-powered flights operated with an Embraer 190.[167] Two years prior, the airline had operated over a six-month period an Airbus A330–200 powered by biofuel from Amsterdam to Aruba and Bonaire.[168] KLM is a world leader in the use of biofuels,[169] and is also seen as a leading corporate citizen in the airline industry.[170] Were it not for CSR, the airline's costs commitment to biofuels might not be as significant; this is clearly a case where a strong focus on CSR has pushed an airline to take concrete actions to reduce GHG emissions.

15.9 CONCLUSION: CSR BEST PRACTICES CAN ENCOURAGE AIRLINES TO GO EVEN FURTHER IN THEIR EFFORTS TO REDUCE GHG EMISSIONS

This chapter has shown many examples where more efficient practices have resulted not only in reduced GHGs but also in reduced operating expenses for

163 Ibid. at 23. The progress is possible in part due to Finnair's replacement of Airbus A-340 4 engine jets, with the brand-new Airbus A-350 XWB. The latter carries 20 percent more cargo and passengers and is 25 percent more fuel efficient than the former.

164 Ibid. at 25. This has not yet happened.

165 KLM Takes Care, "Biofuel because" (February 2, 2015), https://klmtakescare.com/en/content/biofuel-because- last accessed October 22, 2017.

166 KLM, "KLM to operate biofuel flights out of Los Angeles" (September 8, 2016), http://news.klm.com/klm-to-operate-biofuel-flights-out-of-los-angeles last accessed October 22, 2017. The biofuel is mixed with kerosene as the cost of daily transatlantic flights using biofuel only would be prohibitive.

167 KLM, "KLM launches new series of biofuel flights from Oslo to Amsterdam" (March 31, 2016), http://news.klm.com/klm-launches-new-series-of-biofuel-flights-from-oslo-to-amsterdam last accessed October 22, 2017. The European Commission contributed funding for biofuel research and Embraer used the flights to compare the efficiency of kerosene with biofuel.

168 KLM, "KLM launches transatlantic biofuel flights from Amsterdam to Aruba and Bonaire" (May 16, 2014), http://news.klm.com/klm-biofuelflight-aua-bon last accessed October 22, 2017. The European Commission contributed funding for biofuel research.

169 See NRDC, "NRDC airline scorecard: First-ever ranking of airline biofuel use" (February 3, 2015), www.nrdc.org/media/2015/150203-1 last accessed October 22, 2017.

170 See Air France, "Air France-KLM takes care corporate social responsibility report 2015" (June 9, 2016), http://csrreport2015.airfranceklm.com/web/app.php/en/en/pdf last accessed October 22, 2017, at 26.

airlines. However, its objective has been to identify those situations where management has made decisions that reduced GHG emissions without necessarily improving the bottom line. SAS CEO Jan Stenburg's 1995 decision to buy aircraft with cleaner-than-required engines is an example of an investment that was not driven solely by financial concerns, but focused also on minimizing the airlines' impact on the environment. Finnair's recent decision to replace its thirsty A-340s with fuel-efficient A-350s is an investment not only in more efficient aircraft, but in aircraft with far fewer GHGs per passenger/km. Finally, airlines like Air Canada and KLM are spending money exploring biofuels, fully in the knowledge that such fuels will be far more expensive than kerosene for the foreseeable future. However, both know that without research biofuels will never replace Kerosene, and the promised GHG reductions will remain elusive. Thus, their commitment to biofuel is a bet on new technology and backing for an alternative to kerosene that may power the airline industry in the decades to come. From the SAS decision of 1995 to KLM's 2016 experiments with biofuels, CSR is showing that the market alone does not drive every policy. To the extent that CSR will drive airlines to exceed the business as usual scenario of market pressures and pending regulatory requirements, it will also propel the progress upon which the airline depends to thrive.

Conclusion

Reflections on the ICAO, Sovereignty, and Supra-State Governance

Brian F. Havel

I am grateful to my new colleagues in the McGill Institute of Air and Space Law – professors and graduates alike – for having collaborated to produce this important collection of essays. As climate change tightens its hold on global public policy, this book has addressed many timely issues affecting the sustainability of an industry that finds itself in the vortex of the climate change debate. Moreover, the authors have placed these issues in the broader context of the allocation of public power between traditional State sovereignty on the one hand and new models of global (and sometimes regional) governance on the other. These themes of governance will resonate with every scholar or practitioner whose work touches upon the fields of public or private international law.

The more specific sphere of governance selected in this volume is that of the Convention on International Civil Aviation (the *Chicago Convention*), as well as the institution that operationalizes the Convention, the International Civil Aviation Organization (ICAO). Indeed, the Introduction states unabashedly that the capacity of the Convention and of the ICAO to authorize and adapt to the imperatives of new public policies like sustainable development is "[a] central concern" of what follows.[1] Moreover, the ICAO and its chartering treaty are particularly compelling sites for a project that explores the viability of supra-State governance.

Virtually since its inception, the international aviation industry has been exceptional in its degree and quality of supra-State regulatory oversight. There is no global treaty on railways or automobiles and trucking, no "International Rail Transport Organization" or "International Automobile and Trucking Organization" within the United Nations system, no network of bilateral,

[1] Introduction.

regional, and global agreements that regulates these other transport industries, nor have these sectors been allowed an *a priori* exemption from the regulatory infrastructure of world trade, including the General Agreement on Trade in Services. Only the international aviation and maritime sectors were singled out in the United Nations Framework Convention on Climate Change[2] and in Article 2(2) of the later Kyoto Protocol[3] for special treatment outside the multisectoral framework arrangements intended to apply to all other industries.[4]

With special treatment, of course, comes special scrutiny. As a public symbol of globalization and industrialization, aviation has tremendous visibility and can easily be targeted as a potential environmental villain. The more this sector is once again exceptionalized by the global community of States, the more attention is focused on the means by which it will respect the mandate to suppress its contribution to global climate change. The complexity of the sector, moreover, means that different agents could have been chosen to administer the selected regime, as the European Commission noted.[5] Airports, for example, could have acted as aggregators for polluting activity, with an economic signal transmitted through landing charges. The wide variety of approaches to those charges, and the consequent risk that signals about carbon emissions reduction would be too easily distorted, appeared to dissuade the Commission from that approach. The ICAO, as the Kyoto Protocol's named custodian for a global sectoral approach, made the deliberate choice that those directly in charge of aircraft investment decisions and operations – the world's commercial airlines – should be the frontline administrators for any global regime. It is therefore the airlines themselves that will be entrusted with the environmental sustainability of the international aviation industry.[6]

2 See *United Nations Framework Convention on Climate Change* (adopted May 9, 1992, entered into force March 21, 1994) 1771 UNTS 107.

3 See *Kyoto Protocol to the United Nations Framework Convention on Climate Change* (adopted December 11, 1997, entered into force February 16, 2005) 2303 UNTS 162.

4 On the history and current prospects for regulation of environmental protection in the international maritime industry, including the role of the International Maritime Organization (the ICAO's sister specialized UN agency), see J. J. Smith, "Inspirations from Sustainable Maritime Development," Chapter 15.

5 See European Commission, "Impact assessment of the inclusion of aviation activities in the scheme for greenhouse gas emission allowance trading within the Community," SEC (2006) 1684.

6 The reader should also be aware that all of the international aviation sector's stakeholders (airlines, airports, aircraft manufacturers, air navigation bodies, and so on) advocated and supported an ICAO-generated global emissions regime. See Realwire, "Aviation industry commitment to action on climate change," https://www.realwire.com/writeitfiles/PositionPaper_ICAO-ASBY_2013_mediumres.pdf last accessed October 30, 2017; ATAG,

In that context, the editors have assembled an intelligent study of airline carbon emissions regulation that recognizes and addresses the problem of sustainability without problematizing the airline industry as *hostis humana generis*,[7] a rogue industry matching the cigarette manufacturers in low public esteem. Negative rhetoric of that kind echoes loudly in social media and elsewhere, and includes British environmental activist George Monbiot's notorious canard that the only foolproof way to control aviation emissions is to murder the industry that generates them.[8] But whether or not the international aviation industry is guilty of a moral failing, the contributors to this volume have focused solely on the legal and policy prescriptions that will slow the industry's carbon airprint while allowing airlines to continue to operationalize their national and global networks.

This dual focus is not only an iconic example of smart regulation;[9] in the present context it reflects also how "sustainability" carries a double connotation that is actually written into the *Chicago Convention*. Thus, Article 44 of the Convention charges the ICAO with sustaining the industry, *sub nomine* "international civil aviation," and in so doing to assure the public benefits of

"Aviation industry makes strong call for action at ICAO assembly" (Press Release, September 19, 2013), atag.org/our-news/press-releases/67.html last accessed October 30, 2017. The selection of the commercial airline industry to implement the regime was not intended to exclude the panoply of other measures, including new aircraft technology and more efficient air traffic management, that non-airline stakeholders would be expected to contribute toward a lowering of overall levels of emissions. The airline industry would naturally anticipate that its costs of implementation would be partly offset by these other contributions. See Realwire, "The global flightplan: Reducing emissions from the international aviation sector through carbon-neutral growth from 2020" (Paper to UNFCC COP 19 Climate Talks, Warsaw, November 2013), https://www.realwire.com/writeitfiles/PositionPaper_ICAO-ASBY_2013_mediumres.pdf last accessed October 30, 2017.

7 "The universal enemy of mankind," an epithet once applied to piracy. See B. F. Havel and G. S. Sanchez, *The Principles and Practice of International Aviation Law* (Cambridge: Cambridge University Press, 2014) at 182 –83.

8 See G. Monbiot, *Heat: How to Stop the Planet Burning* (London: Allen Lane, 2006); see also G. Monbiot, "On the flight path to global meltdown," *The Guardian* (September 21, 2006), www.theguardian.com/environment/2006/sep/21/travelsenvironmentalimpact.ethicalliving last accessed October 30, 2017.

9 See ICAO, "Working paper presented by IATA on smarter regulation: Unlocking the promise of aviation in Latin America at the 6th meeting of the North American, Central American and Caribbean directors of civil aviation," NACC/DCA/06-WP/12 (ICAO North American, Central American and Caribbean Office: Bahamas, May 10–12, 2016); ICAO, "Working paper presented by IATA on smarter regulation: Ensuring that no country is left behind," A39-WP/140 (August 5, 2016); OECD, Regulatory Policy Committee, "Recommendation of the council of the OECD on regulatory policy and governance" (2012); European Commission, "Communication from the commission to the European Parliament, the Council, the European Economic and Social Committee and the Committee of the Regions" COM(2105)215.

"safe, regular, efficient, and economical" air transport service. Most, although perhaps not all, of the contributors to this book would now add "environmentally sound" to Article 44's domain of public benefits.[10] The ICAO's dual mission of advancing the industry while ensuring wider public benefits has not proven incoherent over the decades since the Organization was established, and it could scarcely be said to include the kinds of drastic measures that commentators of Monbiot's ilk have also advocated, such as strict individual traveler caps on the use of short-haul and long-haul air travel. Indeed, the ICAO has managed increasingly well to align the two poles of industry and public benefits sustainability.

The ranges of carbon emissions that are attributed to air transport – mentioned at various points in these essays – run from 2 to 6 percent depending on the chemistry of the atmosphere and the atmospheric conditions involved.[11] Again, however, the contributors to this work have not switched law and policy for science. They have made an assumption that the scientific question of aircraft carbon pollution is settled to the extent that prophylactic and remedial responses have become public policy orthodoxy. Indeed, as a *political* matter (rather than from a scientific point of view, which is not the claimed expertise of any of the contributors) the book's chapters subscribe to the findings of climate change science, including published research of UN bodies like the Intergovernmental Panel on Climate Change, that anthropogenic greenhouse gas emissions are destined to cause eventual catastrophic damage to the planet's ecosystems. The most recent scientific findings continue to toll the same warnings.[12]

As South Africa's delegation argued in earlier ICAO debates on aviation emissions control, the path to compliance with the Organization's Kyoto mandate was bound to expose the considerable distance between simply having a mandate for action and the exercise of the *leadership* needed to

[10] On the question of how the ICAO and the Convention have evolved to embrace the challenges of environmental sustainability, see *infra* Note 15.

[11] And, as noted in the Introduction to this volume, "[a]viation would have been the 17th largest emitter of CO_2 in 2010, if international aviation were a 'country.'" See Introduction, *supra* Note 1.

[12] See NOAA Earth System Research Laboratory, "The NOAA annual greenhouse gas index (AGGI)" (updated Spring 2017), www.esrl.noaa.gov/gmd/aggi/aggi.html (The index indicates a 40 percent rise in the greenhouse gases having the most influence on earth's temperature since 1990); J. Blunden and D. S. Arndt (eds.), "State of the climate in 2016," *Bulletin of the American Meteorological Society*, 98 (2017), online: ametsoc www.ametsoc.net/sotc2016/StateoftheClimate2016_lowres.pdf last accessed October 30, 2017.

carry out that mandate.[13] Emissions reduction has been perhaps the most stringent test of the ICAO's functional capacity, and readers of this book will have gained a deep insight into the Organization's operational ethos as it labored (or better, struggled) to compose a workable consensual strategy. After all, as Alejandro Piera's analysis in Chapter 12 made abundantly clear,[14] taking jurisdiction over upper-atmosphere carbon discharges represents a quantum leap in the scope of environmental oversight within the ICAO system. Localized environmental damage has long been regulated in the ICAO's Annex 16. But greenhouse gas emissions in the upper atmosphere are not only inherently a vastly more complex public policy issue (including not least the "attribution" of emissions responsibility for transborder or high seas air services), but eventually may circumscribe traditional State sovereignty through juridicalizing the "atmosphere" as a common resource of mankind.[15]

Returning to themes of international governance, in the remainder of this Conclusion I will make some observations about a "meta"-theme that is implicit in several chapters of this book and is worth exposing here in more explicit terms: the continued viability (or sustainability) of the idea of supra-State governance in an age that many consider to be punctuated by a resurgent nationalism and a more emphatic assertion of traditional sovereignty. The sustainability of supra-State governance is obviously a more abstract question than that of environmental or sectoral sustainability (hence the "meta"-theme). But each of these concepts is nevertheless symbiotic because a failure of appropriate governance will severely compromise any project for transnational emissions control as well as the international aviation industry's compliance with its environmental mandates. Relatedly, as the director of an academic center for international air law that is located and thrives in Montreal, cheek-by-jowl with the ICAO, it seems appropriate for me to extend the meta-theme of governance sustainability to offer some brief comments on the ICAO's contribution to global governance – and on the ICAO's own sustainability as a global institution – as reflected in part in its adoption of CORSIA.

[13] See ICAO, "Working paper by South Africa on South African position on consolidated statement of continuing ICAO policies and practices related to environmental protection – climate change," A37-WP/251 (2010); ICAO, "Working Paper by 54 African states on the Position of African States on Climate Change," A38-WP/272, 38th Sess. (2013).

[14] See A. Piera, "Getting to global cooperation: The ICAO and climate change," *supra*, Chapter 12.

[15] See Havel and Sanchez, *supra* Note 7, at 227–28.

The global governance meta-theme that I perceive in this collection of essays seems opportune in a time when the robust nostrums of the Posner/Goldsmith school of realism hold new sway in public international law.[16] That circumstance may be the result in part (and maybe in large part) of the ascendancy of the Trump Administration in the United States. Two of President Trump's most senior appointees, Director of the National Economic Council Gary Cohn and National Security Adviser H. R. McMaster, early in his Administration authored a remarkable apologia that seeks to theorize the President's solipsistic actions on behalf of America as a boon for the world. The title of their opinion piece, "America First Doesn't Mean America Alone,"[17] is not by itself tendentious, but the body of the piece immediately pivots to "a commitment to protecting and advancing our vital interests." Despite pledging in parallel to "foster cooperation and strengthen relationships with our allies and partners," Cohn and McMaster fix boundaries to international cooperation by disavowing the world as in any sense a "global community," seeing it instead as an "arena where nations, nongovernmental actors and businesses engage and compete for advantage." The United States, they conclude, brings to this competition "unmatched military, political, economic, cultural and moral strength. Rather than deny this elemental nature of international affairs, we embrace it."[18]

The softer interpretation of the Cohn/McMaster thesis is to imagine it as an awkward embrace of Harold Koh's model of "transnational" law, which (in my view) seems to explain the normativity of international law as a vast political *agora* where nations and enterprises engage in daily rituals of cross-border exchanges that ultimately become routinized and solidified as law in the ordinary sense.[19] Like Koh's, theirs might therefore also be a "transactional" view of international law, if one were seduced by their reference to the world as an "arena." But of course, it is naïve to try to detect normative common ground between Koh and the President's counselors. The latter are steeped in realism, and even Hobbesian realism ("the elemental nature of international affairs"), where brinkmanship rather than cooperation has primacy as the mode of engagement between States.

[16] See generally J. L. Goldsmith and E. A. Posner, "International agreements: A rational choice approach," *Va J Intl L*, 44 (2003).

[17] G. D. Cohn and H. R. McMaster, "America first doesn't mean America alone," *The Wall Street Journal* (May 30, 2017), www.wsj.com last accessed October 30, 2017.

[18] See ibid.

[19] See H. H. Koh, "Why do nations obey international law?" *Yale L J*, 106 (1997), 2599.

Despite the unexpected arrival of Trumpian realism, the evidence of the present collection of essays is that State practice in the international air transport "arena" continues to evolve toward a divesting of sovereignty rather than the opposite. We can freely stipulate that Article 1 of the *Chicago Convention* enshrines a 1seventeenth-century "Westphalian" vision of sovereignty. Indeed, I have elsewhere characterized Westphalian sovereignty as representative of a *noli me tangere* ("do not touch me") exercise of absolutist State rights,[20] as well as somewhat ironically as "probably the only incontrovertible principle of international law."[21] From this volume of essays, however, I have gleaned that the ICAO's manifesto for the future of carbon emissions reduction – no matter how the Organization may be faulted for inevitable compromises and institutional shortcomings – signals that an epistemic community of international aviation professionals remains capable of subverting the claims of States to a narrow, egoistic, and even ethnocentric vision of sovereignty.[22]

Of course, we will not likely see a formal repeal of Article 1 of the *Chicago Convention*.[23] The substantive message of that Article is actually close to its centennial, if we link it to its predecessor formulation in the Paris Convention of 1919.[24] The ideology of Paris/Chicago sovereignty remains pervasive and is easily observed, for example, in the desire of States to reserve blocks of airspace exclusively for military purposes. The broad understanding of Statehood, too, has hardly changed, and Walter Laqueur's sardonic portrayal of a State (published in the *New York Times*) as an organism having a television system, a police force of at least 100, a budget to maintain a least one delegate at the United Nations, and a national airline, still strikes a piquant note even after nearly forty years.[25]

[20] B. F. Havel, "The constitution in an era of supranational adjudication," *NCL Rev*, 78 (2000), 257 at 329.

[21] B. F. Havel and G. S. Sanchez, "Toward an international aviation emissions agreement," *Harv Envt'l L Rev*, 36 (2012), 352 at 357.

[22] Former UN Secretary-General Boutros Boutros-Ghali has stated that the time for an absolute vision of sovereignty has passed and that, in any event, "its theory was never matched by reality." UNSC, UN Secretary General, "An agenda for peace, UN Doc A/47/277, 47th Sess. (June 1992) at para. 17.

[23] For the discussion by Steven Truxal of how Art. 1 represents an "extreme" or "ultra" sovereignty see S. Truxal, *Economic and Environmental Regulation of International Aviation: From International to Global Governance* (Abingdon: Routledge, 2017) at 49.

[24] *Convention Portant Reglementation de la Navigation Aerienne* (Convention Relating to the Regulation of Aerial Navigation) (adopted October 3, 1919, entered into force May 31, 1920) 11 LNTS 173, Art. 1,

[25] Quoted in B. Gidwitz, *The Politics of International Air Transport* (Lanham, MD: Lexington Books, 1980) at 21.

With all that said, however, we can also observe that sovereignty has diachronic as well as synchronic dimensions, captured in the late Professor John Jackson's useful comparison between the coexistence in London of two sibling museums, the Tate Britain and the Tate Modern, and the emergence in international affairs of a "Sovereignty" and a "Sovereignty Modern."[26] Jackson's re-plotting of sovereignty offers a more nuanced appreciation of a doctrine that, while it has not been eviscerated in its traditional understanding, has nonetheless evolved to reflect a more "functional" view of State interests, of shared good governance among States, and indeed of the European notion of *ordre publique*.[27] Paul Fitzgerald and Md Tanveer Ahmad, in their chapter on sustainable flight management, crystallized this diachronic point in arguing that the dominance of environmental concerns, coupled with frequent availability of more direct air routings, should encourage States to take a fresh look at why airspace is still being allocated using the piecemeal openings and closings of traditional sovereignty.[28] The ICAO's regulatory nous, in fact, slices sovereignty into thick sets of functional responsibilities, so that a perfectly rational paradox emerges whereby State sovereignty is recast (and in some sense restored) as the capacity of States to *divest* themselves of pieces of sovereignty precisely in order to achieve some of the functional purposes that at least in part justify the concept of airspace sovereignty in the first place.

Cohn and McMaster did alight upon one important feature of Sovereignty Modern in their broadside against the community of States: In a sense, everything *is* negotiable when States tackle large questions of public policy and the delivery of public goods. But in this collection of essays we did not see any suggestion of a Trumpian arrogation of power, but rather an almost diffident attempt at the *allocation* of power between global, regional, or State institutions. In a modern iteration of sovereignty, moreover, *de jure* allocations of power are helpful but not always dispositive; reading its charter, we are not going to expect the ICAO to fix potholes on the streets of Chicago (or of Montreal, as I now find), but we certainly do expect the ICAO to superintend global air safety. But even textual prescriptions do not foreclose newer responsibilities. States, their inter-State organizations and their allies in civil society

[26] J. H. Jackson, "Sovereignty- modern: A new approach to an outdated concept," *Am J Int'l L*, 97 (2003), 782.

[27] See Truxal, *supra* Note 24 at 56.

[28] See P. P. Fitzgerald and M. T. Ahmad, "Sustainable flight management and aviation," *supra*, Chapter 3. Indeed, Fitzgerald and Ahmad believe that environmental concerns may become so dominant in international public policy that they will justify Professor Nicolas Matte's prediction in 1981 that State sovereignty would become "conditional upon the freedom of international movement." (citation omitted).

remain in a continuing search for allocative responsibility. Governance is no longer the cognate of sovereignty, and the reverse can also be true. Global institutions can (and do) evolve to accomplish what they are allocated to do but also what they may never have been allocated to do. The ICAO in recent times has enlarged its "functionality" to include intelligence distribution concerning conflict zones as well as comprehensive security and safety audits of its membership,[29] and stewardship of aircraft carbon emissions is now its most publicly daring allocative step.

Erwin von den Steinen, writing in another place, proposed that the metes and bounds of "sovereignty" in the *Chicago Convention* were not solely established by the peremptory language of Article 1: He also invoked the preamble to the *Chicago Convention*, which refers to "nations and peoples" rather than to States and sovereignty (a usage that portended the coming end of colonialism).[30] But even adding von den Steinen's insight to the prior argument about the emergence of a Sovereignty Modern (with the ICAO as its prime exemplar), an important caveat remains. It remains extraordinarily difficult to impose global change in *any* sector of public or economic affairs.[31] The ICAO's expanding functionality could be derided as anomalous in that it coincides with an emerging multipolar world where the kind of "mega-multilateralism"[32] that produced the *Chicago Convention* is in retreat (and we are long past the zenith of the institution-building capabilities of Western power).[33] Indeed, three of the authors in this book anticipated the emergence of a process that they style "minilateralism," comprising regional and transregional experiments in environmental cooperation such as a proposed – though unrealized – linkage of the EU and Australian ETS regimes.[34] The

29 ICAO, "Conflict zones information sharing repository: Risks and threats posed to civil aviation operation over or near conflict zones," www.icao.int/czir/Pages/default.aspx last accessed October 30, 2017; ICAO, "Global aviation safety plan (GASP)," www.icao.int/safety/Pages/GASP.aspx last accessed October 30, 2017 (facilitates the sharing of sensitive information relating to safety between member states).

30 See E. von den Steinen, *National Interest and International Aviation* (Alphen aan den Rijn: Kluwer Law International, 2006), at 34.

31 "[H]ow do you effect global change? It turns out that it's really difficult. If we can't reform FIFA [the world's football steering body], my goodness, how can we deal with nuclear proliferation or carbon emissions or trade?" S. Kuper, "Why Sepp Blatter is a genius," *Financial Times* (May 22, 2015) (quoting Roger Pielke, professor of political science at the University of Colorado).

32 M. J. Hoffman, *Climate Governance at the Crossroads: Experimenting with a Global Response after Kyoto* (Oxford: Oxford University Press, 2011).

33 See generally H. Kissinger, *World Order* (New York, NY: Penguin Press, 2014).

34 See J. W. Lee, B. Mayer, and J. Wheeler, "Aviation and sustainable development: Some perspectives from the Asia-Pacific," *supra*, Chapter 7. In these kinds of scenarios, say the

COP21 agreement reached at Paris in December 2015[35] is already shadowed by the threat of sabotage from the Trump Administration, imputing a geopolitical risk that the ICAO's emissions initiative will itself come to seem not bold but quixotic.

In the conceptual setting of this book, however, broader doubts about the resilience of Sovereignty Modern may be somewhat *hors de combat*. Many of the contributors here were substantially concerned – whether explicitly or implicitly – with how the ICAO, a "septuagenarian" global institution,[36] has adapted itself to situations where its realm of governance is no longer entirely vouchsafed by the language of its founding charter (the *Chicago Convention*). From the outset, these authors (in my view) have privileged a dynamic theory of treaty interpretation, aligning the venerable Convention with the Sustainable Development Goals of the United Nations.[37] The ontological premise of the present collection of essays, as revealed in the Introduction,[38] is that the *Chicago Convention* is a "living" document and as such must be read purposively. Accordingly, any objective of public policy (such as sustainable development[39]) that is adopted by ICAO's member States will slide seamlessly into the interpretive context for the Convention. How far this conflation of the Convention with the Sustainable Development Goals is in harmonious alignment with the exegetical principles of the Vienna Convention on the Law of Treaties (as the Introduction asserts[40]) is certainly contestable.[41] Nevertheless,

authors, the ICAO would only need to broker a deal among regional clusters rather than attempting to orchestrate a global infrastructure.

35 See *Paris Agreement* (adopted December 12, 2015, entered into force on November 4, 2016), https://unfccc.int/process-and-meetings/the-paris-agreement/the-paris-agreement last accessed October 30, 2017.

36 The word choice is Alejandro Piera's: A. P. Valdes, *Greenhouse Gas Emissions from international aviation* (The Hague: Eleven International Publishing, 2015), 117.

37 See Introduction (citing to U.N. Gen. Res. 70/1 on the 2030 Agenda for Sustainable Development).

38 See ibid.

39 A number of authors in this book have chosen to rely on the 1987 Brundtland Report for a workable definition of this concept: cf. E. Conway and A. De Mestral, "International civil aviation and sustainable development: The application of WTO law," *supra*, Chapter12 ("sustainable development is understood as 'development that meets the needs of the present without compromising the ability of future generations to meet their own needs") (citation omitted). Wrapped into this notion of sustainable development are principles of collective State responsibility and communalized environmental protection: Conway and De Mestral (citation omitted).

40 See Introduction, *supra* Note 1.

41 The Introduction, it must be said, makes powerful arguments why the *Chicago Convention* embraces environmental sustainable development both textually and purposively; but see Piera, "Getting to global cooperation," *supra* Note 15 (suggesting that, for the ICAO, the

while this is not the place for an extended comparison of dynamic and textualist theories of treaty interpretation, it is worth reflecting for a few moments on the public international law implications of the ICAO's "leaning into" additional responsibilities and functions.

Many of this book's contributors have presumed or argued that the Convention is not immutable scripture but is an adaptable, flexible, even protean instrument. That is obviously a dialectical position that resonates in US constitutional jurisprudence, in the work of the Appellate Body of the World Trade Organization (WTO), and indeed in the respected "living tree" scholarship that attends the Constitution of my new home in Canada.[42] Despite the recent skittishness of WTO Appellate Body members concerning evolutive interpretation, that approach is surely a natural epistemological consequence of big international agreements where the signatories are unlikely to revisit the texts within a foreseeable time period.[43] Unlike the WTO, however, the *Chicago Convention* has not been subject to the changing moods and neuroses of supranational judicial interpretation. The ICAO's expanding portfolio of responsibility has emerged from the "functional" initiative of its member States – or more accurately, of its Montreal-based permanent officials. The Organization's history reveals early beginnings where it developed the apolitical, technical, and mutually beneficial rules of global aviation that flow directly from the mandates of the Convention (the rules that regulate aircraft registration or jurisdiction over the high seas, for example). The purpose of this early rule-making was to remove informational asymmetries in the mutual aeronautical relationships of the member States. If, for instance, States were free to license pilots and crew according to autonomous standards and procedures, trans-border air services would be encumbered by the massive logistics of evaluating the risks posed by licensed aviation professionals (or aircraft) from other States. The ICAO

development of air transport might be thought to prevail over environmental protection, given that the *Chicago Convention* does not mention the environment). On issues of treaty interpretation, including use of subsequent agreements, there is no better source than R. K. Gardiner, *Treaty Interpretation*, 2nd edn. (Oxford: Oxford University Press, 2015).

42 See *McCulloch* v. *Maryland* 17 US 316 (1819); *United States – Import Prohibition of Certain Shrimp and Shrimp Products* (1998), WTO Doc WT/DS58/AB/R (Appellate Body Report), docsonline.wto.org last accessed October 30, 2017; Hon. J. R. J. Sharpe, "The Persons Case and the Living Tree theory of constitutional interpretation," UNBL J, 64 (2013), 1 [HEINONLINE]; *Edwards* v. *Canada* [1930] AC 124; *Re Same-Sex Marriage* [2004] 3 SCR 698, 2004 CanLII 79 (SCC); *Brown* v. *Board of Education* 347 US 483 (1954).

43 Indeed, the approach adopted in the UNFCCC is based on the idea that States should limit themselves in the foundational diplomatic instrument to broad formulations and seek incrementally to accomplish the real work of implementation in subsequent regular conferences of the parties. See Havel and Sanchez, *supra* Note 7, at 225–26.

established the baselines for professional authorization using common standards and benchmarks (some of which are actually provided in the Convention itself) to define the terms upon which States would accept the training and operational practices of other States. In doing so, the ICAO "dramatically cut[] the transaction costs associated with updating technical standards for an industry that experiences continuous and dramatic technological change."[44]

To be sure, for most of its history the ICAO trod cautiously in the arena of *economic* regulation, cleaving to its technical mandates as its member States engaged bilaterally with one another to create a labyrinthine network of air routes. In a sense, the notorious bilateral system (the "Chicago system" as I have elsewhere called it[45]) mocked the commonality of purpose that the ICAO had fostered in building its air navigation and safety annexes.

Although, as noted earlier, the ICAO expanded its remit to include several new areas of responsibility in the non-economic sphere – from hijacking and terrorism to noise and carbon pollution – a trajectory of ever-expanding functional responsibility was by no means inevitable. Regionalism has become a continuing threat to the monolithic global model, as the WTO experience has demonstrated.[46] So also are shifts in political, economic, and social sentiment, some or all of which may encourage States to find alternative vehicles for cooperation or even to retrench into their national systems. Laurence Helfer's thoughtful study of the UN-affiliated International Labor Organization (ILO), for example, reveals an organization founded in 1919 but almost on the brink of extinction in the post-1945 period as internal Cold War clashes erupted, new institutional competitors such as the UN Economic and Social Council gained influence, and prolonged economic prosperity and the rise of capitalism altered the structure of many labor forces.[47] In subsequent decades the ILO abandoned its prolific output of proposed (but sparsely ratified) treaties and other international instruments and limited itself to a defense of a core group of labor protection standards.

44 B. F. Havel and J. Q. Mulligan "International aviation's living constitution: A commentary on the Chicago Convention's past, present, and future," *Issues in Aviation Law and Policy*, 15 (2015), 7.

45 See B. F. Havel, *Beyond Open Skies: A New Regime for International Aviation* (Alphen aan den Rijn: Wolters Kluwer, 2009), 5.

46 On regionalism and the EU's emissions trading initiative, see Introduction. For analysis of regional governance initiatives in aviation emissions reduction, see also Lee, Mayer, and Wheeler, "Aviation and sustainable development: Some perspectives from the Asia-Pacific," *supra* Note 35. and K. W. Chen, "Sustainable development, aviation, and open skies," *supra*, Chapter 6.

47 See L. R. Helfer, "Understanding change in international organizations: Globalization and innovation in the ILO," *Vand L Rev*, 59 (2006), 649.

How, then, can the ICAO's more expansionist history be explained? Were new responsibilities literally "foisted" on the ICAO[48] because of exogenous causes (such as criminal acts against aviation, or in response to US and EU unilateralism in imposing their own safety and security audits or, in the case of climate change, because of the actions of the States Parties to the Kyoto Protocol or international pushback against the EU's unilateral ETS?[49]) Or was this faster pulse of activity the result of endogenous causes, where States become gradually familiar with the operational tempo and capacity of an international organization and willingly (and at the subtle urging of its officials) devolve more responsibility to it as new circumstances arise? For the ICAO, exogenous and endogenous causes appear to have worked in tandem so that States in search of responses to huge transnational problems recognized the efficiency of relying on the ICAO's accumulated expertise. The climate change mandate, despite its distributional challenges,[50] suggests member State confidence in the ICAO's proven and continued capacity to gather information, to monitor performance, and ultimately to pull together an extremely broad agreement.

****

There is, of course, no guarantee that CORSIA will succeed, given its long projection into the future,[51] nor can it be excluded that geopolitical events will force a revival of other sites of regulation, especially at the regional level.[52] Indeed, it would be foolhardy to conclude this book by assuming that

48 Havel and Mulligan, *supra* Note 45 at 18; given that I used the word "foisted" in that prior article, I was interested to read David Chen's phrase "saddled with" in his chapter, also in relation to the ICAO's charge from the *Kyoto Protocol*: We both appear to think that the ICAO might have preferred to pass this cup. See Chen, *supra* Note 47.

49 See Piera, *supra* Note 15.

50 It is important to recall the distributional and equity challenges posed by a global response to aviation emissions. These challenges have been well-vented in this book, including a reminder in Nicole Gonzales' chapter that developmental inequities added much complexity to the design of the global regime. Alejandro Piera, also, warned of a perception that climate change could be perceived as a "European" problem only. See Piera, *supra* Note 15. Perhaps the distributional and equity challenges of global management of traffic rights was wisely avoided in the *Chicago Convention* itself, but to some degree that does beg the question as to why the ICAO in 2016 saw itself as fit for the even more distributionally complex task of creating a communalized global system for the regulation of aviation emissions. See Havel and Sanchez, *supra* Note 7, at 378 (discussing the distributional implications of a US/EU emissions agreement). To the ICAO's great credit, it managed to persuade its membership that it is.

51 See M. T. Ahmad, "Global civil aviation emissions standards – from noise to greener fuels," *supra*, Chapter 2.

52 Alejandro Piera's chapter emphasized that some of the ICAO's challenges in executing CORSIA will be endemic to its own institutional structure: There is a visible "disconnection," he notes, between the Organization and the member States that are neither members of the

CORSIA definitively resolves the problematics of global aviation carbon emissions or that the ICAO's historical mandates to its membership have been universally respected.[53] And although the ICAO has opted to make CORSIA the direct burden of the commercial airline industry, the industry itself has long noticed the political importance of emissions control and has even positioned itself as a separate site of privatized "lawmaking" activity in the sense imagined by the late Professor Roderick Macdonald.[54] For example, the international airline industry's flagship representative organization, the International Air Transport Association (IATA), appointed a senior legal adviser to oversee its membership's emissions policy[55] and has committed the sector to autonomous initiatives including carbon-neutral growth from 2020 and a 50 percent cut in carbon emissions by 2050 compared with 2005 levels.[56] IATA, therefore, provides a "private" counterpart to the ICAO's public intergovernmental regime, although both organizations collaborate closely on emissions policy and regulation and exploit their physical adjacency in Montreal to do so.[57]

IATA's initiatives show an economic sector that has been prepared to acknowledge political reality rather than contest scientific orthodoxy.[58]

ICAO Council nor participants in the technical work of the Organization. Piera, "Getting to global cooperation," *supra* Note 15.

53 See e.g. ICAO, "Safety report on universal safety oversight programme- continuous monitoring approach results" (2013 – 2016). Ahmad had caustic words to describe past ICAO compliance and the facility (and perhaps equanimity) with which States do not discharge their obligations of notification to the ICAO (irrespective of whatever might be their actual substantive compliance with ICAO mandates). See Ahmad, "Global civil aviation emissions standards," *supra* Note 52.

54 See generally R. A. Macdonald, "Unitary law re-form, pluralistic law re-substance: Illuminating legal change," *LaL Rev*, 67 (2001) 1113.

55 The title of the position is Director Aviation Environment and the current holder of the post is Michael Gill.

56 IATA, "Policy: Climate change," www.iata.org/policy/environment/Pages/climate-change.aspx last accessed October 30, 2017; see also IATA, "A global approach to reducing aviation emissions," www.iata.org last accessed October 30, 2017; IATA, "Bold industry commitment on environment" (Press Release No. 26, June 8, 2009), www.iata.org/pressroom/pr/Pages/2016-02-09-01.aspx last accessed October 30, 2017.

57 IATA's Articles of Association include a mission statement that calls expressly for collaboration with ICAO. See "IATA, *Articles of association*, Art.1V (3)," www.iata.org/about/Documents/articles-of-association.pdf last accessed October 30, 2017.

58 With that observation in mind, the reader might wish to peruse the chapter written by Paul Fitzgerald and René David-Cooper, who advocate including an aviation emissions component in the modern doctrines of Corporate Social Responsibility. See P. P. Fitzgerald and R. David Cooper, "Corporate social responsibility in the aviation industry," Chapter 15. I would add, however, that not all airlines thrive on business models that respect social norms: some EU low-cost carriers have a different view of how to sustain what Fitzgerald and David-Cooper call "consumer appeal."

Moreover, as David Zingg and Omer Gülder demonstrated in Chapter 1, the international air transport industry also promotes technology-based carbon reduction through complementary and combinable strategies that include design refinements, operational efficiencies, biofuels (as to which Zingg and Gülder provide the *mot juste* for the conversion of vegetable oils into biodiesel, namely, "transesterification"), and other technological improvements.[59] Indeed, environmental officials at the U.S. Federal Aviation Administration have long advocated operational strategies such as streamlined airport taxi movements and air traffic management *in place of* complex market-based regimes such as CORSIA.[60]

Still, despite the reality that the ICAO is not the sole progenitor of normative or technical control over global aviation emissions, the meta-theme of global governance is convincingly shown in the ICAO's recent history. The international airline industry, seemingly always pitted against meddlesome regulators, is hoping to win political dividends by announcing voluntary codes of carbon restraint and by touting its investments in fuel and operational efficiency. But the heavy lifting of a worldwide global emissions agreement, secured despite the potential for a centrifugal collapse in the face of distributional and equity challenges, remains the ICAO's special achievement. In a world geopolitical system where global governance is more and more rarely a reflex response to major policy challenges, the ICAO has shown that serious supra-State regulation can continue to coexist with regional and national institutions. In this book, the reader will have gained an understanding of why 191 governments not only bolstered the historical exceptionalism of international aviation by designating the ICAO to barter a global emissions deal, but of why they still believe that the ICAO will succeed in doing it.

59 See D. W. Zingg and O. L. Gülder, "Technology developments and renewable fuels for sustainable aviation, Chapter 1. Relatedly, it is worth reading Zingg and Gülder conjointly with Fitzgerald and Ahmad, Chapter 3, to watch how the latter authors propose efficiencies in flight management techniques if States would yield some sovereignty to "as-the-crow-flies" air services routings (an application of the "Sovereignty Modern" precepts mentioned in this Conclusion): P. P. Fitzgerald and M. T. Ahmad, "Sustainable flight management and aviation," Chapter 3. Fitzgerald, in a later chapter, suggests *inter alia* that environmental concerns should be added to the criteria for assessing the legality of airline joint ventures (including an "up-gauging" requirement). See P. P. Fitzgerald, "Seeking global environmental harmony in aviation," Chapter 13.

60 US, Federal Aviation Administration, "Aviation environmental and energy policy statement (2012)," www.faa.gov/about/office_org/headquarters_offices/apl/environ_policy_guidance/policy/media/FAA_EE_Policy_Statement.pdf last accessed October 30, 2017.

Index